Praise for Stephen R. Bown

"Stephen Bown is emerging as Canada's Simon Winchester."
THE GLOBE AND MAIL

"[A] fascinating biography. . . . As a depiction of an explorer's
life it is intelligent and thrilling."
THE SUNDAY TIMES (UK) on *THE LAST VIKING*

"Bown has drawn on journals, logs, letters and official reports
to piece together a story never fully told before. And what a story."
NEW SCIENTIST on *ISLAND OF THE BLUE FOXES*

"Bown is a meticulous researcher and a gripping storyteller."
CANADIAN GEOGRAPHIC on *SCURVY*

"[A] thrilling must-be-read-at-one-sitting page-turner."
THE WASHINGTON TIMES on
A MOST DAMNABLE INVENTION

"Magnificent."
PUBLISHERS WEEKLY, STARRED REVIEW,
on *MERCHANT KINGS*

STEPHEN R. BOWN

The

COMPANY

THE RISE AND FALL

of the

HUDSON'S BAY EMPIRE

ANCHOR
CANADA

Anchor Canada and colophon are registered trademarks of Penguin Random House
Canada Limited.

LIBRARY AND ARCHIVES CANADA CATALOGUING IN PUBLICATION
Title: The Company / Stephen R. Bown.
Names: Bown, Stephen R., author.
Identifiers: Canadiana 20200241206 | ISBN 9780385694094 (softcover)
Subjects: LCSH: Hudson's Bay Company—History. | LCSH: Northwest,
Canadian—History. | LCSH: Canada—History—To 1763 (New France) | LCSH:
Canada—History—1763-1867. | LCSH: Fur trade—Canada—History.
Classification: LCC FC3207 .B69 2021 | DDC 971.01—dc23

Cover design: Andrew Roberts
Cover image: Frances Ann Hopkins, Canadian (1836–1919), *Canoes in a Fog, Lake
Superior*, 1869, oil on canvas, Collection of Glenbow Museum, Purchased 1955.

Printed in Canada

Published in Canada by Anchor Canada,
a division of Penguin Random House Canada Limited,
a Penguin Random House Company

www.penguinrandomhouse.ca

10 9 8 7 6 5 4 3

Penguin
Random House
ANCHOR CANADA

Contents

PART FOUR: **FALL**

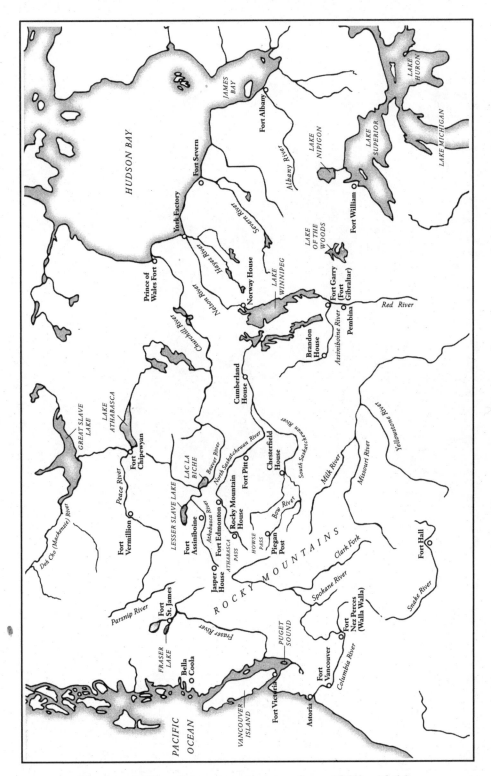

Hudson's Bay Company Territory, c. 1820–1860

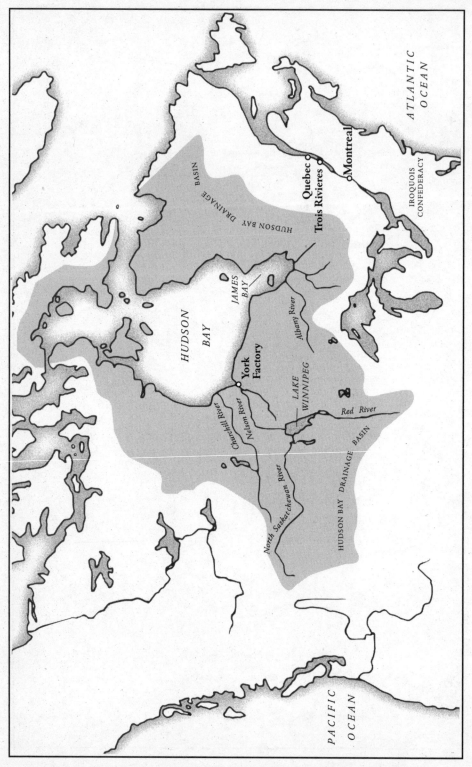

Rupert's Land, the Original Territory of the Company's
Commercial Monopoly under the Charter of 1670

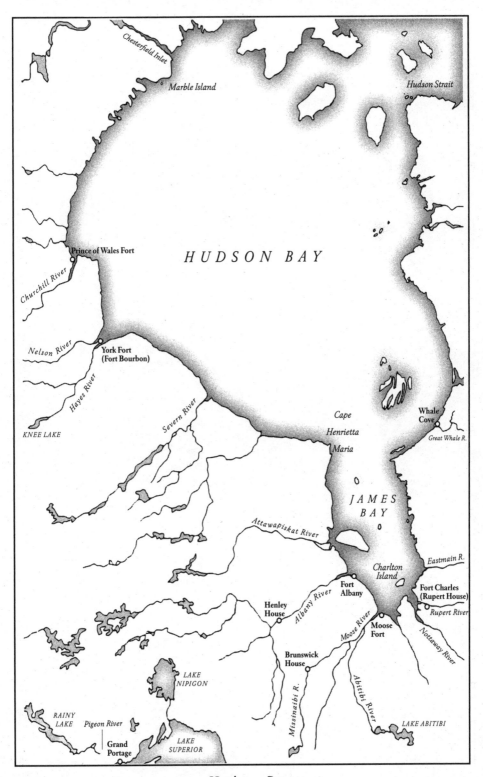

Hudson Bay

INTRODUCTION

In 1670, the Hudson's Bay Company was a small English business with a handful of primitive outposts along the western shore of Hudson Bay, trading practical manufactured goods for furs with the Cree of inland Subarctic Canada. One hundred and fifty years later, its trading posts populated the subarctic lowlands south and west of Hudson Bay, the tundra, the Great Plains, the Rocky Mountains and the misty forests of the Pacific Northwest. The Company, having inadvertently linked into a sophisticated web of intercontinental travel and commerce that involved dozens of Indigenous nations over countless thousands of kilometres, transformed the culture and economy of Indigenous groups from Montreal to Vancouver Island and ended up as the most powerful political and economic force in northern and western North America—even founding the cities of Winnipeg, Edmonton and Victoria, among others.

Yet for most of its existence the Company, governed by several dozen well-connected English aristocrats, seldom directly employed more than five hundred workers. Although the Company was an English corporation, its investors in London and its first employees from the

British Isles, it later became inextricably linked with the peoples of the lands where it operated. It contracted Iroquois and French-Canadian voyageurs from Montreal and Métis from the Red River country. For countless generations its customers, suppliers and contract workers were the Indigenous peoples who were also friends, associates, competitors, wives and extended family to all levels of Company employees. Over time, it became a widespread domestic institution, an indelible part of the economic and social fabric of northwestern North America.

King Charles II had granted his cronies a grandiose charter and monopoly absurd in its scope and geographical misunderstanding—absolute mercantile authority in English law over a territory that encompassed the entire watershed of Hudson Bay, some four million square kilometres of land, over 40 per cent of the later territory of Canada, including all of northern Ontario and Quebec, all of Manitoba, southern Saskatchewan and southern Alberta and a good portion of the states of North Dakota and Minnesota. The region held nearly one third of Canada's water runoff in a vast lowland of swamps, ponds and lakes, and was home to at least ten million beavers, then extremely valuable for their pelts. The Company was not a colonizing enterprise—nothing in its charter had do with missionaries or conquest—but nor was it a purely business enterprise. While commercial transactions for profit were its primary objective for the first century and a half of its existence, it also had other responsibilities, such as searching for the fabled route to Cathay, "by meanes whereof there may probably arise very great advantage to us and our Kingdome."

The interior of North America in the 1670s was bewildering and unknown, and it was decades before the Company began to appreciate the political and cultural complexity of its trading monopoly. Word of the Company's arrival spread quickly, and people began canoeing the rivers to its forts or factories along the Hudson Bay coastline each year. The Cree who dwelt closest to the Company outposts along the bay, and eventually the Assiniboine and Chipewyan, became the brokers of the trade, operating their own jealously guarded monopolies and using the Company as a wholesale distributor, while passing on goods to Indigenous peoples farther inland.

After generations of mutually beneficial trade, knowledge and technology had been shared both ways, and many Company employees, including people of mixed genetic and cultural heritage, had learned the secrets of inland travel and survival. When faced with competition from traders of the North West Company coming west from Montreal in the 1780s, the Company moved inland and competition intensified. For most of its life the Company competed most vigorously for the right to thrive without competition.

The Hudson's Bay Company and the North West Company each sought to dominate the other, with various Indigenous peoples taking sides as the situation evolved, playing the companies off against each other for better terms of trade. The British government forcibly merged the two companies in 1821 under the old name of the Hudson's Bay Company. Eventually its monopoly was extended to the Pacific Ocean, to include the later states of Oregon, Idaho and Washington and the province of British Columbia. By the time the monopoly was rescinded, in 1870, after two hundred years, and the Company's territory transferred to the new country of Canada, the Hudson's Bay Company had realigned the economy of northern North America.

The Company's history is not a story of heroes and villains, though certainly there were heroic and villainous characters; it is much more nuanced. History is not a single narrative, but rather many competing and intertwining narratives blending and striking off from each other. In evaluating such a monumental entity and its profound influence on the development of a large portion of North America, the variables are nearly overwhelming. Do we follow the storyline of the uneducated field workers; the aristocrats and financiers in London; the multitude of Indigenous trappers, traders and entrepreneurs; the predominantly Cree wives of the Company's immigrant European workforce; the

European fur merchants and hat makers; the famous pathfinders and travellers; the governing overseas directors; or perhaps even the hapless beavers? To focus too predominantly on one storyline effectively sidelines others. I have taken a broad interpretation of who the people of the Company were and have cast the net wider, to include a more diverse group of people who influenced, and were influenced by, the Company over the years of its life as a monopoly during the monumental exchange that endured for two hundred years.

PART ONE

ORIGINS

Chapter One

THE GRAND SCHEME

In the fall of 1665, two French *coureurs de bois*, recently arrived from a voyage across the Atlantic Ocean from North America, sailed upriver on the Thames toward the sprawling metropolis of London. They had a business proposition to discuss with English financiers, after having been snubbed by authorities in New France and merchants in New England. They were weary and anxious. Their first ship had been taken by Dutch privateers, who had unceremoniously dumped them in Spain, and it was months before they could gain passage north. Even now the timing was inauspicious. The two men stood at the railing, sniffed the air, and smelled smoke as the buildings on the outskirts of the city drew near. The chaotic urban detritus they beheld was a bewildering juxtaposition to the forests, rivers and lakes they were accustomed to, where life was harsh and unpredictable but the air was at least fresh. As the two men cast their gaze about, they spied burnt-out buildings, deserted streets, looted houses and clusters of ragged fleeing refugees.

Less than a year earlier the city had hummed with over 450,000 people, most of whom dwelt among twisting lanes and alleys that were hemmed with congested timber tenements capped by dingy garrets, leaning precariously like crumbling termite warrens. Discarded trash, human and animal urine and ordure, rotting vegetables and blood from slaughterhouses clogged the open sewers that ran down the middle of the cobbled streets. Flies swarmed the cloying air that was thick with tendrils of competing stenches: soap manufacturers, tanneries and smelters belched smoke and houses burned raw coal for heat, producing a clammy fog that hovered over the city and trapped in the stale exhalations of its denizens. Mounds of rotting refuse were heaped outside the city gates at the verge of shantytowns, the whole place infested with small black rats—rats that were the hosts of fleas, and fleas that bore the bubonic plague bacterium, transferring it to people by biting them and drinking their blood. Plagues had ravaged the city every generation or so since the 1300s, but 1665 saw the worst outbreak in a century. At its height of virulence, in the fall of 1665, this plague was killing more than seven thousand people each week, eventually slaying roughly a quarter of the city's people.

The stench of death permeated the air, and carts lumped with corpses trundled down detritus-strewn roads to dump their macabre loads into plague pits. The dockside regions were the hardest hit, the disease having first arrived on a ship from Holland, and so the boat carrying the two Frenchmen did not stop in London. Clutching perfume-doused handkerchiefs, or nosegays, to their faces, the duo continued upriver past London to the city of Oxford, where the royal court had fled to escape the pestilence. The weary men were taken ashore by Colonel George Cartwright, King Charles's commissioner who had first met them when he was in Boston touring New England after the British conquest of New Amsterdam. Cartwright was astonished at the pair's tales of a great northern or western sea that they claimed to have seen with their own eyes, and he was intrigued by the possibilities. He correctly surmised that his friend Sir George Carteret, one of the king's most respected financial advisors, privy councillor, treasurer of the navy and one of the richest men in England, would want to hear their incredible tale and its promise, or at least premise, of riches.

They disembarked in the venerable university city and were given comfortable quarters amongst the slate-roofed spires and twisting alleys of the old town. Once they had settled comfortably into their temporary abode, they were taken for a series of interviews with prominent members of the royal court that culminated on October 25 with an audience with King Charles II. Charles was a flamboyant hedonist known as the Merry Monarch because of the gaiety and social liveliness of his court. The son of Charles I, who had been beheaded in 1649 at the conclusion of the English Civil War, the younger Charles had spent eleven years in exile in France and the Dutch Republic while England was bowed under the weight of the dour and repressive Puritan rule of Oliver Cromwell. He had returned to become the king of England, Scotland and Ireland only a few years earlier, in 1660.

Cromwellian repression had included the shuttering of theatres and the shattering of stained-glass windows and stone carvings in churches. Sunday amusement was constrained, under the threat of strict punishment, to attending church at one's prescribed local parish. Public frivolity such as dancing around maypoles was frowned upon, as was laughter, lively celebration and all forms of creative expression. Charles immediately brushed aside the dusty cobwebs of Puritan rule and was rewarded with the loyalty of the people; he was a popular monarch in the early years of his reign, even if the state-borne expense for his lavish living was staggering. The relief in the land was palpable, like a clearing of the clouds after a storm. Theatres reopened, with the novel provision that women could stride the stage as well as men, while bawdy comedy and libertine literature prevailed.

A man of good humour and laughter, fond of celebration, sumptuous furnishings and fine clothing, Charles was a great subject of gossip, particularly for his numerous mistresses, seven of whom bore him twelve children. But Charles was also an astute statesman, acknowledged for

reviving the Royal Navy, reforming laws and taxes to encourage commerce and overseas trade, and supporting the arts and sciences. The
Restoration period is known for its soaring flourishes in architecture,
music, theatre and the sciences. King Charles II granted a royal charter
to the Royal Society of London for Improving Natural Knowledge in
1660. Christopher Wren designed St. Paul's Cathedral, the playwright
and poet William Congreve enlivened the theatre with the lively wit of
his plays, Robert Boyle experimented with gases and is regarded as the
first modern chemist; Robert Hooke propounded cell theory and perfected the microscope; Isaac Newton promulgated his profound theories
on gravity and developed the calculus. Charles also nudged the nation
incrementally toward constitutional monarchy. It was the beginning of an
age of unbridled optimism, ripe for new ideas and bold undertakings.

But Charles's dissolute ways were a financial burden. His numerous
mistresses and children and the maintenance of Whitehall Palace
(then Europe's largest, sprawling over twenty-three acres of grounds, with
nearly two thousand buildings of varying and erratic architecture stretching half a mile along the Thames) were a great drain on the nation's purse.
Despite substantial incomes he was chronically short of funds. Not
incidentally, Charles had a keen interest in mercantile concerns, which
were a means to satisfy his insatiable desire for money to fund his
grandiose dreams. The expansion of trade and commerce became
national concerns, and the king had a close relationship with London's
financiers, and he formulated many of his national policies, including
wars, through the lens of commerce. Charles had recently set in motion
the conquest of the Dutch colony of New Netherland, and had authorized
his brother James, the Duke of York, to seize the city of New Amsterdam
from the Dutch West India Company in 1664. The following year it was
renamed New York.

The king was keen to support the expansion of trade in Africa and
India to boost England's economy. Naturally, he was also receptive to a
plan that could make him money while damaging the prospects of the

French, with whom England was frequently at war, by undercutting their trade from the St. Lawrence. During one period of hostilities between 1628 and 1629, an English expedition had seized the fledgling communities of Quebec and Tadoussac and discovered warehouses of fine furs, which they promptly confiscated. The English knew that the prosperity of the French colonial outposts, tiny though they were compared with the English settlements south along the Atlantic, were based on a highly profitable trade in quality furs. The furs from the Hudson River region, by comparison, were of secondary quality, and this trade was dominated by the Iroquois. Other members of the English court also perked up at the scheme put forth by the two French travellers, a scheme that promised to shaft the French in the fur trade while making a profit for themselves, for seldom do patriotism and personal gain so neatly align. The plan was the genesis of one of England's most storied commercial enterprises.

THE TWO MEN WITH THE ORIGINAL IDEA, Médard Chouart des Groseilliers and Pierre-Esprit Radisson, were long-time citizens in New France along the St. Lawrence River and long-time traders with the Indigenous peoples. They were just the sort who might be able to provide knowledge and experience to help the British gain a foothold in the North American fur market, and particularly to access the superior furs from the northern regions. Although there is no record of the meeting between the charming rogues from New France and the colourful English king, their presentation must have left a favourable impression. The king likely was dressed in his habitual cavalier outfit—an enormous, curling wig, puffed silk and brocade doublet, slashed to expose colourful under fabric, embroidered velvet hose and shiny buckled leather shoes—the foppish finery of the time. One hopes that Radisson and Groseilliers had changed their own habitual attire before meeting the king, but knowing their propensity for props and theatre they may not have. A ship's captain described Radisson as "apparelled more like a savage than a Christian. His black hair, just touched with grey, hung in a wild profusion about his bare neck and shoulders. He showed a swart complexion, seamed and pitted by frost and exposure in a rigorous climate. A huge scar, wrought by the tomahawk of an Indian, disfigured his left cheek. His whole costume was surmounted by a wide collar of marten's skin; his feet were adorned by buckskin moccasins. In his leather belt was sheathed a long knife."

Regardless of their attire, they couldn't easily be ignored. The court decided to keep them on salary through the next year in Oxford. The two entrepreneurs fit nicely into the antics of the merry court and provided countless hours of entertainment by elaborating on their past adventures. Both were from France originally and had been drawn decades earlier to the French settlement on the St. Lawrence by circumstance and fortune rather than design. Although partners in many escapades, the two were very different. They were brothers-in-law, one young and charismatic, the other grizzled and contemplative; Groseilliers was approximately twenty years older than Radisson. Both had spent the bulk of their lives on the fringes of French colonial settlement along the St. Lawrence.

Groseilliers was born in Charly-sur-Marne in Champagne, France, around 1618, where his parents managed a small gooseberry farm, Les Groseilliers. He made his way to New France in 1641, when he was around twenty-three, and was initially affiliated with the Jesuit missions near Georgian Bay, learning the traditions and skills of the Huron (Wendat) and even fighting with them against the Iroquois (Haudenosaunee). After the Iroquois drove the Huron from their traditional lands by the early 1650s, Groseilliers set out roaming, west toward Lake Superior, searching for them in an effort to re-establish ties to the fur trade. In 1653, he was back at Trois-Rivières. Life was harsh and precarious in those days and he had already lost his first wife and child by the time he met and married Marguérite Hayet, the older stepsister of a youth named Pierre-Esprit, who had emigrated to New France with his sister Elizabeth.

Radisson, a boastful and charismatic spinner of tall tales, was born near Avignon in southern France sometime in the late 1630s, making him between the ages of eleven and fifteen when he arrived in New France in 1651. According his own sometimes fanciful reminiscences, he was not in the community for more than a few months before he was captured by a roving band of Mohawk (Iroquoian) while out hunting birds. While others in his group were killed, he was taken captive because of his youth and was taken back to their settlement along the Mohawk River in New York, a village of at least a thousand people in dozens of great communal longhouses surrounded by their farms and the ancient deciduous forest. The whole land was "greatly beaten with the great concours of that people that comes and goe to trade with the Flemings [the Dutch]," Radisson recalled. Although the family was headed by a man who boasted nineteen European scalps, young Radisson, owing to his facility with their language and his professed desire to learn their ways, was treated kindly and adopted. In the Iroquoian matrilineal society, it was the matrons who had the final say on adoptions, and Radisson was selected by a woman who wished to replace her recently deceased son. He underwent the ceremony of adoption: his death through ritual torture, and then his rebirth as a Mohawk. His new name was Orinha. He learned to hunt and to speak the Iroquoian language, and he was trained in warfare and taken on extensive raiding forays against neighbouring peoples to the west. For a while he was content with his new life, "desirous to have seen their country."

But his days were overshadowed by constant internal conflict between his divided loyalties. He longed for his former life. One day an opportunity to return presented itself. He was travelling with a hunting party of three Mohawk and a captive Algonquin whom Radisson called the "wild man," a term the Iroquois used to describe the Algonquins. The Algonquin captive persuaded him to help kill the three Mohawk while they slept by crushing their skulls. "To tell the truth," he admitted, "I was loathsome to do them mischief that never did me any." Yet he nevertheless "tooke the hattchett and began the execution which was soone done." The two quickly fled the scene of their murder but after two weeks of travelling north through the woods, they were tracked down and recaptured by the Mohawk. The Algonquin man was quickly killed—they cut his heart out and put his head on a stick, cut off his flesh and "broiled it and eatt it." Radisson was saved only because he disavowed any role in the murder of his Mohawk hunting companions, but he was stripped naked and marched back to his village along with dozens of other captives.

Warriors tied him to a post in the village centre along with twenty or so other captured prisoners, mostly Hurons and a handful of French, and began to torture them. His fingernails were slowly pulled out as he was commanded to sing, he was burned and branded with red-hot implements, his flesh was cut to the bone, and an old man thrust a scorching spike through his foot. Do not despair, his adopted family whispered to him, for they had paid the customary gifts as payment to the families of the dead men and his mother had pleaded for his life. Do not show fear, they said to him, for all the Iroquois peoples despise grovelling and cowardice, but on the other hand do not be too brave or arrogant, as that would be a provocation for more torture, or an excuse for someone to want to eat his heart. Many of the captured Hurons were tortured to death, while others quickly had their heads smashed. Only the youngest were to be adopted.

While Iroquoian society at this time was extremely violent, aggressive and bloodthirsty, with various forms of ritual torture being common, the tortures inflicted upon Radisson were mild and not intended to kill him—it wasn't an accident that he survived; this was just his punishment. Although Radisson was grateful to his adoptive family for saving his life, he never forgave his captives for his ordeal. Once he had healed and rejoined society, he began travelling extensively throughout the territory of the Five Nations of the Iroquois, including a five-month-long expedition visiting the other Iroquois nations (the Oneida, Onondaga, Cayuga and Seneca) and then raiding south and west as far as western Ohio, skirmishing and killing and capturing prisoners. Radisson found himself part of a trading contingent headed to the Dutch outpost on the Hudson River called Fort Orange (renamed Albany after the English conquest of New Netherland a decade later). The governor of the fort offered to ransom Radisson from the Iroquois, but he refused because he loved "my new parents that weare so good and so favorable to me."

Once he had returned to his village, however, he began to have second thoughts, to dwell upon his earlier life in New France and to muse, as he later admitted, that since it "was my destiny to discover many wild nations, I would not to strive against destinie." He soon fled south along the Hudson River back to Fort Orange in the fall of 1653, and made the daunting journey back to New France. With no ship to take him directly there, he was sailed via Manhattan, which he called "a towne faire enough for a new country," Amsterdam and La Rochelle. He then made the voyage back, sailing up the St. Lawrence in the spring of 1654, two years after he had been captured. En route, he had befriended a Jesuit priest who enlisted him to engage in a mission to the Onondaga Iroquois, who were pursuing peace with the French after driving the Huron from their traditional lands.

Radisson's brother-in-law Groseilliers, meanwhile, had continued his efforts to re-establish the damaged relations with the Huron and other scattered peoples in the aftermath of the Iroquois assaults that had driven them west in an epochal demographic displacement that reverberated for generations. He returned from a two-year journey to the region around Lake Michigan, where he had met many different peoples from various cultures whom he had not encountered before, and many peoples who were wandering exiles from the wars with the Iroquois who were attempting to restructure their lives. He gleaned from them that the best fur territory lay to the north of Lake Superior. Nevertheless, the value of the furs he took back to New France in late 1656 was considerable enough for him to begin planning a new expedition despite the huge investment in time and effort to get to the distant lands, not to mention the challenges of overcoming the obvious reluctance of peoples closer to New France to let them pass through their territory, thereby undermining their economic role as middlemen.

By this time, Groseilliers, who was in his late thirties and a hardened traveller, skilled trader and practised cultural interpreter, was persuaded by Radisson, now in his early twenties, and also an experienced traveller comfortable among mixed cultural groups in unfamiliar lands, to hire him for the great expedition planned for 1659. "It is a strange thing," Radisson mused, "when victuals are wanting, worke whole nights and days, lye downe on the bare ground, and not allwayes that hap [lucky], the breech in the water, the feare in the buttocks, to have the belly empty, the weariness in the boans, and drowsiness of the body by the bad weather that ye are to suffer, having nothing to keepe ye from such calamity." Radisson had grown accustomed to adventure and its attendant hardships and would never settle down to a conventional life.

FRENCH MARINERS HAD BEEN TRADING FOR furs intermittently since the second half of the sixteenth century, but it was the founding of Quebec by Champlain in 1608 that marked the transition from a seasonal coastal trade to a permanent enterprise with routes that extended deep into the continent's interior. With a population numbering only in the hundreds, the tiny French colony nevertheless became embroiled in the regional conflicts of the Montagnais, Algonquin, Huron and Iroquois-speaking peoples, with furs and firearms being the drivers of economic and political activity. Algonquian speakers lived primarily in the Ottawa Valley, the Huron farther west around Georgian Bay and in southern Ontario, and the Montagnais in the north of present-day Quebec and around the mouth of the Saguenay River on the Gulf of the St. Lawrence. The Huron were an Iroquoian-speaking people with similarly settled culture but were not part of the Haudenosaunee, or Iroquois Confederacy, to the south and east.

The land was covered in great deciduous forests of oak and maple and elm, interspersed with lakes and rivers. It was humid and hot in the summer and cold and deeply snow-covered in the winter. The more northern Montagnais and Algonquin lived semi-nomadic lives, moving between different regions of their territory according to the season and the availability of animals for food. The Huron and Iroquois, on the other hand, lived in villages of large communal longhouses around fields of corn, squash and beans. Corn was an important trade commodity to northern peoples like the Algonquin. The trade routes were well maintained and regularly patrolled. The lakes and rivers held an abundance of fish, and wild turkeys were plentiful, as were wild game such as deer and migratory geese and other birds. These were affluent societies made even more so in the early days of the fur trade when they had access to European trade goods at cheap prices and, thanks to their role as middlemen, trade with more distant groups.

The 1650s were a time of conflict and upheaval along the St. Lawrence region, the Hudson River and what is today southern Ontario. The Montagnais positioned themselves as the fur brokers, as successive Indigenous peoples would do in time, pushing the trade farther north and west, transporting French manufactured goods inland, trading and then carrying the furs back to auction off to the French. In exchange they demanded firearms to help them in their conflict with the Mohawk of the Iroquois Confederacy to the south—a pre-existing struggle that intensified as the beaver population diminished, causing increasing competition between the Iroquois, the Montagnais and the Huron over who would control trade with the peoples farther west and north. The Hudson River region was never the best beaver territory, and by the 1640s it was mostly trapped out, which led to the "Beaver Wars" of the 1650s and 1660s, as the Iroquois sought to become the only middlemen in the trade, controlling all access to the European fur markets. By 1650, the Huron were vanquished as a political force, the survivors abandoning their lands and fleeing to distant regions.

It was common for young Frenchmen to live, work, travel and learn Indigenous languages and customs to secure alliances and smooth commerce. They were called the *coureurs de bois*, or runners of the woods. The French settlements at Quebec, Trois-Rivières and Tadoussac were traditionally allied with the Huron and the Algonquian-speaking peoples and suffered the animosity and hostilities of the Iroquois. The tiny French colony was entirely dependent upon local peoples for survival—the settlers owed their existence to the conduit they presented to exchange furs for metal implements. These people showed the French how to survive—how to hunt food, avoid scurvy and use furs for winter clothes that were far superior to cloth. Many young men married women from the Indigenous societies to form alliances for protection and to gain access to hunting and trapping grounds. By 1660, the entire French presence in New France was barely 3,200 people, two-thirds of them men, but within a decade it had already doubled. Montreal was founded only in 1642 and for many years consisted of little more than a few dozen families, although it too grew along with the fur trade.

Like the Great Plague of the fourteenth century that arrived from China along the Silk Road and killed perhaps 60 per cent of the European population, smallpox and other newly introduced diseases had an even greater mortality rate among the Indigenous peoples of the Americas. It is estimated that before European contact, the population of Indigenous Canada and the northern portions of the United States was over 500,000, concentrated primarily in the Pacific coastal regions (150,000 to 200,000), the Great Lakes and St. Lawrence valley (100,000 to 150,000), the central aspen parkland (50,000 to 100,000) and approximately 100,000 spread throughout all other regions. People lived everywhere, but not in dense urban societies. Eurasian diseases killed perhaps 80 per cent of the population in some areas, sweeping the land in waves every generation or so as the plague did in Europe, heading into northern and western regions along with European travellers and traders, and dramatically reordering Indigenous North American politics and culture well into the nineteenth century.

In addition to the Eurasian diseases there was competition for access to markets. The French settlements held annual fur fairs and auctions, and soon competition for furs intensified when English and Dutch traders began coming up the Hudson River from New Amsterdam. The Iroquois Confederacy launched aggressive and predatory "mourning wars" to capture younger people of either European or Indigenous ancestry, to be adopted into their society and bolster their declining population. This is why Radisson, being young, was adopted rather than killed.

In 1658, the new governor of New France, Marquis Pierre de Voyer d'Argenson, was rallying the defence of Quebec and Trois-Rivières against Iroquois raids that were disrupting most of the trade and travel between the settlements. Radisson wrote that the Iroquois "were soe strong and so to be feared, that scarce any body durst stirre out either cottage or house without being taken or kild, saving that he had nimble limbs to escape their fury." It was a turbulent time for Radisson and Groseilliers to be involved in the fur trade, but great profits could be made by the bold.

IN 1659, RADISSON PERSUADED HIS brother-in-law to hire him on an expedition to the Far West searching for the source of the best furs, and probably to satisfy his own wanderlust and curiosity. Despite political opposition from various people in the administration of New France, Groseilliers secured a vague permit to leave the community and negotiated a profit-sharing agreement. When the governor demanded they take two servants with them, Radisson, suspecting they would hinder his movements and spy on his activities, replied insolently that he would gladly take the governor along, but not his servants, whereupon the governor grew angry and forbade him to leave Montreal.

This was only a minor setback, and the brothers-in-law decided to leave under cover of darkness. When a group of Huron and Odawa offered to allow Radisson and Groseilliers to accompany them on their return journey west, to make a larger group for safety against marauding Iroquois, Radisson and Groseilliers agreed, and they secretly canoed up the Ottawa River and down the French River to Lake Huron and then west along the south shore of Lake Superior, following the well-travelled route. The two brothers-in-law and their Huron companions ranged far and wide in the Great Lakes region beyond the territory through which Europeans had ventured. The curious duo continued travelling west of the Huron lands along the south shore of Lake Superior and beyond. Here they met many different peoples from three distinct linguistic families and cultures, whose language they did not understand: the Ojibwa (Anishinaabe), the Sioux (Dakota and Assiniboine) on the edge of the prairies, and the Cree from the northern forests.

Eagerly collecting information on the new lands and energized by the thrill of exotic travel, they kept walking and canoeing west until they met the peoples who hunted and fished in the headwaters of the Mississippi and Missouri Rivers west of Lake Superior. They overwintered southwest of Lake Superior in what is now Minnesota, where they were invited to participate in a great "Feast of the Dead" celebration with Huron and Ottawa refugees that included people from "eighteen several nations" including Sioux, Saulteaux (Plains Ojibwa) and Cree. Over one thousand people came together in a great camp where the festivities included smoking ceremonies and ritual gift giving, feasting, drumming, dancing and singing, games and sporting contests. The two men now dug deep into their supplies for goods they had hauled all the way from Montreal and displayed them, both to trade and as gifts, an enticement for future trade. Many had seen these items from the east before, but not the strange people who produced them. Items presented by the Frenchmen included hatchets, knives, kettles, combs, mirrors, face paint and little bells and brass rings for the children; things that, according to Radisson, "were rare and precious in those countries."

There, at the great gathering to celebrate ancestors, alliances were renewed, marriages agreed upon and news exchanged. Radisson paints a vivid portrait of the festivities and the rituals. "The women also, by having a nosegay in their hands, and dance very modestly not lifting much their feete from the ground keeping their heads downewards makeing a sweet harmony." While the men were adorned with feathers and some had bucklers, or shields, "on their shoulders uppon which were represented all maner of figurs according to their knowledge, as of the sun and moone, of terrestrial beasts, about it feathers very artificialy [artfully] painted. Most of the men their faces weare all over dabbed with severall colours their hair turned up like a crowne." From the Cree who had travelled from the northern forests they traded for the glossiest and largest beaver pelts they had ever set eyes upon, and heard tales of great rivers that flowed north to a frozen sea, a "salt sea," perhaps the very sea that maps showed had been navigated by English mariners a generation earlier. Around campfires in the evenings they heard tales of massive herds of bison on the plains and "the nation of the beefe," as they called the Sioux farther west.

In the spring they continued west as invited guests, into the lands of the Sioux at the fringe of the great grasslands, who at that time were still living in villages and growing corn, in the years before they acquired horses and spread out onto the prairie.

The two travellers learned of the great trade fairs in the Mandan villages along the upper Missouri River. People from thousands of kilometres away, from all directions of the compass, congregated to haggle and barter for goods such as northern furs, pipestone, buffalo robes, grease, ochre, obsidian, eagle feathers, porcupine quills, fine leather, pottery, dried corn, wild rice, tobacco, dried herbs, preserved fish, precious stones, decorative seeds, coloured embroidery—and of course to share news of the land. "Every one brings the most exquisit things to shew what his country affoards," Radisson wrote of the great Feast of the Dead during the winter, and this applied even more so to the larger trade fairs along the Missouri.

Attuned to commercial possibility from years engaged in the eastern fur trade, with a knowledge of certain Indigenous languages and customs, and with curious and adventurous dispositions, Radisson and Groseilliers formed the kernel of an idea that would eventually transform northern North America: what if they could tap into this well-developed intercontinental trade network that was lacking in certain goods—primarily metal tools, implements and weapons—that even now were not present in large quantities among the mix of goods generally available. Whoever could gain entry to this economy by understanding the culture and geography could set themselves up financially—and perhaps most important for Radisson and Groseilliers, could do so in a manner that wasn't tedious and plodding but rather daring and exciting.

IN EARLY SUMMER THE TWO TRAVELLERS continued their journey by returning east, this time tracking the northern shore of Lake Superior and then canoeing downstream following rivers through the northern evergreen woodlands, travelling with parties of Ojibwa and then Cree over the established portages, trails and river systems. They were well received by the communities of Cree they met during the summer. "We weare well beloved, and [they] weare overjoyed that we promised them to come with such shipps as we invented." The Cree, those mysterious northern people who dwelt in the heartland of the beaver, were unlike most of the other peoples encountered by the peripatetic pair. They were not semi-sedentary but roamed the forests continuously hunting, and "cloath themselves all over in castors' skin in winter, in summer of staggs' skins. They are the best huntsmen of all America." During the winter they dwelt inland where the hunting was better, and only moved to the coastal regions of James Bay during the summer to take advantage of the superior fishing. "This is a wandring nation," Radisson observed, "and containeth a vast countrey."

Because of the chaos in the trading networks caused by the Iroquois wars in the south, French goods had been coming west and north, passed on from one group to another, by a long and circuitous route that went up the Saguenay River to James Bay and upstream along the Albany River by Lake Nipigon. Groseilliers and Radisson were quickly realizing just how interconnected things were outside the orbit of the fledgling settlements of New France.

Along the shore of James Bay, Radisson and Groseilliers feasted on fat geese, fire-roasted fish and fresh caribou steaks while basking in the hot summer sun and pondering brilliant lingering sunsets. Near the mouth of what is now called the Rupert River they came upon the rudimentary hut that Henry Hudson had constructed in 1610, an "old howse all demolished and battered with boulletts." If Hudson had been there before, ships could navigate there again. The early English mariners from a generation or two earlier had been searching for the source of an inlet to a mighty inland sea or a route through the continent to the nearly mythical South Seas and the Spice Islands. What Groseilliers and Radisson found instead was an El Dorado of rich and thick furs from animals that lived in lands with long, dark winters and deep snows.

WHEN RADISSON AND GROSEILLIERS PADDLED their canoes back to the St. Lawrence on August 24, 1660, leading sixty canoes and perhaps three hundred Indigenous traders, and loaded with a mountain of furs, they were celebrated as heroes. But Governor d'Argenson, out of jealousy and the intransigence of vested interests, insulted them as mere provincials and seized a good portion of their furs on the grounds that they had been trading without a licence, ignoring the fact that these furs might have saved the fledgling community from imminent economic collapse stemming from the strangling of trade by the Iroquois. The adventurers retained barely one-fifth of their profit, and Groseilliers was even tossed in jail briefly. Having claimed a large sum of their profits, the governor then promptly left for France that fall. "The bougre [bugger] did grease his chopps," Radisson noted, "that he might the better maintain his coach and horses at Paris." French colonial authorities then forbade Radisson and Groseilliers from venturing west again, fearful that their exploits might shift the focus of the fur trade away from the St. Lawrence and weaken the struggling colony.

The governor wanted to promote farming and settlement, and so he discouraged the community's men from fleeing to the hinterland—at least without a licence. He imagined that it should be the local peoples who did the travelling, bringing the furs to New France, since that had always worked in the past. Spurned by their own government and annoyed at the corruption and restriction on their activities, the two brothers-in-law, after a failed attempt at restitution in the French courts and a subsequent failed attempt to persuade the French minister of finances Jean-Baptiste Colbert to back them, set off for Boston, in the Thirteen Colonies, as the next best place to seek sponsors for their grand and audacious scheme. But after a few years of vigorous persuasion and a failed voyage led by sea captain Zachariah Gillam that was turned back by ice at the entrance to Hudson Strait, Radisson and Groseilliers decided to accept an invitation to cross the Atlantic and present their case to the English court.

They had a plan that was sure to interest the English: to use ships to exploit the vast beaver preserves surrounding Hudson Bay, bypassing New France altogether and dealing directly with the Cree who dwelt in the heartland of the beaver. Ocean-going ships could easily transport a greater quantity of furs than flotillas of canoes with tricky and time-consuming portages. Groseilliers and Radisson intrigued and inspired the English courtiers. Smooth-talking Radisson boasted about his life in the wilderness of Canada: "We weare Cesars, being no body to contradict us," he proclaimed. He regaled the gentlemen of the court with the tale of their journey to the Far West, and of his plan for a series of forts along the bay that would be situated web-like to attract Cree trappers and traders, to bring their wares close to where English ships could load them and haul them across the Atlantic to London, where they could be processed and distributed throughout Europe. The scheme would bypass altogether the tangled logistics and disruptive conflicts of the St. Lawrence–Great Lakes region, which in any case was controlled by France, and gain access to the heart of the continent and its well-established networks of trade.

Radisson and Groseilliers pointed out that the English East India Company, founded in 1600, was showing renewed profits with its monopoly on trade to India, and was yearly dispatching thirty ships around the Cape of Good Hope in Africa and across the Indian Ocean. Was not Hudson Bay first explored by an English mariner? The brothers-in-law had even found his abandoned fort. Here, far to the north, were to be found pelts of the finest quality, from a source free from profit-sapping middlemen, and without the complex logistics that hamstrung New France. Perhaps they could even cut off the fur supply to the St. Lawrence, damaging French political and economic interests and making a profit for themselves in the bargain. It was almost too good to be true.

Radisson and Groseilliers had inadvertently revived the old English dream of a Northwest Passage. In the spring of 1610, Henry Hudson, a veteran of three earlier voyages in the employ of the Dutch, which resulted in the exploration of the navigable Hudson River, was employed by a consortium of English merchants to captain a single ship, the *Discovery*, and scour the northern coast of Labrador and Baffin Island for a trade route to the silk, spices and gems of those distant and mysterious lands in the Orient. The voyage was plagued by discontent from the outset. According to the testimony of the surviving mariners, the first suggestion of a mutiny was apparent before they had even departed Iceland. Hudson's officers quarrelled, the catalyst for discontent being the mate Robert Juet, who was irritable, fearful and constantly muttering. And Hudson wasn't a good leader, except perhaps in bravery and stubbornness. Ignoring the squabbling of his officers and the growing discontent of the crew, he blithely ordered the *Discovery* onward and was convinced he had located the secret sea route to the Orient when he sailed into a "great and whirling sea." He had found what is now called Hudson Strait, a turbulent thrashing waterway over seven hundred kilometres long that leads into the ice-infested northern reaches of the great inland sea now known as Hudson Bay. The *Discovery* sailed along the east shore of the bay as far south as James Bay until the season grew late.

Despite being provisioned only for one season, Hudson relentlessly pursued his dream, ignoring the protests of his crew and the better judgment of his officers. Late in November, when the "nights were long and cold, and the earth covered with snow," the *Discovery* was iced in for a nocturnal Arctic season near the mouth of the Rupert River, where Hudson had his carpenter build the cabin that Groseilliers found fifty years later. Not surprisingly, the winter sojourn was notable for scurvy, lack of food, punishing winds, dark and cold and deteriorating morale.

The *Discovery* was finally freed from its icy entrapment in James Bay in June 1611. Jaws dropped when, despite a perilous shortage of provisions, Hudson commanded the ship forward on his quest for Cathay. The crew, partially starved, sick and fearing for their lives, mutinied. They set Hudson, his young son and seven others (the weak and debilitated) adrift in a small boat in the vast, frigid and unknown waters of the bay, according to court documents, "without food, drink, fire, clothing, or any necessaries, and then maliciously abandoning them, so that they came thereby to their death, and miserably perished." Juet then ordered the *Discovery* to set sail for England. It was not a pleasant trip home, however, and only eight of the thirteen mutineers survived near starvation during the Atlantic crossing. The bedraggled, malnourished wretches were not received in London as heroes, but neither were they punished for the crimes of mutiny or murder, as their information was deemed too valuable to put at risk.

The excitement surrounding the discovery of Hudson Bay, and the belief that a Northwest Passage had finally been located, prompted the formation of a new British company possessing the optimistic name the Company of the Merchants of London, Discoverers of the North-West Passage. Even though Henry Hudson had advised against the feasibility of a Northwest Passage from Hudson Bay even if one existed, Hudson Bay became the focus of several other voyages in the early seventeenth century. "If the Passage be found," Hudson observed, "I confess there is something gain'd in the Distance, but nothing in the Navigation, allowing that this Passage falls into the South Sea; as if it does not, little good is like to ensue of it, because of the hazard of Cold, of Ice, and of unknown Seas, which Experience must teach us."

Nevertheless, in 1612 Thomas Button set off to discover the Northwest Passage while searching for Henry Hudson and to rescue him if he still lived. The Button expedition was also iced in. The mariners spent a wretched winter at the mouth of the Nelson River, during which many of the crew almost perished from the debilitating ravages of scurvy and the punishing Arctic winds. Button forebodingly named the region Ne Ultra, which in Latin translates as "go no farther"—which he did, quickly returning to England.

Perhaps the most peculiar, and most audacious, of all the Hudson Bay voyages was an informal competition to reach the Orient in 1631. Captain Thomas James and Captain Luke Foxe (commanding the *Henrietta Maria* out of Bristol and the *Charles* out of London, respectively) raced across the Atlantic and into Hudson Bay, each vying to be the first to deliver a letter of greeting to the Emperor of Japan with a proposal of commerce, written in English and signed by King James I. Dreams of commercial riches must have been overwhelming to have led James and Foxe—inexperienced in polar exploration and having never been to Hudson Bay—to launch off on such an ambitious voyage when others had so recently failed in the same endeavour. But the idea of a Northwest Passage was a preoccupation, nearly an obsession, for English merchants and the Crown.

James and Foxe were opposites in upbringing, education, personal philosophy and general demeanour, which naturally led to mutual animosity.

Their respective books *The Strange and Dangerous Voyage of Captain Thomas James* and *North-West Foxe* reflected their personalities. James was the learned, whimsical gentleman, a lawyer and an amateur poet. "Many a Storme, and Rocke, and Mist, and Winde, and Tyde, and Sea, and Mount of Ice, have I, in this Discovery, encountered withall; many a despaire and death had almost overwhelmed mee," began James in the style that permeates the entire manuscript.

Foxe, on the other hand, was the practical and pragmatic observer. Married for two decades, he was a man of experience but little formal education. Stubborn and opinionated, he admonished his crew for smoking tobacco and for laziness, among other things. Foxe defended his decision to return after a single season, pointing out the damage to his ship, the expense of sailors' salaries and other practical considerations. If there is "more required (I meane in discovery)," he wrote, "who is so pleased may set forth the beginning of May, and satisfie their desire this nexte year, with ship newly repaired, newly manned with fresh men, and untainted with skurvie, crampe, or cold paines, but more and better able to performe the enterprize then the Winterer can be. To conclude: I referre it to the judgement of reasonable discretion, whether it may be held fit that I should suffer."

Both James and Foxe narrowed in on the west coast of Hudson Bay as the most likely location to find a passage west to the court of the Japanese emperor. Foxe heeded the advice of Button. Despite his disastrous winter near the Nelson River, the aging Button, in his demented optimism, pronounced to Foxe: "I do confidently believe there to be a passage, as I do there is one between Calais and Dover or between Holy Head and Ireland." Consequently, Foxe planned to concentrate his searching in northwestern Hudson Bay and he steered his ship into what is now called Foxe Basin. But after scouring the coast, squinting through his eyeglass and probing promising inlets, he had found no west-leading waterway. Perhaps his greatest failing was that he returned without dramatic incident, declaring "further search of a passage this way was hopeless." His sponsors were not amused to hear that the wealth of Cathay was not within easy reach, and he had no compensating tale of daring and suffering to attract public sympathy. Foxe was branded a coward, his reputation was irreparably damaged, and he died within a year of the publication of his book.

James settled on a more southerly region of coast. He based his decision on the travel account of Jens Munk, the Danish explorer who endured an excruciating and demoralizing winter near the Churchill River in 1619. Munk's expedition was utterly ruinous. Only three survivors returned to Denmark: Munk, an old man and a young boy. Throughout the dark winter, the other sixty-two sailors and officers had slowly expired "with great pains in the loins, as if a thousand knives were thrust through them. The body at the same time was blue and brown . . . and was quite powerless. The mouth, also, was in a very bad and miserable condition, as all the teeth were loose, so that we could not eat any victuals." The corpses were unceremoniously piled on a nearby hilltop and covered in stones. The unlikely trio defrayed the agonizing debilitations of scurvy by sucking withered roots and grasses found near the Churchill River.

Almost twenty years later, in August 1631, James cruised near the mouth of the Churchill River, "the very place where the Passage should be, as it was thought by the understandingest and learnedest intelligencer of this Business," but after failing to find a west-leading waterway, proceeded to follow the western coast of Hudson Bay south into what is now known as James Bay. James was not as experienced in seamanship or navigation as Foxe, and he damaged his ship looking for a harbour on Charleton (now Charlton) Island. In November, despite the work of the crew, the *Henrietta Maria* remained unseaworthy, and James realized that the season was too far advanced to navigate the ice of the bay. In order to protect the damaged vessel from further deterioration, he decided to scuttle the ship and settle in for the winter. The winter was a horrifying nightmare spent huddled in three drafty huts on the wind-lashed beach while the dreaded scurvy spread through the crew. During the dark nights, James could hear "the miserable groanings, and lamenting of the sicke men all night long, enduring (poore soules) intolerable torments." The following July, leaving four dead under small mounds of stones, they managed to refloat their vessel and sail away, arriving in England in October 1632.

Neither James, Munk nor Foxe encountered any Indigenous people during their voyages because, as Radisson noted, during the winter the Cree return inland to escape the punishing wind and ice and lack of animals for food. Owing to the disastrous experiences and wasted funds, no other English ships sailed Hudson Bay for over three decades. But memories of these early English expeditions, however fruitless, were revived by Groseilliers and Radisson's claims of having canoed down a river from the "North West into the South Seas," and then returned on a different river "North east into Hudson Bay." Their boasting, vague promises and musings rekindled the old English obsession with a Northwest Passage, and seemed even more exciting in combination with the prospect of a good profit in commerce with the Cree, the eponymous woodsmen of the north, along the coast of the great inland sea that had already seen so many dramatic English adventures.

Chapter Two

ROYAL BEGINNING

T he man who stares boldly from the portrait looks down his long nose with a saturnine expression, like a dyspeptic judge at a tedious hearing. Bedecked in the exaggerated finery that was in vogue in the English court, he looks distinctly uncomfortable, as if the entire ensemble was painted on afterwards, an artistic facade obscuring his regular attire. It presents an image at odds with his usual pursuits as a cavalry commander, naval admiral and empirical investigator. Born in Prague, a veteran of the savage Thirty Years War that ravaged Europe until 1648, Prince Rupert of the Rhine served as the head of the Royalist cavalry during the English Civil War, earning a reputation for aggressive and bold manoeuvres. Brave, daring and handsome, he was a heroic figure used in pro-government propaganda. He even ran as a roguish privateer in the Caribbean. Rupert was an archetype of the mid-seventeenth-century cavalier, with a well-deserved reputation for dash and daring and for fashionable mistresses. Banished from England after the defeat of the Parliamentary forces and the death of his uncle, Charles I, in exile he was a staunch supporter of his first cousin, later King Charles II.

After the restoration of Charles II to the throne of England in 1660, Rupert was rewarded with both a position on the Privy Council and several titles, including Duke of Cumberland, Earl of Holderness and Count Palatine of the Rhine. His temper and rashness had been tempered with a more thoughtful and considered demeanour, and as the years passed Rupert earned a reputation for aloofness, a difficult fellow who was never fully comfortable with his life in London or with his ambiguous role within Charles's inner circle. One of his contemporaries gave a less than flattering portrait of the duke in later life: he was "brave and courageous even to rashness, but cross-grained and incorrigibly obstinate . . . he was polite, even to excess, unseasonably; but haughty, and even brutal, when he ought to have been gentle and courteous . . . his manners were ungracious: he had a dry hard-favoured visage, and a stern look, even when he wished to please; but, when he was out of humour, he was the true picture of reproof."

In his youth a student of mathematics and military architecture at the University of Leiden, with a wide-ranging interest in science and technology, he became a founding member of the Royal Society. A substantial portion of his royal apartments in Windsor Castle were transformed into a giant laboratory for scientific experimentation. His specialties were mathematics, hydraulics and metallurgy, with a focus on their military applications. Dubbed the "philosophic warrior," Rupert is also remembered for the epithet engraved on the chapel where he was buried, which waggishly proclaims: a "soldier's life is a life of honour, but a dog would not lead it." Rupert was also a well-regarded artist and a noted tennis player—one of the best in the country, according to the diarist Samuel Pepys. His broadly curious mind also took an interest in politics, geography and commerce. His interest in Groseilliers and Radisson may have been because he recognized the strategic importance of beaver fur as a military staple; it was nearly waterproof and was invaluable as a covering to keep ammunition for guns and cannons dry.

In that first year after the plague, while the two French explorers were receiving a government pension and housed nearby, Rupert was taken by their bravado and listened intently to their boasts about the quality and quantity of beaver pelts in the northlands. He perked up when they described the size of copper outcroppings they claimed to have seen, and he began to imagine the commercial and strategic possibilities of the Hudson Bay trade. If it was as feasible as Radisson and Groseilliers intimated, it would provide needed government revenue, access to valuable resources and, as a bonus, thwart French colonial ambitions. He began recruiting a coterie of like-minded investors, courtiers, statesmen and financiers to contribute to a voyage to Hudson Bay to test the theory. For this first voyage, Rupert persuaded the king to lease to them, for a paltry sum, a small two-masted ship called the *Eaglet*, and they purchased an even smaller ship, the *Nonsuch*, which was barely five metres wide and sixteen metres long (and possibly named after one of Charles's famous mistresses, Barbara Villiers, Lady Castlemaine. Her celebrated beauty knew non-such competition and Nonsuch was apparently her sobriquet).

None of Rupert's notable and influential investors were familiar with the fur trade, but several had connections to past English enterprise in the Americas, including John Kirke, whose father had been one of the organizers behind Thomas Button's failed 1612 expedition to Hudson Bay as part of the Company of the Merchants of London, Discoverers of the North-West Passage, and whose daughter Radisson later married. While Rupert brought the company of adventurers together to dream and to cough up the capital, his business advisor and personal secretary, the calculating and disliked James Hayes, took care of the detailed preparations for the expedition. While some profit was no doubt enticing, the amount of money invested by these exceedingly rich and influential members of the king's inner circle was tiny in comparison to their fortunes. It's just as likely that they merely had a desire to be part of the ongoing saga of English history of sailing to the northern bay, an entertaining and amusing vicarious adventure that wouldn't cost them too dearly, or perhaps not at all if it proved profitable.

But with Groseilliers and Radisson, nothing ever seemed to go as planned. No sooner had London begun to recover from its recent bout with the first horseman of the apocalypse, plague, than galloped in a second horseman: fire. After a hot and dry summer, the Great Fire of London started inconspicuously in the early morning of September 2, 1666, in a bakery on one of the numerous laneways of the congested city, a city constructed almost entirely of wood and heated and powered by wood. The flickering orange blaze lit up the early-morning sky, yet would have been quickly doused by the admittedly unprepared and ineffective fire brigades but for the strong easterly wind that coaxed the bakery fire into a raging inferno. Within hours, flames leaped between buildings and streets and reduced whole neighbourhoods to ash before anyone could properly evacuate. The fire eventually consumed about 13,200 houses and 87 churches, including St. Paul's Cathedral, leaving vast tracts of the old city in smouldering ruins and many thousands of bewildered refugees.

While London rebuilt after the fire, the voyage was delayed. Radisson and Groseilliers must have been frustrated with yet another impediment in their years-long plans. But the intrigue over the planned voyage to Hudson Bay spread and drew in a larger circle of interest. Courtiers must have talked, and the excitement at the prospects must have seemed great or at least interesting, or perhaps the possibilities seemed abundant in this time of geographical mystery when North America in particular still held the possibility of a sea route through it to Asia and the fabulous wealth of the Spice Islands. Wind of their proposal to the English king apparently travelled far. In November 1666, an agent named Elie Godefroy Touret was imprisoned in London for trying to persuade Groseilliers and Radisson to switch their allegiance to the Dutch.

It was the Dutch who thwarted Groseilliers and Radisson in June of the following year, when the famous admiral Michiel de Ruyter led a fleet against the Royal Navy near the end of what is now called the

Second Anglo-Dutch War. The Raid on the Medway, near the mouth of the Thames, is considered the Royal Navy's worst defeat, with numerous ships destroyed, damaged or captured. De Ruyter's raid also disrupted commerce during the crucial sailing window for the Hudson Bay expedition. The dangerously ice-choked and turbulent "furious overfall" of Hudson Strait was safely navigable only in the summer and the delay meant that the season was too far advanced to risk a voyage, so the expedition was put off for another year. Because the sailing conditions were essentially unknown, apart from the few-decades-old reports of earlier English mariners, Rupert and his investors wanted perfect conditions to test the viability of the route for regular commerce. A successful outcome was far from assured, and the venture could easily be seen as speculative and dangerous: a voyage to a largely unknown destination to conduct commerce with an unknown people whom only Radisson and Groseilliers had claimed to have met.

But the spirit of the age was one of irrepressible optimism after the smothering years of Puritan rule, and so these nods to realism meant delays rather than cancellations. British aristocrats viewed the little-known hinterlands of northern North America much as the Romans viewed the Celtic tribes of Britain before they invaded the northern island sixteen hundred years earlier—a relatively harmless people with primitive technology, about whom they knew little nor cared much about except as it might prove advantageous to engage with them commercially. And it was only Radisson's and Groseilliers' woods experience and knowledge of the local customs and languages that made the voyage to trade for furs in Hudson Bay possible in the first place. In addition to speaking French, English and some Dutch, between them Groseilliers and Radisson knew several dialects of Algonquian and Iroquoian, Sioux and some Cree. They were both comfortable in confusing and awkward social settings and familiar in a general sense with Indigenous North American ceremony, diplomacy and customs of commerce. At the time of its financial founding, they were by far the Company's greatest asset.

Finally, nearly eight years after they devised their audacious scheme to realign the fur trade, Radisson and Groseilliers were ready to sally forth down the Thames to Hudson Bay. On the morning of June 3, 1668, the ships hoisted sails at Gravesend and passed the gathered nabobs as they headed out to sea. Radisson sailed aboard the *Eaglet* while Groseilliers sailed aboard the *Nonsuch*, which was captained by Zachariah Gillam, the Boston captain who had attempted a voyage with the two adventurers years earlier. The *Eaglet* carried more provisions and equipment and planned to overwinter and return the following summer, while the *Nonsuch* intended to accompany the larger ship, drop off its cargo and quickly return the same season.

The two small ships were heavily loaded and rode low in the water, their holds stuffed with all manner of items deemed useful to trade with the Cree, as determined by Radisson and Groseilliers. The two Frenchmen were given great latitude in running the commercial aspect of the operation. The instructions called on the ships' captains to "use the said Mr. Gooseberry and Mr. Radisson with all manner of Civility and Courtesy and to take care that all your Company doe beare a particular respect unto them, they being the persons upon whose Credit wee have undertaken this expedition." Foreseeing concerns arising from their French nationality, and English mariners not wanting to take direction from foreigners, the instructions were explicit that they were to be in charge. Although the instructions also predominantly described discovery, the potential for mineral deposits, locations for settlement and a permanent fort, and the discovery of the passage to the South Seas as further objectives, these were public relations gestures: returning with a hold full of furs was the primary goal.

Well out to sea to the northwest of Ireland, the flotilla was hammered by a terrifying storm. A "sudden great storme did rise and put us a sunder," Radisson wrote. "The sea was soe furious six or seven hours after that it did almost ouerturne our ship, so that we were forced to cut our masts rather than cutt our lives." Radisson and the *Eaglet* limped back to London, while Groseilliers and the *Nonsuch* pushed on alone. That winter, Radisson put himself to use writing his memoirs at Prince Rupert's request and charming the backers of the expedition, including later eloping with and marrying the daughter of Sir John Kirke, whom he apparently "deluded and privately married." Kirke was a prominent London man of business, one of the original financial backers of the expedition and later of the Hudson's Bay Company.

THE SMALL FIFTY-FIVE TON *Nonsuch* cruised safely through Hudson Strait and proceeded south into James Bay, where they located a good harbour at the mouth of what they called the Rupert River after their patron. There they cut down some small trees and hammered together a primitive dwelling for the winter, stuffing the chinks between the logs with grasses. It was the first commercial depot built in Hudson Bay, and Groseilliers called it Charles Fort after their even more important patron, the king. It was later renamed Rupert House and became the village of Waskaganish in Quebec. Tutored by a woods-man of Groseilliers's talents, the men quickly finished the fort and then fished and hunted ptarmigans, passing the winter in monotonous health apart from some mild cases of scurvy. Groseilliers instructed them in the usual local Indigenous custom of treating scurvy with bitter spruce beer.

In the spring, following their usual pattern, various Cree bands began to return to the coast and were naturally surprised to see visitors settled in at the mouth of the river. Soon word spread that the visitors were there to trade, and over the summer around three hundred Cree came to the fort and bartered their winter fur coats for the axes, needles, metal scrapers, various firearms, gunpowder, tobacco, ropes, saws and other metal goods that were rare and valuable to them and normally expensive since they otherwise had to acquire these goods from other traders, principally the Montagnais, who dealt directly with the French traders farther south in Quebec.

The Cree were a numerous, semi-nomadic people whose habitual lands were the forested fringe around the bay. They were renowned for their hunting prowess, and for most of the year lived inland in decentralized bands of up to twelve people, or two related families. Commercial minded and entrepreneurial, they quickly became avid suppliers and traders and were closely linked to the Company's fortunes, spreading west along with the trade in the eighteenth century. Despite being the Company's principal traders, except during the brief summer months when they journeyed to the coast, knowledge of their culture and customs remained superficial to the Company Baymen in their forts until the eighteenth century, when the trade settled into a predictable and stable pattern. Even Groseilliers knew little of the woodland Cree whose lands he was visiting,

In mid-June, the *Nonsuch* made ready to depart the "bottom of the bay," as the region became known, and reached London three months later after an uneventful voyage. They had found no passage to the South Seas, but they had vindicated Groseilliers's and Radisson's claims that the fur trade from Hudson Bay would be profitable. In stark contrast to other expeditions, the ship had returned without suffering horribly and with a hold of valuable beaver pelts. Calculating profit and loss is not easily done for such a pioneering entrepreneurial venture, but after the cost of the goods, the wages of the employees and the repairs to the ships, especially the *Eaglet*, were accounted for and balanced against the prices fetched on the London fur market, the investors were pleased. From the desolate and gravelly shores of the northern bay, these bales of slick and shiny pelts would be turned into coats, felt hats and other stylish and fashionable accessories for status-hungry socialites, courtiers and financiers who rode their carriages and strode the streets in the better parts of town garbed in this latest symbol of wealth and sophistication. The demand certainly existed, and the supply could only improve with knowledge of the route, the climate and the people. The new enterprise was poised to gain access to a region that seemed custom-made for the fur business—a network of river systems that sprawled web-like from Hudson Bay and James Bay, deep into the interior of the continent—a transportation and travel network well developed by centuries of use by Indigenous peoples, with a climate cold enough that beaver grew luxuriant pelts in winter, and rugged terrain that limited population and permanent settlement.

While the original investors immediately began planning another voyage for the next summer and commissioning a ship for that use, the *Prince Rupert*, backroom negotiations were under way to determine the governing structure of the new enterprise that seemed to have such a promising future. There were always political considerations. In this case King Charles II weighed his friendship with King Louis XIV of France, who secretly provided Charles with a portion of the money that enabled his extravagant expenditures independent of the English Parliament. In April 1670, Louis had granted a monopoly to a Dutch adventurer named Laurens Van Heemskerk, who claimed that he had made a voyage to the South Seas through Hudson Bay. Van Heemskerk's claims to the French king were just a fabricated fistful of stories he had heard from Groseilliers, and were part of the effort to lure the two Frenchmen back into the service of France, to prevent the English project and with it English expansion. The French did not want an English presence north of their St. Lawrence settlement to squeeze them pincer-like between the already much larger English settlements to the south along the Atlantic.

But Rupert's persuasion, and indeed the enterprise's glowing prospects, swayed Charles. After delaying for months, on May 2, 1670, he agreed to grant to his cousin Prince Rupert and seventeen fellow court-ier-adventurers a charter giving to them the "Sole Trade and Commerce" of Hudson's Bay as "true and absolute Lordes and Proprietors" of the region that included "all those Seas Streightes Bayes Rivers Lakes Creekes and Sounds in whatsoever Latitude they shall bee that lye within the entrance of the Streightes commonly called Hudsons Streightes together with all the Landes Countryes and Territoryes upon the Coastes and Confynes of the Seas . . . aforesaid." The charter was handwritten on five calfskin, or deerskin, parchment pages and is about seven thousand words long. Rupert kept it under lock and key in his private quarters before it was moved to the Company's headquarters in London. The document was beautifully illuminated with illustrated borders on each side of the page and at the top. An illustration of King Charles II appears in the top left corner of the first page, and his royal seal, a green-tinted wax disk, certified the document's authenticity. The territory, of unknown extent and geography, was named Rupert's Land.

Charles II had granted his cronies a grandiose monopoly absurd in its scope and geographical misunderstanding—absolute mercantile authority in British law over a territory that encompassed the entire watershed of Hudson Bay, some four million square kilometres, over 40 per cent of the later territory of Canada, including northern Ontario and Quebec, all of Manitoba, southern Saskatchewan and southern Alberta and a good portion of the states of North Dakota and Minnesota. Since no one from England or any other European nation had been there and there were no maps, it would be generations before they had a clear idea what the grant entailed. The king appointed his cousin Rupert, perhaps for a fee, the first governor of the Company of Adventurers of England Trading into Hudson's Bay. The governor was to be assisted by a committee of seven well-connected gentlemen.

The charter for the Company was based upon those for other similar monopolies then in vogue in Europe. The Dutch West India Company owned plantations in the Caribbean and in New Netherland (recently captured by the English and named New York), the Dutch East India Company held a Dutch monopoly over the spice trade in Indonesia, and the English East India Company held a similar charter for trade and commerce in India. The charters essentially created monopolies that protected the investors against competition within their jurisdiction, so that they could operate risky ventures without having to worry about merchants from their own nation undercutting or interfering with their operations.

Given that the Company of Adventurers of England Trading into Hudson's Bay was a perilous and uncertain operation never attempted before, and that it would pay political dividends as well as monetary ones, King Charles justified it. That nearly all the investors were friends, acquaintances and relatives made it all the easier. The initial investors included the powerful and influential of the realm, luminaries such as Christopher Wren and Robert Boyle and other titled and rich members of London's nobility and financial elite, including six members of the Privy Council and the king's brother James, Duke of York. The Company still had to pay taxes, and its operations would provide a hitherto non-existent market for English manufactured goods, as Charles sought to broaden British commerce from its dependence upon the Dutch and the Baltic region and to counter the expansion of New France. The Company was a means of tapping private capital to pursue foreign policy.

The Company was not a colonial enterprise—nothing in its charter had to do directly with conquest, but neither was it purely a business enterprise. While commercial transactions for profit was the primary objective for the first century of its existence, the new entity would also be saddled with a few minor obligations, such as continuing to search for the route to the Spice Islands in Asia. Put forth in the preamble of the charter were also a few vague non-committal obligations, for example to establish permanent commercial outposts "by meanes whereof there may probably arise very great advantage to us and our Kingdome." The king wanted to ensure that once unleashed, the Company could still be held accountable in some way for its activities, or that at least it would have a patriotic obligation not to turn a blind eye to any geographical discoveries that were of no use to it as a merchant company but may have political or commercial value to England. The Company always had a legal responsibility of loyalty to the Crown that was not imposed on any other purely commercial entity operating out of London.

Nevertheless, settlement was never of any interest to the Company, and for a hundred and fifty years it avoided, or actively opposed, even admitting any Europeans other than its own employees from travelling its domain. If Company agents encountered any other travellers or business representatives, they were empowered to confiscate all the goods and property of the offending individuals, paying half the value to the king and keeping half themselves for their trouble. Since they were burdened with the costs of defending their monopoly, this was deemed reasonable compensation. The Company was given, or burdened with, the full authority and responsibility to uphold justice between English subjects within Rupert's Land, without recourse to appeal to the government across the Atlantic, and tasked with the job of outfitting and supporting its own armed forces to defend its interests. Charles II wanted the taxes but not the responsibility.

Nor was the Company enflamed by missionary zeal. The charter has no provisions for proselytizing the people within their commercial monopoly, although the Colonial Office issued a set of guidelines for the Company afterwards, almost as an afterthought, to make sure the "true and absolute Lordes and Proprietors" hadn't been given too much power. The guidelines strictly forbade the Company from any activity that would inflame relations between the English and any Indigenous peoples, and tasked it specifically with policing the actions of its employees and severely punishing them if they caused any damage to the goods, persons or possessions of any people within the boundaries of the charter. They were also urged to provide instruction in the Protestant religion to any who requested it. In any case, nothing was ever done with this vague urging apart from a single chaplain dispatched for a few years in the 1680s, and another chaplain who visited the Hudson Bay posts for a single year a decade later. Business was business, and the Company was preoccupied with making money, not the spread of cultural values.

But neither was the Company given any diplomatic guidelines regulating how its agents should or could interact with the people living in the lands of their commercial monopoly. They were specifically not to make war with any other Christian nation or monarch (by which was meant European, and specifically French, since there were no others anywhere nearby or even potentially nearby). Beyond the requirement to not embarrass the king or embroil the kingdom in an expensive conflict as a result of its profit-seeking actions, the Company operated independently. It was tied to the English monarchy with a feudal-like governing structure of responsibilities, obligations, oaths and ceremonial functions, but otherwise was left on its own. The Company was, however, in addition to other exotic gifts to the king, required to pay for this royal privilege with a ceremonial presentation of two elks and two black beavers "whensoever and as often as Wee our heirs and successors shall happen to enter into the said Countryes." This peculiar symbolic rent to the king was never once paid, since no English or British monarch, nor any of the aristocratic London investors or governors, ever visited the Company's domain until the twentieth century, many decades after the original monopoly charter had ceased to have any force and the Company was merely a business operating within the Dominion of Canada.

Rupert, now in his fifties, had deep ties to London's financiers and was becoming ever more interested in promoting English commerce; he had recently been asked to lend his support to and christen the cornerstone of London's newly formed Royal Exchange. He and the other key investors schemed and planned throughout the winter of 1670. They envisioned annual flotillas of ships crossing the Atlantic from England loaded with knives, saws, kettles, utensils, mirrors, muskets, pots, axes, sewing needles, gun shot, gunpowder, wool cloth, beads, tobacco, brandy and other tools and sundry implements that would find welcome along the shores of Hudson Bay.

The plan was to make a series of forts or factories (so named because the factor, or agent, would be in attendance) at suitable locations along the frozen shore of the bay, near the mouths of the principal rivers so that it would be easy for Cree and later other Indigenous traders to reach them in the spring after they hunted beaver during the winter when pelts were thickest and when they were inland anyway following their usual semi-nomadic cycle. The Company's trade season fit ideally within the existing way of life of the Cree. But it also suited the Company's traders, since they could do business in the late spring and summer, load the ships and sail away before ice closed the bay for the winter. The Company's long-term business plan was to have a permanent workforce stationed in the bay to maintain constant contact with the local peoples, so that each year ever more could be persuaded to make the journey to trade, to build long-term relationships.

But the new world the Company entered in the 1670s was bewildering and unknown. Even with the help of Groseilliers and Radisson and their knowledge of Cree and Ojibwa culture they had gained from travelling through the territory, it was decades before the Company began to appreciate the politically and culturally complex world of their trading monopoly. Groseilliers and Radisson understood the bonds of ritual kinship that were needed to secure ongoing relationships, to foster trust and respect. They were both skilled in trade rituals and knew what type of items were in demand and the prices that could be charged. With this knowledge, the Company launched into its project with verve and optimism. People began canoeing the rivers to the Company's outposts on the coast each year, and the Company steadily increased the number of those posts. The trade was immediately profitable for both sides and conducted largely in a peaceful and mutually beneficial way, with ever-increasing quantities of beaver flooding the London fur markets, and from there onward to merchants in Amsterdam and France.

IT WAS A SEEMINGLY RANDOM flight of fashion that began the dramatic expansion in commerce between the English, French and many of the Indigenous peoples of North America. Furs have always had value in winter for warmth, and to a lesser extent had value for their water-resistant properties, but it was their use in the manufacture of felt that drove the demand in Europe. Felt was developed originally in central Asia as an excellent insulating and waterproofing material for tents and tarps; it was also used in ancient times by Roman legionaries as padding under their armour. In seventeenth-century Europe, felt was primarily used in the manufacture of hats, an ever-changing fashion accoutrement that became an indispensable signifier of prestige and social identity first for gentlemen and ladies and then, as the century progressed, for nearly every status of person. The style of hat signalled the level of prestige and the profession of the wearer. Picture the distinctive tricorne or Continental hat; or the cocked hat of the navy; the dignified stovepipe Regent, or top hat, of the financiers; and the somewhat amusing Paris Beau beloved of the young urban rake. Ladies' hats had their own hierarchy of frivolity, complexity and expense—and attendant etiquette and social flourishes that governed how a hat was worn and with which accessories, how it was donned and with which distinctive and noble gesture it was removed.

In general, the waterproof and durable beaver felt hat, which could be dyed and moulded into a bewildering variety of shapes, was perfectly suited to symbolize and reflect the desires of an increasingly stratified and mercenary society. People were marked by their hats, the prices of which were well known and appreciated. Since it took about three to four worn beaver pelts to make enough felt for a single hat, some hats were so pricey that they were carefully tended and repaired for years and then passed down as inheritances. Even wealthy people kept inferior spares to be worn in inclement weather, saving their best beaver for notable occasions—or at least occasions when others might note the quality and make of their hat.

Felt was made using heat, moisture, pressure and mercury nitrate to shrink the fur fibres so that they matted together. Hatters spent long hours toiling away in their poorly ventilated tenements, inhaling clouds of mercury fumes as they bent over their felt-making apparatus, combing, pressing and steaming the pelts into the desired consistency and shape. Mercury was eventually discovered to have debilitating effects on the hatter, causing a type of poisoning called erethism, or mad hatter disease, which was characterized by tremors, depression, delirium, memory loss and hallucinations. Hatter wasn't a profession or trade conducive to a long and healthy life, but nor were many other occupations of the era, and the dangers were poorly understood while the pay could be high.

By the early eighteenth century, London was not only the principal depot for the wholesale warehouses of prime beaver pelts from the best beaver preserve in the world, but by a coincidence of history it was also becoming the global centre for hat manufacture, which for centuries had been based in northern France. Seventeenth-century Europe was riven with religious conflict between Catholics and Protestants. Many of the felt and hat manufacturing trades were dominated by French Protestant Huguenots. In the mid-1680s, they began to flee their homes and cross the English Channel to escape religious persecution. They settled in the vicinity of London and brought with them the secrets of their trade, so that soon the best hats in Europe made from the best beaver pelts from North America originated in London. The most distinguished French nobility, and even Catholic cardinals, ordered their distinctive hats from Protestant hat makers in London.

FUR HAD ALWAYS BEEN THE KEY economic driver behind French settlement in the St. Lawrence, just as it would be the driver of the Company's monumental expansion. The Jesuit priest Father Le Jeune wrote in 1634 that the Montagnais "say that [beaver] is the animal well-beloved by the French, English and Basques, in a word, by the Europeans." When he was a guest travelling in their country, Le Jeune "heard my host say one day, jokingly, 'The Beaver does everything perfectly well, it makes kettles, hatchets, swords, knives, bread; and, in short, it makes everything.' He was making sport of us Europeans, who have such a fondness for the skin of this animal and who fight to see who will get it; they carry this to such an extent that my host said to me one day, showing me a very beautiful knife, 'The English have no sense; they give us twenty knives like this for one Beaver skin.'"

Castor canadensis, the North American beaver, is the largest rodent in North America. Chubby, with dark brown fur, they weigh on average around forty-five pounds, with a range of between twenty-five and seventy pounds, increasing in size along with the latitude. In the Far North, old beavers have been recorded over a hundred pounds in weight. They fell trees to construct dams to flood waterways into ponds or small lakes where they construct hummock-shaped lodges with twigs, stones and mud. A land dominated by millions of beavers, as much of North America was, takes on distinct characteristics. The numerous ponds and flooded areas increased biodiversity by providing habitat for fish and waterfowl, while the clearings in the forest supported large game and a host of other species. In addition, when stewed in a broth, beaver was an important food source.

Beavers had long been nearly extinct in Europe and their pelts had to be shipped from Siberia, processed by Russian craftsmen and sold into Europe at inflated prices by Russian merchants. The beaver from the Hudson River region and from the St. Lawrence was never the highest quality, and the animals had quickly become depleted so that most of the beaver being traded to the French was passing through multiple hands, ultimately coming from farther north and west. But the region bounded by the Hudson's Bay Company's commercial charter contained between ten and twenty million beavers, making their monopoly in theory extremely valuable. (There were upwards of a hundred million beavers throughout North America.) The Company's monopoly contained nearly half the world's supply of fresh water, it was swampy and low with innumerable lakes and ponds, and it was covered in aspen and birch forests, prime beaver food, and sectioned by rivers that drained toward Hudson Bay from deep in the interior. There could be no better habitat for beavers anywhere on the planet, and no better location for a trading fort than at the terminus of the rivers that flowed toward the bay.

English ships in Hudson Bay were certainly a threat to the economic prospects of New France. For the Cree it meant much easier access to goods that could be obtained more cheaply than if they traded their furs to the Montagnais, Ojibwa or others to take to the distant St. Lawrence for sale. As Groseilliers predicted, the woodland Cree whose lands encompassed the drainage basin of Hudson Bay were by far the best beaver hunters, living in the best beaver habitat, and they did indeed clothe themselves in winter in "castors' skins." A beaver skin that had been previously worn was particularly valuable and was given the moniker "made beaver," which became a standard conversion for other items. Everything was priced in a value of made beaver. All the English goods for sale at Company outposts and all the other types of furs and country goods offered for sale by the Indigenous populations were first converted into a quantity of made beaver. But what does "made beaver" signify?

For generations Russian furriers had perfected a method of refining furs by combing and separating the soft and plush under-fur, or "wool," from the coarse outer hairs. The wool was suited for felting because of thousands of tiny barbs that cause it to become matted together when pressed. The stiff outer "guard" fur was used in the making of fine fur coats and accoutrements. Naturally, the Russians were secretive about the process, and until it was discovered by English furriers in the later eighteenth century, most furs brought into Europe from North America had to be repacked and shipped east to Russia for processing before the under-fur was shipped back to be refined into the felt hats that fashion dictated. Some furs, however, were able to bypass this costly and time-consuming Russian processing. The long, cold winters of the northlands caused the beavers to put on thick, lustrous coats; and for the same reason the Cree, and other people yet unknown to the Company, wore their own beaver coats for many months of the year. Wearing their coats, with the fur facing inward as was the custom, for all these months as they went about their business caused the guard furs to separate and drop out—eventually making the fur coat lose its value as a winter garment suitable for a rugged way of life but gain immeasurably in value to English and French traders.

Any beaver coat worn for any length of time was worth far more than a pelt from a freshly trapped and skinned beaver. It became a source of amusement to the traders how valuable cast-off garments could be at the end of winter, when the Cree were accustomed to tossing them away. The most valuable furs were ones that had been gently used for more than one winter. Used clothing could be easily exchanged for all manner of goods, and as Father Le Jeune recorded, many believed that "the English have no sense" for paying so much for it. Once the Company began sailing to Hudson Bay and trading directly with the Cree, material wealth along the coast rapidly increased.

But the enduring problem from the earliest days was that there were only so many winter coats that an individual could wear, no matter the price to be had from selling them afterwards to credulous foreigners. And so this inspired a new enterprise: local people would surreptitiously purchase the used clothing of people just a little farther distant from wherever the traders were located, and then pass them on—acting as brokers in the trade rather than exclusively as producers. Although this could be a lucrative endeavour, it usually didn't last more than a couple of generations. Either the Company traders found a way around the middlemen who were keeping the prices high, or the people farther inland recognized the true value of their used clothes if they could themselves reach the trading depots. This created a series of short-lived commercial empires. Two of the largest and most successful were the Iroquois Confederacy in the mid-seventeenth century, maintained by the "beaver wars," and the western Cree of the eighteenth century. It was a cycle that had defined the history of the European–Indigenous economic relationship since the beginnings of New France just before

Radisson and Groseilliers' time, and it was a pattern that quickly repli-cated itself for the English traders along Hudson Bay.

HUNTING BEAVER FOR THEIR PELTS long predated the arrival of Europeans. Indigenous people always had uses for the furs of animals, and particularly beaver, for clothing, for sleeping robes and pallets, and for travel coverings for some of the same reasons beaver were hunted to extinction in Europe—their furs were warm and water-resistant. But it wasn't easy to hunt beaver, even for the Cree who were practised at it and lived where these rodents reigned supreme.

There were several main methods for hunting beaver, and each depended upon the season. In the spring, beavers were taken in a trap baited with the wood most beloved by the toothy rodents, the tasty inner bark of aspen and birch. The trap worked like a lobster pot—a cage-like container that was easy to get into but difficult to get out of because of a narrowing of the entrance tunnel. In the winter, the hunters used nets. They would creep quietly onto the ice near a beaver lodge, slice a slit in the ice and lower the net down near the beaver's house, baited with tender bark, and then, according to a Jesuit priest who described the operation, "this poor animal, searching for something to eat, gets caught in a net made of good, strong, double cord; and, emerging from the water to the opening made in the ice, they kill it with a big club."

The most skilful technique, which was most common among the Cree, was to crack open the beaver's lodge with a hatchet. The most impressive lodges, according to a seventeenth-century account, were "two stories high, and round. The materials of which it is composed are wood and mud, so well joined and bound together. The lower story is in or upon the edge of the water, the upper is above the river. When the cold has frozen the rivers and ponds, the Beaver secludes himself in the upper story, where he has provided himself with wood to eat during the Winter. He sometimes, however, descends from this story to the lower one, and thence he glides out under the ice, through the holes which are in this lower storey and which open under the ice." Once the house was cracked open, "these poor animals, which are sometimes in great numbers under one roof, disappear under the ice, some on one side, some on the other, seeking hollow and thin places between the water and ice, where they can breathe. Their enemies, knowing this, go walking over the pond or frozen river, carrying a long club in their hands, armed on one side with an iron blade made like a Carpenter's chisel, and on the other with a Whale's bone, I believe. They sound the ice with this bone, striking upon it and examining it to see if it is hollow; and if there is any indication of this, then they cut the ice with their iron blade, looking to see if the water is stirred up by the movement or breathing of the Beaver. If the water moves, they have a curved stick which they thrust into the hole that they have just made; if they feel the Beaver, they kill it with their big club." Most methods of hunting beaver before and during the early era of the fur trade were variations on these techniques, until Sewell Newhouse of New York State invented the spring-loaded steel leg-hold trap in 1823. Before this invention, it was not an easy task to capture a beaver.

Owing to the difficulty of hunting the animals and the need to wear their fur as a coat for a year, the number of beaver pelts available to trade was somewhat limited even though beavers lived in great quantities in the Hudson Bay drainage basin and across the northwest. "Prior to the discovery of Canada," wrote David Thompson, the famous cartographer and fur trader, "this Continent, from the Latitude of 40 degrees north to the Arctic Circle, and from the Atlantic to the Pacific Ocean, may be said to have been in the possession of two distinct races of Beings, Man and the Beaver. Except [for] the Great Lakes the waves of which are too turbulent it occupied all the waters of the northern part of the continent. Every River where the current was moderate and the water sufficiently deep, the banks at the water edge were occupied by their houses . . . all the lowlands were in possession of the Beaver, and all the hollows of the higher grounds."

Once the steel trap began to be used in the Company's domain, hunting beaver, which had been previously a job of patience, knowledge and skill, became one of merely snowshoeing between beaver ponds setting the traps and returning later to claim the frozen carcass. The leg-hold traps allowed a hunter to kill upwards of a dozen beavers each day rather than each season. Steel leg-hold traps in fact made it so easy to harvest beaver that the populations declined precipitously. A region that once would have provided several generations of commercial quantities of beaver to hunters now could be scoured clean with a few years of dedicated effort and the Company introduced conservation policies to manage the beaver populations within their domain.

BEAVERS WERE IMPORTANT ANIMALS IN the cultural and spiritual traditions of many Indigenous peoples of North America, a source of metaphorical symbolism. In some mythologies they could represent perseverance or hard work and productivity, but also stubbornness. Beavers could be represented as the shapers of the world, a nod to their transformative landscape redesign. Conversely, they could be viewed as selfish for continuously building dams and flooding places without consulting other animals. In the fur trade era, they came to represent wealth or male hunting prowess. To some Plains peoples, such as the Blackfoot-speaking Siksika, Kainai (Blood) and the Piegan, beavers represented wisdom. To other peoples, including the Huron-Wendat and the Iroquois (Haudenosaunee), they were an integral component of the order of clans within communities.

Beavers could occupy symbolic positions in the cosmology and were often used as allegory, the classic example being the Woman Who Married a Beaver, an Ojibwa (Anishinaabe) story in which a woman leaves her people and goes to dwell with her husband, a beaver, only returning to visit her human family periodically. They have children, and the husband and offspring, who also occasionally visit the human world, are killed by hunters but return alive to the beaver world each time with gifts of tobacco and needles and other trade goods. Only upon the beaver-husband's death in the beaver world do the woman and her children return to the human world, bringing with them an important message: always honour the beaver and never discredit or slander them on pain of bringing down a curse of poor fortune at hunting. As part of the hunter's code, beaver bones were often returned to the water in a small ceremony under the belief that animals are caught only when they willingly give themselves, and must be honoured with the proper rituals and thanks for their sacrifice.

BEAVERS BECAME SO VALUABLE TO BOTH Europeans and Indigenous peoples in the seventeenth and eighteenth centuries that numerous engravings of their lives, and the methods of hunting them, could be found in European travel books and maps. The misinformation is amusingly inaccurate. In the tradition of medieval bestiaries that include fanciful and imaginary creatures alongside semi-accurate depictions of actual animals, beavers are depicted with enormous bucked teeth and curiously intelligent and humanlike eyes. Oddly anthropomorphized, they stride erect, carrying log poles toward lodges that resemble communal multi-storey apartment buildings. Sometimes, overactive imaginations showed half-naked men garbed in togas, the stylized depictions of the Indigenous hunters, forming ranks along the banks of ponds or rivers firing long, smoking rifles at humanesque beavers, while the gentle myopic beasts swim and chew at the trunks of large trees, apparently unaware of, or unconcerned with, the presence of the hunters.

Written accounts of beavers had them dwelling in sprawling communal house-villages, speaking to each other and working in organized groups to secure food and build their dome-like dwellings. Some writers claimed that they had social stratification, including the use of beaver-slaves to speed the construction. One early eighteenth-century observer, Pierre-François-Xavier de Charlevoix, mused that "there are sometimes three or four hundred of them in one place, forming a town which might properly enough be called a little Venice." Other accounts had them living in nations and waging war against each other. The fur trader and traveller Samuel Hearne, a man well exposed to the more prosaic lives of the furry flat-tailed denizens of the lowlands, expressed amusement at this attribution of noble traits. In his classic *Journey to the Northern Ocean* he wrote: "I cannot refrain from smiling when I read the accounts of different authors who have written on the economy of those animals, as there seems to be a contest between them, who shall most exceed in fiction . . . Little remains to be added beside a vocabulary of their language, a code of their laws, and a sketch of their religion." Hearne also addressed the claim that the beaver's tail was actually a natural trowel used in the construction of their apartments or for plastering the inner walls. "It would be as impossible for a beaver to use its tail as a trowel," he wrote, ". . . as it would have been for Sir James Thornhill to have painted the dome of St. Paul's Cathedral without the assistance of scaffolding." Nevertheless, Hearne was fond of beavers, and when he was a senior officer at one of the Company's forts in the 1780s, he kept beavers as pets and reported that "they were remarkably fond of rice and plum pudding."

It wasn't just the beaver's pelt that was considered valuable. A seemingly miraculous substance known as castoreum, a yellowish exudate secreted by the teardrop-shaped castor glands, or "beaver stones," located between the pelvis and tail of mature male and female beavers. It was used both as scent to mark territory and to keep their fur greasy and waterproof, and beavers were so attracted to the smell that it was often used as bait in traps. Once removed from the beaver, the castoreum was preserved by smoking it over a fire. Today it is occasionally used in perfume or as an exotic and expensive form of artificial vanilla or strawberry flavouring. In more credulous eras it had other, reputedly beneficial properties. Since ancient times in the Mediterranean, castoreum was variously deployed by physicians as a cure for epilepsy, to induce abortions and to assuage the ravages of tuberculosis. It also had other properties that were suitable to a difficult-to-obtain and expensive medicinal ingredient: it could cure dementia, toothaches and gout as well as relieve headaches and fevers. (Castoreum does contain salicylic acid, the main ingredient in Aspirin, so this last was probably an accurate claim.) According to the writings of the seventeenth-century French physician Johannes Francus, castoreum was also beneficial for improving eyesight, getting rid of fleas, preventing hiccups, promoting sleep and preventing sleep, and of clearing the brain. He also reported that "in order to acquire a prodigious memory and never to forget what one had once read, it was only necessary to wear a hat of the beaver's skin, to rub the head and spine every month with that animal's oil, and to take twice a year the weight of a gold crown-piece of castoreum."

Equally grounded in amusing ancient lore was the beaver's apparent antics when hunted. According to a bestiary from the twelfth century, "There is an animal called Castor the Beaver, none more gentle, and his testicles make a capital medicine. For this reason, so Physiologus says, when he [the beaver] notices that he is being pursued by the hunter, he removes his own testicles with a bite, and casts them before the sportsman, and thus escapes by flight. What is more, if he should again happen to be chased by a second hunter, he lifts himself up and shows his members to him. And the latter, when he perceives the testicles to be missing, leaves the beaver alone." Hence the reason the beaver is called Castor— because it is castrated. Of course, the beaver wasn't castrated, even in this fanciful tale, since the castor glands are not testicles but scent glands. Nevertheless, many hundreds of thousands of glands were shipped to Europe by the Company along with the pelts.

That such a gentle and innocuous creature should inspire such artistic liberty seems unusual, but the money to be had from processing their pelts and castoreum was also unusual. Whether there was any empirical evidence justifying the value of castoreum is open to question. But when has fashion had anything to do with science or proof? Or even common sense? The hunt for beavers was beginning the economic transformation of a continent.

Chapter Three

CLASH OF EMPIRES

After a tedious six-week voyage from London, the three-masted *Wivenhoe* hove to in a flood tide in an estuary off the mouth of the Hayes River. Some men clambered over the gunwales and into a smaller longboat and rowed ashore. One of the men was the new field governor, a formerly rambunctious religious quack named Charles Bayley, who had been serving time in the Tower of London for his heretical rantings. Another was Radisson. They inspected the bleak, gravelly beachhead that Groseilliers suspected might lead directly into the heart of an unknown continent, performed a perfunctory ceremony and hammered into the ground a plaque affixed with King Charles's royal coat of arms. Then a squall forced them to retreat back to the *Wivenhoe*. They put back out to sea and steered southeast to join the other ship, *Prince Rupert*, captained by Zachariah Gillam with Groseilliers aboard as trader, at Charles Fort, which they promptly renamed Rupert House. They had brought a great deal of supplies in addition to large quantities of trade goods, but it would be fourteen years before workers would expand the premises.

The first order of business was to reaffirm the "league of friendship," negotiated by Groseilliers the year before, with arriving bands of Cree. The trading continued throughout the summer, and Groseilliers and Radisson also hired some of the local men as hunters to bring in the bounty of the land to the small outpost. Deer, geese and other migratory birds, and whitefish livened the dry provisions brought on the ship. Radisson and Groseilliers sent out smaller boats along the coast and began scouting good locations for additional trade forts. Bayley, "the old Quaker with a long beard," began to learn some of the skills he would need as the new governor before the supply ships departed for London in August. Prince Rupert and his secretary James Hayes, in consultation with Radisson and Groseilliers, had devised an ambitious business plan that called for a series of permanent overwintering factories, or forts, serviced by an annual fleet of ships from London that would sail into the bay, service the forts and depart in the same season.

Although it would be nearly a century before the Company ventured inland along any of the rivers to trade, throughout the 1670s the Company expanded its network of outposts at most of the major rivers that disgorged into the bay. Moose Factory, in the south of James Bay, was founded in 1672. Fort Albany, at the Albany River in present-day Ontario, was established in 1679. Farther west and north, along the main part of Hudson Bay, was Fort Severn, founded in 1689. At the mouth of the Nelson River was York Factory, founded in 1684, and farthest north was Fort Churchill (Prince of Wales Fort), founded in 1717. The Company maintained this configuration, with minor variations, until the late eighteenth century.

Under Rupert's stewardship of the finances and Bayley's management of the field operations, the Company was earning significant profits, on an admittedly small capital outlay, and invested everything back into the business to fuel its expansion. In 1684, in its fifteenth year of operation, the Company issued its first dividend to shareholders, a pleasing 50 per cent. But the operation's logistical and financial success was attracting the attention of French political and economic interests who were not as enamoured with the Company's presence as the Cree were. The Cree were receiving better-quality and cheaper goods from the Company posts in the bay than were being offered in the St. Lawrence, and naturally the flow of furs began to shift northward. The Company, although ostensibly an independent business, was always associated with the British Crown—in a royal sense, not just a national sense. Just before his death in 1682, Rupert, in his capacity as a vice admiral, issued a special warrant that granted the Company the right to use a variation of the Royal Navy's Red Ensign as its official flag at its forts and on its ships. No other private businesses were allowed to affiliate themselves so blatantly with the Royal Navy.

After Rupert died, the directors cast their eyes about for a suitable candidate for governor and settled, not on a professional financier or manager from London's financial district, but on the king's brother, James, Duke of York, the likely successor to the throne. The royal connection that had opened so many doors in the past did not shine with the same lustre with James as it had in Charles. While he may have bolstered the support for the monopoly charter, James did little to advance the Company's interests beyond lending it his name and title. He proved a lackadaisical and indifferent, if not mildly hostile, patron, since he had competing fur investments along the Hudson River valley in New York, and he was also a Catholic desirous of maintaining his relationship with France's King Louis XIV. James's ceremonial governorship lasted barely two years before he resigned to become England's new king, which itself lasted only a handful of years until he was forced to flee the country in 1688, replaced by his Protestant daughter Mary and her Dutch husband, William of Orange.

So soon faced with a vacancy in the most important position of governor, the directors again plumbed for politics rather than acumen, choosing John Churchill, first Duke of Marlborough. A powerful aristocrat and one of the greatest generals in British military history,

Churchill deployed his influence to the Company's benefit by providing for marines to serve aboard Company supply ships and for the Royal Navy to occasionally defend Company interests in Hudson Bay. He staved off growing challenges to the Company's monopoly (from a group of American fur merchants, the London-based Skinners' Company and the Company of Feltmakers), and reaffirmed the charter in 1690 by obtaining parliamentary sanction, preserving the Company's status and prestige as well as its links to the Crown. The political gambit proved valuable, if not in dividends from profits, at least by insulating the Company from pesky competitors. Its foothold on the bay was tentative and survival was never assured.

THE FIRST FRENCH TRAVELLERS TO Hudson Bay were spies. Since the Company was founded in 1670, French colonial authorities had been sending agents north along the rivers leading to the bay to intercept Cree traders heading to the Company's outposts and either trade with them or persuade them to head south instead. The Company's presence had reduced the flow of northern furs to New France to a trickle, a situation that threatened the economy of the small but growing community, and soon provoked aggressive tactics to disrupt the competition. It would be dangerous to allow the English to establish a trading alliance with Indigenous partners that was to the north, thereby pincering New France between two English commercial and political networks. The commerce in New France was further undermined when a smallpox epidemic that began in Quebec, brought on ships from France, worked its way inland along the St. Lawrence to Montreal and over the next year as far as the upper Great Lakes. The disease also spread along the northern rivers, wreaking severe damage among the Montagnais and Algonquin, and then south into Iroquoian territory. The diminished population meant that there were fewer people to hunt the beavers and wear the skins.

On the other hand, Bayley's unexpectedly calm and measured approach to the Company's business was profitable and notable for the absence of any drama. Groseilliers and Radisson, however, seemingly destined never to be satisfied, observed Bayley with squinted eyes. The pious Quaker, his earlier zealotry moderated by his time in prison, could hardly be expected to have got along with the garrulous and scheming French adventurers. They felt that he didn't give them the respect they deserved, especially regarding their repeated urgings that the Company venture inland along the rivers to create more trading posts closer to the source of the furs. But they were not entirely trusted by the English, who feared that their allegiance would one day return to the country of their birth, if it had not already secretly done so. Radisson wrote that Bayley "scornfully rejected all our advice in order to follow that of others which clearly would ruin the establishing of the trade, and on every occasion they demonstrated that they regarded us as useless people who, in their view, they no longer needed and who merited no recognition." The tensions between the English and the two French rogues rose particularly from the ranks of the ordinary English seamen, who had a reputation for being drunken and disorderly and for being impervious to common sense when dealing with the Cree or respecting French foreigners. Yet Radisson and Groseilliers were the main traders and cultural brokers, indispensable to the enterprise.

In 1672 the Jesuit missionary Father Charles Albanel, then fifty-five and apparently already a withered old man, departed Tadoussac in three large canoes with two companions and sixteen Montagnais guides to see for himself what the English Company was up to. The arduous journey involved two hundred portages around deadly waterfalls and eventually took them down the Rupert River to James Bay. Albanel encountered no English, as they were off hunting, so he devoted himself to trying to convert the local people to his religion before he headed back south. He concluded that it was clearly not a viable trade or travel route. But in January 1673, Albanel again made the journey, this time with the specific objective of meeting up with Radisson and Groseilliers and persuading them to return to the service of France. He arrived in August with a small contingent but was captured by Bayley and sent to London on the supply ship.

In London, Albanel urged Radisson and Groseilliers, who were in the city for the winter, to abandon the Company, arguing that it wasn't treating them very well anyway. Radisson nodded in agreement, "though only after having resisted doing so for a long time." Despite the former "bad treatment" at the hands of the French, a payment of 400 golden louis d'or settled the matter. Radisson later claimed that the sum was merely used to pay their debts that had increased under the parsimonious patronage of the Company. Radisson forfeited his pension and abandoned his English wife, the former Mary Kirke. "All my friends know that I loved my wife tenderly," he wrote in his defence after he and Groseilliers snuck across the Channel to France, where they had been promised a favourable reception. It was not to be. "They made us wait fruitlessly for a very long time," Radisson recalled, before being perfunctorily ordered to return to New France, where political squabbles continued to block their ambitions. The French authorities were content that the two traders were no longer working for the English Company, but were also distrustful because Radisson had left his wife in London. He was ordered to bring her to France, but her father wisely prevented her from departing the country.

Groseilliers shrugged and went back to his home in Trois-Rivières. The much younger Radisson, now unemployed and separated from his wife, continued to lead a life of intrigue and adventure. He managed to get a placement as a midshipman on a French naval expedition to attack Dutch colonies in West Africa and the Caribbean. As was typical for him, it ended in great adventure but little profit—shipwreck and rescue but the loss of all his booty.

Back in Paris in 1679, he strove to return to the fur business. The Company rebuffed his overtures of service, and he was also snubbed by France because his wife remained in London. They "could see that I still had English sentiments," he recalled, ". . . and that I ought not to expect they could trust me, nor that they would give me the slightest employment." Radisson sought a meeting with the pious and stern Charles Aubert de La Chesnaye, Montreal's first true financier and the founder of a business empire in fur, fish and farming. La Chesnaye was a man striving for social respectability, which he sought to achieve by the accumulation of wealth, even while living modestly. He was on a trip to Paris when he met Radisson in 1679 and urged him to join in a new venture for winning over the Cree, and Hudson Bay, to the French. He called his grandly ambitious venture La Compagnie du Nord, which was conceived as a challenger to the Company in the north. Radisson was promised a quarter of the profits for taking on a leadership role. By 1682, Chesnaye and Radisson had procured two ships and twenty-seven men to sail to Hudson Bay under Radisson's command. The plan called for them to return to the patch of beach that Radisson had claimed for the King of England with Bayley a decade earlier and establish a permanent trading outpost.

Remembering his and Groseilliers's audacious inland adventure from fifteen years before, Radisson was aware that the greatest store of prime furs lay to the north and west of Lake Superior, and that the Hayes or Nelson Rivers were likely the best arteries of travel to reach those distant lands. The expedition would include his nephew Jean-Baptiste Chouart, Groseilliers's son, an experienced trader of twenty-seven. Radisson wrote that Chouart was experienced in wood travel and that "all his life he had frequented the lands of the wild men and acquired great experience in trading with them."

But now, after over a decade of business in Hudson Bay, the Company was also ready to act on this long-standing concept of inland expansion. The time when the only ships plying the bay were English was drawing to a close.

Radisson's two small ships, the first French ships to sail through Hudson Strait into the bay, arrived at the mouth of the Hayes River on August 21, 1682, after about six weeks at sea from the St. Lawrence. They sailed upstream along the mighty Hayes River for about twenty-three kilometres. Radisson already knew that the Nelson and the Hayes Rivers joined upstream briefly before separating and heading inland along slightly different trajectories. The narrow peninsula that separated the mouth of the two rivers was called Port Nelson. The Nelson was the larger river, but canoe travellers from the interior almost always switched over to the Hayes because it was less turbulent and easier to navigate safely. For this reason, a trading outpost at the Hayes would be far more practical and useful than one at the Nelson.

As Radisson, his nephew Chouart and another man headed inland to try to encounter some Cree, Groseilliers began constructing a fort on the south shore of the Hayes. After eight days of canoeing inland, about forty leagues, Radisson spied a furtive young man hunting a deer, but when he called out the man ran off. Radisson lit a large fire during the night, and the next morning nine canoes, with a total of twenty-six people, rounded a headland and came within hailing distance. They were Muskego, or Swampy Cree. Radisson invited them to his fire and distributed gifts of knives and tobacco. To the chief he gave a musket, powder and shot and a blanket for the man's wife. During the evening and the next day, he made several speeches and negotiated an informal treaty of friendship with them. "While making him the gifts I told him that I took him for my father. He adopted me for his son by covering me with his robe." Radisson then accepted their reciprocal gifts of their old beaver robes and urged them to spread the word that he would soon be open for business downriver.

Back at the encampment where Groseilliers had made progress on a rudimentary fort, Radisson was shocked to hear cannon fire from the north. He and two men headed along the shore in a canoe and discovered, to his great surprise, a group of traders, who began to read to him a few garbled words in Cree from a book. Radisson determined that they were from Boston, having sailed aboard a ship called *Bachelor's Delight* with a crew of fourteen. The captain was young Benjamin Gillam, nephew of Zachariah, the captain of the Company's first ship, the *Nonsuch*. They had arrived at the Nelson only a few days earlier. Zachariah Gillam was then captaining his own ship for the Company, the supply ship *Prince Rupert*, and was himself en route to the same region.

Radisson boldly asked under what charter or authority they were here, and mentioned deceptively how he initially thought that they were one of his other ships and that he was established nearby with military forces "sufficient to prevent them from trading." He implied that his men were even now building a fortified encampment near his other two ships to the south. Radisson advised the young captain to pack up and leave, and then asked to come aboard the *Bachelor's Delight* to eat and talk. Charming and charismatic as ever, he bluffed his way into a group, where he quickly became the dominant member. He was scouting and assessing the ship's defences, already making a plan to "seize his ship, which was a lawful prize, since it had no commission to trade from either France or England."

As Radisson was canoeing back to his own camp, he and his men spied another, much larger ship sailing toward the river's mouth. As it was late in the evening, Radisson lit a large fire on the shore to trick the new ship into stopping its voyage upstream to where the Bostonians had settled. The ship slowly reduced sail and stopped for the night just offshore. Radisson shrewdly added up the total numbers of men in the three separate groups and calculated that, although the two English ships were not affiliated, the English certainly outnumbered his small French contingent. In the morning he determined that the new ship was the Company's annual supply ship, the *Prince Rupert*, with the new overseas governor, John Bridgar, on board.

When a boat with six men rowed ashore, Radisson took up an arrogant, defiant stance, boldly displaying his arms, while his men hid in the bushes nearby. He loudly claimed that the *Prince Rupert* was not permitted to land. They asked who he was, since he was dressed like a Cree and had spoken in their language. "I am a Frenchman who tells you to withdraw," he pronounced, and added that the land had been claimed by the King of France. His men then came forth from the woods and gestured as though there were others nearby, implying that their force was more formidable than it was. Radisson accepted an invitation to board the *Prince Rupert* to dine and discuss the situation. He naturally demanded that two English hostages remain onshore to secure his liberty. Over dinner, Radisson boasted that he had two ships, with another still coming, and had many men already spread throughout the region and others building a fort. The season was advanced, by then mid-September, so obviously they would all be overwintering in the vicinity. After seeing that the English intended to build a fort at the very spot the *Prince Rupert* had stopped, Radisson departed and returned to his encampment and to Groseilliers, who had been hunting and stockpiling deer and white ptarmigans purchased from the Cree.

TEN DAYS LATER, RADISSON RETURNED TO the Nelson River to investigate the goings-on and discovered that the *Prince Rupert* had become stuck in mud and was tilting with the tide. He noted that the Company men were disorganized and in a poor situation. He then travelled overland to the Bostonian fort upriver. He alone knew what was going on. The Bostonians and the Company men were unaware of each other, and he intended to keep it that way by controlling all the information. The Bostonians in particular were between a rock and a hard place, since they had no government charter and were therefore trespassing on the Company's trade district. Radisson spoke Cree and had also made alliances with the local peoples. He was in control of the situation and scheming to play the parties against each other to his benefit.

On October 21, disaster struck the *Prince Rupert*, furthering the drama. Because the ship was stuck in the mud, the crew was unable to move it to a safer location for a winter harbour. Ice encrusted the tilting vessel, and during a mighty storm it was dragged out into the bay and destroyed. It sank quickly, with nine men aboard, including its captain, Zachariah Gillam, leaving only eighteen of the Company's men alive on the shore, with little provisions, goods or equipment.

Over the next several months, Radisson deftly manoeuvred events to his liking. He and a small band snuck into the Bostonians' primitive fort and captured it. Then he burned the Company's rudimentary fort. He discovered the governor, Bridgar, "in a pitiful state, having drunk himself into a stupor." Bridgar had been "mistreating" many of the Company's employees and they wanted to defect and join Radisson and the French to better survive the winter. Although the two ships commanded by Radisson and Groseilliers were also damaged by the shore ice, in the spring the men were able to saw them apart and assemble one mostly seaworthy vessel from the combined pieces. They dispatched the two English crews in this vessel to join up with Company outposts south in the Bottom of the Bay. The only ship, of the four wintering near Port Nelson, that withstood the ravages of the winter was the *Bachelor's Delight*. Radisson and Groseilliers commandeered it for themselves and loaded it with around two thousand prime beaver pelts. They sailed away in late August, once the bay was reasonably free from ice, leaving the young Jean-Baptiste Chouart in charge of seven Frenchmen and the ongoing operation of La Compagnie du Nord.

Radisson was in good spirits as they sailed east through Hudson Strait and then south to New France, where they arrived without incident in October 1683 expecting to be hailed as heroes. But in Quebec, in an echo of the previous ill-usage that had driven him to the English, the governor confiscated the ship and demanded a 25 per cent tax on their furs. Infuriated, Radisson boarded a ship to France to argue his case, but soon was caught up in European politics. The news from Hudson Bay had preceded his arrival, and King Louis XIV and his court were preoccupied with appeasing English complaints that Radisson had captured English personnel in a time of peace and burned their forts, which he certainly had done. Radisson and Groseilliers became pawns in the imperial game. At the time, Charles II's brother James (later King James II) was France's best hope for re-establishing the Catholic religion in England, so agitating the Company's commercial backers, who either were having or had

a cozy relationship with prominent aristocrats and other politically connected individuals, was now considered poor foreign policy.

The Company's directors in London, however, must have recognized
Radisson's incomparable competence as a leader and a fur trader, based
on his audacious actions at Port Nelson during the winter of 1682–83.
They persuaded him to travel to London and rejoin the Company, and
he resolved, according to his own account, "to cross over into England forever, and to commit myself so steadfastly to His Majesty's service and
the nation's interests that no other consideration would ever be able to
disengage me." He smuggled himself out of France with the help of the
English ambassador, who was working at the urging of James Hayes.

Radisson's bargaining position was strengthened when he revealed to
the Company committee that his nephew, Jean-Baptiste Chouart, had
remained at La Compagnie du Nord's fort at Port Nelson. Chouart was
in charge of the ongoing trade with the Cree and had likely amassed a
valuable hoard of furs by now, which were just waiting to be shipped
back and sold, hopefully in London. When Radisson was presented to
court, he promised the new King James II his "inviolable fidelity" and
that he would work "at the very risk of my life" exclusively to advance
the Company's interests.

The next summer, Radisson was again sailing to the bay, this time in
the service of the Company, aboard a ship aptly named the *Happy Return*.
He cruised up to the settlement he had helped organize and build the
previous summer with the Company's flag flying from the mast, and
caused some consternation and confusion when he stepped ashore to
greet his fellow compatriots and persuade them to turn over the fort and
all its vast wealth of furs to the Company and to sign on themselves.
Radisson, with his silver tongue, had no great difficulty in persuading his
nephew and the other French and the Cree that it was all for the best.

The summer of 1684 was a banner year. Around seven hundred Cree
canoed down the river from the interior to trade at the new post, which
would eventually be named York Factory and become the Company's

largest and most important outpost. They collected nearly twenty thousand pelts, not all of superior quality. (Radisson managed several more
years with the Company, which bestowed upon him a distinctive title of
dubious authority: Superintendent and Chief Director of the Trade at
Port Nelson.) As he departed the bay at the end of the season in 1684,
Radisson, without knowing it, crossed paths with a French ship again
financed by Chesnaye and La Compagnie du Nord that wintered in the
vicinity but was only able to trade for a meagre quantity of furs.

If not for political interference, Radisson and Groseilliers would have
become enormously successful entrepreneurs in New France, which
highlights the role of social class and politics in securing any sort of
business success at the time. The pair were repeatedly thwarted by
French colonial authorities who wanted control of economic activity
related to the trade in the colony: a sort of supply management system
that would keep prices high by preventing an overabundance of beaver
flooding the market. Radisson and Groseilliers violated the custom that
determined who should be permitted to engage in commercial activity.
Radisson, never entirely trusted by the English, particularly in the 1680s
with the rise of anti-Catholic and anti-French sentiment surrounding
the succession, and not politically connected enough to secure a long-
term senior position with the Company, eventually retired to London
to a sporadically paid Company pension. He would die there in 1710
with a bounty on his head offered to anyone who would return him to
Quebec to face punishment. Groseilliers's fate is unknown.

THE COMPANY'S NETWORK OF FORTS IN southern and western James
Bay had been operating profitably for years, serviced by annual ships.
Efforts from New France to lure the Indigenous peoples to trade south
instead of north had repeatedly failed. Instead of being at the end of a
supply chain that stretched south to the St. Lawrence, the Cree, whose
territory hugged the rim of the northern inland sea, were now at the
start of a supply chain that ended along their coast. Instead of receiving

the least for their furs, they now received the most with the least effort. Others, instead of having to deal with middlemen to get their beaver furs, the best in the world, to market, now had to deal with the Cree to gain access to the Company posts. It was a dramatic shift in power. But it was a shift of short duration.

The challenge to the Company's undisputed presence in Hudson Bay came within a few years of Radisson's taking control over La Compagnie du Nord's operations that he had founded at Port Nelson. It came not by sea but overland from New France, and it would plunge the Company's fortunes into a deep trough from which it wouldn't crawl out for nearly two and a half decades. The Company had paid its first dividend only in 1684, the year Radisson rejoined the enterprise and brought in all the furs traded by his nephew, and it continued to pay dividends between 25 per cent and 50 per cent until 1690, when the demand for furs declined precipitously. No further dividends were paid for twenty-seven years, while the Company struggled on, verging on financial collapse.

The cause of the disruption was war. Marine captain Pierre de Troyes and his company of reinforcements sailed up the St. Lawrence and disembarked at Quebec in August 1685. With him aboard the ship was the new governor of Quebec, Jacques-René de Brisay, Marquis de Denonville. The governor was quickly persuaded by La Chesnaye and La Compagnie du Nord that it would be in their interest to launch a military expedition overland north to the Company's outposts at the Bottom of the Bay. They pointed out that in 1679 Father Albanel had already made the overland journey north to the Company's posts and had reported upon their great weakness: that they were built to resist the cold, and perhaps attack from the water, but they were not built to resist the arms of those who might attack them from the land.

In February 1686, de Troyes was commanded to take his military band north to attack the English traders and dislodge them from the bay. The troop included thirty professional French soldiers, around seventy young French Canadians who were accustomed to overland travel, among them several skilled tradesmen such as a blacksmiths and carpenters, and a handful of interpreters and guides, probably Montagnais. Among the group was the young Montreal-born officer Pierre Le Moyne d'Iberville, who would for the next decade be one of the greatest thorns in the Company's side. They set off from Montreal, then a small town, through the snow, dragging their supplies and weapons on sleds, including thirty-five large canoes for use in the summer. When spring melted the snow, they canoed up the Ottawa River to Lake Temiskaming and then paddled downstream along the Moose River to the shore of James Bay by mid-June. It took them eighty-two days of struggling over treacherous portages and waterways along the little-known and arduous route.

Technically the French and English governments were at peace, and the sixteen men at Moose Factory were aware that no ships could arrive until later in the summer due to sea ice. They were not prepared for a band of attackers coming overland. They also were not military men but rather carpenters, blacksmiths and traders. The fort was a wooden palisade-style enclosement with a tower and a handful of small cannons, pointed toward the sea. Attacking at night while everyone slept, d'Iberville and his brother Jacques snuck into the fort by climbing the outer walls. After tying down the three cannons, they opened the gates and called for their compatriots to rush in. A torrent of screaming men ran from the woods through the gates and subdued the bleary-eyed defenders, who had no interest in risking injury or death by fighting. De Troyes, however, was surprised at the enthusiasm of his Canadian woodsmen. "I discovered that I had great difficulty trying to stop the assault of the Canadians who, screaming like savages, demanding the opportunity to use their knives." It was all over in a couple of hours.

The local band of Cree who were nearby had done nothing to alert the Company employees inside the fort to the presence of French aggressors because they were annoyed at the behaviour the local trader. Despite the admonishments, advice and instruction of Radisson (who was still resident at Port Nelson as chief director of trade) on the diplomatic protocol that was required in dealing with the Cree, and later other Indigenous peoples, the Company didn't consistently teach local traders of the importance of local ceremony and customs and the need for reciprocal bending of culture. The local peoples were changing their lives a little to accommodate the Company's logistical needs and they certainly expected the Company to likewise accommodate their needs, something that happened inconsistently, depending on the personality of the local trader. Cultural and ceremonial relationships were important in the fur trade, more so than in other business transactions, and the Company could have avoided a great many problems in its early years if it had been more assiduous in selecting traders more attuned to the nuances and expectations of a different culture.

De Troyes quickly prepared his men for the next target, Rupert House, a further 120 kilometres to the northeast along the coast of James Bay. It was the Company's first outpost, established in 1670. He left forty men behind at Moose Factory to guard the prisoners. At Rupert House, they again attacked at night. While the bulk of the French force scrambled up and over the walls using a forgotten ladder that was leaning against the outer wall, d'Iberville canoed out to the Company's supply ship *Craven* and, after shooting and killing a sleeping man on the deck, stamped his feet to awaken the civilian sailors and hit them in the head with the butt of his gun as they clambered up through the hatch from below. Now with a large ship and its cannons at his disposal, de Troyes burned the fort and then decided to assault the Company's largest and most important outpost, Fort Albany. The captured men were taken as prisoners back to Moose Factory.

Fort Albany is not visible from the sea. The attackers, by now exhausted and bedraggled and subsisting on local herbs, approached in the evening, cruising around looking for it. Just as they were about to give up in frustration, ironically it was the sound of the fort's sentry firing the evening gun to announce all's well that alerted them to its location. This more substantial outpost was built of squared timbers and occupied a defensive outcropping overlooking the river. The French cruised up the river silently and began the assault just as dinner was being served. Shot poured through the walls into the dining room, where one bullet smashed the decanter as a servant poured wine and another nearly struck the wife of Henry Sergeant, the overseas governor, as she sat for her meal. (Sergeant was the only governor permitted to bring a wife across the Atlantic until George Simpson did the same a century and a half later.)

During the ensuing battle, Sergeant offered little encouragement to his men: "For Severall tymes Wee asked him if Wee should fire or Contrive some meanes to oppose the French; his answer allwayes was doe what you please." Sergeant then went into a panic and threatened that if the men, all civilians, didn't do more to defend the fort, the Company would refuse to compensate them for lost limbs or to look after their wives and children if they were killed. The Company didn't hire soldiers, and these men had no military training, having signed on to be craftsmen, traders, sailors and tradesmen. It is hardly surprising that morale was minimal, and the men raced to the cellar when the furious horde of attackers began screaming and chanting "Vive le Roi!" while launching over forty volleys of shot in an hour, including from the cannons of the captured ship, which had been sailed up in front of the fort.

In a brief pause in the firing, the attackers heard a hollow echo of their own cries, which they soon realized came from the cowering Company men mimicking their patriotic chant from the cellar where they had taken refuge. The resident chaplain soon appeared at the gates waving a lady's apron affixed to a pole. When they convened to discuss the terms of surrender, Sergeant brought along a fine bottle of wine and began with a joint toast to the faraway kings of their nations. He agreed to leave de Troyes everything except for personal possessions, turning over the fort without having fired a shot. Most of the prisoners were then taken to the outpost on Charleton Island, where they were retrieved by a Company supply ship months later and taken to Port Nelson.

Leaving the irrepressible d'Iberville in charge with forty men, de Troyes retraced his route back to Montreal, where he was regaled as a hero and promoted. The news of the victories quickly crossed the Atlantic and gave Louis XIV a secret bargaining chip against James II during their negotiations to settle grievances between the two nations in December 1686. The Treaty of Peace, Good Correspondence and Neutrality in America called for all property to remain in present ownership—but the English didn't yet know that the Company's three oldest James Bay posts were now in French hands and the Company retained only Port Nelson and a recently established outpost at the Severn River. Its original hub-and-spoke trading structure at the Bottom of the Bay was destroyed. The valuable furs, however, were still in storage at the captured forts. D'Iberville soon grew bored and decided to set off for France himself the next spring. After a quick crossing, he secured command of a small frigate, the *Soleil d'Afrique*, and sailed the next summer back to the bay to claim the stock-piled furs.

At Fort Albany, d'Iberville, not yet thirty years old, had not quite finished loading his ship's hold with the previous year's prize in pelts when two large Company ships—the eighteen-gun *Churchill*, named after the new London governor, and the frigate *Yonge*, crewed by eighty-five men and the new overseas governor, Captain John Marsh—sailed near on a mission to reconstruct Fort Albany and re-establish the prof-itable trade network at the Bottom of the Bay. Perhaps thinking that the French had done their damage and departed, they were ordered not to engage in any battles but only to fire back if attacked. Showing more of the tactical, strategic brilliance and ruthless subterfuge that had allowed him to take over all of the Company's southern outposts the previous year, d'Iberville had removed the channel markers that guided ships safely from the bay upriver to the fort. Now the Company ships cruised upriver, only belatedly noting that the usual markers were missing, and one of the ships soon ran aground on the river bottom. The men began furiously unloading cargo and workers to lighten the load and free the ship. D'Iberville meanwhile had positioned snipers along the shore and ordered them to take pot shots at the Company's labourers.

D'Iberville had only sixteen men with him and one small ship, the larger *Soleil d'Afrique* being at Charleton Island. He was massively out-manned and outgunned and essentially trapped upriver of the Company force, so he decided to deceive the larger force with bluster. In his favour, sickness raged on the *Churchill* and the *Yonge*, including the dreaded scurvy, and morale was poor. With a greater knowledge of the land and a commanding view of the English activities, d'Iberville observed hunt-ing parties leaving into the bush and sent his men to intercept them, capturing the captain of the *Yonge*, William Bond, as soon after other groups, including the contingent sent to negotiate for Bond's release. Seeing disorder and lack of leadership in the congregations of English near the stricken ships, d'Iberville moved cannons into place and began lobbing cannonballs into the camp until they surrendered.

It was another victory showing d'Iberville's military brilliance and underscoring just how unprepared the Company was for any conflict, being a commercial enterprise and not having any trained naval com-manders or soldiers. They were in the Bay for business, whereas d'Iberville was there for battle. The Company's assessment of the con-flict was a warning to the men at Port Nelson: small numbers of French at the Bottom of the Bay had "taken an English Fort and three ships whereof one of good force with divers prisoners, this seemed hardly Credible at first, but proved too trew afterwards, For Bond & his mate Foolishly wandering to hunt Partridges, were themselves caught Like woodcocks, & then by subtle degrees our Factory shipps & goods surprized, to the perpetuall shame of the nation."

But in politics, as in physics, an action has, if not an equal, certainly an opposite or opposing action. The outposts in the Bay were to change hands repeatedly. In 1688, James II was overthrown in the Glorious Revolution and fled to France. When England and France officially declared war in the spring of 1689, d'Iberville's depredations against the

Company's unarmed civilians were among the English grievances. The Company's commercial activities and its presence in Hudson Bay became a target for even more aggressive assaults, not just from the St. Lawrence but from across the Atlantic. As Governor Denonville of New France had observed in 1685, Port Nelson was valuable because the Cree, and indeed all the as yet unknown peoples in the western regions, controlled access to the best beaver pelts, and the entire trade would fall into the hands of the English since the Indigenous people "will not have far to go, and will find goods at a much lower rate than with us." There was no feasible way for the French to supply the captured bay forts from the St. Lawrence.

Unable to compete commercially, the governor sought a military solution. In 1690, after several years of attacking English settlements, d'Iberville headed north from Quebec with three small ships. This time, Port Nelson was the prize. But the pickings weren't as easy as in the past—the Company had secured the services of a huge thirty-six-gun warship from the Royal Navy and it lay offshore. Knowing when he was outmanoeuvred, d'Iberville skittered quickly away south and managed to seize Fort Severn instead, loading the accumulated furs and departing after destroying it, leaving the Company with a single outpost, York Factory at Port Nelson.

In 1692, while staging an invasion of England to restore the former king James II to the throne, the French navy suffered a devastating defeat by the Royal Navy at the Battle of La Hogue, on the Normandy coast. Twelve French warships were destroyed along with numerous small vessels, which ended the invasion. With the Royal Navy in command of the seas, the London Committee commissioned three frigates and a smaller vessel to launch an assault to retake Fort Albany. In charge was a long-time Company servant named James Knight, a former carpenter who had risen to chief factor of the fort in the early 1680s, and a man who was to have an unusual and distinguished career with the Company until his death in his seventies in 1720.

Knight's squadron arrived in the bay late in the season and wintered hidden along the eastern coast, crossing to Fort Albany in late June the next year to find the fort apparently abandoned. As his two hundred trained marines advanced, however, guns began firing from the fort in oddly irregular bursts before abruptly stopping during the night. Knight advanced again when all was quiet and he discovered the fort deserted and in poor repair. The lone occupant was a bedraggled and insane former blacksmith chained in a cell. The other five pitiful defenders had deceived Knight's force by loading all of the guns of their starved and dead comrades and firing them to gain themselves time to flee south and escape under cover of darkness. The warehouse was stuffed full of a vast trove of pelts collected over the previous years that they had been unable to ship out. When faced with Knight's force, the skeleton garrisons at the other forts at the Bottom of the Bay all fled, leaving the Company fully in charge again.

But it was to be a short-lived victory for the Company. On September 14, 1694, d'Iberville, vowing revenge but unable to secure ships the previous year, arrived at York Factory, along the north bank of the Hayes River, with two small frigates. As the pre-eminent Company outpost, York Factory boasted thirty-two cannons and other armaments such as mounted swivel guns. The staff consisted of fifty-three traders, clerks and labourers. The defenders, however, were not as formidable as the armaments. The Company had boldly named them the Independent Company of Foot, but they were little more than regular civilians who had received rudimentary instruction in how to shoot together. Their appetite for military engagement did not match that of d'Iberville's trained French troops. As the cannons had been rigidly placed to permanently point to the water, over the next few weeks d'Iberville unloaded cannons from his ships, placed them out of range of the fort and prepared to bombard the place. At a parley the next morning, the Company men offered to surrender under one condition: that d'Iberville allow them a good night's sleep first. He obliged. Then, as promised,

the Company men marched out and the French marched in. The pitiful
exiles were left to fend for themselves before being shipped under guard
to France the next summer. During the winter, scurvy took a toll on
both the French and the English.

But the outpost, which d'Iberville renamed Fort Bourbon, was not
done being a pawn in the game of empire, and in 1695 it was again captured by the English, this time by two Royal Navy frigates rather than
by ineffectual Company workers. Then d'Iberville returned. During the
winter of 1696–97, he was in Newfoundland where, after landing at
the French capital of Placentia, he famously marched overland to the
Avalon Peninsula and on to St. John's and in a series of raids acknowledged as much for their ruthlessness as their effectiveness, destroyed
thirty-six fishing villages and displaced the people to hardship and starvation. After four months, and just before a large contingent of English
soldiers arrived, he was ordered north again to Hudson Bay, where he
launched his most famous assault during what has become known as the
Battle of Hudson's Bay.

D'Iberville's fleet of five ships included the forty-six-gun *Pélican*, a
formidable warship. After three weeks navigating the fog and ice floes
of treacherous Hudson Strait, one ship foundered and sank while the
others were scattered. Ever bold and optimistic, d'Iberville pressed
ahead alone in his flagship southwest across the bay to York Factory.
When he arrived in early September the fort seemed abandoned, so he
sent a shore party to investigate. While he paced the deck of the *Pélican*
waiting, and worrying about the many men below deck who were down
with scurvy, he spied a cluster of sails in the distance and sallied forth to
meet them in more open water, thinking they were the remainder of his
own squadron. As he drew near, a cannon fired a shot across his bow,
and he knew it was the Royal Navy come to the Company's defence. The
squadron consisted of the fifty-two-gun warship *Hampshire*, under
Captain John Fletcher, and two heavily armed Company supply ships,
Royal Hudson's Bay and *Dering*, with another sixty-two guns between

them. D'Iberville, trapped between the enemy squadron and the cannons at the fort, had little room to manoeuvre. As he always did, he decided that offence was the best defence, and though outnumbered, he ordered his ship ready for combat, opening the gun ports, clearing the deck and running out the big cannons.

The bay had never seen anything as terrifying and spectacular as two European warships blasting each other with broadsides. The standard naval tactic of the day was for the opposing ships to sail past each other, getting as many of their guns to bear as possible, which were almost exclusively on the sides (which is why when they fired it was called a broadside). And this is what happened soon enough between the two big ships. At first the *Pélican* cruised ahead during a running fight with sporadic cannon fire, with small shot ripping at the rigging and wounding sailors. The captains bellowed, sailors heaved on the ropes, hauling sails to catch the wind, and the ships turned for battle. The *Pélican* and the *Hampshire* slid closer, and when abreast pounded away at each other, the acrid smoke of gunpowder billowing and stinging the eyes. The air was filled with the pop of small guns while the big guns boomed, deafening the gunners. Splintered wood from the ships' hulls flew randomly, skewering men, who screamed in pain, blood pouring from their wounds and making the deck slick with their gore. The ships were so close that the men could see each other's faces and bellow insults across the choppy water. Captain Fletcher spied d'Iberville through the smoke and demanded his surrender. Naturally he refused. The ships let loose a final broadside, the *Pélican*'s perfectly timed to rip holes in the *Hampshire*'s hull right at the waterline as it rolled with the swell. After no more than three ship lengths, the *Hampshire*, water gushing in through the great gashes, foundered on a hidden reef and sank so quickly that all hands were sucked to their doom, screaming, in the frigid waters of the bay.

The smaller Company ship *Royal Hudson's Bay*, belatedly entering the fray, came close and let fly a single broadside at the *Pélican* and then, badly damaged from the return volley, struck her flag and surrendered. The *Dering* took advantage of a gust of wind and fled south to Fort Albany. A storm had been brewing, and while d'Iberville aboard the *Pélican* was preparing to board the *Royal Hudson's Bay*, the storm drove the damaged ships toward the stony shore. The *Royal Hudson's Bay* was washed onto a sandbank and the men scrambled overboard and waded through wind-whipped spray to the bleak beach. The *Pélican* was badly damaged and rudderless. D'Iberville ordered all three anchors heaved overboard, but they merely dragged through sand while the current and wind spun the wreck of a vessel and lodged it onto a sandbar many kilometres offshore. As the wind howled, the sailors roped together a raft from the wreckage, placed their wounded comrades aboard and attempted to float ashore, swimming through the foaming seas. Perhaps eighteen more men drowned before the survivors dragged themselves from the frigid water. As they stood huddled and shivering in the wind the other ships in d'Iberville's fleet cruised into sight and prepared for yet another siege of York Factory.

The resistance put up by the Company men was but a whimper. The ships came close and unloaded their guns to the beach, while d'Iberville's troops fired at the defenders on the ramparts. The governor, Henry Baley, flew a flag of surrender, and soon he and the other Company men collected their possessions and dolefully departed the fort to fend for themselves in the nearby forest as winter set in. D'Iberville left a small garrison and hastily sailed home with the fort, now called Bourbon again, in French hands.

The Company's greatest adversary, d'Iberville never returned to the bay after his ten years harassing and destroying the Company's trading outposts in the service of France. In his time the greatest soldier born in New France, d'Iberville went on to explore parts of what is now Louisiana along the Mississippi River and to lead French forces during Queen Anne's War in the Caribbean, where he died of fever in 1706 at the age of forty-seven.

French forces made one final attempt to retake Fort Albany, the Company's sole remaining outpost, in 1709. A force of around a hundred French woodsmen and Mohawk mercenaries from the St. Lawrence made the arduous overland route, but the garrison of twenty-seven, warned of the advance by a Cree trader, fought off the attack, inflicting heavy casualties. Fort Albany was the only year-round post still operated by the Company at the time, the others having been destroyed or in French hands, and the Company lacked the resources to rebuild in the face of possible further French assault. And so it remained for the next sixteen years—with the Company in charge of trade at the Bottom of the Bay while the French retained Fort Bourbon. The Company's charter giving royal monopoly sounded as grand as the day it was written, but reality was more edifying—the Company's sole tangible asset in Hudson Bay was a handful of primitive wooden cabins surrounded by palisade-style defensive walls and a sparse handful of employees, far outnumbered by the local Cree who visited to trade.

PART TWO

RISE

Chapter Four

THE QUIET MONOPOLY

In the summer of 1714, James Knight, the new governor in Hudson Bay, and Henry Kelsey, the new deputy governor, disembarked from their ships and strode from the stony beach to inspect the company's old premises at York Factory, which the French had renamed Fort Bourbon sixteen years earlier. According to the provisions of the Treaty of Utrecht signed between England and France the previous year, Company property in Hudson Bay was to be returned. Knight and Kelsey were appalled at the state of the venerable depot. It was now manned by a mere nine people, who were living in a wretched state. The timbers of the old fort had been allowed to rot, the foundations to crumble. The occupying French had done no maintenance for most of their tenure, perhaps because they also had been unable to profitably sell most of the region's beaver pelts owing to the war.

Knight, the irascible dreamer, reported that "the place as wee are come to is nothing but a confused heap of old rotten houses without form or strength, nay not sufficient to secure your goods from the weather nor fit for men to live in without being exposed to the frigid

winter my own place I have to live in this winter is not half so good as
our cowhouse was in the bottom of the bay & I have never been able to
see my hand in it since I have been here without a candle it is so black
& dark cold & whet with all nothing to make better but heaping up
earth about it to make it warm."

Years earlier, in 1690, Kelsey, a man with an affinity with the Cree and
an uncommon curiosity toward Indigenous peoples, set off with several
Cree companions southwest from York Factory on an expedition to
drum up business, "to call, encourage, and invite, the remoter Indians to
a trade with us" along the bay. Loaded with samples of the trade goods
on offer at Company posts, they canoed upstream along the Nelson
River to Lake Winnipeg, wintered along the Saskatchewan River near
The Pas, Manitoba, then traversed west across the Saskatchewan River
out onto the Great Plains near Saskatoon. There Kelsey beheld a sea of
gently rolling hills covered in tall grasses and interspersed with islands
of aspen forest. It was a great open land of fresh winds, sprawling vistas,
thundering herds of bison and plentiful elk and deer.

The number of people living in the aspen parkland was much greater
than in the harsher scraggly subarctic black spruce surrounding the bay.
Hardly a day went by that Kelsey didn't see or encounter someone. He
witnessed the spectacle of mighty bison herds and was shocked at the
sight of grizzly bears. Ever dutiful to his employers, he recorded that
"there is beavour in abundance but no Otter." He met many people he had
never encountered before and who had never visited any of the Company's
posts, including members of a western group he called the "Naywatamee
Poets" who were probably either the Mandan or the Atsina, members of
the Blackfoot tribes whose language he didn't understand and whom the
Company wouldn't encounter again for half a century. There were no
horses at the time; horses wouldn't migrate this far north until the
mid-eighteenth century. Kelsey exhorted some of these Plains people to
come east to trade at the Company's posts. But they looked askance at
Kelsey's Cree companions and their guns. Not to mention that it would

have been a mighty year-long journey to the unknown shores of Hudson Bay. They knew they would never make it that far. Kelsey returned east after a three-year journey, but the Company did nothing to follow up on his information because of the war with France.

The war had caused a glut of furs in the Paris market, which drove down prices in Europe, and this coincided with the decline in the French hat industry when many of the Huguenot hatters fled to England to avoid religious persecution and the industry shifted to the environs of London. In 1697, Louis XIV decreed that, to prevent the price of fur from declining further, thereby causing a loss of colonial revenues derived from the 25 per cent tax imposed in Quebec, all French fur outposts in the region west along the Great Lakes, with the exception of Fort St. Louis along the Illinois River, must close. The decree sought to restrict the supply of furs on the market, to help reverse the price decline. The colonial government issued no new trading permits and officially forbade any French colonists from the St. Lawrence from travelling to the west, but relented somewhat when their Indigenous allies threatened to trade north with the Cree instead, stoking fear they would form new and permanent alliances with the English. *Coureurs de bois* continued to rove the region of the Great Lakes, maintaining their deep cultural ties to Indigenous peoples as they had for generations, but to avoid the fur quotas they began secretly selling their furs in Albany instead of Montreal, as did the Iroquois and their trading allies, and competitors the Wyandot and Ottawa from the Great Lakes regions. The presence of the Company at the Bottom of the Bay, which threatened to direct commerce north, put serious strain on the relationship between New France and their Indigenous allies.

But by the end of the war, the Company itself was also bowed by the financial burdens of its unprofitable military activities. The dilapidated state of York Factory when James Knight reclaimed it in 1714 was a mirror of the financial state of the Company's entire enterprise. No dividends had been paid since 1690. There had been erratic payment of wages and pensions, including Radisson's, and the Company had taken out loans to service existing debt. The Company remained solvent only because of the reputation and lineage of its shareholders. It was in serious need of a revitalization. The Company was a tiny entity in terms of its impact on the English economy: though it held a monopoly over Rupert's Land, nearly half of the furs sold at auction in London still came from other sources trading through Boston or New York.

But with the ascension of new governor Thomas Lake, and after 1712 his son Bibye Lake, both aristocratic and well-connected London barristers and financiers, the Company was slowly set on sound financial footing. With the decline of hostilities in the early eighteenth century and the rejuvenation of economies in Europe, the stage was set for stability along the bay and a greater demand for its chief saleable commodity. Bibye knew that with peace the Company could once again flourish.

AN AGGRESSIVE TRADER, particularly when it came to negotiating his salary and performance bonus from the London Committee, James Knight had returned to London in 1697 after his term at Fort Albany and had invested his substantial earnings into Company stock. He was awarded a position on the committee for his loyalty and insights and was the natural choice to lead the expedition to retake possession of York Factory from the French commander Nicolas Jérémie. Then in his seventies, in an era when people usually died young, Knight commanded the fort with a strong hand, suppressing the supply of alcohol, railing against cursing and improper language, and frowning at sexual liaisons between his men and the Cree women. He believed it was his personal responsibility to ensure the moral righteousness of the community.

Knight quickly determined that it would be impossible to repair the dilapidated structures, and he prevailed upon London purse strings to fund the construction of a new fort about a kilometre downstream. When that was nearing completion in October 1715, he declared the new premises to be "the best lodging as ever Man had in this country."

For many years there would be ongoing work by a succession of labourers in response to the increase in trade and employment, including new storage rooms, expanded palisade fences and walkways, new kitchens separate from the main house, a smithy and a powder depot. The climate around York Factory was harsh, colder and darker in winter than at the outposts in the Bottom of the Bay, and permafrost meant that it was always under construction.

Knight's first season was the most challenging of his tenure. A timid ship captain in 1715 had failed to locate the inlet of the Hayes River and sailed the coast for weeks, sometimes within sight of the men in the fort, before retreating back to London without unloading any supplies. Knight surveyed the ragged turnips and potatoes in the fort's gardens, counted the scruffy sheep and goats that nibbled on the scraggly vegetation within the rustic fencing surrounding the fort and knew it would be a tough winter. The problem was compounded when, after word spread that the English Company was now in charge of the fort again, trade picked up from the general lack of interest and neglect of the French. Many hundreds of people arrived only to be shocked when Knight told them there was almost nothing to trade. After the journey they had made, they became angry and frustrated at the prospect of a return trip empty-handed, particularly without gunpowder for hunting. By the next year, perhaps a thousand sullen and anxious Cree were camping in the vicinity waiting on Knight's promise that the Company ship could arrive at any time. It was only the arrival of a small supply ship in the fall of 1715 that prevented outright starvation, but the tension fully resolved in August 1716, when the new ship arrived with a full hold of standard trade goods.

With peace in Europe, trade in Hudson Bay slowly returned to a predictable pattern that would prevail for generations. The Cree didn't care too much about who was technically in charge at the forts; it was trade disruption that was frustrating. The lack of consistency and availability of goods was vexing to people who had made a weeks-long trek to a particular fort only to be disappointed. The scheme that Radisson and Groseilliers had originally conceived could now reassert itself. The original business plan was sound, the logistics favourable, and it had only been war that had prevented the Company from flourishing. From its perch along the western rim of Hudson Bay, the Company would finally be able to take advantage of and expand upon thousands-of-years-old Indigenous trade and travel networks along waterways that wended their way deep into the interior of the continent.

The Company's strategy was to offer consistent good-quality goods as an inducement to people to make the journey to their forts with beaver pelts, and for the most part the Company posted consistent but unspectacular returns. With financial and political stability, and the guarantee that forts would be operating and well stocked, the Cree canoed in ever greater numbers down to the forts each spring, and the annual ships arrived from London to resupply and carry home the velvet booty on a predictable schedule. Soon the Cree were joined by Ojibwa from the south and Chipewyan from the north in being drawn into the Company's commercial orbit. The Company, however, had little interest in learning about the lands beyond its immediate posts or the people who lived there. They were perched on the edge of a foreign land for the sole purpose of doing business.

In 1718, Bibye Lake convened a meeting with the Company's thirty-five shareholders to announce the good news of a 10 per cent dividend, the first in twenty-eight years and the first in what would be an unbroken string of dividends for the next sixty years. Under Bibye, the Company was transformed from a ragged, erratic enterprise subject to piracy and attack from French national forces, barely solvent trying to defend its interests, anxiously waiting each year to see if any of its supply ships would arrive, into a thriving wholesale entity with prime beaver shipped regularly to London for resale throughout Europe and Russia. One of the key requirements that the rich and shrewd Bibye demanded from employees above all else, apart from avoiding all non-commercial activities, was secrecy. Bibye knew that negative public sentiment could undermine their monopoly. Monopolies were always open to criticism, and others such as the Royal African Company, South Seas Company and the English East India Company had recently weathered storms of negative publicity. The Hudson's Bay Company was a small enterprise by the standards of the day, puny compared to the English East India Company, then still decades away from its glorious but violent rise under Robert Clive to become ruler of most of India.

The economic and social fallout from the collapse of the South Seas Company was fresh in the news. More formally known as "The Governor and Company of the merchants of Great Britain, trading to the South Seas and other parts of America, and for the encouragement of fishing," the South Seas Company was the focus of a speculative stock investment bubble that the government had supported as being safe and secure. People had been urged to exchange their government debt annuities for shares in the company. When the share price rose, people rushed to trade in more government debt, since the return on South Seas stock was greater, and this drove the price higher. Ostensibly, the South Seas Company was a public/private partnership that was granted a monopoly to trade in South America and the South Pacific. But since Britain and Spain were at war, there was very little chance of any trade happening, since these were then Spanish territories. The South Seas Company was plagued by accusations of insider trading and bribery. Many who were "in the know" made fortunes, while others were left holding the empty bag when the stock crashed in 1720. Once the bubble burst, there was widespread dissatisfaction with political corruption, and authority figures in general were derided. "Monopolies are absurd, inconsistent, and destructive," argued one disgruntled commentator, capturing the tenor of the times. "Never yet was a Monopolized Trade extended to the degree of a Free one; therefore any Country abounding in Monopolies must decline in Trade."

Bibye Lake wanted to avoid any scrutiny into the increasingly profitable activities that were occurring along the distant reaches of Hudson

Bay. Shareholders, the London Committee instructed, were not to talk about the Company's rising prospects; share transactions were to remain quietly private; there would be no public record of shareholders or directors; Company servants were required to sign oaths of secrecy, and a portion of their pay was reserved for payout only upon retirement after years of tight-lipped service; letters home from the bay were scrutinized; employees were searched for pelts and written information when they boarded ships for home; and ships' captains' logs and reports were kept private. Bibye's vision was for the Company to prosper unobtrusively while drawing no attention to its monopoly and attracting no competitors. The London Committee issued its decrees, and the rising shipments of quality furs quietly grew. It was almost as if the Company didn't exist apart from a handful of mysterious ships that arrived each year at the London docks and quickly unloaded a nondescript cargo into a warehouse.

WHILE JAMES KNIGHT LAID THE GROUNDWORK for the Company's bland stability after the Treaty of Utrecht, he himself was a bit of an unpredictable rogue and a peripatetic dreamer. Soon after he had assumed control of York Factory from the French in the summer of 1714, and began his ambitious construction and renovation projects, he was already turning his mind to increasing the Company's trade with people who lived farther north. Despite the provisions of the Treaty of Utrecht that established the primacy of the Company in Rupert's Land, French traders, with Huron and Algonquian supporters, had constructed small trading outposts on several rivers leading north to the Bottom of the Bay, particularly along the Albany River. They were diverting trade to the south by intercepting canoes before they reached the Company's outposts. Although the goods they offered were not the same as those of the Company, the diversion was enough for Knight to realize that short of an expensive military operation, there was no way for the Company to expand trade in that direction. He turned his attention instead to the lands north and west of York Factory. He didn't know much about the peoples of this region, since they seldom came to York Factory out of fear of attack from the Cree. He called them the Northern Indians, otherwise known as the Chipewyan. Knight knew of their existence only as female slaves of the local Cree.

Early on the morning of November 24, 1714, a lone "near starv'd" young woman stumbled into a party of goose hunters who were weaving their way between the rolling hills running parallel to the banks of a creek a little way inland from the fort. She had a remarkable story to tell. For generations there had been hostilities between the Cree and the more northerly Chipewyan, with raids and captive-taking being common, and the Cree generally having the greatest success owing to guns and knives they obtained in trade at York Factory (or Fort Bourbon or Port Nelson, as it had been called in earlier decades). The Cree were defending their position as middlemen, and warfare and raiding between the two groups was escalating. The Chipewyan woman, named Thanadelthur (Jumping Martin), belonged to a clan whom the Cree called the Slaves because they were so often captured by Cree raiders. They dwelt as far west as Great Slave Lake and Lake Athabasca. Thanadelthur had been captured by a Cree raiding party in 1713, but escaped with another young woman, and they were headed north to rejoin their people. Unfortunately, their escape from captivity happened as winter was beginning to grip the land. The only food they could find was from snaring the occasional rabbit. They felt the storms and cold keenly without shelter. Exposure and hunger broke their spirits and they got lost, finally deciding to turn back to save their lives. Her companion soon perished, and Thanadelthur was walking toward York Factory alone when she was found and taken to the fort. While she was recovering from her ordeal, she saw first-hand the source of the goods and weapons owned by the Cree, and when she met James Knight, the chief factor, she enthusiastically described the quality of the furs in her distant homeland and urged him to send an expedition.

What really made Knight perk up was when she described a yellow metal that lay on the ground in a certain region of her homeland. Seeing how Knight reacted, she frequently brought it up, telling tales of people with handfuls of what surely must have been copper or gold that inflamed Knight's imagination until it became his driving passion. She persuaded him to send some traders north to the Churchill River and hoped there wouldn't be too much trouble with the Inuit. Knight later wrote that "she tells me that they promised her when she was there last that they would get a great deal of copper to bring down against we settled at Churchill River and that there would be a great many there next spring to look for us, if any of the Indians did make their escape from the Iskemays." The Chipewyan were known to the Cree both for their witchcraft and for lives that revolved around the migrating caribou in subarctic black spruce and tundra. They were adept at snowshoe travel and good at fishing, but had never before used canoes and had never had direct access to any of the new and exotic goods that arrived in Hudson Bay in the Company's ships. The Inuit—the Iskemays—were their habitual enemies, as were the Cree.

Knight knew that having an interpreter and cultural liaison would be vital to his newly forming plans, and he was particularly enthusiastic about Thanadelthur, for she was obviously intelligent, brave and resourceful. Although Knight never describes her physical appearance, according to Dene oral history she was attractive, vivacious and an uncommonly gifted orator. Knight was amused with her enthusiasm and respected her opinions, but also soon discovered that she had a strong will and a temper. She agreed to work toward making peace between her people and the upland Cree, and Knight assigned her to go on a trade mission with a trusted lieutenant, William Stewart. In June 1715, Knight called together the Company men and the local Cree for a ceremonial feast and persuaded them that peace with the Chipewyan was necessary and that they should gather a contingent to go along with Stewart to make overtures to the west. Knight promised the Chipewyan "Large presents of Powder, Shot & tobacco with other necessaries" to assuage their reluctance to venture into the lands of their enemies, and to seemingly undermine their own economic, social and political superiority by bringing them into the economic orbit of the Company.

On June 27, the delegation of around 150 set off in a dispersed cluster. Thanadelthur was the real captain of the expedition, while Stewart served as the Company's representative and as a witness tasked with keeping her safe, "to take care that none of the Indians Abuse or Misuse the Slave Woman." Stewart was also instructed to keep an eye on the trade goods Knight reserved as presents for Thanadelthur, which she intended to distribute to her people and inform them of his plans to establish a new trade fort north along the coast at the Churchill River. Thanadelthur kept everyone focused on the task, urging them on and haranguing them for their perceived failings. Stewart later told Knight that he never saw "one of such Spirit in his Life. She kept all the Indians in awe as she went with and never Spared in telling them of their Cowardly way of Killing her country Men, that he was Often Afraid that they would have killed her had I not given such strict charge not to Abuse her." Knight had also instructed Stewart to be on the lookout for any yellow metal and to take detailed notes.

The large band travelled generally north and west to the vicinity of eastern Great Slave Lake, but by October the weather was freezing, the game was scarce, and the travel with snowshoes was exhausting. The large contingent eventually split up into smaller bands in order to survive, to search for animals over a greater area and avoid starvation. Many turned back as the season advanced, and only a dozen or so Cree pushed on to search for Thanadelthur's people. One winter day they came upon the scene of a massacre, where it seemed that some of the Cree who had separated from the group earlier had attacked and killed nine Chipewyan. The dozen remaining Cree with Thanadelthur and Stewart, fearing that they would be blamed for the killing and attacked by vengeful Chipewyan while greatly outnumbered, readied to flee. Seeing the entire enterprise disintegrating around her, Thanadelthur stood upon a rock and launched into a speech in Cree. She beseeched them to set fear aside and remain at the camp for ten days, while she pressed on searching the land for a band of her people alone. The Cree trading captain, who remains nameless in all the records, looked about the snowy, barren landscape of frozen plains and stunted spruce and nodded his agreement. They made a rudimentary fortification, lit a fire and settled down out of the wind in a nervous patience. Stewart remained with them, urging them to stay calm and promising to intervene to prevent, if he could, an armed assault on the camp.

Thanadelthur continued wandering the frozen landscape searching for evidence of her people for many days. When she found a large band of over a hundred, she sought out the leaders and laid out her plans, speaking continuously for days until she was "hoarse with her perpetual talking," urging them to come with her back to the camp and make peace with the Cree to gain access to the Company's goods. She had seen the items that could be obtained in trade and knew how some of these items would be of inestimable benefit to both men and women alike, easing life in their harsh homeland. On the tenth day, in a perhaps apocryphal twist on the story, she returned to the Cree camp with two Chipewyan men, while about a hundred of her people remained in a camp farther away. The trio waited until Stewart signalled to her that it was safe to approach. According to legend, she climbed upon a large rock and gestured the larger band of her people forward, singing with joy as they came toward the Cree camp—on the final day before the Cree were to return east. A famous 1952 painting by Franklin Arbuckle shows a fictional version of the event. Thanadelthur stands in the centre of a small copse of spruce, gesticulating and beseeching, with both groups of people arrayed on either side of a campfire over which cooking pots steam. Breath steams from her mouth, snow blankets the land, and the sun is low in the winter sky. The Cree are adorned with beadwork and hold guns upright, while the Chipewyan hold bows and are garbed in skin clothing with fur-rimmed hoods. William Stewart stands to the side, an observer but not an actor in the events, wearing similar clothing but with a red winter tuque to distinguish him from the others.

To drive home the necessity of the peace treaty, "she made them all stand in fear of her as she scolded at some and pushing of others that they all stood in fear and forced them to ye peace. Indeed, she has a Divellish Spirit," Knight wrote afterwards, "and I believe that if there were but 50 of her Country Men of the Same Courage and Resolution they would drive all the Northern Indians [Cree] out of their Country." Ten Chipewyan returned to York Factory with the Cree, including Thanadelthur's brother. They arrived in early May 1716, and then devoted the summer and fall to learning how to prepare beaver skins and other furs to the Company's requirements. The entire group remained near York Factory for the winter. Despite the peace treaty, the Cree and Chipewyan still eyed each other suspiciously and feared secret attacks. The Chipewyan were billeted with some of the Cree, and they taught each other their languages, attempting to overcome their mutual animosity. Thanadelthur, her brother and another woman remained inside the fort, learning more about the Company and its bay-based operations and teaching Knight and some of his men about the Chipewyan way of life so that mutually advantageous trade could develop.

Thanadelthur was anxious that the relationship between her people and the Company be successful, as a means of subverting the power of the Cree and perhaps to make their own lives easier with new tools. When one of her compatriots slyly suggested that efforts to prepare the pelts might not be necessary and that they could try to pass off substandard ones, she "ketcht him by the nose Push'd him backwards & call'd him fool and told him if they brought any but Such as they were directed they would not bee traded." Even old Knight once became the focus of her temper. He had given her a gift of a small kettle and then noticed that she had apparently traded it away. When he confronted her, she reputedly became enraged. "She did rise in such a passion as I never did see the Like before," he wrote, and threatened that she could order her people to kill him if he ever ventured north to the Churchill River. The next morning, she presented herself tearfully to him, proclaimed that he was like a father to them all and promised that he would never fall to harm. Soon the governor was consulting her on his plans and attentively listening to her stories of mineral deposits, a "yellow mettle," which he surmised must be gold. She knew what to say to interest him, and when she discussed the topic with him and he proffered his proposals, she would "Presently Give her Opinion whether it would doo or not."

During her time at the fort in the fall of 1716, Thanadelthur devoted herself to learning English and married one of her Chipewyan companions. She made plans to return to her people and spread the word that Knight had promised to establish the new fort farther north. She persuaded Knight to name her brother as the trading captain to her people. But her plans never came to fruition. That winter was particularly harsh and life at the fort, being unlike "their Natural way of Living," caused her and several others to come down with an unknown illness notable for a high fever. "Ye Northern Slave Woman has been dangerously Ill and I expect her Death every Day, but I hope she is now a Recovering," Knight reported optimistically. But although Knight did all he could to alleviate the suffering from the sickness, she and the others worsened. She called the young English servant Richard Norton, who was supposed to accompany her inland in the spring, and urged him to not fear her people, telling him that her brother would protect him. When she died on February 5, Knight wrote, "I am almost ready to break my heart." He later reflected that "She was one of a Very high Spirit and of the Firmest Resolution that I ever see in any Body in my Days and of great Courage and forecast. Also Endoued with an extraordinary Vivacity of Apprehension."

Knight was worried that her death inside the fort might provoke suspicion and fear. He distributed presents to the Chipewyan party, held a ceremony and made plans for Thanadelthur's brother to take young

Richard Norton with him into the interior to plan for next year's trade. Knight did manage to find another interpreter who spoke Cree, Dene and some English, but complained that her services cost "above 60 skins value in goods."

That summer a group of Company men, including Knight, sailed north to the Churchill River as promised. The region around Churchill, with its barren, rocky and wind-lashed shores, makes York Factory look balmy in comparison. They could hardly find a suitable spot for a dwelling, and when Knight found the sooty remains of a burned and abandoned hut, believed to be that of the Danish commander Jens Munk which, he sardonically remarked, "they found so badd that After they had built it I believe they was so Discouraged that they sett it afire to Run away by the light of it." He had found York Factory bad compared with the more southerly posts, but Churchill, at the edge of the treeline, was ten times worse. Not the least problem was the insects. "Here is now Such Swarms of Small Sand flyes that wee can hardly See the Sun through them . . . They flye into our Ears, Nose, Eyes, Mouth and down our throats . . . Certainly these be ye flyes that was sent as Plagues to ye Egyptians as caus'd a Darkness over the Land and brought such blotches and boils as broke out all over them into sores." Soon they were covered in scabs and could barely open their mouths after a couple of weeks. It was also, he wrote, a land without fish, fowl or venison. This clearly was not his favourite place, yet the lure of precious metal had become nearly a mania to him, according to the gossip around the bay.

When the Company established its most northerly post, Fort Churchill, at what is now called the Churchill River, in 1717, it was supposed to alleviate the conflict between the Cree and the Chipewyan at York Factory, but it inadvertently contributed to a conflict between the Inuit and the Chipewyan. The increase in trade also shifted the politics of the region in other ways. The guns that the Chipewyan obtained in trade in the coming years did, more than anything else, halt the Cree advance into their territory. And, as the Cree were doing in more southern territories, the

Chipewyan soon began to create their own commercial empire by acting as brokers to more distant Athapaskan-speaking peoples near the Mackenzie River. The Chipewyan also began to sporadically use canoes where possible in regions of their territory to better transport goods to and from the new outpost, which later in the century would be rebuilt into a stone fortress and renamed Prince of Wales Fort.

KNIGHT HAD BECOME OBSESSED WITH the tales that Thanadelthur had spun and the mythical source of copper or gold. His attention drifted ever northward. He also ruminated over Thanadelthur's enticing description of a great inland sea that lay fourteen river crossings to the west, beyond the copper hills. Could this be the sea route to the Orient through a Northwest Passage? Born around 1640, Knight was by this time a greybeard, nearing eighty, and obviously had no intention of retiring to England, though he had amassed a fortune during his many decades of service with the Company. Perhaps he had been too long gone from his native land, after nearly fifty years along the bay, to ever reintegrate. He certainly was rich, but, like nearly all the bayside officers and governors, he was not a born gentleman. He began his career as a carpenter. Perhaps he loved the rugged life along the bay and the daily adventure it entailed too much to ever give it up. Perhaps he just enjoyed being in command, or perhaps he was suffering from dementia or just wanted one final adventure or a great quest worthy of his waning energy and attention. Given his age and wealth, he certainly wasn't fascinated with the gold because he needed money.

Whatever the reason, in 1718 Knight boarded the Company supply ship at the end of the season and sailed through ice-clogged Hudson Strait across the Atlantic to London. He resigned as governor of York Factory and presented his case for an expedition. Knight had set the Company's bayside operations back on the path to prosperity and had genuine weight with the London Committee, as he assured them of easily obtained mineral riches, the same tales that Thanadelthur had told to him.

For Bibye Lake and the other committee members, people other than their own employees poking around the shores of their commercial monopoly was precisely what they wanted to avoid; quiet, unobtrusive and profitable stability is what they sought. After the many decades of war, they wanted to focus only on activities that paid for themselves. Nevertheless, when Knight threatened to take his proposal elsewhere if they refused him, the London Committee reluctantly voted to finance an expedition to the far north of Hudson Bay. Knight was instructed to take two ships, the hundred-ton frigate *Albany* and the much smaller sloop *Discovery*, and search for mineral mines along the coast north of the Churchill River. He would have a crew of twenty-seven, plus officers and passengers. He was to plant the Company's flag to record discoveries and keep an eye out for the Strait of Anián, the elusive waterway that would lead west to the balmy shores of the Spice Islands. The ever-optimistic Knight brought a collection of "Cruseables, Melting Potts, Borax &c for the Trial of Minerals," as well as two huge iron-bound chests for holding the gold and copper ore he confidently predicted lay in those barren northern lands.

This preoccupation of Knight's, and to a lesser extent the Company's, with precious metal seems odd, but one can't help but wonder how history would have unfolded if anyone had found copper or other metals in the vicinity of York Factory or Fort Churchill and begun mining and processing the ore. The knowledge and skill of metalwork would have spread throughout the country, undermining the Company's single greatest asset—its otherwise unobtainable supply of metal implements.

In 1719, the year after the Company paid its first dividend in two decades, Knight's ships weighed anchor at Gravesend, waved to the Company's dignitaries who had congregated for the ceremony and raised a glass as they slipped downstream—and slipped from the pages of history. The first conclusive evidence of their disaster wasn't uncovered for nearly half a century, despite dozens of ships sailing in the vicinity and occasional reports of wreckage and stories from the Inuit.

Company officials didn't bother with any direct search for Knight when he failed to return from his explorations, and in fact showed a curious lack of interest in the loss of such a well-manned and expensive expedition. The same summer, Henry Kelsey, who had taken over as governor in the bay after Knight resigned, sailed north along the coast from Fort Churchill. His mission was not to find and rescue Knight but to exchange two slaves (either Cree or Chipewyan) for two Inuit, whom he wanted to bring back to Churchill to teach them to be interpreters and cultural ambassadors, to increase trade at the most northern fort. During this expedition and several others, he uncovered no evidence of Knight. His investigations seem to have been rather perfunctory, perhaps owing to his dislike of his old boss, who had accused him of private trading and theft. No search expedition was organized until 1722, too late for the stranded sailors.

Knight's expedition had met with disaster during the first winter. Both of his ships ran aground while attempting to harbour for the winter on Marble Island, a tiny wind-lashed and barren outcropping of rock seven kilometres off the coast in northwestern Hudson Bay, only four days' sailing north of the Churchill River. The men met a ghastly death from frostbite, scurvy and starvation. In 1769, the Company adventurer Samuel Hearne found on the shore the crumbled ruins of a brick building and mounds of coal, a cannon and shot, and a rusting anvil and spied the wreck of the two ships beneath the clear cold waters of the inlet. He learned from the Inuit the melancholy tale of the final days of the doomed mariners. "Sickness and famine occasioned such havock among the English, that by the setting in of the second Winter their number was reduced to twenty." By the following year, only five men remained. These survivors "were in such distress for provisions that they eagerly ate the seal's flesh and whale's blubber quite raw, as they purchased it from the natives. This disordered them so much, that three of them died in a few days, and the other two, though very weak, made a shift to bury them. Those two survived many days after the rest, and frequently they went to the top of an adjacent rock, and earnestly looked to the South and East, as if in expectation of some vessels coming to their relief. After continuing there a considerable time together, and nothing appearing in sight, they sat down close together, and wept bitterly. At length one of the two died, and the other's strength was so far exhausted, that he fell down and died also, in attempting to dig a grave for his companion." There is speculation that some mariners must have sailed from the island in one of the long-boats, but no evidence of it has been found.

Almost two decades after the tragic event, critics of the Hudson's Bay Company such as Arthur Dobbs (an avid enthusiast for polar exploration and a merchant in favour of abolishing the Company's monopoly) accused Company officials of directly contributing to the failure of the expedition through negligence in order to forestall further search for a Northwest Passage. Dobbs proclaimed that the Company deliberately sabotaged the Knight expedition, fearing that the discovery of valuable mineral deposits or a navigable trade route east would end their lucrative trading monopoly in Hudson Bay. Years later, in 1752, a Company employee named Joseph Robson wrote that he had heard that "some of the Company said upon this occasion, that they did not value the loss of the ship and sloop as long as they were rid of those troublesome men."

Chapter Five

THE CHILLY RIM
OF THE BAY

Hudson Bay is an enormous inland sea possibly created by an ancient meteorite, and the stony shore curves like a great bowl cut from the interior of the continent. The bay is connected to the Atlantic Ocean by a single inlet through Hudson Strait, a 750-kilometre-long and 150-kilometre-wide waterway known for turbulent and erratic currents and ice chunks that make it perilous for sailing ships. The ice chunks choke the waters for most of the year, continuously drifting south from the permanently frozen northern reaches and limiting navigation to a few short months. The bay is colder and icier than the Arctic Ocean despite being much farther south, because of its isolation from moderating ocean currents.

The Hudson Bay Lowlands region that encircles the south and west of the bay is a mostly flat and semi-swampy region cut through with rivers, creeks, lakes and ponds, all with gentle gradients and slow-moving waters that begin deep in the interior of the continent and meander thousands of kilometres to their exodus into the bay. The Albany, Severn, Hayes and Nelson are the principal rivers, each with its own drainage basin, and each had a Company fort stationed where they entered the bay. The Nelson is by far the largest river, draining Lake Winnipeg, nearly 650 kilometres southwest. The Nelson's drainage basin is enormous and encompasses most of the southern half of the provinces of Manitoba, Saskatchewan and Alberta. From Lake Winnipeg a continuous river system stretches over two and a half thousand kilometres west along the Saskatchewan River system and south along the Bow River, both leading west to the height of land in the Rocky Mountains. The smaller Hayes River, which exits into the bay near to where the Nelson does, is placid and good for canoeing close to the terminus near York Factory, but inland it is riddled with rapids, waterfalls and gorges and was never a significant canoe route. Winters in the lowlands are cold, long and dark, while summers in the south and west of the bay are chilly and short, but bright. The strip of land adjacent to the coast is nearly tundra in that it is barren and rocky and wind-lashed.

The muskeg and boggy terrain made overland travel in the summer difficult. The Cree and the Chipewyan subsisted on the migrating caribou herds, seasonal fish and a multitude of migratory birds. The rivers were abundant with brook trout and sturgeon. Polar bears came ashore in the spring and roamed the land with their young until the fall, when they again ventured out onto the ice floes. Population density close to the bay was never as high as it was in the interior to the south.

Farther inland, the terrain changes to the Canadian Shield, a much larger landscape of hard rock gouged by glaciers that is also laced with rivers, creeks and swamps, all interconnected and generally flowing east or northeast toward the bay. Waterways were the true highways of transportation and travel. The Shield is also densely covered in small spruce. Travellers walked along the frozen rivers, sometimes using dogs and sleds in winter, and canoed in summer. In the spring breakup and the fall freeze, travel was dangerous and arduous and rarely undertaken, limiting communication in those seasons. In late April or May, the river flows cracked the uniform blanket of ice, sending torrents of bergy water out into the bay, yet sometimes pushing the ice ashore. Farther north, around Prince of Wales Fort, the breakup occurred later, by mid-May, and not until June farther north. Fall freeze-up was likewise staggered from early November in the northernmost zones through early December for the lands southwest of James Bay. In the southern regions north of Lake Superior and in the Boundary Waters region to the west, fishing, maple sugar and wild rice were abundant, and later corn was cultivated as the Ojibwa took up the practice from the Huron in the late seventeenth century. In contrast, the northern coast was characterized by big-game hunting and fishing and a more dispersed population.

For most of the eighteenth century, the Company operated a string of posts at the Eastmain River, Moose Factory, Fort Albany, York Factory and Churchill (later renamed Prince of Wales Fort), and even later Henley House and Fort Severn. The population of bay-bound men amounted to around 250 to 300. The Company funded no inland explorations and maintained no inland posts. The daily operations of the outposts remained remarkably the same until the late eighteenth century. The management of personnel, the prices and the general mix of goods sent out from London was coordinated and decided upon in London, with input from the chief factor of each post and the resident governor in the bay, who was usually stationed at York Factory.

Each August and September, the supply ships, usually three of them, delivered their supplies and collected the furs, then turned around and braved the treacherous crossing of the bay and wended their way through the erratic currents and ice-choked waters of the Hudson Strait, before crossing the turbulent Atlantic to return to London, for a total voyage time of up to ten weeks. The Company hired competent captains and crews and prized long-term experience to avoid disasters and to maintain proprietary knowledge. Their sailing routes, and their skills with Indigenous languages and customs, were kept secret, as was their knowledge of the timing of the wind cycle and currents and the locations of safe harbours. When the ships reached London in late December, men unloaded the furs into dockside warehouses, and the Company began the process of auctioning them off over the winter. The ships' crews were paid off and future employment offered, and the men whose contracts had ended signed their secrecy agreements before being paid their back salary. Meanwhile, the managers were already planning the next season, pricing and sourcing goods according to the shifting demands of their customers, compiling in warehouses the cargo of supplies to keep the posts operating, and vetting recruits.

For much of the century, the Company's operations were routine, with little drama and with dividends ranging between 8 per cent and 12 per cent, until 1783, when another conflict with France halted them for a few years.

If the finances and routines in London were boring and predictable, life at the forts fell into the same category. Living at the Company's posts was harsh compared with anything in the British Isles. The trading outposts offered little protection against the cold. They were mostly similar to each other in construction materials, shape and purpose, consisting of a semi-defensive, poorly caulked wooden palisade with four bastion towers with cannons and a single large gate. Inside was a collection of heavy wood or stone two-storey buildings. Over time the cleared lands around the forts became littered with a haphazard collection of workhouses, cookhouses, cooperages and other facilities for work that didn't need to be inside the fort when the threat of French attack was low or non-existent. These were not military forts and they had no professional soldiers. The men at each fort were under the command of the chief factor and several other officers, including a second-in-command. Others were the sloopmaster, a surgeon and a handful of clerks, with the bulk of the population being labourers, including skilled tradesmen such as a blacksmith, shipwright, tailor, cooper and mason.

In winter it was a land where vinegar froze solid and a scorching red-hot cannon ball, heated before sleep, could barely keep a window from freezing. Wine froze when poured from the bottle and hoarfrost covered the interior walls. Snowdrifts up to four metres deep were not uncommon.

There were freezing winds, a lack of firewood, tedious jobs and monotonous foods, except for the seasons when birds could be hunted or when Cree hunters brought in venison or caribou. James Isham, a senior officer at various posts during his long career along the bay, wrote of his time at York Factory in winter with a grim fortitude. "The Wall's of our housses we here Live in are 2 foot thick of stone,—the windows small with 3 inch wooden shelter's, which is Close shutt 18 hour's Every Day, in the winter,— four Large fires are made in Large Brick stoves (Build for that purpose) Every Day." When the coals burned down, the chimney was capped to keep the heat in, but the resulting smoke "makes our heads to ac'h, and Very offencive and unholesome." Four or five hours later the inside of the fort's main rooms had become covered in thick ice that had to be chipped off every day with hatchets.

Complaints of the cold fill the journals and reports of the Company's servants along the bay, with temperature recordings as low as minus forty Celsius. Storms and brutal cold were the most commonly recorded aspects of weather. Samuel Hearne described one particularly punishing winter storm at Churchill in early March: "a violent snow came on the NNW and lasted four days without intermission. The snows were higher than the house—consequently, all the windows of the upper as well as the lower storey were entirely blocked up . . . Our stone walls are at present of little use, for both men and horses can come over them with as much ease as through the gate. The depth of drift in the yard is about twenty-two feet." There were accounts of exposed limbs nearly freezing overnight, ink turning solid in the well, hail the size and ferocity of musket shot and winds powerful enough to blow men away.

The men didn't just huddle indoors all winter. Most worked outdoors, engaged in activities such as making barrels, repairing wooden structures, hunting for birds, cutting trees and hammering metal items, as well as, of course, organizing, sorting and bundling furs. Sometimes they trapped on their own, hunted for deer, went fishing or went on short trips with Cree or Assiniboine parties to fell inland timber that could be rafted downriver when water levels were low. Isham described how they looked when they ventured out to do their winter tasks, bundled in layers of flannel, leather and fur. When gearing up for a journey to hunt, the men looked "more Like Beasts than men," he noted, with "a bag upon the back, with a tin pot and hatchet by the side, with a Beard as Long as Captain Teache's"—the famous pirate Blackbeard—"and a face as black as any Chimney Sweepers."

Summer's bright long days contrasted with the dark and cold stormy winter. But the short balmy season was not without its detractions, the great abundance of mosquitoes and sandflies being the most notable. The permafrost meant that the land never fully dried, remaining swampy and covered in a multitude of shallow lakes and ponds, which were prime breeding grounds for all manner of biting insects. Gardening and bird hunting, otherwise pleasurable activities that got the men outdoors, could become intolerable when a new swarm hatched. Sometimes work had to be halted due to an increase in the swarms after a humid rain or when the wind off the water died down. Men would mash them off of their arms and legs and faces when they emerged from the brush and rushed across the open land toward the fort. They kept fires burning constantly, hoping that the clouds of smoke would drive the bugs away, or applied seal oil to their faces and hands. Men's heads puffed up from the toxin of thousands of bites. James Isham wrote that the "sand fly's are so thick a man Can not see his way for them, Even if a man open's his mouth he is Lyable to be Joack't." James Knight complained that "where they light is just as if a spark of fire fell and raises a little bump which smarts and burns so that we cannot forbear rubbing them as causes such scabbs that our hands and faces is nothing but scabbs." Sadly there was no escaping this maddening but thankfully short-lived period of pestilence.

August was when the supply ships arrived with recruits. It was an exciting time of celebration, of men arriving and leaving and new foods and luxuries. A separate supply ship each usually serviced York Factory and Prince of Wales Fort, while a third ship sailed south to supply both Moose

Factory and Fort Albany. Smaller boats would shuffle goods between smaller forts such as Eastmain. The turnaround between unloading supplies and loading furs was short, owing to the sailing conditions in the bay. Whenever sails were spied on the horizon, the sleepy posts burst into action, with everyone working long hours so that the captain could turn around and depart by late August or very early September, in time to clear Hudson Strait before it became too dangerous.

The offloaded goods were vital to survival, as each fort or factory had to operate as an isolated community for most of the year. The clerks kept precise records scrawled with goose quill pens. Each item that arrived, whether for trade or use by the fort, was checked off and inventoried as soon as it was taken ashore and placed in the warehouse. Once the ships sailed away, taking friends and colleagues who often waved goodbye forever, the post settled in for the quickly arriving winter and a season of monotony. The men collected firewood, hunted birds and generally passed the time until the first snows covered the land, which made overland travel easier and safer. Then came winter and all its dark days, legendary storms and freezing nights. With spring came the arrival of the Indigenous traders with their own winter's work in collected pelts packed into their canoes.

The Company learned quickly to sign men on for terms of three to five years, with the most important stipulation that they not engage in private trade. Private trade, of course, undermined the Company's business, and although many engaged in secretive private trade over the years in a small way, the punishment was not usually severe, since the Company needed skilled men with experience. They couldn't really be sent home, since that was expensive and many would have gladly returned before their tenure was up. The Company offered a significant raise for anyone renewing a contract for another three- to five-year term. Salaries were low, set at perhaps one hundred pounds a year for a senior officer to as low as six to ten pounds a year for the least skilled or youngest labourer. But the men's expenses were also low, since room and board were provided, and they had nowhere to spend their salary except at the warehouse. Many workers opted to have their wages paid out at the end of their term. Sometimes the Company offered bonuses for exceptional service such as surveying, or hazardous jobs like blasting rocks. A season engaged in these dangerous jobs could earn a labourer additional pay equal to an entire year's regular wages.

The temptation to engage in private trade and augment their wages was always strong, and the Company never managed to stamp it out completely. From as early as 1686, the London Committee sent directives to the bayside governor to search for and confiscate contraband furs that were being smuggled out with the connivance of the ships' captains. In a letter to Governor Henry Sergeant at Moose Factory, the committee informed him, "We know very well Governor Nixon before you Did it. But we never did approve thereof . . . We know presents from Indians Doe arise from presents first from them to the Indians, and what are the presents but of our owne goods. Therefore judge you to whome all furrs belong."

Further, Sergeant was ordered to "strictly watch all ship Masters & others of our Servants that come home, that they doe not presume to bring home any furrs wither single or for lyning of coates, if you finde any such you shall take them away there and put them into our Warehouse." But it proved impossible to entirely prevent the practice, and every generation there seems to have been a scandal involving a connivance of officers and ship captains to carry illicit furs to London or to smuggle brandy or other suitable liquor to the bayside posts. It was considered a serious problem and was one of the reasons the Company at first was reluctant to encourage closer relationships between their employees and the Cree and Ojibwa traders who travelled to or lived near the forts.

The Company supplied a great quantity of the men's food, the remainder consisting of "country food," or fresh meat, which was sometimes hunted by the men when they had time or inclination, but more often by Indigenous hunters. The rations included copious quantities of salt pork and beef, flour, lard, dried peas, bacon, hard cheese, butter and oat-meal. Particularly important for their diet were wild geese in the fall and spring, often salted for later eating, ptarmigan netted in winter and arctic char, which also were frequently salted and saved. Salting, drying and freezing were the only preservation methods. The fort traded cari-bou and deer meat from the local Cree who knew how to hunt them by the dozens, spearing them from their canoes as the herds crossed rivers. A typical breakfast was fried fish or steak, while dinner could include any number of roasted, braised or boiled meats, including rabbit, duck or partridge, in addition to seasonal treats such as berry tarts and cheese washed down with madeira or port, or porter and spruce beer. The pro-tein-heavy diet kept the men strong and in general ready for arduous physical work in sometimes extreme conditions. (Most were already considerably hardier and in better health than those at home in the British Isles.) The Company often erred on the side of abundance when it came to calculating each man's food allotment, and so they frequently had more than they could eat. Not surprisingly, they secretly traded the surplus with Indigenous peoples.

The only fresh vegetables in their diet were those grown in the fort's gardens. Since the growing season was a scant sixty days despite being a similar latitude to London, and the soil shallow, the variety and quan-tity of vegetables was limited. The Company regularly sent over seeds for radishes, potatoes, peas, turnips, cabbage—tough, hardy northern fare—but also lettuces and mustard. Anything that would help the men become more self-reliant saved them money, after all. It was often a challenge to grow these crops reliably, since no farmers were ever sent over, and many of the men weren't interested. Even the position of gar-dener was misleading, since they generally knew little and followed written instructions from head office. The climate and soil weren't ideal for agriculture in any case. Grain often failed to ripen, although turnips, peas and radishes could be harvested regularly. Dandelions proved hardy and plentiful and "having grown pretty luxuriant, made most excellent salled to our roast geese," wrote William Wales at Prince of Wales Fort in 1768. Not a native species to North America, dandelion has become ubiquitous, the bane of lawn-proud urbanites, but back then it was a valuable dietary supplement. Spruce beer was the best scurvy treatment, and the London Committee was interested in the beverage common to many Indigenous peoples that had been adopted by the Baymen, "that Juyce that you tap out of the trees which you mixt with your drink when any one is troubled with the Scurvy."

Although it wasn't easy and had plenty of setbacks, the London Committee continued to send seeds as well as livestock such as sheep, goats, cattle, pigs and horses—hardy varieties from Shetland. Surprisingly, cattle survived well most of the time but suffered horribly during poor years. Cats were also imported to kill the innumerable mice that infested the forts. Edward Jarvis wrote a letter to John Thomas at Moose Factory in 1785 asking about the availability of a spare cat: "We are over run with mice and have a boar cat who can do nothing among them they are so very numerous, would be glad if you could spare a she Cat I would return her or a kitten or two."

Other local items that regularly graced the dinner tables at the forts included herbs and vegetables traditionally harvested by the Indigenous peoples who dwelt nearby. They shared the knowledge and also brought in these items for trade. A multitude of wild edible vegetables—savoury, astringent and sweet—enlivened meals and provided vital nutrients. These included Labrador tea, wild celery, wild garlic, wild leeks, rock lichen, arrowhead (small starchy tubers), nettles, burdock and an abundance of other shoots, tender roots and leaves eaten raw, added to stews or used to garnish roasted meats and fish. Berries and currants grew in abundance throughout most regions.

Life at the forts was highly structured, and mealtimes were no exception. There were times of frenetic activity and long days when the men worked to exhaustion, followed by seasons in which spare time was abundant, so a lingering meal was part of the routine to prevent social disintegration and keep morale from sliding. Dinner was a semi-formal affair for the officers or senior managers, with multiple dishes each night and a much greater portion of the scarce vegetables. They toasted each other with wine or brandy at meals, and arguments were forbidden at the table. The regular garrison had a more monotonous fare taken from giant communal pots, and beer or cheap spirits to have with it. One Company officer, Andrew Graham, who lived at multiple forts in the later eighteenth century, was known for his amusing and trenchant observations on natural history, social customs and daily life. He pointed out the glaring differences in the two mess tables that occasionally was the cause for grumbling and muttering. The officer's table "is always handsomely supplied with provisions, very seldom having less than three dishes; and on particular occasions fourteen or sixteen . . . The officers have wines and French brandy plentifully allowed them; and the men London porter, and British spirit [gin] served out at the discretion of the Chief."

The Company strove for an almost military structure for daily life and routine, with the officers and men having separate living quarters and separate eating rooms and the day's work blocked out into regular segments like on a ship, with strict rules for behaviour and language in an effort to preserve authority and order. Unruliness would be deadly in the harsh climate, not only to the men who would be unprepared to deal with climate, natural disasters or disruptions in the Company's supply ships, but also to the Company's profits. But the effort to instill or replicate a class system similar to that in British society was never fully successful, since the officers were not born gentlemen but merely successful and competent long-term tradesmen or clerks rather than well-connected dilettantes.

It took constant effort to keep the men busy in the slower months. Cards, games, a few musical instruments and some books for the literate helped while away the time when storms kept them trapped in their drafty, smoky cabins. Hardly surprising that heavy drinking was also part of bayside life, particularly during the dark, cold winter. English brandy, which was merely raw gin coloured with iodine or molasses, was a staple ration for the men as well as a trade good. Many were the complaints of drunken labourers, sloppy at their work and annoying with their loud and turbulent antics. There was always the fear that drunk night guards would burn buildings down through negligence or that inebriated workers would injure themselves, chopping into a leg with an erratically swung axe or crushing their fingers between logs.

Keeping group morale high was a perpetual issue. The same small cohort trapped and crowded in unpleasant conditions, rehashing the same discussions, prejudices and conflicting opinions over and over led to arguments. Arguments and booze led to disobedience and fights and sickness. The Company was always searching for recruits who could weather the winter without drinking and fighting. One of the earliest governors in the bay, John Nixon, begged the London Committee "to send me Some country lads, that are not acquainted with strong drink, that will worke hard . . . and are not debauched by the voluptuousness of the city."

The Company tried to get young apprentices who would sign on for seven years (to save on the high cost of transporting people across the Atlantic and back and because salary raise negotiations happened only when a contract concluded) and who were suited to harsh northern living. To avoid the risk of hiring crew who might prove unhappy and turn to drink, they looked to Lowland Scots and Orkney Islanders, people from a cluster of bleak rocky islands off the northern coast of Scotland where life was harsh and economic prospects were poor. For many of these young men, work at an isolated outpost in distant Hudson Bay was more promising and profitable than remaining at home. The Orkney Islanders were generally quiet, hard-working and obedient, if clannish, uncurious and prone to small-scale smuggling. By 1730, the Company's mostly nameless transient bayside workforce came from these two locations.

Excessive alcohol consumption was a problem within the fort, as it was among the Cree and Ojibwa, several hundred of whom lived surrounding the main forts. Unlike the Baymen, they had no experience with intoxicants as powerful as brandy or rum, and the frustrations of a small group living constantly together, nurturing their resentments and animosities and grudges, came burbling up with alcohol's lowered inhibitions. James Isham observed of the Cree delegations to York Factory that they "are given very much to Quarrelling when in Liquor having Known two Brothers when in Liquor to Quarrell after such a manner, that they have Bitt one another nose, Ears, and finger's off . . . They are also Very Sulky and sullen, and if at any time one has a Resentment against another, they never show itt, till the Spiritious Liquor's work's in their Brains, then they Speak their mind freely."

Spirits were in great demand as payment for hunting, in ceremonial exchanges and in payment for furs. Throughout the eighteenth century the Company made frequent attempts to restrict or regulate the dispensation of liquor, but these efforts were never uniform. The main obstacle to instituting a more consistent prohibition was that it was impossible to regulate alcohol completely within the factories for their own employees, and they feared that if denied alcohol completely the Indigenous traders would take their business to the French, in spite of the greater travelling distance and inferior trade goods. Potent alcohol was a recurring problem for all who congregated at the Company's posts; this was a society struggling to develop the social infrastructure and accepted behaviours needed to regulate and control the actions of people under the influence of the new intoxicants. Isham later observed that a custom had evolved whereby men who planned on drinking would send away the women and children along with all the guns and knives. Most of the problems between the employees and officers at the factories also had to do with the abuse of or smuggling of liquor.

The most striking thing is that none of the decision makers on the London Committee ever visited the bay, apart from James Knight, and the yawning gap between reality and theory was also part of life at the outpost. Whether it be admonitions to grow more vegetables, to get more work done during each season, to trade for more furs by exhorting the Cree to work harder, or to get their employees to urge Indigenous peoples from farther inland to breach the Cree hegemony and trade directly at the fort, many directives had to be politely ignored. Life at the factories along the bay revolved around its own unique set of customs and activities, borrowing from Indigenous practices whenever convenient, accommodating Indigenous customs whenever possible and generally creating its own society that was derived from cultural and geographical necessity rather than rigid London imperatives.

One directive from the London Committee to John Nixon must have made his eyes roll when he read it at Fort Albany in 1680. A helpful suggestion on how to save money on food rations, it revealed just how little was appreciated in London of life along the bay: "Upon Hayes Island where our grand Factory is, you may propagate Swine without much difficulty, wch. is an excellent flesh, and the Creature is hardy and will live where some other Creatures cannot." These types of directives were written by well-meaning dandies, upper-class financiers and aristocrats who had never been to Hudson Bay and experienced its primitive outposts, harsh climate and poor soil, but also had never worked outside the rarefied palatial offices and manors of upper-class English society— people, in short, who ought not be telling servants how to procure their food on a remote distant continent, where they were visitors in a bewildering and deadly land, perched precariously along the rim of a geographical and cultural *terra incognita*.

On the one hand, there was the London Committee, with its directors planning grand strategy and issuing orders that occasionally indulged in the penchant for micromanagement, and then there were the people who worked for the Company in the outposts with the geographical and climatic constraints of the Subarctic and who worked with, or were friends with or even married to, the Indigenous people of that land. The Company had official policies, but the people bayside interpreted those policies and adjusted them to reality.

RELATIONSHIPS WITH THE HOSTS OF THAT foreign land were at the heart of life and business at the posts. Not only were the local, or Home Guard, Cree often hired for jobs as labourers, hunters, guides, seamstresses, cooks and interpreters, but sexual and romantic relations between Indigenous women and Company men were common. In the earliest days of its operations in the late seventeenth century, the Company's directors issued proclamations to its officers to prevent or obstruct these relationships. "We are very sensible that the Indian Weoman resorting to our Factories are very prejudiciall to the Companies affaires," the committee wrote to John Nixon in 1682, "not only by being a meanes of our Servants often debauching themselves, but likewise by embeazling our goods and very much exhausting our Provisions, It is therefore our positive order that you lay your strict Commands on every Cheife of each Factory upon forfiture of Wages not to Suffer any wooman to come within any of our factories." For obvious reasons, this directive from aristocratic directors, comfortable in their estates in London and surrounded by their families, was not only foolish but unenforceable, human nature and social needs being what they are.

There was always a difference between what London directors wrote in their letters as official policy and what chief factors enforced for themselves and their men. Money was usually at the crux of it. Workers who spent many years of their lives in what amounted to remote work camps wanted to improve their lot as much as possible, while the managers didn't want responsibility for families. But, as Graham noted, "the Company permit no European women to be brought within their territories; and forbid any natives to be harboured in the settlements. This latter has never been obeyed."

But the Company soon appreciated the benefit of having close ties with their Indigenous trading partners and quietly began supporting intimate liaisons. The shift in opinion was based on the realization that these relationships were not a financial drain but rather an asset. Unofficial diplomatic marriages between Indigenous women and Company employees became common, with Indigenous women seeking kinship ties for more favourable trading privileges, while single Company men sought female companionship and an introduction to the life and customs of the land. In a practical sense these were alliances for mutual aid, companionship and support, both social and economic, much like marriages today. Women also performed vital domestic tasks around the factories, such as making moccasin shoes, sewing clothing and netting snowshoes.

Regardless, there wasn't as much "debauching" going on as certain prudish directors feared. Although various forms of prostitution existed at the forts, most relations were not casual or promiscuous; rather, they resulted in many long-standing unions, which as a general rule were arranged according to the customs of the local peoples. A Company man refusing an offer of a local marriage could be considered an insult that could damage the Company's business interests. Country marriages, as they were called, became more common throughout the eighteenth century and resulted in large numbers of children of mixed parentage, biologically and culturally, dwelling around the forts. They were "country born" or "citizens of the bay" if English, while the French later called these mixed-heritage children Métis or *bois-brûlé* (burnt wood).

Country marriages often lasted many years but were sometimes a cause of great pain when children were sent away for schooling or when either parent died, leaving them culturally adrift, or when the trader retired, abandoning his wife or children to their people. The women left no written record of their experiences or thoughts, so it's impossible to know exactly what they thought or what motivated them. As was the custom, a widowed or divorced woman returned to live with her extended family, sometimes relieved to be rid of an annoying or otherwise unsuitable mate, other times grieving. As many examples of relationships existed along Hudson Bay in the eighteenth century as there are today, from loving and intimate to cold and calculating, from mutually loving to mutually exploitive.

Mixed liaisons became common, if unofficial, and continued for generations. James Isham, one of the most insightful sources of information
on bayside life in the mid-eighteenth century and a man with a Cree
wife and son, described the children of mixed parentage as being "pretty
Numerous" and said they tended to be "fine Children . . . streight Lim'd,
Lively active." When he died in 1761, after three decades along the bay,
Isham bequeathed his estate to his son, Charles Thomas Price Isham,
who also worked for the Company. Lisette Umfreville, the daughter of
trader Edward Umfreville and his Cree mistress, had her eye on John
Rowand, the great-girthed future chief factor of Fort Edmonton. When
his horse returned to the fort riderless one afternoon, she leaped into
action, grabbed her own horse and rode out to rescue him, finding him
alone and in pain from a broken leg. As she nursed him back to health
they fell in love, and when they married *à la façon du pays*, Rowand
adopted her three surviving children from a prior marriage and received
a herd of horses as her dowry. He called her "my old friend the mother
of all my [seven] children," and they remained together for the next
thirty-nine years, until she preceded him in death in 1849.

When the trader Daniel Harmon married a Cree woman, Elizabeth
Duval, in 1805, he admitted that his plan had been to see that she was
secure and then leave her behind, but that after fifteen years together he
couldn't. "The union which has been formed between us, in the providence of God, has not only been cemented by a long and mutual performance of kind offices, but, also, by a more sacred consideration. . . .
We have wept together over the early departure of several children, and
especially, over the death of a beloved son. We have children still living,
who are equally dear to us both. How could I spend my days in the civilized world, and leave my beloved children in the wilderness? The thought
has in it the bitterness of death. How could I tear them from their mother's
love, and leave her to mourn over their absence, to the day of her death?"
Another of Harmon's diary entries is a window into domestic life at the
forts: "I now pass a short time every day, very pleasantly, in teaching my

little daughter Polly to read and spell words in the English language, in which she makes good progress, though she knows not the meaning of one of them. In conversing with my children, I use entirely the Cree Indian language; with their mother I more frequently employ the French. Her native tongue, however, is more familiar to her, which is the reason why our children have been taught to speak that in preference to the French language." When Harmon quit the fur trade in 1819, after stints working at various forts and over the Rocky Mountains in New Caledonia, the couple retired together to a town in Vermont with their children. Many other traders and voyageurs opted to remain with their families in the vicinity of the trading posts.

So many of the Orkney Island labourers had taken Indigenous wives over the generations that by the 1770s there was a school on the island of South Ronaldsay, founded by William Tomison, dedicated to these children of the bay, although most children of mixed parentage were raised and lived along the bay, especially the girls, and joined their mother's family if their father died or went back to Britain. Many of the children educated at South Ronaldsay returned for careers with the Company. As a distinct society formed around the posts, neither fully Indigenous nor English, the Company also employed many of the mixed-heritage children who grew up along the bay, both the boys and the girls. By the end of the eighteenth century, London was sending out schoolbooks to be used by the children of their employees, and by 1806 the children were being taught "reading, writing, arithmetic accounts."

By the nineteenth century, the Company drastically reduced its recruitment of young apprentices from the British Isles, ending a practice that had been in place for well over a century. There was no longer a need for them, as the new mixed-heritage communities around the Company's posts filled all these positions. Factory boys, as they were sometimes called, did the work of maintaining the communities through fishing, hunting, gardening, tending domestic animals, writing and record keeping, felling timber, carpentry, coopering, and sailing the smaller sloops. The trading forts became like villages of blended culture, law and genetics—meeting places—and the Company could not survive without the services of the men as hunters and labourers and the women for making and maintaining clothing, cooking and translating. The Home Guard Cree were increasingly drawn into the economic orbit of the Company's forts, such that their way of life soon depended upon access to European manufactured goods. By the mid-eighteenth century, the Home Guard were the hundreds of people who lived more or less permanently around the Company forts, while the Upland, or trading, Cree were those who came in for the annual trading ceremony.

It was nearly a practical impossibility for the people in the fort to distance themselves from the Cree who lived near the fort after generations had become culturally and economically enmeshed with the routines and the people. Although the situation varied between forts and varied over time according to the personality of the latest chief factor or governor, for the most part the Company's London Committee turned a blind eye to the social activities of the bay so long as they didn't cost them anything. One failed experiment in leadership occurred at Fort Albany in 1752. After several generations of traders had made their careers and lives at Company outposts, they appointed Orkneyman John Isbister to be the new chief factor. He had previously been a senior officer at Churchill. Whatever his other attributes, Isbister was not a diplomatic or astute leader. Rigid and autocratic, he didn't see his outpost as a community of civilians engaged in a mutual commercial exchange that required diplomacy and cultural acceptance. Rather, he viewed it as more of a military outpost, and ordered the men to fall in line as if they were in a garrison during war, in strict accordance with the written official directives of the London Committee. He used the strap and other punishments to enforce his moral code, a code that included no alcohol and no fraternizing with Indigenous women. Meanwhile he secretly tried to keep an Indigenous mistress himself, which irritated both his employees and the local people and challenged social customs that had prevailed for generations.

Isbister's reign was also marked by the Company's first tentative attempt at sending men inland. French traders had established a rival fort about 170 kilometres upstream along the Albany River, and since their actions were damaging Fort Albany's trade, Isbister was ordered to set up a small satellite fort at the junction of the Kenogami River to counter the commercial threat and to remind people to canoe down to Fort Albany for better prices. Henley House, as it was called, was a strategic location where the Cree habitually gathered before they headed downriver to Fort Albany. Unfortunately, Isbister had his lieutenant William Lamb enforce his own social policies at the small outpost, to disastrous effect.

Following the example of his boss, Lamb apparently kept two women, including Won a Wogen, the daughter of Wappisis, a former Albany trading captain. According to custom, the exchange of women was meant to convey reciprocal morally sanctioned social rights and obligations, including generosity and friendship. A woman's family would gain special status at the fort, including the expectation of shared food. It was a form of kinship. When Wappisis and his sons, Sheanapp and Snuff-the-blanket, and son-in-law Annsoet arrived at the palisade in December 1754 with over a dozen other family members, they received a cool reception from Lamb, who at first welcomed them but then ordered them to leave the fort and camp outside, a grave insult to the dignity of Wappisis and a breach of the social compact, especially as Lamb kept his daughter Won a Wogen and the other women inside with him (whether with their consent or against their will is not recorded). Lamb was violating the custom for even the most casual of country marriages.

Wappisis felt cheated, and not for the first time. At Fort Albany, Isbister had insulted Wappisis once before by refusing him entry to the fort, which had been granted to him and his family under the previous chief factor. Refusing to let him inside and offering none of the usual food, or even a show of respect, was culturally obtuse and poor business practice. Messing with the entrenched bayside domestic customs would

never have been good for trade in the long run, something understood
by most of the Company's bayside people if not by the London
Committee. But Isbister was a man who interpreted his duty to the
letter, and seemed to fail to appreciate that disturbing the unique blend
of customs and responsibilities that regulated the interactions between
the Cree and the Baymen could have unforeseen consequences.

Wappisis was also an unsavoury character. He had earned the sobriquet "the land pirate," and had a reputation for waylaying other
Indigenous traders en route to the fort and stealing their furs. He was a
sort of bandit chieftain who depended upon fear and intimidation to
maintain his power. The affront to his dignity was a blow to his personal
reputation and a demotion of his status, and he took matters into his
own hands, in the name of justice, as he saw it, for the domestic and
sexual exploitation of the women. Wappisis watched from his camp as
Lamb sent men out to work in the forest, and then, with Snuff-the-
blanket, snuck up and shot Lamb in the head. They then killed the other
four men inside the fort and hid their bodies beneath some old logs.
They remained at the fort trading or giving away the stock and then
departed after ransacking the place, but leaving the structures intact.
Wappisis threatened everyone not to reveal what he had done or he
would kill them.

When news of the attacks on the fort arrived at Fort Albany months
later, Isbister concluded that the French must have attacked the outpost,
since there was a rumour that the French were offering money for proof
of dead English traders. When Wappisis arrived with his entourage at
the end of May, Isbister thought his story and behaviour odd. He
claimed that Henley House was taken in January and that he had seen
Indigenous men allied to the French hanging about. Isbister became
suspicious of Wappisis's boasting, which was met with awkward silence
from the other people. Soon, frightened witnesses secretly emerged to
tell the true tale. Wappisis was a feared and not terribly liked person,
and the plunder of the fort and the disruption of trade had caused

hardship and the starvation of several children who were dependent upon the fort for supplies.

Isbister invited Wappisis and his two sons into the fort, and they entered "very gaily." They were shocked when he ordered them to be seized and confined in separate rooms. Isbister then went outside and fired two shots into the air and then went to each of the three men, saying that the other two had confessed and had been killed so there was no point in denying the murders at Henley House. All three confessed. When Wappisis heard he had been deceived he raged, straining at his ropes and threatening to kill Isbister.

Once Isbister determined that the Home Guard Cree had no affinity for Wappisis and that many also had been victims of his depredations in the past, and in fact thought it was good that the pirate had been apprehended, he sought the advice of his own council and the officers at Moose Factory. There had never been any murders or violence of this sort in the previous eighty years, so there was no precedent for how the Company was supposed to deal with the situation. Weighing the opinions, Isbister ordered Wappisis and his two sons to be hanged.

The Henley House murders were the first time the Company sought to impose its own authority rather than Indigenous dispute-resolution customs, but it seems that Isbister, despite his role in creating the problem, handled the situation with a deft blend of ceremony that satisfied his own men and the Cree. Although Wappisis was not an honest or well-respected leader, if Isbister and Lamb hadn't been such hypocrites in their abuse of the unwritten social compact that smoothed international relations between the peoples along the bay, it seems likely that the whole episode could have been avoided. At the time, the Company had no particular authority to dispense justice over anyone other than their own employees, even according to the terms of their charter, and for the first century of its life the Company generally treated the Cree, Assiniboine, Ojibwa and Chipewyan on a nation-to-nation basis, rather than as a colonial enterprise. The capture and hangings caused no animosity in relations or decline in trade because the punishment generally conformed to the Indigenous custom and understanding of being a just retribution for the murders—Isbister was believed to be within his rights to seek restitution for the murders of his men. Nevertheless, the post was soon closed for fear of further retribution by Wappisis's extended family, who avoided Albany for many years afterwards. Henley House was abandoned, and the Company made no more efforts to move farther inland after such a terrible setback.

With no police force and no strict social order, occasionally a disciplinarian chief factor could face a near mutiny—certainly the London Committee's official orders needed to be interpreted with a great deal of flexibility to conform to local customs. The prevailing attitude that developed at each fort was specific to a group of men living in isolation from their country for years at a stretch. Apart from a brief period of intense labour when the supply ship arrived and letters could be exchanged, they had no contact with anyone other than their compatriots at the fort and the local people. They adapted, learned new ways, and were exposed to a culture very different from their own. Neither local nor British justice could be followed entirely, and the general policy was not to interfere in any of the goings-on between Indigenous peoples. But when it affected Company employees, a sort of hybrid justice system prevailed, mostly following the customs of the Indigenous people but with a gloss of English ceremony, to obtain the desired outcome. The relations between the Company and its Indigenous customers and employees was complex and constantly evolving as the generations passed.

Chapter Six

BEYOND THE BAY

On a fine but otherwise unremarkable mid-eighteenth-century day in June at York Factory, Chief Factor Andrew Graham was roused from his desk by a sudden commotion among his men and calls for his attention. Around the bend of the Hayes River came at least a dozen canoes, paddling abreast with the central boat and its six occupants flying a pole with the Company flag, similar to the Red Ensign, in the stern. The people in the boats were attired in their cleanest and best clothing, and as they approached, they loaded muskets and fired into the sky. Graham gave the word and his men likewise saluted the arriving brigade with a thunderous fusillade of fowling guns and a few small cannons.

The canoes pulled ashore and dozens of people began unloading supplies and setting up camp in the clearing by the river's edge. Three men separated from the busy group and marched up the embankment to the fort where Graham walked out to welcome them. The chief, or trading captain, and his two lieutenants, often sons or relatives, were wearing their finery: red or blue coats with white shirts, tall woollen stockings and buckled shoes. Their heads were adorned with feathered hats tied around the forehead with a colourful sash, pirate-style, the ends hanging down to their shoulders.

The dignitaries introduced themselves, and the group walked into the fort and into a drawing room, where they sat on wooden chairs, according to their rank, around a central table upon which had been placed pipes and tobacco. Everyone smoked quietly for several minutes. Graham later described the meeting. "The Silence is then broken by degrees by the most venerable Indian, his head bowed down and eyes immovably fixed on the floor, or other object. He tells how many canoes he has brought, what kind of winter they have had, what natives he has seen, are coming, or stay behind, asks how the Englishmen do, and says he is glad to see them. After which the Governor bids him welcome, tells them he has good goods and plenty; and that he loves the Indians and will be kind to them. The pipe is by this time renewed and the conversation becomes free, easy and general," while baskets of bread, fruit and cups of brandy were passed around.

While these pleasantries were being exchanged, Company servants outfitted the trading captains and their lieutenants with a set of new clothes, similar to the ones they were wearing, pricey and distinguished. Then the trading captain and his lieutenants led the Company officers in a procession back through the gates of the fort to the camp in the clearing and took them into a ceremonial tent whose floors were covered in clean birchbark and fresh beaver pelts. There they were seated in places of honour while the Company servants brought more bread and prunes. The trading captain, or chief, launched into a speech of welcome and good wishes and then ordered a senior member of the tribe to distribute among the people gathered outside the welcome gifts from the Company's chief factor: brandy, bread, dried fruit and tobacco. After these rituals were complete, the chief and the lieutenants were invited to breakfast inside the fort with the Company officers, and afterwards the trading room was opened to them for inspection. The first item of trade was brandy.

After a couple of days of singing and dancing and general celebration, each family in the band prepared their host a gift of furs and presented it to the chief factor, and the two sides settled down to the business of exchange. One final ceremony was the smoking of the calumet pipe, to renew the league of friendship. Graham noted that "smoking the calumet is necessary to establish confidence, it is conducted with the greatest solemnity . . . The Captain walks in with his calumet in his hand covered with a case, then comes the lieutenant and the wives of the captains with the present, and afterwards all the other men with the women and their little ones. The Governor is genteely dressed after the Indian fashion, and receives them with cordiality and good humour. The captain covers the table with a new beaver coat, and on it lays the calumet or pipe; he will also sometimes present the Governor with a clean beaver toggy or banian to keep him warm in the winter." The trading captain then presented the gift while the senior people sat in chairs in silence until the chief factor took the pipe and lit it.

More speeches followed the ceremonial smoking, along with proclamations of friendship and loyalty, as the trading captain and the governor each related the past year's major events: deaths, births, marriages, the condition of the winter and notable occurrences, troubles and hardships. Most important were the promises that each would be generous and fair to the other. The actual trade was conducted by each individual through a window or wicket at the warehouse, with the trading captain observing the proceedings.

After days of celebration, ceremony, negotiation and trade, usually lasting about two weeks, the chief factor presented final parting gifts to seal the end of the season and ensure that everyone was satisfied with the events. These could be a new pipe and tobacco, dried fruit, a hunting gun with powder and shot, fishing hooks, hatchets, thimbles or brandy to take away. The senior women, who often tended to be healers, were taken with their husbands into a special room where they were presented with a small red leather trunk that contained "a few simple medicines such as

the powders of sulphur, bark, liquorice, camphorated spirit, white oint-
ment, and basilicon, with a bit of diachylon plaster." The purpose of each
item was explained, if it wasn't already known, which it usually was since
the women's memories were "very tenacious." Sometimes goods were
given to the chief to take inland to those who couldn't make the journey.
"I can from personal experience," Graham noted, "affirm that a large
stock of goods are indiscriminately given away yearly to natives that are
in want, occasioned by sickness etc." It was important to maintain
goodwill for the business to prosper, as well as for common decency, and
as Graham noted, the Cree "are a good natured people and very susceptible of wrongs done them."

The most elaborate ceremony was reserved for people who travelled,
often long distances, to the trading fort and not just the Home Guard
Cree, who had a much closer relationship with the Company's forts. The
most formalized ceremonies, like the ones described by Graham, were
held at York Factory, which accounted for over half the Company's
revenue in the mid-eighteenth century and attracted at least five or six
hundred Cree each year in several large trading groups. The Eastern
Cree arrived in small groups at Eastmain, the smallest fort, and traded
less and departed without fanfare.

The Indigenous trading captains held an important position of responsibility as arbiters and brokers, based on their ability to smooth relations
between their own people and the Company traders, a role similar to a
chief factor's. It wasn't a hereditary position. The trading captain was
elected each year to be the head of a collective bargaining unit, although
they sometimes retained some of this authority throughout the year in
anticipation of the future season. The Cree trading captain Wappenessew,
or Wapinesiw, led annual fleets of between twenty and thirty large
canoes, with up to four people in each, to York Factory for decades and
was, Graham said, "a person of prime consideration . . . and his influence
is very extensive." The Chipewyan captain Matonabbee was known as
"the great northern Leader" and personally led over a hundred traders

and trappers every year to Churchill in the 1770s. The Cree Attickasish was another well-known and esteemed trading captain who managed an extensive business circuit for many years. The trading captains were as important and well known in their communities as the chief factors were to the Company, and maintaining good relationships with them was vital to the Company's success.

Sometimes Company men who were less experienced traders, or who were new to the job and didn't speak any of the Indigenous languages well, or perhaps who had a poor understanding of the ritual function of gifts at the start of a commercial transaction, saw the gifts distributed to the trading captains at the conclusion of each year's business as bribes or merely as a material stimulus to trade. But the excess gifts given to the trading captains to distribute at their discretion served other important social functions, such as maintaining social cohesion and the common welfare of the larger group. "All gentlemen that are acquainted with the natives in Hudsons Bay," observed Graham, "know that it is not altogether by giving large presents to the leaders that will gain a trade, but by an affable, kind, easy behaviour to the whole body of natives; for as all natives are master over their own families they give no ear to the leader if they have any disgust to the fort."

From the earliest days of the trade people could tell when the ceremony was insincere. Radisson reported in 1684 that the Cree at Port Nelson were annoyed that "the Frenchmen of Canada made gifts to them in order to oblige them to open their bundles." Insincerity in the ceremony of trade resulted in declining trade at forts if there was a perception that the customs were being abused to hasten trade, while sidelining all the other less tangible reciprocal responsibilities that went along with it. The annual visit to the forts to trade became an important aspect of the calendar. The Indigenous trappers or traders spent weeks, perhaps even months, travelling to the Company outposts at considerable effort, and sometimes hardship, and faced a return journey of equal duration. They were not about to trade quickly and leave. They wanted to mark the significance of the journey and prolong the pleasures.

Credit was also an entrenched custom of the Company's trade from the earliest years. The trade, with its elaborate ceremony and ornamental customs that proclaimed and required mutual respect and obligations, matched the complexity of life in general. Owing to the fact that life was capricious and unpredictable—that years of good seasons could be followed by a disastrous year—it benefited both parties to allow for the vagaries of fate to dictate the terms of trade. The people demanded, and the Company complied, that trading partners would be advanced an "outfit" for the winter that could include knives, shot, powder, nets and cord or rope, as well as some of the ubiquitous and coveted twists of Brazil tobacco. The Company's traders then would expect that they would be given first opportunity to get the furs the next season, but also to take responsibility for the losses if the season was poor and offer support in times of need. This arrangement of mutual obligation required a great deal of trust and respect by both parties: for one, that their material needs would be looked after in times of need, and for the other, that the loan of equipment and supplies would eventually be repaid. These were serious social contracts. The famous trader and traveller David Thompson remarked on one occasion, "On taking the necessaries which they require for the winter season, several of them, especially those advanced in life, have made a bargain with me, if they should die in the winter, I should not demand the debt due to me in the other world; and to which I always agreed."

Many Indigenous people viewed the relationship as one with the individual person with whom they were dealing, not the Company in general. It was personal, symbolically familial and based on ceremony and ritual. Sometimes, if a chief factor retired or was transferred to another fort, people believed they no longer owed their debts, a situation the Company sought to avert for obvious reasons. There were reports of some people taking advantage of the credit system by moving between posts and never repaying, but there were also credible accounts of Company traders under-measuring goods like gunpowder, watering down brandy, cutting cloth short or assessing beaver pelts at less than their value.

For the most part, however, the fur trade at the Company's outposts along Hudson Bay in the eighteenth century was stabilized by the social contract that resulted in mutual benefit. The trade was more like a treaty or an alliance, with plenty of unspecified future mutual obligations of support and responsibility. Although this relationship began with Radisson and Groseilliers and the Cree of the Hudson Bay Lowlands, as the Company expanded its operations it found that this general style of commerce resulted in less friction and conflict and better returns.

By the early nineteenth century, though, this relationship began to break down as competition developed between the French and English traders. As they each sought to gain the most furs for the least merchandise, the various inland Indigenous peoples played the competing traders against each other, and certain Indigenous groups also sought their own commercial empires as middlemen. When dealing with such a long period of history spanning many generations, no single summary can convey the totality of the relationship as it evolved over time, but for many generations the ceremony described by Graham at York Factory governed trade along Hudson Bay.

THE FUR TRADE HAD AN ENORMOUS INFLUENCE on the material culture of Indigenous groups. The Cree, Dene/Chipewyan, Ojibwa and Assiniboine who frequented the Company's posts throughout the eighteenth century, although different culturally and linguistically, shared a similar basket of technology and material culture. They hunted with bows made from willow, used sinews for thread and fishing line and the bone tips of antlers for thimbles, burned fat for lamp fuel, and tanned or softened hides for buckets, packs and bags, clothing, boots, lashings, tents, drums and mitts. Nearly every part of an animal such as a caribou was fashioned into something useful or fulfilled a decorative purpose. Likewise, feathers held ceremonial value, and hollow bird bones became flutes and smoking pipes. Furs kept them warm. The land provided everything, but not necessarily in abundance or with consistency—life could be easy one year and harsh the next without warning; the changing seasons could bring feast or famine. And it was enormously labour intensive to create all these tools derived from animals.

To a people who lacked iron technology, even a crudely sharpened piece of metal could be a valuable implement. When Radisson began trading for the Company along Hudson Bay, he noted the value placed upon a piece of iron and how useful a single knife could be as a tool for basic living. "And having noticed that one of them used a small piece of flat iron to hack away at his tobacco," he wrote of the beginning of a trading ceremony, "I asked him for this piece of iron and threw it into the fire. That surprised all of them . . . I assured them that they would no longer lack anything, as long as I was among them," he boasted. "And at the same time, I removed the dagger that I had at my side and gave it to the one whose piece of iron I had thrown away." On this occasion, Radisson easily filled his canoes with worn beaver clothing in exchange for his stock of metal tools and weapons. It was the beginning of a relationship that would endure for centuries in its essential characteristics, even while the balance of power shifted over the generations to favour the Company. The fur trade was successful over such a long period because it provided both partners with items of value.

The Company, and the fur trade in general, influenced the North American economy far beyond the rim of the bay where it operated its trading forts. When eyes faced east and scanned the rising sun in the morning, they knew that was the direction from which came exotic foreign goods and guns. Even if they didn't travel to the bay themselves, all knew the direction from which these goods came, often traded many times between peoples as they filtered their way west through the interior of the continent. The land was occupied by many dozens of ethnic groups, each with their own ancient and shifting alliances, unsettled grudges and political and economic aspirations. Fluid, dynamic and

complex, the cultural landscape wasn't easy to understand, and was certainly not one that could be controlled in any way.

But the fur trade, as a form of mutual exploitation, had many benefits.
The manufactured items that the Company offered made life easier, and
proved to be economically important, since they could be traded farther
afield at any time, and could dramatically shift the status quo in warfare.
The guns, hatchets and knives, and even metal arrowheads, altered the
balance of power in favour of those who had them and made hunting
easier and more successful—including the hunting of more beaver to
obtain more metal tools and implements. Brass kettles, pots and pans
rapidly replaced ceramic, bark and hide vessels, making cooking astonishingly easier and faster because metal pots could be placed or held
over an open fire without damage, simmering stews and soups for hours
without requiring much attention. Cloth made from cotton and wool was
also a highly prized item, as it had different characteristics than furs and
leather. It was lighter, dried more easily and was more colourful (although
not as durable or warm). Seemingly frivolous items such as coloured
glass beads and decorative lace were also valued for novelty and fashion.
About two-thirds of the dollar value in furs went toward items of necessity
or practicality, while one-third was spent on "superfluous" items (probably
a similar ratio to today's households). By the mid-eighteenth century,
European manufactured goods were found throughout the interior of
North America and had become nearly indispensable in some regions.
Over time the trade of guns and metal implements changed the culture
and politics of Indigenous peoples as far away as the Rocky Mountains,
while beaver pelts changed the culture of England and Europe, with
ever-changing styles in the universal felt hat commanding continual
financial outlays.

As trade settled into a more predictable pattern for the Company
and trading volume increased, it caused great upheaval in Indigenous
societies—many of which were as yet unknown to anyone in the
Company—that reverberated across the interior of the continent. The

Home Guard Cree who dwelt closest to the Company forts and factories along the bay, and eventually the Assiniboine, quickly set themselves up in business as brokers, middlemen of the trade, operating their own jealously guarded monopoly on trade with the Europeans, and transporting and trading goods at inflated prices to those farther inland in exchange for their worn furs. They resisted the movement of European traders into their lands and managed their political and economic hegemony for generations.

The markup could be extreme. In 1766, Andrew Graham reported that an "Archithinue" man, a member of one of the Blackfoot peoples of the western plains, arrived with a Cree trading party to York Factory. He told Graham, through an interpreter, that Cree traders "came amongst them and bought up their furs, giving them a gun for fifty wolves or beaver, six ditto for a hatchet, twenty ditto for a kettle, four for a knife and so on . . . He was surprised to see me and the trader give a gun for fourteen beaver, a hatchet for one beaver, a large kettle for eight beaver etc." The Cree traders bought furs from the Blackfoot and other people at a much-reduced rate year after year, and then transported them by canoe to Company outposts and sold them for profit. Graham sat the man down and tried to persuade him to bypass the Cree and make the journey to York Factory himself the next year, but the man demurred. He told Graham that he never would come again because "he did not like to sit in the canoe and be obliged to eat fish and fowl," foods with which he was unfamiliar and didn't enjoy. For this young man, the epic journey from his home within sight of the Rocky Mountains across the continent to the edge of Hudson Bay was for adventure and to satisfy his curiosity, not for economic reasons. He was a tourist, and he wanted a souvenir, a frilly laced hat. When Graham asked what he would use it for, he replied that it was a gift for his father, "who would wear it when he rid on horse-back in pursuit of the buffalo."

TRADE ROUTES THAT HAD EXISTED FOR centuries grew larger and more vibrant with the increased economic opportunities, while the currency needed to pay for the new items, beaver pelts—and especially used or pre-worn beaver pelts—became indispensable, reordering economic activity and ways of life even in the most remote regions. Guns and ammunition obtained from the Company, for example, were extremely valuable and wended their way south and west, while horses flowed north from Mexico and the southern U.S. The Mandan communities along the upper Missouri became the hub of the trade, as they had been the trade destination for centuries.

But the trade also drew European culture farther inland, and people soon became dependent upon the items that beaver could buy. The Home Guard Cree, and later some Assiniboine and Ojibwa who dwelt in close proximity to the Company's forts, soon lost the skill to hunt and travel as they formerly had done and were dependent upon the Company just as the Company was dependent upon them. They developed market skills or commercial trading skills instead of nomadic survival skills, a trend that grew more prevalent throughout the eighteenth century. The trade also provided the economic incentive for warfare and increased economic rivalry and inter-group warfare, and the more powerful weapons made warfare more deadly. The realignment of the economy and the shifting politics in turn caused cultural and demographic shifts.

The Assiniboine (a Siouan-speaking people), whose traditional territory spanned from Lake of the Woods west to the Saskatchewan River, had for ages been at war with the Dakota Sioux, whose territory was farther south. As the Assiniboine obtained metal weapons and guns from the Cree, who had obtained them from the Company posts at the Bottom of the Bay, they had an advantage in the continuing conflict. That is, until French traders began extending their networks west of Lake Superior. By the mid-eighteenth century, the escalating warfare made peaceful life difficult in the disputed territory west of Lake Superior toward the Plains and the lower Red River. The majority of the Assiniboine eventually abandoned parts of their homeland and moved west, taking up bison hunting in the aspen parklands and grasslands.

The Ojibwa later migrated into the former Cree territory of north-western Ontario. The Cree, on the other hand, expanded northwest from the forests of northern Ontario and increasingly dominated the Nelson River region that led to York Factory and the great river systems that spread to the southwest. As they continued their northward and westward expansion in pursuit of beaver, the Cree infringed upon the Dene and Chipewyan, who retreated from the military superiority of their southern neighbours, until the late eighteenth century, when devastating waves of disease reduced the Cree population and their capacity as a military power and they retreated from the northernmost territories they had taken from the Chipewyan and began to move west and south to the grasslands and parklands around the North Saskatchewan River. For generations the Cree had positioned themselves economically as intermediaries or traders, rather than trappers, so when the Company moved inland to compete with the North West Company, the Cree also had to move inland, and many took jobs as provision hunters for the expanding fur trade network. Other people even farther west, such as the Beaver and the Sekani, along the Peace and Athabasca Rivers, were also pressured to move west.

These political and cultural migrations were happening throughout the interior of North America long before the Company had any idea about these distant peoples and who they were or any geographical knowledge of the vast territory that lay generally west of their lonely outposts. The Company barely maintained more than a few hundred factory-based employees whose knowledge of the interior was based mostly on news they obtained from Cree traders and others who had made the journey to their outposts. Only in the later eighteenth century, after a century of operations, was the Company drawn inland. They had resisted altering their business plan for generations, until change was forced upon them by competition from French traders from Montreal.

THE MOSTLY CREE FUR BROKERS WHO were responsible for a majority of the Company's business managed the price differential between what they paid inland peoples for furs and what they knew they could resell them for at the Company posts. They were well aware of the prevailing prices being offered at various posts and could make the decision to travel farther to some posts to secure a more favourable deal, resulting in some posts running out of supplies while others were overstocked at any given time. The standard rates were a base guideline for both Indigenous trading captains and chief factors rather than an absolute price list, and these basic rates fluctuated between posts and over time according to the whims of the London fur market, competition with the Montreal traders and the composition of furs the trappers brought in each year. In order to smooth the transaction once everyone had agreed upon what they wanted, the Company established some baseline values for furs and certain key items, sometimes referred to as the standard of trade. The goals were to reduce haggling time, to avoid a situation where each post sold items for different prices based solely on the whim of its chief factor, and to signal to the Indigenous people what they could expect, since different items obviously cost the Company more to acquire and transport.

Fort Albany in James Bay, for example, had to be more competitive on price than York Factory on the western coast of Hudson Bay because French traders had established outposts along the rivers leading to the Bottom of the Bay. In general, whenever there was competition from the traders from Montreal, the Company was forced to lower its prices, provide more gifts as incentives to make the journey to their posts, or improve the quality of its goods. But trade with the Company was prevalent even among peoples who also traded inland with the itinerant French traders because of their frequent shortage of trade goods and lack of larger or heavier items. Certain goods were difficult to transport thousands of kilometres inland by canoe and portage, but were easy for large ships to transport directly from London to the western coast of Hudson Bay. The Company could offer items for cheaper prices because of its efficient transportation route that brought goods into the heart of the continent in bulk. At Fort Albany in 1733, a single beaver pelt could be exchanged for twenty fish hooks but only one brass kettle. The famous Hudson's Bay point blankets, quality wool blankets noted for their indigo stripes, were added to the trade mix in the late eighteenth century and were immediately popular, sometimes amounting to half the trade goods passing through some Company outposts.

The prices of all trade goods were set in values of made beaver, with other animal pelts, such as squirrel, otter and moose, quoted in their made-beaver equivalents. It might require two muskrat pelts to equal one made beaver most of the time, but the value sometimes shifted according to the fluctuations of fur prices in the European markets. A made beaver had specific definitions, at first being a pelt that had been worn as clothing, with an unworn pelt being worth less. By the late eighteenth century, once the Russian technology for separating the inner fur became widespread, the definition of made beaver changed, and pelts no longer held a premium for being worn as winter garments but still had to be properly prepared. Much later the Company introduced its own currency, with each coin stamped with the symbol of its made-beaver equivalent, and these coins were accepted at face value in any Company post as if a person had brought in actual beaver pelts.

The standard of trade at Fort Albany in 1733 shows what one made beaver could purchase:

Item	Amount per Made Beaver
Beads (Coloured)	¾ lb.
Kettle, Brass	1
Lead, Black	1 lb.
Gun Powder	1½ lb.
Shot	5 lbs.
Sugar	2 lbs.
Tobacco, Brazil	2 lbs.
Ditto Leaf or Roll	1½ lbs.

Thread	1 lb.
Vermilion	1½ oz.
Brandy	1 gallon
Broad Cloth	2 yard
Blankets	1
Flannel	2 yard
Gartering	2 yard
Awl Blades	12
Buttons	12 dozen
Breeches	1 pair
Combs	2
Egg Boxes	4
Feathers, Red	2
Fish Hooks	20
Fire Steels	4
Files	1
Flints	20
Guns	[1 for 10 to 12 pelts]
Pistols	[1 for 4 pelts]
Gun Worms	1
Gloves, Yarn	1
Goggles	2
Handkerchiefs	1
Hat, laced	1
Hatchets	2
Hawk Bells	8
Ice Chisels	2
Knives	8
Looking Glasses	2
Mocotagans (Curved Knives)	2
Needles	12
Net-Lines	2

Powder Horns	2
Plain Rings	6
Stone Rings	3
Scrapers	2
Sword Blades	2
Spoons	4
Shirts	2
Shoes	1 pair
Stocking	[1 for 1¼ pelts]
Sashes, Worsted	2
Thimbles	6
Tobacco Boxes	2

When the goods were of inferior quality or when the preferred items were not in stock, Indigenous traders were not shy about making their displeasure known. Thomas McCliesh, writing from Fort Albany in 1716, informed the London Committee of the type and quality of goods that were in demand and that he required. He wanted smaller kettles ("for it is impossible for an Indian to carry them [big kettles] in their canoes nor draw them in sledges through the woods in winter"), shorter guns (which were easier to transport through the forest) and brandy so he could compete with the French traders who had established a post several days' travel upriver and serviced it by canoe brigade along the Ottawa River to Lake Abitibi. "I can have more done towards the encouragement of the trade in small furs for a gallon of brandy than for forty beaver in any other goods in the factory: it is become so bewitching a liquor amongst the Indians especially with those that use the French," who traded liberally in potent brandy. He then admonished the committee: "I have had several complaints from the Indians of the badness of our cloth this year, and not without reason on their side, for the baize is as thick as it is; they matter not the fineness or the coarseness provided it is thick."

McCliesh also complained to the London decision makers about the people doing comparison shopping with more southern French posts. "Never was any man so upbraided with our powder, kettles and hatchets, than we have been this summer by all the natives." Especially "all those Indians that has traded with the French." In 1739, Governor Richard Norton sent back a stock of one hundred sword blades from Churchill with the somewhat snarky admonition that he had requisitioned bayonets, not sword blades, to suit a specific need of his customers and that "if your honours do not conceive the difference, the natives do." Unpopular goods sat in the warehouse and eventually rotted or rusted and had to be shipped back to London at great expense, so the Company had to be particularly careful to attune their goods to the wishes of their customers and their specific tastes and requirements.

ANOTHER ASPECT OF THE GREAT EXCHANGE that transformed the land beyond the bay was infectious diseases. Disease followed in the wake of the fur trade, and having an unknown and mysterious provenance, wreaked enormous cultural and economic damage among Indigenous peoples. At first the connection between disease and the fur trade was not immediately obvious, owing to the gestation time before symptoms presented. The diseases in the region where the Company operated were not often epidemic. The diseases carried on board ships from London were no longer infectious by the time the vessels reached Hudson Bay after a ten-week voyage. Nevertheless, Company factors frequently mentioned fevers, sickness and mortalities, including reports from the interior, and sicknesses originating with the "French Indians," the Ojibwa.

The inland fur brigades of voyageurs in the later eighteenth century were a link connecting the inland Indigenous peoples to the eastern urban disease vectors of Montreal, Quebec and Boston—and, later, all the large and rapidly increasing populations of the English colonies along the Atlantic. The shorter sailing time from London to these regions, and the large domestic population, kept a constant level of infection within the urban population, ready to spread with travellers. Letters and reports from Company traders frequently made reference to the diseases coming north and west along rivers from farther east in the Great Lakes region: "much afflicted with sickness," "a great sickness," "a great Mortality," "Dyed last winter with Ailements," "as mortal as if they had the Plague," "a very Remarkable Sickness and Casualtys" reads the depressing litany. When the fur trade from Canada was thrown into disarray after New France was conquered by the British in 1760, there was a period of about seven years when eastern traders did not venture beyond the shores of Lake Superior, a period that saw a corresponding decline in the instances of disease reported at the Company's posts along the bay.

Epidemics afflicted all peoples the Company dealt with—from the Chipewyan and Inuit in the north to the Cree, Ojibwa and Assiniboine in the south and others farther distant—and although it isn't always possible to know the specific sicknesses, the most common were small-pox, influenza, measles, whooping cough and "great colds." Overall the frequency of the epidemics that are mentioned would have left a devastating legacy of orphans, widows and men who had lost all or most of their family. In addition to the immediate physical loss for individuals was a loss of community throughout entire regions as populations declined. The repeated waves of sickness inflicted upon groups—a seemingly endless sequence of mourning and sorrow in a changing world—would have more than offset any material benefit from the trade goods obtained through contact with foreigners, had such a trade-off been understood or available. The theory of germs and infectious disease was not even conceived until the mid-eighteenth century. European physicians still sought to balance the four "bodily humours" through bloodletting and other dangerous and ineffectual treatments. Even a practical cure for something seemingly as simple as scurvy was not implemented in the Royal Navy until 1795, and ships arriving at Company posts were still filled with scorbutic sailors. The disease was virtually unknown to Indigenous populations, who had knowledge of appropriate local foods to eat in each season.

Often, the disease itself wasn't the ultimate killer. Epidemics induced starvation. In a semi-nomadic hunting society, where stockpiles of food were quickly depleted and there was limited contact between dispersed extended family groups for much of the year, it often wasn't possible for people to help each other by supplying surplus food. When a band was unable to hunt because of sickness, there was no way to seek help from other people. Survival depended upon having able-bodied family members regularly doing the work, and a dispersed population over rugged terrain increased the mortality of diseases by preventing aid to the sick. Many who might otherwise have survived a sickness perished instead from starvation and exposure. This quickly led to a fatalistic attitude. Company trader William Walker wrote in 1781 that "they are frightened of going nigh one to another as soon as they take bad, so the one half for want of indulgencies is starved before they can gather Strength to help themselves. They think when they are once taken bad they need not look for any recovery. So the person that's bad turns feeble that he cannot walk, they leave them behind when they're pitching away, and so the poor Soul perishes." Many travellers, including such astute observers as David Thompson, wrote of how the men in particular, when under the influence of a raging fever, would throw themselves into the freezing water, and thereby perish from exposure.

Because of low population density, the epidemics rarely spread throughout large regions at the same time. As a result, epidemics were perceived not as a universal problem but rather as something local, sporadic and unexplainable. And owing to the time lapse between contact with a contagious individual and the onset of serious symptoms, it was difficult to make a direct connection. The larger epidemics, such as the 1737–38 smallpox outbreak that was particularly devastating to the Ojibwa around the Lake of the Woods and to the Cree to the northwest of Lake Winnipeg, had a dramatic effect on culture and economics. It precipitated the northward migration of northern Ojibwa so that after mid-century they were in a position to be making the journey to Company outposts along the bay with minimal interference from the Cree. Epidemics also caused other migrations and amalgamations of cultural groups, sometimes into polycultural refugee villages, and sparked raids against neighbouring peoples to capture female slaves to bolster their population, similar to the "mourning wars" of the Iroquois a century earlier.

Sometimes an outbreak of disease caused warfare between groups, as the devastation was blamed upon traditional enemies. On May 25, 1728, trader Joseph Myatt wrote from Fort Albany that, following the previous years' disease outbreak, "this morn Eight Curnoes of our home Inds fitted out from here in order to goe to war with the Esquomays, I Endeavored all I could to oppose it, but in vain, for severall of the Home Inds being Disordered the last winter they attribute all thos things to the Mallice of their enemies." Others recorded similar incidents of reprisal that were blamed upon the sorcery of enemies.

The records of Company managers at several outposts, particularly York Factory, Prince of Wales Fort and Fort Albany, detail waves of disease every several years. Fearsome and unknown, the epidemics mysteriously snaked through the land following travellers and rivers, striking without warning and without remedy. An epidemic could kill up to half of one tribe and yet leave a neighbouring group unscathed. One Company trader at Fort Albany, Anthony Beale, wrote to a colleague in 1712 that the "country is very much altered to what it was formerly for we have had many sick this winter." There are accounts of parties as large as one hundred men canoeing from north of Lake Superior to Montreal, being exposed to what was likely smallpox, and then dying on the return journey, only a few ever returning to their home.

Company outposts were frequently called upon to assist whenever the outbreak was within travelling distance. There are descriptions of

Indigenous traders showing up at the outposts either sick or starving and requesting aid for their families farther inland who were too ill to make the journey themselves. The Company, through the compassion of its local agents if not the distant London Committee, offered considerable aid to the stricken people out of practical and humanitarian motivation. Many knew each other after years of annual visits and transactions during which they shared news of the land and perhaps even of extended family. When a disease epidemic raged through the land and killed people, the directors in London, when they later learned of it, might have viewed it as a looming labour shortage or a decline in trade furs, but for the employees who lived along the bay it was a different thing altogether.

But even from a purely business perspective, the Company could hardly thrive if its customers and contract employees were dead. Owing to the nature of the fur trade, in which relationships, trust and ceremonial bonding were vital aspects of the commercial relationship, the Company and its employees, many of whom had Indigenous families and in-laws, could hardly turn a blind eye to the suffering and death caused by these waves of disease. In June 1751, York Factory chief factor James Isham recorded the effects of a spreading sickness, writing that "one cannoe came down the River, brought the unwelcome news of 2 Indns Dying, I am sorry to hear of the Death of many Indns since last June." During one bad spell of sickness at York Factory, Isham recorded fifty-four deaths of Indigenous people he knew in just a single year between July 20, 1757, and September 14, 1758: "Esinepoet, his wife, 2 girls & a boy," "Wittechap & his wife Shissohon," "Memimetahasu—Leader of the Severn Indians," "Mistekanass, wife & 2 children," "Cabetekishew's old wife & boy." In April 1783, at Fort Severn, after smallpox raced downriver to the fort, one of the officers spoke with two families who had come downstream to trade and reported that "they have seen but one Indian during the Winter, that they are all dead Inland, these very deeply marked with the small pox, one of them has lost all his Children by it except one poor Boy, which is both blind and Lame, and they have been obliged to haul him all the winter." Epidemics never struck in evenly spaced intervals but arrived seemingly at random. Some bands were left untouched while others were nearly entirely killed, leaving orphaned dependents, broken families, unfathomable sorrow and an unknowable fear of the future.

The most significant epidemic to strike the region was smallpox in 1779–83. On a different scale than any other epidemic, it originated in Mexico and spread north along with the new trade patterns that had arisen with the widespread domestication of horses several decades earlier. Before horse travel, the lack of north–south rivers and the great distances had prevented diseases from flowing from the south. Now, mounted riders travelled far more quickly than people on foot and infected neighbouring peoples hundreds of kilometres distant before realizing they were infected themselves. This epidemic crossed the Great Plains and entered the territory of the Company eastward via the Saskatchewan River and the Red River and then progressed to the more southern regions. The pestilence eventually swept as far north as Great Slave Lake and over the mountains to the Pacific but petered out before reaching east of Lake Superior.

This particular epidemic was so virulent that it depopulated entire bands or tribes, leaving no survivors. Particularly hard hit were the Ojibwa and Woodland Cree along the Nelson, Hayes and Albany river systems. Chief Factor William Tomison canoed between northern Lake Winnipeg and York Factory along the Hayes River, and nearly everyone he met along the once busy river system was sick, dying or dead. The news of the land, including accounts from far to the west and south, was of widespread devastation. At York Factory, Matthew Cocking tried to prevent the disease from spreading farther by trying to shield the local Home Guard or Swampy Cree, who were in the Company's employ, from the contagion. He sent men upstream along the river to warn arriving Cree or Ojibwa away from the fort. He offered to send his own men out to meet them instead. He prevented boats from travelling between the Company's other posts along the bay, and issued instructions to other forts to "keep a strict look out, that none of the Home Guards come to the factory but keep at a proper distance . . . Should you find the disorder has attacked any of them, do all in your power for their preservation." His actions were effective for a while but were interrupted by the arrival of a French warship that conquered the fort, the first hostile action since d'Iberville's assaults nearly ninety years earlier.

Similar scenarios were repeated many times throughout the eighteenth century and into the nineteenth as the diseases swept through. It was a widespread custom among the Cree and Ojibwa to dispose of furs after a sickness, out of fear that the goods may have been contaminated. A trader from New France, La Vérendrye, noted that "those who escaped made a stop and threw into the river, according to their custom, all the beaver, pichoux, marten, etc., belonging to the dead as well as their own, so that the shore was lined with them and the portages full, all of which was a loss." Disease was damaging to the livelihood of the survivors as well. By the nineteenth century many people instinctively knew to avoid the North West Company (and later the Company's) fur brigades from Montreal and Grand Portage that wended deep into the country. The brigades consisted partly of men of mixed or Indigenous ancestry and could carry diseases quickly across the inland lakes, spreading death in their wake. People learned to self-quarantine themselves, hiding in the deep woods until brigade season was over.

Like the plague that afflicted London witnessed by Radisson and Groseilliers in 1665, infectious diseases were far more prevalent everywhere than they are now with effective medical treatments, inoculations and preventative strategies such as basic hygiene. But these European diseases were unknown to the inhabitants of North America and for a time were disproportionately virulent and all the more terrifying due to their mystery, speed and lethal outcome. Throughout the eighteenth century enormous political and cultural upheaval among nearly all

Indigenous peoples was directly caused by exposure to European-originated diseases that resulted in a constantly changing political and cultural mosaic, territorial migration and economic setbacks. The seemingly endless waves of epidemics were like cascading dominoes knocking each other over in an erratic sequence across the continent, even reaching peoples who had no direct contact with English forts or French traders, as the familiar world disappeared. Some peoples, such as the Assiniboine, recovered their populations rapidly, while others, such as the Cree, were much slower to regain their numbers; in some bands the men died disproportionately, yet in others it was the women and children. Each generation was repeatedly attacked by community-destroying diseases, a bewildering mystery of unknown origin, with no known cure and only vaguely understood methods of transmission.

Edward Jenner didn't show that infection with relatively harmless cowpox could provide immunity to smallpox until 1796, and he didn't publish his first article on it until two years later. By the early nineteenth century, the Company was sporadically attempting to introduce smallpox vaccinations at various of its posts, with mixed results, but it was wasn't until 1838 that the London Committee sent a directive to Governor George Simpson informing him of their plan to introduce smallpox vaccinations to all the Indigenous peoples who regularly traded at Company posts, which at this time stretched from Hudson Bay to the Arctic to the Pacific Northwest. Using the Company's highly structured distribution system, the smallpox vaccine quickly filtered throughout the country. In many instances, the vaccine was given directly to the Indigenous traders with instructions to administer it to people who did not make the journey to the posts. While other diseases continued to ravage the landscape, smallpox, the most virulent and feared, at least was mostly averted by the 1840s, at least among people associated with the Company.

There is no doubt that disease spread inadvertently through the activities of the Company, the fur trade in general, and most specifically with the canoe brigades from Montreal. It was instrumental in spreading contagious diseases that were unknown to North American Indigenous populations and which had a dramatic bearing on the cultural, political and economic makeup of the territory. The devastating waves of epidemics became particularly acute after the completion of the Erie Canal in the eastern U.S., which gave disease an easy transportation corridor from the large population centres along the Atlantic coast directly to the Great Lakes, and then farther west via steamboats along the Missouri and Mississippi Rivers that also took American settlers—and their diseases—west in the 1830s and 1840s. Not surprisingly, the diseases then spread north into the territory where the Company operated. But even in the late eighteenth century there was significant population decline among the peoples of Rupert's Land, in some regions up to 80 per cent.

There was also, after a century of harvesting, a decline in beaver and other fur-bearing animals in the lands close to the forts. Beaver had been harvested for generations in these regions and along the main river systems leading to Hudson Bay. Even the London Committee, with its static and staid commercial operations along the rim of the bay, had to expand its imagination and consider sending employees into the country in quest of furs, to circumvent the Indigenous mini monopolies that were sapping profits. But commercial opportunity alone would never have been a powerful enough inducement for the Company to risk conflict with the Cree, who had good multi-generational relationships with the Company yet were quite aggressive in defending their commercial hegemony. It was the depopulation caused by epidemic disease throughout the eighteenth century that gave the Company the need and ability to move inland to compete with the French traders who also were moving inland and undercutting their trade from the south.

After a century of contact, technology had been exchanged both ways: not only did European metal goods bring local peoples into the iron age with knives, axes, kettles and guns, but they in turn provided their European commercial partners with the means to venture inland, with clothing, snowshoes, bark canoes, toboggans and the knowledge of how to survive in the country. Company men also now had the cultural facility—the language and customs—to expand their limited horizons.

The Company was faced with the commercial necessity of changing their corporate culture from passive contentment to aggressively seeking opportunities inland. In a reversal of the usual corporate pattern, the Company was moving from unexciting stability to unpredictable growth. In the mid-eighteenth century, for the first time since Kelsey's travels in 1690, the Company cast its gaze to the western interior and reluctantly authorized the expense of sending several explorers west into what was, to them, still an unknown land.

Chapter Seven

GREAT PLAINS AND
BLOODY FALLS

The biggest threat to the company's monopoly in Hudson Bay emanated from the geographical musings and political agitations of a choleric Irishman named Arthur Dobbs. The wealthy son of a prominent civil servant, Dobbs moved to London and became an intimate of the city's prominent courtiers and financiers. His favourite topics were free trade and the Northwest Passage, and the Company blocked the pathways leading to both of his dreams. An amateur hydrographer, he had analyzed the tide levels in Hudson Bay and fixated upon the prevalence of whales that seemed never to exit into the Atlantic through Hudson Strait. Therefore, he concluded, the Northwest Passage must exist, in spite of the explorations a century earlier by Button, Foxe and James.

The passage must exist, therefore two things became apparent to Dobbs stemming from this inalienable belief: since the passage must run through the territory of the Company's famous charter, the Company was either negligent in its requirement to explore its exclusive commercial territory or they had already discovered it and were withholding the knowledge to protect their fur trading business. The possibility that the fantastical passage, the darling of England's past, lay within easy grasp drove him to distraction, and he began publicly denouncing the Company's charter and accusing them of not fulfilling their obligation to explore their territory. Whereas the Company just wanted to quietly prosper, Dobbs was inclined toward conquest and colonization of foreign lands and the destruction of the secretive fur monopoly.

Dobbs persuaded the Royal Navy to fund a voyage of exploration in northwestern Hudson Bay, the first of many Royal Navy expeditions in search of a Northwest Passage and the beginning of a quest that would reach its apogee in the nineteenth century. Christopher Middleton, a Hudson's Bay Company veteran known for his work on magnetic variation in the bay and a fervent believer in the existence of a west-leading passage, was placed in charge of two Royal Navy vessels, the *Discovery* and the *Furnace*. His crew were a pack of rogues, violent criminals and scoundrels rounded up by the press gang, and they were kept in check only by the presence of armed marines stationed throughout the ships.

In 1741 they set off to ascertain the feasibility of a sea route to the Orient exiting from northern Hudson Bay or Foxe Basin. The Company reluctantly bowed to pressure from the Royal Navy to provide assistance during an overwintering before the big push north. Robert Pilgrim, the chief factor of Prince of Wales Fort, the new stone fortress being built at the mouth of the Churchill River about ten kilometres upstream from the old Fort Churchill, hadn't been told of this arrangement and, fearing a French attack, fired guns across the bows of the ships as they manoeuvred close. A faux pas to be sure, to fire upon the Royal Navy, but relations soon improved when the new chief factor arrived, the talented and observant James Isham. Middleton and Isham shared a convivial winter sampling the seemingly bottomless cup that flowed from the Navy's liquor cabin. They discussed natural history and the latest scientific developments, while numerous days were set aside for festivities. Christmas alone lasted two weeks, with copious grog issued daily to the entire crew to help pass the dark, cold days.

Middleton set off in June 1742, with his crew suffering from scurvy, caused by an over-reliance on rations, and so debilitated that most of them lay below deck in their hammocks while only a few were able to muster the strength to climb the rigging and set the sails. Hardly surprisingly, they solved few geographical mysteries that summer. Middleton concentrated his search in the vicinity of Wager Bay, west of Southampton Island, and found no navigable channel or passage leading from Foxe Basin. Middleton then returned to London to report his findings. This was not the outcome desired by his patron, Dobbs, who firmly believed in the reality of an Arctic sea route west (and desperately wanted to end the Company's monopoly). They accused Middleton of accepting a bribe from the Company of £5,000 "to return to their service, and not to go the Voyage, or to go in pursuit of it to Davis's Streight, or any other Way that he was ordered upon, he thought himself sure my not doubting his integrity." Dobbs publicly attacked Middleton and ruined his reputation so that he was never again given a senior command. He died in poverty several years later.

While Dobbs's motives may not have been completely altruistic, his claims had enough credibility that, in spite of the protestations of the Company, in 1745 the British Parliament offered a £20,000 reward for the discovery of a Northwest Passage leading from Hudson Bay, available to anyone not affiliated with the Royal Navy. Privately funded voyages of exploration, however, in addition to being extremely pricey, generally do not pay off for investors. Dobbs was one of the only people interested in the reward. A persuasive and single-minded champion, he put together a consortium and two ships, the aptly named *Dobbs* and the *California*, captained by shipmasters who had sailed on Company supply vessels. They sallied forth from London and wintered near York Factory, where the captains quarrelled and generally mismanaged the enterprise, with a little help in that regard from Isham, who had recently been reposted to York Factory from Prince of Wales Fort. After having been criticized for being overly helpful to Middleton a few years earlier, Isham took a

sterner approach to the new enterprise. Not only did he fire a few cannons
to signal his disposition, but he had ordered men to remove the depth
markers so that one of the ships ran aground at low tide. He wouldn't
allow them to camp near the fort and grudgingly helped them set up
some tents in which they spent a miserable winter. After a fruitless and
tepid investigation of the north coast, the ships slunk home, their metaphorical tails between their legs.

Yet Dobbs persisted. In 1749 he persuaded Parliament to convene a
select committee to investigate the multitude of complaints against the
Company by merchants drummed up by Dobbs. The committee heard
testimony or read documents of competing opinions of twenty-two
witnesses, including both loyal and disgruntled Company employees.
Dobbs himself promised that if the Company's monopoly charter were
revoked, prosperity would reign. Some of the fantastical and unrealistic
things he promised included that the nation would have access to the
South Seas (in spite of the recent failures) and that along Hudson Bay
would arise a mighty timber harvesting enterprise (despite others
pointing out the lack of timber along the mostly barren shoreline). He
also claimed, falsely, that the Company annually posted a 2,000 per cent
profit, despite his competing claim that the Company was generally
incompetent and lazy. One of his paid lackeys, Joseph Robson, a former
stonemason at Prince of Wales Fort, proffered the famous quip that "the
Company have for eighty years slept on the edge of a frozen sea."

Common sense prevailed, and Dobbs was dismissed as a malcon-
tent and delusional dreamer who ignored the complexities and
expenses of running such a sprawling and distant enterprise in a harsh
climate in a foreign land where cultural sensitivities ruled. Dobbs's
assertion that a tenfold increase in business could happen right away
under different management was hardly credible. There was some
truth that a monopoly restricted entrepreneurial activity, but Dobbs
damaged his own case with his gross overstatements. Nevertheless,
the Company was tasked with producing some documentation of the

extent of their commercial monopoly as defined by the charter. Why did they deserve such a vast charter of unknown extent if they just huddled around the bay like frogs sunning themselves on the banks of a giant pond? The Company reluctantly agreed to finance some more inland exploration. Dobbs grumbled and retreated in ill humour to his Irish estate. He was eventually appointed the governor of North Carolina, where he died many years later.

One of the unintended developments that arose from Dobbs's near-fanatical public assaults on the Company was that they began, first, to devote some effort to charting the coastline around their posts and announced a new inland expedition to satisfy the critics, and, second, to investigate the rumours regarding the infiltration of French traders into the hinterland of their commercial purview. Many Indigenous traders had been talking about these interlopers selling brandy from ramshackle outposts along some of the rivers leading to the bay. Previously the Company had refused to even allow their employees to travel inland beyond a few days' distance, claiming that it was dangerous and unpredictable, which it was. It would also be an uninvited intrusion into the traditional lands of various Indigenous peoples upon whom the Company was entirely dependent. Nonetheless, this existential threat to their comfortable and profitable monopoly demanded action. The numbers of traders at York Factory was declining, as was the quality of the furs brought in, and the obvious conclusion was that the French traders in the interior were responsible by intercepting people along the rivers to Hudson Bay and skimming off the best furs.

In 1754, the London Committee authorized the second expedition in the Company's history. A former smuggler then employed at York Factory as a net-mender, Anthony Henday was a vigorous man with a reputation for being bold, enterprising, an ideal trade emissary. Like Kelsey sixty years earlier, Henday hitched a ride with a band of Plains Cree returning to their home in June after the trading season. His guide was Attickasish, a respected trading captain and leader, travelling with two dozen companions. They paddled up the Hayes River, crossed northern Lake Winnipeg and entered the Saskatchewan River, where "the Musketoes were intolerable giving us no peace day nor night," and which they planned to follow west into the domain of the Archithinue, or Atsina (Blackfoot Confederacy).

As they emerged into rolling aspen parkland, Henday observed deer, elk, mighty herds of bison and large packs of wolves. At the end of July, they neared Paskoya (The Pas, Manitoba) and Henday spied the first French post. "I don't very well like it," Henday noted, "having nothing to Satisfy Them on what account I am going up the Country and Very possibly they may expect Me to be a Spy." Two men met him civilly at the riverside and invited him back to the fort. The "Master" Chevalier de La Corne had gone down to Montreal with the furs and was not in residence, and some of the men demanded to see Henday's letter of justification for being in the country and told him that they would apprehend him and hold him until they received further instructions—an arrogant proposition considering they were themselves visitors in the land and had no moral or legal authority. Feeling nervous, Henday went and spoke to Attickasish, who just "smiled and said they dared not." Sure enough, he rejoined his armed Cree companions without incident the next morning as they boarded their canoes and paddled upriver on their way west, as the French traders watched them go.

The rolling aspen parkland of the Plains was teeming with animals, particularly when they passed through burnt-out areas where the Blackfoot had lit grass fires to improve bison feeding grounds. (The name Blackfoot derives from the colour of their feet and shoes, which turned black when they walked through these burned grasses.) Like Kelsey before him, Henday met many Indigenous people and noted that the population was much larger than farther north around the bay. There were plenty of animals for hunting, including innumerable birds, deer, elk, moose and bison. He found "berries the size of black currents and the finest I ever eat" and "cherry trees," probably saskatoons. The grasslands were interspersed with islands of aspen, copses of elder and occasional clusters of spruce or pine.

Henday, Attickasish and their entourage pressed on overland across the prairie for weeks. In early September, along the south bank of the North Saskatchewan River near present-day Battleford, Saskatchewan, they met a large group of Assinepoet (Assiniboine). "I gave their leader half a foot of Brazile tobacco," Henday recorded, "and smoked with them: They were very kind and made me a present of some tongues, and a bladder full of fat." This was just one of numerous similarly friendly encounters as they wandered across the land. Henday wrote of encouraging everyone he met to travel to York Factory for good trade opportunities, but he was mostly politely rebuffed by people claiming that "we are conveniently supplied" by the French fort, which offered poorer quality goods but didn't require several months of travel. Attickasish was silent. He had his own plans.

By mid-September, they were in the vicinity of present-day Red Deer, Alberta, and within sight of the Rocky Mountains. When he was ahead scouting, Attickasish met two Archithinues, Siksika of the mighty Blackfoot Confederacy that ruled what is now the western prairies and foothills. They informed Attickasish that their main tribe was farther west following the bison herds. The group continued west, and the next day Henday recorded something astonishing that he had never seen before: a vast shambling herd of "Buffalo so numerous, [we were] obliged to make them sheer out of our way." On October 1, seven Blackfoot warriors wearing bison robes and carrying bone-tipped spears rode into their small camp and demanded to know whether they were friends or enemies. Once the warriors ascertained the foot travellers were harmless, they rode off to announce them to their main camp.

The main settlement was a bustling centre of hundreds of people living in over two hundred large painted lodges arranged in two rows with a main thoroughfare between them. Hundreds of fettered horses grazed the tall grasses surrounding the community. Scores of people, horses and dogs swirled about in the dry heat of a clear fall day, many eager to glimpse the strangers as they were escorted down the thoroughfare. They were ushered through the throngs to an impressive lodge at the end where "a great many dried Scalps with fine long black hair, [were] displayed on poles." A flap door was opened and they were ushered inside, where fifty elders were sitting comfortably about a white bison skin upon which the chief sat. The Leader, as Henday called him, motioned for Henday to stand by his side. He then produced several ceremonial pipes that were passed around in comfortable silence, and soon there was contented puffing while tendrils of smouldering sage incense wafted about and patches of sun came in through the openings above. A group of women brought in woven baskets of boiled bison steaks and tongues, a delicacy, with savoury herbs. Henday didn't speak Blackfoot, but Attickasish did. He told the gathered elders that Henday was sent from the "Great Leader who lives down at the Great Waters, to invite his young men down to see him and to bring with them Beaver skins, & Wolf skins, and they would get in return Powder, Shot, Guns, Cloth, Beads, etc." The Leader grunted and puffed but made little answer to Henday's entreaty. He didn't need to. It was self-evident. Hudson Bay was thousands of kilometres away. To get there required many weeks of canoe travel through lands dominated by armed Cree jealous to protect and maintain their trading lands and their jobs as brokers.

The next day, Henday was again summoned to meet the Leader in the great lodge, and a more specific answer was given to him: his people ate bison, not fish; they didn't use canoes but rode horses; rumours were of many who suffered greatly from starvation on the journey. They were the mounted lords of the western plains, and would remain within their domain. "Such remarks I thought exceeding true," Henday admitted. He had after all been on the road with Attickasish and his band for four months or so across lakes, down rivers and over the grasslands. Moreover, the one item he could always count on to curry favour, the Company's dark and rich Brazil tobacco, failed to impress. "They think nothing of my tobacco," he wrote tersely, "and I set little value on theirs," which they cultivated in small sunny gardens shielded from the wind by aspen trees.

Henday and Attickasish spent several more days as guests in the camp. As he wandered about, Henday observed the daily goings-on and wrote ethnographic observations, which were of obvious interest to him, including descriptions of daily life, domestic activities and rituals. "They appear to be under proper discipline," he wrote of the armed warriors, "obedient to their Leader: who orders a party of Horsemen Evening and Morning to reconnoitre, and proper parties to bring in provisions." Henday observed that he "saw many fine Girls who were Captives." Of the women he noted that "their clothing is finely painted with red paint; like unto English ochre, but they do not mark nor paint their bodies." Other simplistic ethnographic observations ran along the lines of: "they follow the Buffalo from place to place: & that they should not be surprised by the Enemy, encamp in open plains. Their fuel is turf, & Horsedung dryed." Henday was most impressed with the mighty herds of bison that covered the prairie and sounded like thunder as they passed. He was taken on a hunting trip by several young Blackfoot. "I went with the young men a Buffalo hunting, all armed with Bows & Arrows . . . So expert are the Natives, that they will take the arrows out of them when they are foaming and raging with pain, & tearing the ground up with their feet & horns until they fall down." He noted self-deprecatingly that he was happy just to have managed to stay atop his horse, an animal not seen along the bay and that he had never ridden before.

Henday soon moved off to explore the land a little farther west and spent the winter in the vicinity of where the famous Rocky Mountain House would later be situated. In January he and his troop headed north, past what is now called Sylvan Lake toward where the Sturgeon River joins the North Saskatchewan downstream of modern Edmonton. Here they remained, building canoes for the return journey, which they embarked upon at the end of April.

After weeks of paddling along the North Saskatchewan River east back to the bay, in an otherwise uneventful journey, Henday finally gleaned the most important commercial secret of his sales trip so far. Many people waited along the shores to trade their furs to the Cree for the Company's goods that Attickasish and his compatriots transported. They pulled ashore, bartered and negotiated, sealed deals and made promises. The Cree who had brought Henday along with them were specialized merchant adventurers of their own. When Attickasish and others promised Henday that they would surely encourage everyone to make the trip to the bay, it was with a wink and a nudge. "If the Archithinues and Assinepoets could be brought down to trade," Henday wrote, "the others [Cree] then would be obliged to trap their own furs, which at present two thirds of them does not." The inland economy was more complex and nuanced than Henday or the Company had realized. "I have no hopes of getting them to come to the Fort," Henday admitted. He expressed similar sentiments and variations on this theme throughout his journal of the journey.

By the time Attickasish's flotilla arrived at York Factory with Henday, it had swollen to around sixty heavily laden canoes filled with Cree traders and their goods. An epic expedition for Henday, worthy enough to bestow his name to modern-day buildings, roads and monuments along the route, was merely an annual business cycle for the Cree traders. Each year Attickasish and other leaders, before him and after, made similar journeys buying furs from people deep in the interior of the continent and transporting them to the coast of Hudson Bay, where they sold them and used the proceeds to purchase Company goods, which they in turn used to acquire more furs the next year. It was a profitable round of trade. Perhaps there should be a highway in north-central Manitoba, Saskatchewan and Alberta named the Attickasish Commercial Route. A traveller rather than an explorer, Henday nevertheless provided one of the few written accounts of life in these regions at the dawn of the horse era.

There was one incident on the return journey that caused Henday concern, as it related specifically to the Company's economic interests. Henday was frustrated when the troop stopped to visit several French outposts along the river, including the one at The Pas where he had feared being incarcerated by French traders the previous year. These posts offered brandy and traded for many of the best and lightest furs, leaving only the lesser-quality ones to be hauled the distance to the bay. "The French talk several Languages to perfection," he lamented. "They have the advantage of us in every shape; and if they had Brazile tobacco . . . would entirely cut our trade off." This was a bit melodramatic and an exaggeration, since the Company offered other useful goods that were unavailable from the French traders, but an increase in the French presence would be a blow to trade volume and profitability.

After Henday presented his report, the Company, or those within it who were curious enough to read the details, finally were enlightened with a glimmer of understanding into the complex culture and economy that existed just beyond the subarctic spruce surrounding Hudson Bay. Some of Henday's claims were met with guffaws, particularly the notion that the distant plains were populated with skilled equestrians. The interior of the continent was dynamic, but the Company was becoming an ossified institution cashing in on the diminishing returns of its legacy enterprise. It was still profitable, but in decline. After Henday's expedition, the Company sponsored dozens of inland expeditions, including a few more by Henday, in the hope of stimulating an increase in the trade along the Saskatchewan River. But these were small forays with the primary objective of encouraging Indigenous peoples to make the journey to the bay, small-scale marketing expeditions that ended in small gains in keeping with the Company's ambitions. Henday left the Company several years later when they refused to promote him beyond his position of labourer.

While demand for pelts had increased in Europe, the Company began to fear, accurately as it turned out, that the French traders from the St. Lawrence were strangling their commerce by meeting the Indigenous trappers and traders along inland canoe routes before they reached the Company's forts along Hudson Bay. The Company was saved, however, by events beyond its control.

In 1755, the Royal Navy began intercepting French supply ships to the St. Lawrence and Louisiana, and the slow suppression of Atlantic commerce during the Seven Years War squeezed the profits from the French inland expansion and the posts were soon abandoned. When Quebec surrendered to British forces in 1759, the French fur trade withered, leaving the Company in command of the inland trade in a position of undisputed commercial dominance. The conquest of New France by the British meant that the Company faced no large-scale competition for the better part of a decade, leaving it once again as a monopoly while trade increased along the bay.

The Company could expect to reign supreme since the Union Jack now flew along the St. Lawrence, but its confidence that the British government would uphold its monopoly was misplaced. The pot of gold at the end of the rainbow didn't last long. By the end of the 1760s the old trade routes from the St. Lawrence were again being plied by the huge transport canoes of a new enterprise. Montreal became the hub of this ambitious business, which was now also financed by capital from London. French translators and voyageurs remained, but the leadership had changed. Rather than a colonial enterprise subject to the petty regulation and political meddling that had hamstrung the French fur trade since the days of Radisson and Groseilliers, it quickly became more professional and profit-focused, with each season's enterprise being financed and organized by different partnerships and investment syndicates.

IN 1732, SIR BIBYE LAKE, head of the London Committee, had grand dreams for the northern trade from Fort Churchill. The fort was far enough north to be free from competition from French traders originating along the St. Lawrence, ideally situated to capture the trade from the northern Cree, Chipewyan and Inuit, and would be a good base for northern exploration and to support the whaling industry. It could perhaps even be an unassailable depot from which to supply the Company's other operations and would become especially important for the discovery and processing of as yet undiscovered minerals such as copper or gold. He ordered an impressive stone fortification to be erected to replace the wood palisade that had been constructed by James Knight back in 1717. Unusually for Lake, spending money appears not to have been his prime concern. The new fort proved staggeringly expensive to build and wasn't completed for over forty years, but it did satisfy the company's requirement to fortify Rupert's Land per the terms of the charter.

Oddly situated at the most northerly of the Company's bayside outposts, in the most inhospitable climate, with the least access to wood and other materials, and the most challenging hunting, the new fort was to be the crown jewel of the Company's trading empire, so stout and indomitable that the French could never capture it—the French threat being the only opposition in the bay that could ever warrant such a lavish outlay of funds. The proposed depot was to be a four-pronged star-shaped fortress, designed for defence. The stone walls were to be up to twelve metres thick, including a dressed stone exterior, and nearly five metres high. Forty cannons were to be mounted on its walls—one for each of the employees that eventually worked there. It was a ridiculous and foolish display of power and wasted resources for a region that never attained half the furs brought in to York Factory farther south and never succeeded in accomplishing any of its strategic or commercial objectives. Exposed to the freezing winds, the stone contraption was ever plagued by drafts, impossible to keep warm and expensive to maintain as the arctic winds clawed at and destroyed the masonry. It was a miserable place to live, except for the factor's house, which was stately and large enough to host the officers for twice-weekly dinner parties. Called Prince of Wales Fort, it was an ostentatious symbol of misplaced priorities and a domineering, ogre-like lump on the snow-blanketed landscape.

It was here, sometime in either 1736 or 1737, that a boy was born to a Chipewyan father employed by the Company as a hunter and labourer and a mother originally brought to the fort by Cree traders as a slave and sold to either the father or to Richard Norton, the chief factor. The boy was named Matonabbee, and he was destined to become one of the greatest explorers of the north in the eighteenth century. When his father died, and perhaps his mother, the lad was adopted by Norton and his Cree mistress and lived at the fort during the early years of its construction. In 1741, when Norton died and was replaced by James Isham, the boy's male relatives took him to live with them in their migratory life following the caribou. His winters were spent sheltered in the forested areas around lakes and streams, while his summers were devoted to trekking across the open terrain of the Barren Lands. He returned to Prince of Wales Fort in the 1750s, whereupon his unusual skills were recognized and he was hired as a hunter of geese and game and worked as a wood feller and labourer. Matonabbee's upbringing was unique in that he learned the languages and customs of the Home Guard Cree, the inland Chipewyan and the English workers at the fort, which was a multi-ethnic meeting place where cultures blurred, and where Matonabbee developed the cultural fluency and insight that set him apart. He grew to understand what the Company valued and how they approached their negotiations, as well as how the Cree and the Chipewyan understood the land and each other. Tall, muscular, handsome and charismatic, Matonabbee rose to prominence as the principal chief among the western Chipewyan for many years.

In the late 1750s, Matonabbee was selected by the new chief factor of Prince of Wales Fort, Moses Norton (the possibly part-Indigenous son of Richard), as an ambassador and mediator from the Company to the "Athapuscow Indians," a group who spoke a dialect of Cree and dwelt in the vicinity of Lake Athabasca and Great Slave Lake—a little-known land many thousands of kilometres to the west. These people had no access to the Company's outposts except through the more southern Cree fur brokers or by travelling for many months through the territory of their enemies, the Chipewyan (or through Chipewyan intermediaries). On his first cultural and trade expedition, Matonabbee met "several tents" of Athapuscows who held captive a Chipewyan trader named Keelshies and his family. Matonabbee persuaded them to release the captives, but they claimed as payment for this act all of Matonabbee's goods and all six of his wives. Other tales of Matonabbee tell of his escapes from other dangerous situations involving Cree or Athapuscows as he navigated the treacherous cultural animosities between peoples and the tricky and unfamiliar geography, including one instance where he suspected a band of Cree of planning his death. He grabbed up his gun, rushed out of the tent to confront them and proclaimed, "I am sure of killing two or three of you, and if you chuse to purchase my life at that price, now is the time; but if otherwise, let me depart without any farther molestation."

By the mid-1760s, Matonabbee had made several expeditions to the distant lands and had cultivated relationships with the various leaders. His life was spent roving and making business contacts as an agent of the Company, all the while building his reputation as the pre-eminent Chipewyan leader in the vast territory. He reported to the Company that the distant lands were rich in prime beaver. On one of these trips, in 1767, Matonabbee and another man, Idotliazee, brought back at Moses Norton's request a lump of copper from a land with three rivers that ran between two copper deposits. Moses took the copper to London and presented it to the London Committee. The old men became fired up on the dream of valuable minerals and luxuriant beaver and ordered Moses to send out another expedition, this time with a Company man who could take scientific measurements and assess the situation.

MATONABBEE AND HIS ENTOURAGE WERE returning to Prince of Wales Fort in the fall of 1770 when he encountered a small band of bedraggled travellers, an Englishman and two Cree, who were not faring well on the Barrens. One of the men, Samuel Hearne, recalled that Matonabbee quickly "furnished me with a good warm suit of otter and other skins." Hearne gratefully accepted the offer to travel back to Prince of Wales Fort with Matonabbee, and that night Matonabbee "made a grand feast for me in the Southern Indian [Cree] style, where there was plenty of good eating, and the whole concluded with singing and dancing." Hearne was immediately impressed with Matonabbee. "In stature, Matonabbee was above the common size, being nearly six feet high, and, except that his neck was rather (though not too much) too short, he was one of the finest and best proportioned men I ever saw. In complexion he was dark, like the other Northern Indians . . . His features were regular and agreeable, and yet so strongly marked and expressive, that they formed a complete index of his mind; which, as he never intended to deceive or dissemble, he never wished to conceal." The two had many discussions as they travelled across the flat, snow-covered landscape east toward the coast.

Hearne related to Matonabbee the woeful tale of failure that had led to his distressing predicament on the Barrens. This was already Hearne's second attempt to reach the distant lands where lay the fabled copper mines. In November 1769, a year after discovering the remains of the Knight expedition in northern Hudson Bay (and hearing the melancholy tale of the mariners' demise), Hearne had been ordered to set off from the fort with a large group consisting of two Company employees, two Home Guard Cree and a band of Chipewyan, but had returned ignominiously within a month. As there was no viable canoe route, Hearne's plan had been to walk overland on the frozen ground, but the meagre supply of provisions was depleted quickly and the hunting was so poor along his chosen route that he quickly faced starvation. Hearne's first guide, Chawchinahaw, deserted the party barely 320 kilometres from the fort, and without food or guidance Hearne wisely abandoned his quest.

The next month, Moses Norton appointed Connequese to be Hearne's guide. Connequese, however, had little social standing with other Chipewyan in the region and was an incapable leader, negotiator and guide. Hearne's party on this second foray included two Home Guard Cree, but they became lost in the region of the Dubawnt River and were robbed by a passing band of Chipewyan. Although Connequese refrained from outright robbery or extortion himself, because of his ineptitude Hearne retreated in a ragged state, and was pondering his next move when he chanced upon Matonabbee. Matonabbee smiled and pronounced that Hearne's failure was predictable in light of his incompetent guides, and he offered to take Hearne to the copper mine region right away, especially if Norton and the Company could be persuaded to pay for the trip, including his own salary.

Matonabbee also jocularly admonished Hearne for not bringing any women with him, and suggested that Norton was a fool for allowing an expedition to proceed without women. He pointed to his six wives trudging nearby under heavy packs and said, "When all the men are heavy laden, they can neither hunt nor travel to any considerable distance; and in case they meet with success in hunting, who is to carry the produce of their labour?" Women, Matonabbee continued, "were made for labour; one of them can carry or haul as much as two men can do. They also pitch our tents, make our food and mend our clothing, keep us warm at night; and, in fact, there is no such thing as travelling any considerable distance, or for any length of time, in this country without their assistance." Not only were women so indispensable for travel, Matonabbee claimed, perhaps with a wink, but they "are maintained at a trifling expense; for as they always stand cook, the very licking of their fingers, in scarce times, is sufficient for their subsistence." Hearne could only agree with his charismatic companion, but later wrote that he suspected that rather than subsisting on the lickings of their fingers, the women helped themselves to food "when the men are not looking."

The two men were fast friends by the time they had reached the fort, and they had agreed to embark on what would become one of the great adventures in Arctic history.

THE FORMAL PORTRAIT OF Samuel Hearne from later in his life shows a slightly puffy-looking dandy with artificially coiffed hair and a sad or imploring look in his eyes. The portrait may have been reflective of who Hearne had become, but it was not representative of who he was when he met Matonabbee. Hearne was about twenty-four years old at the time, muscular and robust, and around six feet tall. Though he had no experience travelling or surviving in the Subarctic, he was tough and determined. He had led a vigorous life of action since joining the Royal Navy as a "young gentleman" midshipman at age eleven in 1756. He served the duration of the Seven Years War under Samuel Hood, participating in battles, blockades and bombardments from the Mediterranean to France until the war ended and he was discharged in 1763. He was accustomed to rotten rations, stress and danger. By 1767, Hearne was mate on the Company's sloop *Churchill*, based out of Prince of Wales Fort and sailing north to the lands of the Inuit. He also served as mate on the Company's whale ship *Charlotte*. In his off time, when the bay was iced and sailing was impossible, he earned a reputation for energetic outdoor activity and skill at snowshoeing. He also enjoyed the friendship of Andrew Graham, a senior officer with a great interest in natural history, and William Wales, a mathematician and naturalist resident at the fort as a guest sent by the Royal Society to observe the transit of Venus. Natural history of the land and navigation, which was heavily dependent on mathematics, combined with athleticism and bravery and curiosity: Hearne was the natural candidate to fulfill Norton's dreams of a copper mine and perhaps even the fabled Northwest Passage.

Although Matonabbee would be the obvious leader of the expedition, Hearne, owing to his higher rank in the Company's hierarchy and his formal training in navigation and astronomy, has been credited with its leadership. Hearne also wrote a superb account of their adventures, the people they encountered and his observations on the natural world. The epic of Matonabbee and Hearne is yet another historical example of the most literate actor in a drama gaining a disproportionate amount of the fame, as their story is told and retold rather than forgotten. Acknowledging Matonabbee, however, does not discredit Hearne. Hearne was tasked with keeping a journal and making astronomical observations for mapping. He was curious, brave and tough, and he allowed himself to be led into a strange and dangerous land, where he barely spoke the language of any of the peoples, under the protection of Matonabbee for his life. The expedition was conceived by Moses Norton, financed by the Company and led by Matonabbee following his well-trodden commercial route. Hearne was the map-maker and the chronicler.

During the course of their eighteen-month walkabout, Hearne, a keen observer of people, gained a penetrating insight into Matonabbee's personality: "In conversation he was easy, lively, and agreeable, but exceedingly modest; and at table, the nobleness and elegance of his manners might have been admired by the first personages in the world; for the vivacity of a Frenchman, and the sincerity of an Englishman, he added the gravity and nobleness of a Turk." Hearne continued: "I have never met with few Christians who possessed more good moral qualities, or fewer bad ones." Matonabbee also seems to have been a philosopher by nature. For example, in response to Hearne's claim that the Chipewyan seemed to be the "happiest of mortals," Matonabbee responded that of course this was true—they have "nothing to do but consult their own inclinations and passions; to pass through this world as contentedly as possible, with no painful fear of punishment in the next." Adding to Matonabbee's list of admirable qualities was Hearne's observation that "he was remarkably fond of Spanish wines, though he never drank to excess." But in spite of his admiration for his friend,

Hearne noted some darker elements to Matonabbee's character. "As no man is exempt from frailties, it is natural to suppose that as a man he had his share; but the greatest with which I can charge him, is jealousy; and that sometimes carried him beyond the bounds of humanity." Hearne was to see many sides of his friend's character during the course of their expedition.

HEARNE AND MATONABBEE SET OUT with high hopes in December 1770, once again walking rather than canoeing, since this far north there were no materials with which to build canoes and, in any event, the rivers generally flowed in the wrong direction, to the north rather than to the west. Matonabbee had his entourage of cooks, servants and his bevy of wives who hauled the heavily laden sleds over the icy grounds, as well as nine children. Their objective was to continue generally west to the Coppermine River by the summer, and then build canoes to take them north to see the Arctic Ocean. Matonabbee kept a gruelling pace throughout the dark arctic winter, and Hearne nearly dropped from exhaustion and suffered frostbite and swollen, painful feet. Hearne was in awe of the harsh beauty of the Barren Lands, the windswept hummocks of tundra, where dwarf spruce struggled for centuries to grow to the height of a person, the limitless white plains a desert of dry, crusty ridges and undulating snow, where the permafrost descended below the surface. Even in the brief burst of life that was summer, the land was dotted by soupy potholes of muskeg, shallow lakes and rivers. The endless sun of summer saw the exuberant chaos of life, from wildflowers and spongy moss to swarms of mosquitoes and flies so thick they blocked the sun. Vast caribou herds thundered across the expanse in tune with the seasons, north from the shelter of the southern forests to give birth in the spring, and back south again for the winter. The spring and fall were the seasons when untold millions of migratory ducks and geese clouded the sky and peppered the ponds.

After three months of hard travel, Hearne was impressed by his friend's seemingly inexhaustible store of knowledge of "everything that would contribute either to facilitate or retard the ease of progress of travelling" in these parts of the world. Food was alternatively in great abundance or non-existent as they lurched from fast to feast. Storms lashed, soaking them and freezing, with no possibility of erecting a tent. They gnawed raw musk-ox off the bone and chewed on gummy caribou stomach.

On May 3, Matonabbee led the band to the shores of modern-day McArthur Lake (Clowey Lake), a seasonal meeting place where over two hundred Chipewyan had congregated for the changing season, to construct canoes from the bark of birch trees. It had been unseasonably rainy, and Hearne was deflated. He also grew nervous with the crowds, as he was here an outsider in a strange community thousands of miles from his fort. He came to the sobering realization that it was only Matonabbee's fame and position that ensured his safety and that he was "under the protection of a principal man." Hearne didn't really understand the source of Matonabbee's respect, but he soon witnessed how authority and deference were earned in Dene Chipewyan society.

As soon as they had set up their camp along the shore of the lake, Matonabbee began making the rounds. He brought forth supplies such as powder and shot and other items from the Company's stores that his wives had hauled across the Barren Lands. His generosity was a component of the ritualized gifting whereby Matonabbee showed himself worthy of respect by distributing exotic items. He became the big man and the leader, so prosperous that he could afford to share. Matonabbee also engaged in commercial trade, distributing Company goods in exchange for furs that would be hauled back to Prince of Wales Fort in his ever-nomadic round of trade. Matonabbee occupied an important role in the informal hierarchy of the Chipewyan. Hearne didn't have anything to distribute, and Matonabbee told the others not to pester or molest him, which in their eyes firmly established Hearne as subordinate to Matonabbee. Hearne was, however, free with his tobacco, which according to custom was readily and freely offered, and he soon lamented that over half of his substantial stock was gone.

The dreary, windy weather persisted, delaying the construction of the canoes until June 1, when finally, a large group began paddling north down the Coppermine River, leaving the women and children behind. Along the route they encountered members of other groups, and the contingent swelled to around 150 Chipewyan and a dozen or more Copper or Yellowknife (a different tribe of Dene-language speakers, the farthest inland Chipewyan group), in addition to Hearne and two Home Guard Cree. Hearne noted that the river was shallow and so riddled with shoals, falls and rapids that it would be useless for navigation in anything larger than a small canoe, one that could be hauled overland around the obstacles. Whatever lay in the north, transporting it would be problematic.

Wild animals were plentiful, and the group sometimes stopped for several days to hunt musk-oxen and deer whenever they needed food, splitting and drying the meat by the fire before they pushed north again. A hundred and fifty people was a large number in the northern region, and a stable supply of food was never guaranteed. Hearne saw the group slowly getting larger and heard discussions that he didn't understand. He then saw each man making himself a wooden shield and painting it, along with what he describes as other "warlike" preparations. Their shields were painted "some with the figure of the sun, others with that of the Moon, several with different kinds of birds and beasts of prey, and many with the images of imaginary beings." He soon realized that it was not just coincidence that all these seemingly unrelated people chose to accompany him north to the supposed place of copper. It wasn't to help him in his quest. It was a war party, bent on an attack on their ancestral enemies, the Inuit.

When the war band spied a cluster of five large domed skin tents, arrayed around a cataract, on July 17, Hearne knew what was about to happen. He tried to argue against the attack but was hushed with derisive proclamations of his cowardice. Once he realized that he was merely a piece of extra baggage being carted along on a mission unrelated to his own, Hearne began to placate them by claiming that he "did not care if they rendered the name and race of the Esquimaux extinct" but that he didn't see the necessity of killing them without cause. He stated that he would defend himself and his companions in the event of an attack but wouldn't join the assault himself. "I came to consider that it was the highest folly for an individual like me," he wrote, "and in my situation, to attempt to turn the current of a national prejudice which had subsisted between those two nations from the earliest periods." Hearne learned that warlike antagonism and attacks between these people were common and had endured since before anyone could remember. When he later asked, they offered many reasons for the state of warfare, such as shamans using supernatural power to cause disease or ill fortune, or the theft of wives. But in practical terms the underlying cause was that they were all competing for the same territory at the same times of the year, for hunting caribou and for the prime fishing places along the rivers.

Matonabbee, who was naturally the war leader, told the party to conceal themselves behind a low-lying ridge of rocks covered in "crooked and dwarfish" trees. Just before the assault they painted their faces black or red or in vertical stripes and tied their hair back. Some of the men disrobed and others merely removed their jackets and shoes. When these ceremonies were complete, they crept closer, with their shields and weapons ready. As it was always light at this time year so far north, they patiently waited until all the Inuit were asleep before dashing across the open ground to fall upon them.

Screeching and whooping, they clubbed and stabbed the Inuit as they emerged naked and confused from their tents and tried in vain to escape. "The shrieks and groans of the poor expiring wretches were truly dreadful; and my horror was much increased at seeing a young girl, seemingly about eighteen years of age, killed so near me, that when the first spear struck her side she fell down at my feet, and twisted around my legs, so that it was with difficulty that I could disengage myself from her dying grasps." Hearne tried to beg for the girl's life but was sneered at and rebuffed as the killer "looked me sternly in the face, and began to ridicule me, by asking if I wanted an Esquimaux wife." The girl wasn't dead yet and began "twinning around the spears like an eel" in agony until a man stabbed his spear into her. She struggled to ward off the blows even while bleeding to death from the spear that pinned her to the ground.

Soon after the massacre of twenty men, women and children, Matonabbee's band, still fired up on battle lust, spied another camp of Inuit across a branch of the river and began firing their guns at them. These people had never encountered guns before, and "when the bullets struck the ground, they ran in crowds to see what was sent them, and seemed anxious to examine all the pieces of lead which they found flattened against the rocks," until one man was shot in the calf and cried out in pain and they fled, abandoning all their tents, which Matonabbee's warriors soon overran and plundered. They grabbed one unfortunate old man who was slower to escape, and twenty of them stabbed and hacked away at him until he was dead. They destroyed all the possessions of both camps, took the food and the copper tools, the only thing they considered of value.

Hearne was sickened by how Matonabbee and the others had turned so "brutish" and how they desecrated the bodies afterwards. The episode exerted gruesome authority over his thoughts for the rest of his life and he never could "reflect on the transactions of that horrid day without shedding tears." Hearne had seen plenty of brutal and violent warfare while serving with the Royal Navy, so his lifelong distress probably stemmed from the fact that it was civilians who were killed rather than soldiers.

The next day, Hearne and a contingent put their small canoes into the river and continued north to the mouth of the Coppermine River, and he became the first European to view the Arctic Ocean. A few days later he was taken to see the elusive copper mines. The mines proved to be a disappointment and an anticlimactic conclusion to his journey. The rumours of precious metals were based, not surprisingly, on speculation and desire rather than tangible evidence. During an afternoon of searching, Hearne unearthed only a single clump of rough copper weighing about four pounds, amidst "an entire jumble of rocks and gravel." Copper obviously existed, since the Inuit had plenty of copper tools and utensils, and there was evidence that it had been extracted in the past, but it was not abundant, and certainly not in any way economically viable for the Company, owing to the distance from Hudson Bay alone.

It took almost another full year for Hearne and Matonabbee to return to Prince of Wales Fort. The journey included travelling as far west as Great Slave Lake in mid-winter, and Hearne became the first European to see the enormous body of water, the second-largest lake in Canada's Northwest Territories. (Great Bear Lake, farther north and west, is slightly larger.) At approximately 470 kilometres long and between 20 and 203 kilometres wide, the lake is renowned for its fishing and for being the deepest lake in North America. It is named after the Athapaskan group whom the northern Cree, their frequent opponents, called the Slavey. Along the route, Matonabbee completed some marketing and business with another group of Dene-speaking people called the Dogribs, or Tlicho, before they continued their gruelling trek across the lake at a narrow point, and then south through the Athapuscow lands, all part of the biennial business circuit that Matonabbee had pioneered eight years earlier. The ceaseless wandering over rugged terrain took a toll on Hearne's feet. His boots were worn ragged from the stones that pierced his soles, his toenails peeled and bled, and each step during one agonizing stretch left behind bloodstains.

In all, Matonabbee took Hearne over eight thousand kilometres in a giant loop and gave him an unprecedented opportunity to observe the political, economic and cultural life beyond the bay. During the course of the eighteen-month journey, Hearne did not find the fabled Northwest Passage. Neither was the Hudson's Bay Company able to establish a mining or trading operation at the Coppermine River.

Returning from his extensive perambulations, Hearne speculated that the continent of America was much wider than many people imagined and that his journey had "put a final end to all disputes concerning a North West Passage through Hudson's Bay." Though it was by now a familiar refrain, Hearne's practical observation did not "put a final end" to the dream of a Northwest Passage.

WHEN HE RETURNED, Hearne was still a young man, and his adventures with the Company were far from over, but his attentions, and the Company's, would be directed no longer to the north and the rumoured copper mines, but to the south and west, where the encroachments of the French traders from Montreal were undermining the Company's carefully constructed business plans. In 1774, the Company sent a group of men, under Hearne's command, inland along the Nelson River to construct a new fort, called Cumberland House, to better assess the situation in the interior. Hearne selected a prime spot on Pine Island in the Saskatchewan River, about a hundred kilometres upstream from the French fort of Paskova, which today is the site of modern The Pas in northern Manitoba. From here the Company could easily transport goods from Fort York after a forty-day paddle of about 725 kilometres, and the new outpost could be easily accessed by people navigating the Saskatchewan and Churchill river systems. At first it was a primitive log cabin structure with a leaky roof and a smoky interior, but it was profitable. Despite the competition from dozens of small independent Canadian traders along many of the rivers, Hearne led a flotilla of thirty-two fur-laden canoes to York Factory the next spring.

The construction of Cumberland House, the second inland trading fort established by the Company after Henley House, was intended to deal with a long-simmering threat to the Company's business interests that arose from southern traders based out of Montreal encroaching upon their territory. It was a small outpost, but, after a hundred years of being limited along Hudson Bay, it was the beginning of a new era in the Company's story.

The Company's directors knew they could no longer wait for their customers to make the long journey to them. Now they had to go to their customers. The new business structure would be bad for the Cree middlemen, and certainly represented a change from the Company's long-standing commercial policies. But the new merchants from Montreal, a growing city that was under British control now that the Seven Years War was over, were again making inroads after a decade of disruption, and the Company knew it had to do something about it or wither on the vine.

PART THREE

ZENITH

Chapter Eight

THE NOR'WESTERS

A fter the first successful season at Cumberland House, Hearne received a directive from London that he was being promoted to be in charge of Prince of Wales Fort, a post he took up officially at the age of thirty in January 1776. The previous chief factor, Moses Norton, had died in December 1773. Hearne had never liked the man, claiming that he "was known to live in open defiance of every law, human and divine," and that he "always kept a box of poison, to administer to those who refused him their wives and daughters." Hearne also called Norton a "selfish debauchee" and a "notorious smuggler" who reputedly had at least six mistresses in addition to his wife in London, whom he rarely saw.

Hearne succinctly recorded the manner of Norton's death from inflamed bowels, claiming that even while Norton was in "excruciating pain" he remained mean and jealous to the end. Squinting across the dim room from his deathbed, he spied one of his officers holding the hand of one of his young mistresses near the fireplace. He marshalled his ire and spat out in his tremulous voice, "God d——n you for a b——h, if I live I'll knock out your brains." He then subsided into the bed, his energy spent, and "a few minutes after making this elegant apostrophe, he expired in the greatest agonies that can possibly be conceived." As a gift to the people of the fort, something to remember him by, Norton left ten gallons of English brandy to be consumed by all upon his death. So, at least until the booze ran out, Norton was not as universally hated as Hearne claimed.

There was one thing about Norton that Hearne did appreciate: his daughter Mary. Mary was born to one of Norton's Cree mistresses sometime after 1760 and was raised in the fort. Perhaps spoiled by her overprotective father, she never learned any of the skills or customs of her mother's people; nor was she sent to England for an education. Nevertheless, Hearne was clearly smitten with her and gushed in his journal that she possessed every "good and amiable quality, in a most eminent degree" and was "dutiful, obedient, and affectionate to her parents; steady and faithful to her friends; grateful and humble to her benefactors; easily forgiving and forgetting injuries; careful not to offend any, and courteous and kind to all." When Hearne returned to Prince of Wales Fort after founding Cumberland House and took up the command of the fort and its thirty-eight Company employees, he at some time took Mary as his country wife. For years they led a quiet life but had no children. Hearne tended to his pet beavers and slowly worked on the notes of his travels and his observations on natural history and Chipewyan life.

His friendship with Matonabbee continued, and Matonabbee brought in huge quantities of furs to the fort during the 1770s. So respected was Matonabbee as a trader and a leader that in 1776 he arrived at the fort at the head of over three hundred Chipewyan, who were carrying the furs of countless others, a haul that included around five thousand made-beaver equivalent in furs. Their sledges also carried over seven thousand pounds of butchered venison and musk-ox for the fort's provisions. Matonabbee's arrival always provided a break from routine, but on this occasion the usual daily life at the fort ground to halt, as for the next nine days everyone worked constantly to deal with customers. The trades-men were busy mending pots and kettles, the armourer repaired guns, the tailors mended and made coats. Although Hearne and Matonabbee were friends, Matonabbee bargained hard, demanding four hundred made-beaver equivalent in goods personally for his work as a rainmaker, the man who drummed up the business. After the trading began, he requested another seven hundred made beaver as gifts for his people inland. Hearne was annoyed when Matonabbee threatened to take his business to the "Canadian traders" the next year unless his demands were met. In the end, Hearne had no choice. He had seen the inland competition and knew that business once lost to the traders from Montreal would not soon return. "I was glad to comply with his demands," noted Hearne succinctly.

Matonabbee continued as the prime leader doing his circuit of the distant lands, but 1776 proved to be the peak of his efforts. Each season thereafter, more people were drawn into the orbit of the Company's competitors. The Canadians were becoming increasingly proactive and aggressive, but the Company could still offer better prices and a more varied collection of goods, including bulky items such as copper kettles, pans and pots. Nevertheless, the number of furs making their way to all the posts along the shore of the bay was in decline. Matonabbee had met with one of these inland traders, a man named Peter Pond, and done some business with him in 1778 in the Athabasca country, the land where Matonabbee had taken Hearne a decade earlier. The increasing competition between the two companies took on greater urgency as a result of political events beyond their control.

IN 1778, FRANCE DECLARED WAR AGAINST BRITAIN, coming to the aid of the American colonies that had rebelled the previous year in their quest for independence. A localized insurrection quickly escalated into a global conflict involving each country's far-flung outposts and colonies.

On April 12, 1782, at the Battle of the Saintes in the Caribbean, a mighty French fleet under the command of Comte de Grasse and Louis de Bougainville, with thirty-three ships of the line, was defeated by a thirty-six-ship British fleet commanded by Sir George Rodney and Sir Samuel Hood. The British victory thwarted the invasion of Jamaica and broke French naval power. Over 3,000 French were dead or wounded and another 500 captured in five ships, including the flagship *Ville de Paris*, compared with 243 British dead and 816 wounded. While the majority of the French fleet scattered, a small contingent of three ships, the seventy-gun *Sceptre* and two smaller frigates of thirty-six guns, with nearly three hundred marines, was ordered to cruise north to Hudson Bay and destroy British commerce, which meant the Hudson's Bay Company. The commander was Jean-François de Galaup, Comte de La Pérouse, a distinguished young commander who had been a junior officer during the early years of the Seven Years War, serving on several supply expeditions in the Caribbean and at the Siege at Louisbourg. The hope was perhaps to inflict damage on an unsuspecting, poorly defended target and use it as a bargaining chip in peace negotiations. Once again, the Company had the dubious distinction of being a private enterprise getting waylaid by European politics, with the Indigenous peoples paying the highest price.

In early August, the trio of ships entered the treacherous Hudson Strait and headed directly toward their first target, Prince of Wales Fort, through swirling fog and a sea scattered with huge icebergs. By August 8 the ships hove to offshore from the battlements of the impressive-looking stone fortress, unfurling their flags. Arriving so late in the season, La Pérouse knew that he had less than a month before the bay and Hudson Strait became impassable with ice, so time was of the essence—especially if he wanted to take other Company outposts. The fort remained silent, almost deserted, so La Pérouse dispatched six longboats to survey the waters and landed 150 marines ashore. Sill there was no activity. La Pérouse sent one of his officers and a drummer up to the gate to suss out the situation. The gates flew open and a man hoisted a pole with a white tablecloth affixed to the top and nervously walked out. La Pérouse was stunned. Hearne had ordered a complete surrender before a single shot had been fired.

What La Pérouse didn't know was that while the fort looked impressive, appearance was deceiving. Most of the cannons were decades old and were cracked and useless. Hearne had only thirty-eight Company men with him—coopers, cooks, traders, blacksmiths, tailors and other non-military folk—to face the overwhelming French military force. Hearne had served in the Royal Navy for years and knew that it would have been suicide to fight against such a force with a civilian garrison; the French warships could have easily blasted the fort from the water, destroying it and killing the men fairly quickly.

La Pérouse and his men swarmed over the fort, plundering everything except for the personal possessions of the Company employees. Hearne kept a detailed list of the items seized, which included more than 7,500 beaver skins, 4,100 marten skins and an astonishing 17,350 goose quills. The French forces destroyed the fort's cannons, bombarded and exploded the stone buildings, walls and internal structure wherever possible, loaded all of the Company prisoners aboard their ships, Hearne among them, and weighed anchor for the next destination: York Factory. Unfortunately, Mary, along with many other of the Home Guard Indigenous peoples, had fled inland when they beheld the overwhelming force of French naval power. The flotilla sallied forth without her, leaving the destroyed fort, and its dependent support population, behind. A few weeks later, on August 25, La Pérouse repeated the manoeuvre at York Factory, except that the Company supply ship, *Prince Rupert*, escaped with the furs before the French arrived. Once the furs were safely off to London, Governor Humphrey Marten, seeing the formidable French force, surrendered.

The second-in-command, Edward Umfreville, was not enthusiastic about the surrender, though the fort had only sixty men, none of whom

were soldiers, two dozen cannons and some swivel guns. Perhaps hoping
to save his reputation, or to denigrate the governor, Umfreville wrote
that "during their approach, a most inviting opportunity offered itself to
be revenged on our invaders, by discharging the guns on the ramparts.
But a kind of tepid stupefaction seemed to take possession of the
Governor at this time of trial, and he peremptorily declared that he
would shoot the first man who offered to fire a gun." It seems that under
the circumstances surrender was the most prudent course of action for
a small group of civilians facing a powerful military force, but Umfreville
was in a dudgeon and he detailed his opinion on how humiliating it was
to surrender "without one officer being consulted . . . To a half-starved,
wretched group of Frenchmen, worn out with fatigue and hard labour,
in a country they were entire strangers to." He fumed that the factory
could have been defended by a more stalwart governor who possessed
"resolution and good conduct."

Perhaps, but there were also ten times as many French soldiers as
Company men and they were heavily armed and trained military pro-
fessionals in a national navy, rather than untrained tradesmen. La
Pérouse's concern was that the local Cree would join the conflict, as they
were undoubtedly better potential guerrilla warriors, but they had sen-
sibly drifted away into the forest to wait out the conflict rather than be
shot at or captured.

La Pérouse's forces burned anything wooden, plundered what they
could, loaded the ships and set off for home before the winter began
closing in the land and the water. The only thing left undamaged was a
cache of gunpowder and shot for the Cree, so that the conflict wouldn't
deprive them of the ability to hunt during the winter—a kindness not
extended at Prince of Wales Fort. La Pérouse also showed himself to be
a man who could rise above the conflict. Umfreville recorded that he
was "an honour to his nation, and an ornament to human nature. His
politeness, humanity and goodness secured him the affection of all the
Company's officers." In Hudson Strait, he set the prisoners loose in a

small boat that had been captured in the assault, the Company sloop *Severn*, and they returned to England on their own. Owing to inexperience, La Pérouse lost fifteen men to drowning, and several boats of provisions sank during the voyage. La Pérouse was also a man of great learning, who several years later would leave on a voyage of scientific and geographical discovery in the Pacific, similar to Cook's earlier voyages. La Pérouse read Hearne's journal of his adventures in past years, and, though he was a prisoner of war, respectfully returned the manuscript to him and urged him to seek a publisher.

Hearne and Marten, the two defeated chief factors, presented their woeful tale to the London Committee, who no doubt listened with dejected resignation. The loss to the Company was significant, and they halted dividends for the next four years as they struggled to rebuild their enterprise. But both chief factors had their positions renewed and were immediately sent back to their forts to rebuild, arriving aboard supply ships in the summer of 1783. Hearne's return was the most horrible. Prince of Wales Fort was in ruins, and tragedy had befallen many of the Chipewyan and Cree who dwelt near the fort. In addition to the hardship resulting from the destruction of the commercial outposts, the Indigenous peoples around both York Factory and Prince of Wales Fort suffered from the devastating smallpox epidemic that had originated in Mexico and spread north through the interior, killing by some estimates 80 per cent of the local groups of Chipewyan and perhaps as many as half the inland population to the west of Hudson Bay. There were abandoned encampments, empty tents flapping in the wind, and dead bodies littering the land. Many of the survivors resorted to seeking out the posts of the inland Canadian traders. Although Hearne eventually built a new wooden post called Fort Churchill several kilometres upstream along the Churchill River, the scale of trade at Churchill never recovered. Hearne himself never recovered either.

Most sickening to Hearne was that when he went ashore to see the ruins of the fort and begin searching for people, he learned that Mary had perished from exposure or starvation, as did many others that dreadful winter, without access to the goods and supplies from the Company, particularly gunpowder and shot for hunting. She had fled when the French warships arrived, not knowing that the fort would be destroyed and that all the people would be taken prisoner and shipped to England. Hearne blamed her father "for bringing her up in the tender manner which he did, rendering her by that means not only incapable of bearing the fatigues and hardships which the rest of her countrywomen think little of, but of providing for herself." Although Mary had a small annuity from her father, and was provided for by Hearne, once the fort was attacked, the Company's employees sent as prisoners to Europe and the supplies plundered, she was left destitute and without access to any of the resources she had grown up with, while lacking the skills of her mother's people.

Hearne's epitaph for her was an excerpt from a poem by Edmund Waller.

> *Stranger alike to envy and pride,*
> *Good sense her light, and Nature all her guide;*
> *But now removed from all the ills of life,*
> *Here rests the pleasing friend and faithful wife.*

Hearne also soon learned that his friend Matonabbee had hanged himself that winter. Hearne could offer no explanation for the strange event. The speculative Hearne wrote, "This is more to be wondered at, as he is the only Northern Indian who, that I have ever heard, put an end to his own existence." But Hearne, for all his interest in the customs of the Chipewyan, seems never to have grasped fully the importance of ritual gift giving. Matonabbee wasn't a traditional band leader. The respect and authority he commanded depended upon his status as the middleman, smoothing the trade between the Company and the inland people. The traditional reciprocity culture of the Chipewyan had been magnified beyond the usual custom by the Company and their miscellany of exotic items, the products of the global manufacturing network. Matonabbee's power and status were directly linked to the Company's continued operation and his ability to broker access to its goods. In this environment, Matonabbee used the traditional cultural trappings of the Chipewyan to amass great personal prestige, but this very exposure made him vulnerable. Like a leveraged investment, his fall was as dramatic and precipitous as the rise. With the destruction of Prince of Wales Fort, he lost his position utterly and absolutely, the victim of a foreign war over which he had no control. Because his wealth was not material or durable, but ephemeral and cultural, and based upon his ability to continuously deliver goods, his power within the Chipewyan community vanished once the English vanished so suddenly and shockingly. He had no cache of goods, his wealth was his status, and his status was stripped from him by the arrival of French warships. His livelihood, his authority and even his identity were taken all at once. Matonabbee had no idea that the Company would return to rebuild in less than a year. He suspected that everyone he knew at the fort had been killed in the attack, rather than shipped across the Atlantic as prisoners. As far as he knew, the fort being demolished meant the end of the Company.

Matonabbee's world, all of the cultural and economic relationships that he had spent a lifetime developing, disappeared at the same time as the smallpox epidemic ravaged the land. It was too much and, now that he was middle-aged, he felt that he couldn't rebuild his life, that there was no point in living once his entire place in the world disappeared and so many of his people were dead. Perhaps he was even being blamed for the misfortunes, the sickness and the seeming disappearance of the Company. "The death of this man was a great loss to the Hudson's Bay Company," Hearne wrote in a practical sense, "and was attended with a most melancholy scene; no less than the death of six of his wives, and four of his children, all of whom were starved to death the same Winter."

Matonabbee, more than anyone else, had been responsible for the great quantities of trade that had taken place along the Churchill, but many would now take advantage of his absence and the business he had pioneered.

HEARNE NEVER RECOVERED FROM THE DEATH of his wife and his friend. He failed to flourish personally after constructing the new Fort Churchill, which occupied the same turf that James Knight's first outpost had occupied over six decades earlier. The trade never recovered either, and the new post's prospects were grim, mirrored by its governor's mood. His efforts to rejuvenate it were listless and half-hearted. Hearne's world had ended much as Matonabbee's had: his wife was dead, Prince of Wales Fort was destroyed, his good friend was dead, and all the action and excitement were gone from his life and work. Although not yet forty years old, Hearne descended into a drunken apathy, a shadow of the former vivacity and strength that had taken him on epic adventures. Exciting things were happening in the fur trade, but he wasn't part of them anymore. The Company was disappointed when the trade failed to return and implied that it was Hearne's fault. In any case, after a few years he ended his contract and sailed for London in August 1787.

In London, Hearne lived quietly, offering his services as a consultant to naturalists and to the Company. With the help of his friend the astronomer and teacher William Wales, he revived his interest in telling his story and worked hard at transforming the drafts of his adventure and observations into a polished manuscript. Although he had a working draft of his manuscript for years and had signed a publication deal, the book was not published until several years after his death, probably because the Company didn't want to release information that could prove useful to their competitors in the interior. During this time Hearne became swollen and puffy, symptoms of kidney disease. He died at the age of forty-seven, in November 1792—the same year a famous British sea captain named George Vancouver was surveying the entire Pacific coast of North America from California to Alaska and compiling a detailed chart of the region.

Hearne's posthumously published *A Journey from Prince of Wales's Fort, in Hudson's Bay, to the Northern Ocean* is a charming and lively account of his years of adventure with Matonabbee, a classic of northern exploration literature and an unvarnished window into eighteenth-century life in the northern interior, a region on the cusp of great change. Hearne was a keen observer of the natural world, such as the seasonal behaviour of animals, the types of vegetation and the climate. He had a particular interest in Chipewyan customs and lifestyle. Food was another favourite topic, perhaps because the cuisine on the Barren Lands was so different from the food at the fort, and perhaps because on his adventures he often didn't have enough of it. He detailed the many different methods of hunting and of preparing food, which animal parts were the tastiest or most coveted when herbed, boiled or roasted. He described with relish a common hearty caribou stew, and a venison dish called *beeatee* that was "a most delicious morsel." Similar to the Scottish haggis, it was made using the animal's stomach as a vessel, stuffed with blood, chopped fat, tenderized meat, kidneys and heart mixed with seasonal herbs. The *beeatee* was steamed and smoked over a fire into an aromatic pâté. Hearne found buffalo tripe to be "exceedingly good," while warm caribou blood sucked directly from the bullet hole was "very nourishing." Moose stomach, on the other hand, was "rather bitter." Hearne also savoured raw fish of various types and cuts, which was a common meal of the Chipewyan and remained a mainstay of Hearne's palate for the rest of his life, a fondly remembered delicacy that he would specially request when dining out in London, perhaps to unobtrusively raised eyebrows acknowledging the culinary peccadilloes of the eccentric traveller.

Hearne wrote in detail about the annual life cycle of the Dene-speaking peoples of the Barren Lands, and the difference between the sexes and their respective roles in society. Narrative examples give poignancy to his anthropological generalizations, and his fascinating insights are written in clear, descriptive and vibrant language. When noting the propensity for important or respected leaders to have multiple wives,

Hearne noted dryly that "it has always been the custom among those people for the men to wrestle for any woman to whom they are attached; and, of course, the strongest party always carries off the prize. A weak man, unless he be a good hunter and well-beloved, is seldom permitted to keep a wife that a stronger man thinks worth his notice." Hearne noted that, not surprisingly, since earliest childhood all the men worked at developing their strength and wrestling skills so as to be able to protect their wives, and consequently the family possessions, from the "powerful ravishers," some of whom made a career out of fighting to claim other men's wives. He described the ritualized wrestling matches that gave "the appearance of the greatest brutality" but seldom ever resulted in injury. The fighting style consisted mostly of "hauling each other about by the hair of the head," although there were common subterfuges such as secretly cutting one's hair just before the match. The contest was almost always preceded by theatrical boasting and insults, while during the match the gathered onlookers yelled advice and encouragement, but never intervened, while the "object of the contest" sat "in pensive silence watching her fate." The women were often thrown over the shoulders and carried away, sometimes in anguish, yet "at other times it was pleasant enough to see a fine girl led off the field from a husband she disliked, with a tear in one eye and a finger on the other: for custom, or delicacy if you please, has taught them to think it necessary to whimper a little."

Hearne also reported on the social customs surrounding murder, an act that was a heinous crime and seldom seen. "A murderer is shunned and detested by all the tribe, and is obliged to wander up and down, forlorn and forsaken even by his own relations and former friends . . . and he never leaves any place but the whole company say, 'There goes the murderer!'"

Hearne's journals, while portraying a European view of the "new" lands, also reveal the passive role of Company overlanders during their travels to the interior. Hearne was, at times, primarily a bystander, a recorder of events beyond his control in a land dominated by people with passions, hatreds, alliances and prerogatives of their own. Nevertheless, his book collected for the first time much detailed information on the climate, geography, natural history and the customs of the people of a huge piece of land. It was a collection of observations and evidence-based opinions on the territory that made up the Company's commercial monopoly. Hearne had informed them, "The Continent of America is much wider than many people imagine," the unstated implication being that the potential market was also much larger than most people imagined. When he was on his famous journey to the land of the Yellowknives, Hearne had noted, "The natives, my guides, well knew that many tribes of Indians lay to the West of us, and they knew no end to the land in that direction; nor have I met with any Indians, Northern or Southern, that ever had seen the sea to the Westward."

Unfortunately from the Company's point of view, those unknown distant lands that lay concealed in the mists along the western horizon would be inaccessible to them. The traders from Canada were blocking the path.

SINCE THE TIME OF RADISSON AND GROSEILLIERS over a century earlier, Montreal and the St. Lawrence valley had changed, with many new immigrants from France and a growing farming economy along the river. In the years after the British conquest of New France, the change accelerated. The population surged, no longer restricted to immigrants who were Roman Catholic, and the economy soared with the influx of British financing. There was also a wave of Loyalist migrants who fled from the United States after the American Revolution ended in 1783. The population was about 70,000 in 1765; by 1790 it was over 160,000; and by 1806, 250,000. In the city of Montreal, a fire during the war had destroyed many old buildings, but the flood of newcomers and people from the countryside contributed to a perpetual construction boom and the population in the city exploded from a couple of thousand people to over 6,000 by 1782, and racing ever higher. There were 9,000 people in 1800; 23,000 by 1825; and 58,000 by 1852.

Concurrent with this dramatic increase in the population of people of European descent was the rise of Montreal traders, the *coureurs de bois*. They had been pushing west and north throughout the eighteenth century searching for a Great Western Sea and for new markets wherever they had been positively received by local peoples. The challenge to the monopoly of the Company from these traders ebbed and flowed over the generations, never disappearing yet never seriously challenging. One indomitable wanderer named Pierre Gaultier de Varennes, Sieur de La Vérendrye, wandered as far west as the Black Hills of South Dakota and along the shores of Lake Winnipeg in the 1740s. A charming rogue, La Vérendrye and his sons expanded Canadian knowledge of the western hinterland—its geography, politics and culture of the local peoples. But these gains went unrealized from a commercial perspective because of the huge distance and travel time from Montreal and because of the war and conquest by the British.

The defeat of Quebec by British forces in 1759–60 was believed to have rid the Company once and for all of its pesky competitors, but within the decade the opposite proved true. The lakes and rivers of the interior, the southern part of the territory granted to the Company by its monopoly charter, instead were flooded with canoes dispatched from Montreal, now organized into partnerships and financed by London capital. By the late eighteenth century, in an attempt to capture the trade, the traders from Canada were retracing the old trade and travel routes and establishing their own trading outposts upstream on rivers leading to Hudson Bay. The Cree too were cutting into the Company's profits by aggressively persuading other native trappers to conclude their trade before canoeing the remaining distance to the Company forts.

One of the most important pioneers of the inland trade from Montreal was a colourful character named Peter Pond, an itinerant shoemaker, soldier and sailor who by the 1770s had spent years in the fur trade along the Mississippi River before killing a man in a duel and fleeing north. Pond earned a reputation for his violent temper, passionate and fiercely held beliefs and powerful dreams. By the late 1770s, he was pushing the trade into the distant northwest of the Athabasca country, inspired by tales of the vast quantities of beaver. It was here that he met Matonabbee. Pond already then was skimming off trade and undermining the role of Chipewyan middlemen who, like Matonabbee, made their living collecting and transporting goods from the interior to Prince of Wales Fort. The people were eager to have goods brought to them at a cheaper price without the need for middlemen or their own arduous overland journey to Prince of Wales Fort or York Factory.

In 1778, with the backing of Simon McTavish, a shrewd and arrogant young financier and trader, Pond led sixteen voyageurs in four canoes laden with several tons of supplies on a speculative venture farther north and west, over the twelve-mile Methy Portage that separates the Hudson Bay and Arctic watersheds. A rugged and somewhat unsavoury character, Pond was implicated in two other murders while he mapped important parts of the Deh Cho River system (what would later be called the Mackenzie River), and opened the way for the Canadian traders from Montreal to expand their business into this region, cutting off the Company's lucrative flow of furs. Pond was also the first to write about the bituminous sands around Fort McMurray. After Pond established the new trade route, the Chipewyan for the most part took their business to the new outpost in the interior called Fort Chipewyan, near Lake Athabasca, in the vicinity of where the Peace, Athabasca and Slave converged.

In 1779, the traders from Montreal officially became organized into an enterprise called the North West Company, later colloquially known as the Nor'Westers. For several years it remained a small-scale loose affiliation of Montreal merchants probing the interior with a view to working around the Company's monopoly. They could travel inland, of course, since the territory was not owned by the Company; rather, it was firmly in control of various Indigenous nations. But the North West Company needed to gain access to London's capital markets to finance its expansion, and therefore it had to tread with caution when challenging the British government-sanctioned monopoly.

In 1783, the North West Company merged with several other smaller fur businesses in the expanding city and consolidated its operations into a permanent enterprise with a head office. It was led by Benjamin and Joseph Frobisher, Simon McTavish and other well-financed investors, among them James McGill (whose fur fortune in the 1820s founded the Montreal university that bears his name). The organization and financing originally came from the new influx of Anglo and Scottish Quebecers who arrived after the British conquest, but the enterprise also was managed by French Canadians, and with French-Canadian and Iroquois voyageurs doing much of the heavy paddling and adventuring, although the Scottish leaders also often personally led brigades. In the early nineteenth century, four in five managers in Montreal were of Scottish descent. Alexander Mackenzie, one of the adventurous young partners in the 1790s, reflected on the clannishness of the enterprise and noted that the dispersed isolated nature of communities in the Scottish Highlands demanded self-reliance and loyalty, characteristics that were of great benefit to those leaving home to live in distant isolated trading posts.

Of course, clannish loyalty could be taken too far, and arguably it was so in the North West Company, where in the early nineteenth century most of the senior management was related to Simon McTavish, either by birth or by marriage, including Mackenzie and Simon Fraser, such that it was almost a family business. Contacts and relations were the most important criteria for employment and advancement; outsiders were not welcome. But, to keep the enterprise from stagnating, as profit-sharing partners retired they were required to give up their stock to younger officers, so that the working partners were always labouring for their own interest.

Soon the Nor'Westers were dominating the trade, opening up new trade forts in distant regions farther inland. Because much authority was vested in the inland working partners, they could make decisions and react swiftly to overcome new geographical obstacles and cultural challenges. The wintering partners could take advantage of opportunities in a way that the entrenched and bureaucratic Company, with its rigid command structure and generally low-paid employees who lacked authority, could not. Whereas the employees of the Company could be likened to passive branch managers for distant shareholders, sending their reports back and awaiting instructions from people who had never been in the lands where they did business, the partners of the North West Company were a loose affiliation of individualists who shared in the profits. They were dynamic and entrepreneurial rather than complacent and tradition-bound. When they saw an economic opportunity—to fulfill an unmet demand for a new trading outpost, to pioneer a new, faster transportation route, or to make a trade alliance with an Indigenous leader—they found a way to do it rather than wait for a decision to come from London on the next year's supply ship.

But the long and complex supply lines of the North West Company were a formidable obstacle to securing its dream of a transcontinental fur empire. It was a plan easier to imagine than to execute. Unlike the Company's annual supply ships, the Nor'Westers had to import goods from across the Atlantic to Montreal in the fall, then sort, organize and pack the items for the next spring when they could then be transported west to the interior. The huge birchbark *canots du maître*, the Great Lakes canoes, could be up to twelve metres long, with a capacity for five thousand pounds of goods and a crew of up to twelve. Flotillas of these boats worked their way past the Lachine Rapids, upstream along the Ottawa River to Georgian Bay, then followed Lake Huron to Lake Superior and trailed the coast of that mighty lake to Grand Portage. The voyage could take forty days and involved thirty-five portages. At Grand Portage the inland or wintering partners, who had made a similarly challenging journey from their distant western outposts, met with the Montreal management and financial agents each year to make decisions, share new commercial and geographical information and plan strategy to maximize their trade, which included schemes to cut off the Company.

After a back-breaking portage, the goods were transferred into the smaller *canots du nord*, which were only eight metres long and held no more than half the cargo and passengers, and then worked their way over rapids, falls and portages in a test of endurance and strength from the Lake of the Woods and thousands of kilometres more across the aspen parkland and Canadian Shield to supply the increasing number of trading posts in the northwest. Constructing and maintaining all these boats and associated equipment was an enormous undertaking. Ojibwa craftsmen in the region of Grand Portage became specialized at making the smaller *canots du nord* and other smaller travel canoes and sold them to the Nor'Westers.

The serpentine supply chain was also supported by Indigenous peoples along the route who procured birch rind, cedar root and tree sap needed for routine repairs, and hunted, fished and harvested wild rice, corn and maple syrup. The voyageurs had no time for these activities on their relentless paddle to reach the prime fur territory of the Athabasca region. Paddling from before dawn and into the dark without rest, up to twelve hours a day in the northern summer, required staggering quantities of calories. This included up to nine pounds of meat per day for each voyageur, so taking care of the food supply logistics was one of the most important jobs. From the Winnipeg River north on Lake Winnipeg, up the Saskatchewan River and north again to the upper Churchill River, they relied on Plains peoples to supply them with bison, often dried, pounded and mixed with berries, which was called pemmican. A string of small supply posts was established along the entire route, paying for the services of a small army of Assiniboine and Plains Cree, who often raised prices for their goods and services according to the season and as the enterprise expanded. The North West Company naturally sought to gain their services at the cheapest rate, while the Indigenous contractors sometimes engaged in sneaky tactics such as setting fire to the grasslands surrounding the North West Company supply posts in the fall so that during the winter, roaming bison would stay distant, thus increasing the demand for hunters. Soon trapping furs became a secondary enterprise for these people, as it had for the Cree farther north, as they were drawn into the economic orbit of the fur trade, even while maximizing their remuneration. When the voyageurs paddled back south and east each spring, they followed the same arduous and unreliable route.

Within years, the field partners of the North West Company were yearly pushing farther inland and had stretched their supply chain into regions that previously had only rarely received trade goods from other Indigenous traders. The profits to the partners were enormous, their expansion throughout the northwest quick, and their competition was caught off guard, still imagining that its charter would protect it. By the end of the century, when McTavish was called "the Marquis of the Montreal fur trade," the North West Company was annually distributing huge dividends and the partners were living like princes in their Montreal mansions. The Company, on the other hand, kept dividends low and built up a strategic commercial reserve of working capital that would position it for the conflict ahead—similar to the long-term strategy that had seen it through a century of business, weathering each storm as it presented itself, shrinking or expanding as the conditions dictated and persevering for the time when the sun would shine again.

The main reason the Company was so slow to extend its operations inland, other than bureaucratic dithering and misunderstanding, was that there could be no venturing into the interior without canoes, yet there was a lack of birchbark and other needed materials around either of their two major outposts.

The Company needed a different form of transportation, and they took their inspiration for their famous York boats from a traditional design from the Orkneys. York boats were the technological innovation that eventually enabled the Company's inland expansion to compete with that of the Nor'Westers. The York boat had a flat bottom for easy transport over portages, where it could be dragged over logs on pre-cut roads along the route. Heaving hard on mighty oars attached to the opposite side of the sitter, they could, with enormous strength and a tireless crew accustomed to hardship and discomfort, propel themselves inland, using sails whenever they crossed lakes, which was the only respite for the labourers who toiled like galley slaves to propel the heavy boats against the current. A crew of around six men could power a cargo of up to six thousand pounds. Sometimes, at dangerous rapids or shallow rocky sections, some men got out and used ropes to haul the boat from shore. Beginning in the late eighteenth century, the boats were manufactured at Moose Factory and York Factory (which they were named after), and later at Norway House and Fort Edmonton.

Eventually the Company moved inland from Hearne's Cumberland House and Fort Albany into the region between Lake Superior and Lake Winnipeg, which brought them close to the supply lines of the Nor'Westers. Most of these early posts were unimpressive, shoddily constructed cabins with mud chimneys. They were quickly abandoned and new posts built in other locations. One fur trader wrote in 1796 about Bedford House, near Reindeer Lake, "We builded Log Huts to pass the winter, the chimneys were of mud and coarse grass, but somehow did not carry off the smoke, and the Huts were wretched with smoke, so that however bad the weather, we were glad to leave the Huts." These rudimentary outposts also had a poor selection of goods simply owing to the transportation challenges. As well, and more importantly, the Company was pushing inland west along the North Saskatchewan River system. Manchester House was founded in 1786, Buckingham House in 1792, Edmonton House in 1795 and Acton House in 1799, as well as dozens of smaller posts. By the turn of the century, Cumberland House had become more of a provisioning centre, collecting dried bison, whitefish and venison for distribution to the farther outposts.

Because it now was compelled to take its business to the people, the

Company was forced into a far more complex logistical structure than in its first 110 years of operation. The same basic model applied, in that ships from London continued their annual voyages to the western coast of Hudson Bay to unload the year's trade goods and then reload the furs and other products of the country. But now it was the Company's responsibility to transport the furs from the interior to the bayside factories and to transport the trade goods into the interior without relying upon the unpaid labour of Indigenous peoples or on the flourishing Indigenous transport businesses. In 1786, in recognition of this new reality, the Company appointed William Tomison to be chief factor at York, but in a first for the Company and a signal recognition of the changing times, he was to reside in the country rather than along the bay.

As the years passed and the number of inland posts grew, the bay posts were becoming more like supply depots, of secondary status in authority and direct economic contribution. Competition forced major changes upon the Company, and additional expenses, in both labour and management, than the Company had ever before faced.

EACH OF THE TWO COMPANIES HAD competitive advantages and disadvantages. Working against the North West Company was the fact that the Hudson's Bay Company could get its goods by ship right into the heart of the continent, while the Nor'Westers had to transport their goods from Montreal, far to the south and east. But the Company suffered from a lack of manpower. The near-continuous wars that occupied Britain (the American War of Independence between 1775 and 1783 and the French Revolutionary and Napoleonic Wars between 1792 and 1815) deprived the Company of easy access to young male workers when they were desperately needed to staff the new inland posts. The Napoleonic Wars in particular made it difficult for the Company to recruit young men into the overseas fur trade, and it increasingly hired the mixed-blood descendants of earlier employees to take on roles within the Company hierarchy. The Company still adhered to its policy of rarely employing Indigenous people for full-time careers because it wanted them out in the bush capturing beaver, fulfilling the supply side of the business equation, for which they were uniquely suited. Over time the connotation of "mixed-blood" or "Indian" denoted economic roles and placement in the hierarchy rather than purely genetic or racial background. By the beginning of the nineteenth century, the Company still had barely five hundred employees in North America, although it relied heavily upon the contract services of countless Indigenous hunters, guides and labourers.

The Nor'Westers, on the other hand, drew on Quebec's seventy-thousand-strong local population, whether French or Mohawk-Iroquois. They fielded approximately twelve hundred people along their vast supply line. It was a more expensive and labour-intensive business model, but, as would be seen, the larger numbers would be useful in a fight. The Iroquois were particularly suitable for aggressive conflict, and even the Company began hiring them decades later when the two companies were at war. "I have frequently heard the Canadian and Iroquois voyagers disputed as regards their merits," wrote Company agent Colin Robertson in 1819, "perhaps the former may be more hardy or undergo more fatigue, but in either rapid or traverse, give me the latter, for their calmness and presence of mind which never forsakes them in the greatest danger." If you were in a scrape, you'd want a Mohawk-Iroquois companion, and these men were in great demand in the early nineteenth century.

The life of a voyageur could be harsh and often short, full of danger and extreme living, but many would never trade it for any other, signing on for the next season's work each year for decades and only retiring when they were no longer capable of the rigours of the life. One old man, astonishingly over seventy, reminisced on his life travelling the land as a fur trader. "I have been 24 years a canoeman and 41 years in service; no portage was ever too long for me. Fifty songs I could sing. I have saved the lives of 10 voyageurs. Have had 12 wives and six running dogs. I spent all my money in pleasure. Were I young again, I should spend my life the same way over.

There is no life so happy as a voyageur life."

The two companies' different corporate structures also manifested in their interactions with local peoples. While the Company men were ordered to adhere to basic discipline and to respect various Indigenous customs and ceremony, the more chaotic arrangements of the Nor'Westers allowed for more individual discretion, which meant in some cases developing a greater facility with Indigenous languages and a deeper understanding of local customs. But the "pedlars," as the Company men derisively called them in the early days before they became a dangerous and organized threat, also earned a reputation for bad living and poor relations with Indigenous peoples, the result of the behaviour of a minority tarnishing the reputation of many. As a consequence, they seldom stayed in the same place from year to year for fear of repercussions and kept building new outposts. It wasn't a stable business plan.

Edward Umfreville was an officer of the Company who later shifted his allegiance to the Nor'Westers, hoping for more pay and a better career. More so than almost anyone, he was able to contrast the character of the employees of the two enterprises. "It however must be owned," he mused, "that the Hudson's Bay traders have ingratiated themselves more into the esteem and confidence of the natives than the Canadians . . . The great imprudence and bad way of living of the Canadian traders have been an invincible bar to the emolument of their employers," he wrote in *The present state of Hudson's Bay*, his cantankerous and partly plagiarized tract detailing his years of service with the two companies. He went on in this vein for a while, eventually offering his opinion that the Canadians "have become slaves to every vice which can corrupt and debase the human mind; such as quarrelling, drunkenness, deception, etc. From a confirmed habit in bad courses of this nature, they are held in abhorrence and disgust . . . they are become obnoxious to the Indians."

The Nor'Westers relied on brandy and rum as a staple trade good, items that were easy to transport and high in short-term profit. They had no scruples about pushing it, unlike the Company, which mostly viewed too much liquor as detrimental to business and life in general. Umfreville was disgusted at the effect the trade in hard liquor had on certain Indigenous people, a situation he considered "not at all to the ulterior advantage of the natives, who by this means became degenerated and debauched, through the excessive use of spirituous liquors imported by these rivals in commerce."

While the Company focused exclusively on trade and left every other aspect of life within its commercial territory to its own fate, without any direct meddling in Indigenous societies, the Nor'Westers moved inland and imposed their customs on people, interacting with them in a way that transcended merely economic interest if it would improve trade. Certainly, during the 1790s in certain regions, particularly with the Chipewyan for example, there was a great deal of resentment toward the Nor'Westers, and if it weren't for the smallpox epidemic that ravaged the population in the previous decade, they would have banded together and ousted the invaders from Montreal. Familial ties also no doubt played a role in minimizing violence between cultures that could easily have been in greater conflict. It was a situation of social disruption that would get progressively worse in the second decade of the nineteenth century.

Although the Nor'Westers were making enormous profits and had by the end of the eighteenth century captured the majority of the fur trade from the sleepy factors of the Company, running a stable business was becoming more difficult as each new region became "beavered out" and the fur brigade stretched farther west. Shipping costs alone rose with every mile of travel. A deep rivalry developed between the two enterprises as they each sought to expand westward into the remaining prime beaver regions, setting the stage for a dramatic conflict just as a famous Nor'Wester, Alexander Mackenzie, set off on a series of expeditions that would make his fortune and change the fur business.

Chapter Nine

THE GREAT RIVER
OF THE NORTH

W hen the ice broke up on the rivers around Montreal in early May, it signalled a flurry of activity for the managing partners of the North West Company headquartered in the city. For months they had been stockpiling and organizing goods in warehouses, hiring voyageurs and readying the fleet of *canots du maître* for the epic journey west. When the water was deemed clear, the great flotilla set off on its 1,600-kilometre voyage: upstream along the Ottawa River, over a portage to the French River, and downstream into Georgian Bay, along the shore of the North Channel of Lake Huron to Sault Ste. Marie and then into Lake Superior. At about the same time, the inland partners, who had spent the winter managing operations at the dozens of rudimentary forts and stockades that sprinkled the river systems west of Hudson Bay, set off east in their smaller canoes, hauling the season's cache of furs. The destination for both was Grand Portage.

Built by Simon McTavish in 1784, Grand Portage was a large fortified depot along the northwestern shore of Lake Superior. There the two parties met for a month-long celebration and conference and exchanged

their cargo of manufactured goods for packs of pelts before heading back
to their bases, leaving just enough time for the western field partners to
paddle the jaw-dropping distance back to their outposts before the rivers
froze up again. It was a sprawling community of wharves, warehouses,
workshops, offices and barracks loosely clustered around and within a
massive palisade fort. (In 1805, when it was determined that the original
Grand Portage was located in American territory, the Nor'Westers
relocated their main depot sixty-five kilometres northeast along the
shore to Fort William, present-day Thunder Bay.)

From their perch atop the log towers of the fort's walls, scouts usually
spied the fleet from Montreal in late June, the first of several brigades
of around thirty *canots du maître*, each canoe piled with bundled goods,
with ten paddles uniformly plunging into the water to the tune of a
song. The canoes pulled onto a beach just out of sight and the voyageurs
donned their gaudy blue jackets, scarlet sashes and red tasselled caps.
The captain, or bourgeois, of each canoe donned a sleek beaver top hat.
Appropriately attired for the upcoming ceremony, the men climbed
back into their canoes and as a group dashed in unison toward the fort's
harbour, to the delight of the garrison of onlookers. McTavish himself
always arrived in his personal canoe, gaily painted to distinguish it,
while his voyageurs were the snappiest dressers. He came every year to
preside over the ceremonies and ensure business was done according
to his satisfaction. By the 1790s, more than a hundred transport canoes
were sent out from Montreal each year.

The frontier fur capital was built into a natural amphitheatre of hills
and rocky outcroppings, with a secure harbour below a gated wooden
palisade with walls four and a half metres high and lookout towers.
More than ten buildings were peppered about the enclosure, including
barracks, warehouses, a secure powder magazine and armoury, a counting house, canoe repair facilities and other useful establishments. One
of the most popular was the *cantine salope*, or harlot's tavern, where,
according to early nineteenth-century traveller Gabriel Franchère,

"liquors, bread, pork, butter, and cheese are sold, and where a treat is given out to arriving voyageurs. This consists of a white loaf, a half pound of butter, and a gill of rum." Many commercial women also loitered about the canteen, giving the tavern's name a poignant meaning. Voyageurs who squandered too much of their pay on liquor and began brawling were locked up in the *pot au beurre*, or butter tub, a low-security jail. In the middle of the little village was the Great Hall, which was about ten metres by twenty metres in size, with quarters for the partners appended to either end. Dwarfing all the other buildings, it was used for meetings and as a venue for the dinners that enlivened the evenings during the month of the rendezvous.

Although the fort was capacious, the two camps of voyageurs, the eastern and the western, with up to three hundred men each, spent their nights in their respective camps outside the palisade. "The wintering hands," Franchère wrote, "who are to return with their employers pass also a great part of the summer here [Fort William]. They form a great encampment on the west side of the fort, outside the palisades. Those who engage at Montreal to go no farther than Fort William or Rainy Lake, and who do not winter in the North, occupy another space on the east side. The winterers give to these last the name *mangeurs de lard* or pork eaters. They are also called *comers-and-goers*. One perceives a remarkable difference between these two camps, which are composed sometimes of three or four hundred men each. That of the pork eaters is always dirty and disorderly, while that of the *winterers* neat and clean." Across the river there was also a community of log cabins inhabited by older "worn out" voyageurs who chose not to return to the St. Lawrence and instead had settled with "women of the country" and were supporting their families with gardens of corn and potatoes, supplemented with fish.

Both the eastern and western voyageurs had a dreadful task upon their arrival, before the carousing could begin. The commercial entrepôt was called Grand Portage for a reason: it was an actual portage to get the goods from Lake Superior over to the Pigeon River and the furs from the Pigeon River to the shore of Lake Superior. The distance was approximately fifteen kilometres of rooted, rocky, mucky, slippery drudgery. Each man loaded two sacks of around ninety pounds each onto his lower back and held them in place with a leather strap around his forehead, hunching forward to take the strain onto the head instead of the back. Each man made the journey at least four times, taking a rest every six hundred metres or so at set intervals called poses. Hernias and broken and strained ankles, knees and wrists were common under the punishing loads of the portage. In the litany of voyageur woes, the gruelling job was ranked second only to drowning. After years of this work some voyageurs had oval holes worn in their teeth the shape of pipe stems, from clenching their pipes and smoking as they trudged along in intense exertion.

Yet there were always plenty of men eager to take on the challenging task. Extra pay was awarded for extra loads, and competitions abounded, with many taking three sacks at a time and in some rare instances men even managed four. One astonishing man carried five: Pierre Chimakadewiiash Bonga, a hugely muscled black trapper who was brought to Mackinac Island by his parents' British master in 1782, when he was still a boy, and was freed along with his family when the master retired to Montreal several years later. Bonga married an Ojibwa woman, and the family developed deep roots in the Ojibwa and European societies over the years, with several becoming interpreters, guides and hoteliers, sending children to Montreal for their education. Bonga's sons were also massive men, over six feet tall and more than two hundred pounds—extraordinary for the era. One son, George, in a perhaps apocryphal legend, once carried six hundred pounds strapped to his back and forehead over a difficult portage, but he managed only about one and a half kilometres before collapsing in exhaustion. Whether sporting event or clever way for management to get additional work from the labourers, the grand portage lived in every voyageur's dreams or nightmares.

The *hommes du nord*, the north men who wintered in the distant hinterland, were the pinnacle of the labouring hierarchy. Long-haired and wearing buckskin clothing like the Indigenous peoples with whom they spent their winters, they received higher pay and commanded great respect for the danger and isolation. Their monotonous travelling diet consisted mostly of pemmican, but they nevertheless mocked the easterners for being *mangeurs du lard* for their diet of corn mash and pig fat boiled into a gloopy porridge. Rivalry aside, both the eastern and western voyageurs were elite athletes, not only for carrying their loads on portages but for their ability to paddle for up to sixteen hours a day, from dawn to dark, singing and chanting to keep the pace. According to American traveller Thomas L. McKenney, who followed the Canadian voyageur route in 1825, "They are short, thick set, and active, and never tire. A Canadian, if born to be a labourer, deems himself to be very unfortunate if he should chance to grow over five feet five, or six inches; and if he shall reach five feet ten or eleven, it forever excludes him from the privilege of becoming voyageur. There is no room for the legs of such people, in these canoes. But if he shall stop growing at about five feet four inches, and be gifted with a good voice, and lungs that never tire, he is considered as having been born under a most favourable star."

Once the heavy work was over, the rendezvous at Grand Portage took on the gaiety of a summer fair. Dancing, carousing and quaffing heroic quantities of fiery liquor inevitably led to fights, which in turn led to knife wounds, torn ears, bitten noses, broken bones and pummelled faces. Outside the fort the voyageurs engaged in a chaotic bacchanalia while the officers shook their heads in wonder. They squandered their earnings at the *cantine salope*, signed new contracts for the following year, feasted on foods hard to obtain on the trail such as bread and butter and fresh potatoes, exchanged news from home or the distant northwest, and generally rousted about enjoying their leisure. Meanwhile the partners and managers conferred in the Great Hall, discussing the politics of the lands: England, Montreal and the great northwest; how events would affect their business; what strategies should be employed to continue to blockade the Hudson's Bay Company; what trade goods were in demand; and into which new territories they should expand.

After about a week, the excitement grew as preparations were made to end one season and start another with the annual banquet and celebration. Voyageurs cleaned themselves up, garbing themselves in their finest clothes, many local Ojibwa canoe makers, hunters and their families arrived, and the officers donned their ceremonial silk vests and grey jackets and buckled their swords of office. As dusk approached, campfires were lit along the beaches and in the voyageur camps, and hundreds of candles were lit inside the Great Hall, where dozens of large plank tables had been set out for the feast. First Simon McTavish and the senior officers filed in, followed by all the skilled and more respectable trades such as interpreters, trade managers and important guides. Once they took their seats, the feast began. In the Great Hall, chefs from Montreal served up platters of roast beef, smoked hams and pork shoulder, steaming herbed whitefish and venison, maple sugar, corn and wild rice from the countryside. The fort's garden gave up its precious potatoes and carrots, and the sturdy meal was washed down with imported port and Madeira and a potent rum-and-brandy punch. The mostly Scottish men gorged and guzzled, boasted, bantered and toasted each other, McTavish presiding at the head of the table.

Once the meal lay heavily in their stomachs, the tables were cleared, and the musicians, hopefully having held off on consuming heroic quantities of punch, set up in front of the vast stone fireplace at the head of the room. The doors were pushed open and the waiting throng of voyageurs and Ojibwa, who had eaten outside, filed in and lined up along the walls. Simon McTavish paraded to the middle of the room with the daughter of a local Ojibwa chief bedecked in her finery, the musicians on cue launched into a traditional reel and the ball began. "For musick we had the Bag-Pipe, the Violin, the flue & the Fife, which enabled us to spend the evening agreeably," wrote the American traveller Daniel Harmon in 1801. "At the Ball there were a number of this Countries Ladies, whom I was surprised to find could behave themselves so well, and who danced not amiss."

But all good things must come to an end, and the next morning, bleary-eyed and sleep deprived, the various men of the North West Company set about their first tasks of the new business year. The officers began organizing their brigades, one group for the long haul back to Montreal with a fortune in bundled furs, the other for the gruelling trek back to the trading posts of the distant interior, Fort Chipewyan on Lake Athabasca being the farthest, many thousands of kilometres away. Many of these French-Canadian and Mohawk voyageurs were returning to their inland families.

IN THE SUMMER OF 1788, yet another young Scotsman, not surprisingly related in some way to the men in the clannish company hierarchy, came through Grand Portage on his way to the farthest outpost of the North West Company. His name was Alexander Mackenzie. The American Revolution had deprived Montreal of access to its habitual fur regions to the south of the Great Lakes, and an independent United States was beginning to restrict the commercial activities of British merchants from Montreal.

Mackenzie was born to a poor family on the Isle of Lewis in the Hebrides in 1764. The rocky mist-shrouded hills buffeted by gusty Atlantic winds was a stunningly beautiful but rugged land, prone to poverty and at the prey of distant landlords with little interest in minding the lives of the people who lived there. After his mother's death, and with poor crops and rising rents, the Mackenzie family was displaced from their land, and they emigrated to New York in 1775. A few months after they arrived, they were caught up in the American Revolution, and the elder Mackenzie joined a Royalist regiment while eleven-year-old Alexander was taken in by two aunts who took him north through New York to Canada.

At the age of fifteen, Mackenzie abandoned his schooling to join the fur trade in Montreal, where he found the job of a counting clerk to be boring. But the adventure and profits to be made in distant outposts was appealing. He was sent out to the rudimentary post at Île-à-la-Crosse (in present-day Saskatchewan), where he stayed until 1787. In this capacity he was evidently successful, and by the age of twenty-three he was a field partner in the North West Company, having served at several inland posts. In 1788, Simon McTavish, the "Premier," sent him to the North West Company's newest hinterland trading post, Fort Chipewyan on Lake Athabasca. Mackenzie was by now a handsome young man with ginger hair and a pleasant yet proud countenance. But he also had a burning ambition to better his lot in a hierarchal society, to accomplish something noteworthy, and he was willing to make sacrifices to achieve his goal.

Although Mackenzie was a bold and persuasive leader, he also seems to have had a proclivity toward narrow-mindedness that was at odds with many of the fur traders and travellers who preceded him, a harbinger of the shifting cultural forces that would undermine many of the sensible fur trade traditions that had reigned for over a century but would come under increasing pressure as the nineteenth century progressed. Mackenzie routinely referred to Indigenous peoples as "savages," and with a smug yet unjustified sense of superiority expressed his disappointment that missionaries hadn't had much success in converting the people to his religion. Their work, he lamented, was "obscured by the cloud of ignorance that darkened the human mind in those distant regions." Of course, in the not too distant past the English had called the Scottish savages.

FORT CHIPEWYAN WAS THE North West Company's bulkhead for expansion into the greatest growth region for furs, and the settlement quickly evolved into a smaller version of Grand Portage. Homecoming voyageurs were met with cheering and hugging wives, running children, the distribution of exotic presents, feasting and dancing—without the chefs from Montreal and the bagpipes, but no doubt just as merry. If the weather was poor, the festivities were held in the only building capable of hosting a crowd. Barely eight by seven metres, the grand cabin could be crammed with upwards of 150 men, women and children of varying ethnicities. After the brief celebration, many Indigenous peoples, who were mostly Denesuline or Chipewyan, began arriving, setting up their lodges on the grounds nearby, having come to shop for the new items. It was a festive time, but short-lived, before the people of the fort went back to the business of living and working in the distant primitive outpost.

While in Fort Chipewyan during the long, dark winter of 1787–88, Mackenzie, huddled in the smoky interior of the main cabin, was inspired by tales of a Northwest Passage and other geographical speculations promulgated by Peter Pond. Pond, by now forty-seven and an old man by fur trade standards, had obtained a chart of the Pacific coast of North America, based on Captain James Cook's rudimentary explorations in 1778, and his imagination ran wild with the possibilities of crossing the continent. On Cook's map, Pond zeroed in on an east-leading waterway, in the approximate latitude of Anchorage, that correlated to a vast river that flowed from the west shore of Great Slave Lake north of Lake Athabasca and that he had heard about from the local Dene-speaking peoples. Pond imagined that this river led west and connected to the inlet that he called Cook's River, which disgorged into the Pacific Ocean—that it was in fact the final link in an overland Northwest Passage. Pond made a detailed chart of the known geography and appended his own hopeful, if somewhat fanciful, additions and eagerly showed it to the young Mackenzie. Unfortunately, Pond made a grave error in calculating longitude with his fallible instruments and his lack of formal training in mathematics. Pond's map showed the distance between the two waterways to be a short canoe trip. In reality, it was many thousands of kilometres, although no one knew it at the time.

Pond's vision and ambition became Mackenzie's, as the astute young business-savvy officer understood fully the gains to be had if indeed the Pacific could be reached after a week of paddling from Great Slave Lake. Mackenzie, who was later to claim that the exploration of the river was the "favourite project of my own ambition," prepared to locate this river and follow it to its mouth. After moving Pond's original fur trade cabin to the shore of Lake Athabasca and naming it Fort Chipewyan, Mackenzie then interviewed and hired the people who would guide and travel with him on his voyage.

On June 3, 1789, he led three cargo canoes with five eastern voyageurs and six Chipewyan across the water from Fort Chipewyan on a grand adventure that he later claimed was sponsored by the North West Company. "We were accompanied also by an Indian who had acquired the title of English Chief and his two wives, in a small canoe, with two young Aboriginal people; his followers in another small canoe." The man was called Awgeenaw, or English Chief, because he "was one of the followers of the chief who conducted Mr. Hearne to the copper-mine river"—that would be Matonabbee, who had died in 1782—"and has since been a principal leader of his country-men who were in the habit of carrying furs to Churchill Factory . . . and till of late very much attached to the interest of that company." Awgeenaw also had a good working facility with several local Dene dialects, the Slavey, Dogrib and Beaver languages. On this journey, the women were paddlers and kept the clothing in repair, while the men were hunters and had general knowledge of the region, as well as being interpreters. Mackenzie noted that the Chipewyan were a handsome people, muscular and well proportioned. Their clothing was mostly made of dressed moose skin, or beaver prepared with fur for warmth, augmented by wool accoutrements from trade. The leather was colourfully and artfully painted, and adorned and woven with porcupine quills. Their shirts and leggings frequently were fringed with tassels of leather.

One of the first notable observations Mackenzie made concerned the swarms of mosquitoes and gnats that feasted upon the travellers and drove them to maddening frustration. Nevertheless, the twelve men paddled off down the Slave River during typical spring weather: overcast, windy and cold. One canoe and its supplies were wrecked in rapids before they reached Great Slave Lake, which the remaining explorers crossed and then began rounding along the still ice-bound northwestern shore. They spied a mighty river flowing west, just as foretold, and began paddling with uplifted spirits. Three hundred kilometres passed in excitement with the Rocky Mountains visible on the horizon, before the river abruptly lurched northward. Hoping it was a temporary diversion, the two canoes paddled on from dawn to dusk each day, often covering over 150 kilometres before the men dropped into an exhausted slumber on the shore.

In early July, so far north the sun never set but swirled overhead in a tight circular motion, the two tiny boats were winding their way through the convoluted maze of islands and channels of a vast delta. Growing increasingly dismayed and frightened, Mackenzie grounded the canoes and with a couple of companions set off to climb to the tallest point of land on one of the islands. From this treeless perch he scanned the horizon and beheld a bleak sprawl, the dirty pack ice of the "Hyperborean Sea." He despondently returned to the canoes, now thinking of the Deh Cho River as the "River of Disappointment."

They paddled the remaining distance to the coast, where Mackenzie knew his great gamble to find the Northwest Passage had failed—the body of water was undoubtedly the Arctic, and not the Pacific, Ocean. In a state of reckless abandon, perhaps induced by the unexpected defeat, Mackenzie ordered his canoes into the turbulent sea to give chase to a flock of frolicking beluga whales he'd spotted near the ice edge. The whales were too elusive to be captured, and later Mackenzie related his relief that no ill had befallen the party as a result of his uncharacteristic abandon. "It was, indeed, a very wild and unreflecting enterprise, and it was a very fortunate circumstance that we failed in our attempt to overtake them, as a stroke from the tail of one of these enormous fishes would have dashed the canoe to pieces. We may, perhaps, have been indebted to the foggy weather for our safety, as it prevented us from continuing our pursuit . . . We were in a state of actual danger, and felt every corresponding emotion of pleasure when we reached the land."

Disappointed with his final destination, Mackenzie immediately turned back for Fort Chipewyan, paddling upstream up to fifty kilometres a day, using sails to propel the boats along peaceful stretches of the river and across Great Slave Lake, and arrived on September 12 with the first snows of the season already dusting the land. Mackenzie had accomplished this arduous journey of over 4,800 kilometres in only 102 days. The Deh Cho, what is now called the Mackenzie River, is the largest river basin in Canada and the second largest in North America. From its beginnings in the Rocky Mountains, where it is named the Peace River, to the Arctic Ocean, the Mackenzie is 4,241 kilometres in length and never less than half a kilometre wide. To this day, the region surrounding the Mackenzie River is mostly sparsely populated but features magnificent scenery.

Mackenzie's journey down the Deh Cho was less of a curiosity-driven pioneering expedition into the unknown and inhospitable wilderness as it was a guided tour down a well-travelled waterway in a lightly populated land. Never did Mackenzie go anywhere without his numerous Indigenous guides and translators, and seldom did he travel more than two days without observing inhabitants along the shore of the great river. He was, however, critical of the behaviour of both his guides and his French-Canadian porters, believing them to be inferior to himself in all ways, including appetite and ability to consume alcohol. In one instance that reveals much about his attitude and character, Mackenzie wrote, "I had to watch the savage who was our guide, or to guard against those of his tribe who might meditate our destruction. I had, also, the passions and fears of others to control and subdue. Today I had to assuage the rising discontents, and on the morrow to cheer the fainting spirits of the people who accompanied me . . . The voyaging Canadians are equally indolent, extravagant and improvident when left to them-selves, and rival the savages in neglect of the morrow." Mackenzie never did name his guides and co-explorers, evidently imagining himself superior despite his being an infant in the country without them. In his own proud mind, there was always one shining individual who towered above the others: himself.

Mackenzie struggled with Awgeenaw over leadership even as he tried to lead the man through his own country. On one occasion, Mackenzie accused Awgeenaw of deliberately scaring off from the shore a band of people Mackenzie had wanted to speak with; he berated him for it and claimed that he had every right to be angry. Mackenzie also boasted that he accused Awgeenaw of not hunting out of jealousy, and said "that I had come a great way, and at a very considerable expense, without having completed the object of my wishes, and that I suspected he had con-cealed from me a principal part of what the natives had told him respect-ing the country, lest he should be obliged to follow me: that his reason for not killing game, &c. was his jealousy." Awgeenaw then apparently "got into a most violent passion," denying Mackenzie's claims and refus-ing to hunt or even travel with him anymore. Being led through his own country by a foreigner was too much to bear. Whether or not Awgeenaw was keeping secrets from Mackenzie, perhaps in an effort to create for himself a lucrative role similar to that of Matonabbee years earlier, the next day Mackenzie was forced to approach him and apologize. "I could not well do without them," he reluctantly admitted. For the next two and a half decades, Awgeenaw worked for the North West Company as a hunter and a carrier of goods to distant peoples along the upper Peace River. Later, he was based out of Fort Chipewyan, before he switched his allegiance to the Hudson's Bay Company in 1815, during the time of intercompany conflict and when the big game for food had become scarce from overhunting.

There was one person Mackenzie spoke with on his dispiriting return voyage who was an inspiration and gave him a tantalizing glimpse of what lay farther west. Awgeenaw met some people camped along the shore, and when he called Mackenzie's canoe over, Mackenzie questioned them. The man was a Dogrib who had "left his own Lands [to the west] on acct of some Quarrals," and he understood Awgeenaw's dialect perfectly. He told Awgeenaw, who told Mackenzie, that there was a river to the south and west on the other side of the mountains that was much larger than the Deh Cho and "that the Natives [there] are Big and very wicked, kill Common Men with their Eyes, that they make Canoes larger than Ours, that those at the Entry kill a kind of large Beaver the Skin of which is almost Red . . . he knows of no Communication by water to the above River, those of the Natives who saw it went over the mountains on foot." These distant foreigners also apparently had enormous appetites and could devour a large beaver at a single meal.

MACKENZIE SPENT THE WINTER AT Fort Chipewyan attending to business before joining the southeast brigade to Grand Portage in the spring of 1790. He was vexed that his expedition was hardly mentioned at the gathering. But really, what immediate use was his expedition to a business enterprise that lived and died on its ability to exchange goods for furs? Entertaining, perhaps, but hardly worth writing a song about. Nevertheless, the partners awarded Mackenzie an additional share in the enterprise, and during the next decade the Nor'Westers expanded their fur trading posts northward along the Deh Cho, displacing various Indigenous intermediaries. By the 1820s, the region had become one of the most profitable and valuable districts in their enterprise.

But in 1791, after many months scouring maps and brooding on his expedition and his future, Mackenzie asked McTavish and the other partners for a leave of absence to travel to London and learn mathematics, navigation, astronomy and cartography. He sailed in the fall and did not return to Fort Chipewyan until the fall of 1792, when he was ready to follow up on rumours from various Indigenous peoples he and others had consulted with who described a magnificent river flowing west through the "Shining Mountains." Mackenzie had also read a newly published book by a British sea captain who had been on the Pacific coast searching for sea otters to trade with China, John Meares's *Voyage Made in the Years 1788 and 1789 from China to the North West Coast of America.* Mackenzie had also read books written by Cook's officers who had joined the sea otter trade which contained various rudimentary charts of the coast, each presenting a variation of inlets and rivers that led into the heart of the continent. Surely this was proof that a route must be possible. Mackenzie's plan was to paddle with a small crew up the Peace River to its source in the mountains and then continue west across the continental divide and hope to find a river that he could then follow down to the Pacific Ocean. Mackenzie's partners no doubt hoped that he would unlock the secret to even more fur terrain to fuel the young company's expansion and battle with the venerable Hudson's Bay Company.

On October 10, Mackenzie departed Fort Chipewyan at the head of three heavily laden canoes and began paddling up the Peace River, heading southwest and scouting for a good place to overwinter so as to get an early start the next spring. They selected a spot near the junction of the Peace and Smoky Rivers that Mackenzie's scouts had located and called Fort Fork (present-day Peace River Landing, in Alberta) where they built a small and primitive cabin, the beginnings of another fur trade outpost. During the winter it was so cold and "the frost was so severe that the axes of the workmen became almost as brittle as glass." Yet Mackenzie also recorded his relief when a chinook rolled in—warm, fresh wind that tumbled down the mountains, bringing a taste of the coast to the interior: "the atmosphere became so warm that it dissolved all the snow on the ground; even the ice was covered with water, and had the same appearance as when it is breaking up in the spring." Mackenzie, not aware of the weather phenomenon of a chinook, thought that it might be an indicator that he was close to the Pacific Ocean. In fact, he was eight hundred kilometres from the coast as the bird flies, not that his own journey would be anywhere near as straight and predictable.

Mackenzie was ready to depart to the west on May 9, 1793. Six canoes of furs obtained in the winter's trading were sent back to Fort Chipewyan, and two men were left behind at the fort. The adventuring party included two Indigenous guides from the nearby Dene-speaking Beaver tribe, one of whom was jocularly called Cancre because of his youthful idleness. Also in the party were Mackenzie's younger cousin, Alexander MacKay, and six Canadian voyageurs, Charles Ducette, Joseph Landry, François Beaulieux, Baptiste Bisson, François Courtois and Jacques Beauchamp—two of whom were members of the Arctic Ocean expedition a few years earlier. In general, it was Mackenzie's custom to name everyone on his expeditions except for the Indigenous guides and hunters. They were accompanied by their pet dog, which had no name other than "our dog," but who was nevertheless a companion to all. For this adventure, Mackenzie had a greater preoccupation with accuracy, bolstered by his new knowledge of how to calculate longitude to help him plot his course and keep records. Although they still had to travel light through unknown rugged terrain, Mackenzie brought along a compass, a sextant, a chronometer and a large telescope. He hoped that with more detailed astronomical plotting of the geographic position of Fort Chipewyan, and access to the charts of the Pacific coast, he would be better able to plan his route westward.

Their single boat was an astonishing piece of Indigenous technology: made of birchbark, sealed with pine and spruce pitch and sewn together with willow roots, it was extremely light and durable. "Her dimensions were twenty-five feet long within, exclusive of the curves of stem and stern, twenty-six inches hold, and four feet nine inches beam. At the same time she was so light, that two men could carry her on a good road three or four miles without resting. In this slender vessel, we shipped provisions, goods for presents, arms, ammunition, and baggage, to the weight of three thousand pounds, and an equipage of ten people." After only a few days of paddling through the Peace valley, they were awed by the magnificent scenery through which they floated. The land was coming alive in the warm spring weather. "This magnificent theatre of nature has all the decorations which the trees and animals of the country can afford it. Groves of poplar in every shape vary the scene; and their intervals are enlivened with vast herds of elks and buffaloes." Despite his claiming to have no literary pretensions, Mackenzie evidently spent considerable time on his descriptions. "The whole country," he proclaimed, "displayed an exuberant verdure; the trees that bear a blossom were advancing fast to that delightful appearance, and the velvet rind of their branches reflecting the oblique rays of a rising or setting sun, added a splendid gaiety to the scene . . . The East side of the river consists of a range of high land covered with the white spruce and the soft birch, while the banks abound with the alder and the willow." Soon the snow-capped peaks of the Rocky Mountains appeared close on the horizon, and spirits were high. Ruminants were grazing in the clearings and along the riverbank, including bison with their "young ones frisking about them." But they didn't encounter any people, which seemed odd to Mackenzie. He didn't want to unnecessarily fire guns announcing their presence in case that might spook anyone he hoped to gain information from, so they set loose the trusty dog to chase some bison toward the river. That evening they feasted on roast bison and washed it down with rum as they lounged around a campfire, satisfied with their good fortune. Of course it couldn't last.

Soon they entered the Peace River Canyon, where the sides of the river grew steep and blocked the view, dashing their hopes of an easy float toward the Pacific. Water levels were high with the spring runoff. They were soon facing thirty turbulent kilometres of rapids beneath near-vertical cliffs, where "dangers immediately presented themselves, for stones, both small and great, were continually rolling from the bank" toward where the men hauled the canoe ever westward with ropes, frequently unloading and carrying the provisions. They worked over four portages, thankful for the light canoe, while the river swirled with eddies and back currents. "It was with the utmost difficulty," Mackenzie wrote, "we could prevent her from being dashed to pieces against the rocks by the violence of the eddies." A few hours later they again feared disaster as they plowed along through a turbulent scene where "the river above us, as far as we could see, was one white sheet of foaming water." Men were grumbling and muttering about returning to safety, and the brutal work of hauling the canoe and cargo grew worse when they began encountering a proliferation of three-metre-tall broad-leafed plants that were covered in "small prickles which caught our trousers, and working through them, and sometimes found their way to the flesh." (The plant is the devil's club.)

By May 29, they had cleared the canyon and found themselves amidst snow-covered mountains. (The region is now flooded by the W.A.C. Bennett Dam.) Two days later they came upon a bifurcation in the river, the Finlay River flowing from the northwest and the Parsnip from the southwest. Luckily one of Mackenzie's interpreters, either Cancre or the other Indigenous man whom Mackenzie failed to name, had spoken to an older Indigenous man at Fort Fork before they departed. This man had explored the region and advised them against the northern route, warning him that it wended its way ever smaller and became lost in the mountains. Even though it looked more promising, Mackenzie heeded the advice and opted for the Parsnip, which was a frustrating river to ascend. They made "a very tardy and mortifying progress" over the course of weeks of brutal slogging upstream without encountering any people. Spurred on by the old man's reports of "a carrying place to another large river . . . where the inhabitant's build houses, and live upon islands," Mackenzie urged, cajoled and pressured his team to continue just a little farther. The current was strong and the progress disappointing, the waters still swollen with spring.

Rounding a curve of the forest-lined chute of foaming water in early June, the smell of camp smoke drifted through the air. They scanned the forest. Two men leaped from cover "brandishing their spears, displaying their bows and arrows, and accompanying their hostile gestures with loud vociferations." They were Sekani, the "people of the rocks," a northern interior Athapaskan-speaking Dene people, game hunters with a language and culture similar to other Dene language groups. The Sekani had extensive trade and travel networks throughout what is now the northern interior of British Columbia.

Once the drama of the standoff petered out, Mackenzie asked Cancre to ask them some questions. It turned out that the group consisted of only three men, three women and eight children, who had never encountered European-looking people before and knew of no mighty River of the West such as Mackenzie sought. Yet intriguingly, they had small pieces of iron obtained in trade from other people farther west near the "stinking lake." Apparently, there were only about fifty people in total in the entire region.

Mackenzie passed out a small collection of exotic items—beads, ribbons and bells—and offered them some pemmican to eat and handed out small sugar cubes to the children. He pondered his options while his men lounged and grumbled. He considered returning to the branching of the river and trying his luck ascending the Finlay River, or perhaps abandoning his canoe and striking overland in search of a trail. He suspiciously worried that his information was distorted, by poor interpretation or by the duplicity of either his translator or the people.

The next morning, Mackenzie thought he overheard one of the Sekani say their word for a big river, and so he strolled over and asked the man to sketch for him a map on parchment using charcoal. According to this map, if Mackenzie continued upstream he would encounter a series of small lakes and portages that connected to a small river. Mackenzie hired the man as a guide and they all set off together. Two days later they were crossing one of the small lakes, which was in flood, but they easily found a well-worn trail leading from the far end of the lake up to a ridge now called Arctic Lake. Mackenzie soon realized that he had crossed the height of land, from whence water flowed in the opposite direction, not back to the Parsnip and the Peace to the Athabasca and Great Slave Lake and down the Deh Cho to the "Frozen Ocean." The water instead flowed west, and he optimistically named a small nearby lake Pacific Lake.

The new water system lay before them: streams that led to Pacific Lake. At an old camp they spied cedar baskets with fishing nets and other paraphernalia, which Mackenzie took. Ever the trader seeking to develop new markets, he left in return a knife, flint, beads and awls. Over the next several days, through waters in flood and overflowing their banks, they tried to head west and down through "a fearful detail of rapid currents, fallen trees and large stones" that Mackenzie descriptively named Bad River (now the James River). Once, when Mackenzie got out of the boat to lighten the load, the voyageurs demanded he stay. "With great earnestness," he reported, they "requested me to re-think, declaring, at the same time, that if they perished, I should perish with them. I did not then imagine in how short a period their apprehension would be justified." Fear intensified when the canoe slammed into a rock in the thrashing rapids, pitched sideways, took on water and ground to a stop on a gravel bar before being sucked downstream through the foaming boulder fields, cracking into rocks and knocking the men about. One man grabbed for a small tree on the shore to help stop the plunging of the canoe and was violently yanked out and flung ashore. The roaring rapids and cascades commanded the canoe and tore it asunder, spilling the men and their goods into the torrent. They grasped at chunks of wreckage while being spun downstream gasping for air until the whole shattered rig drifted ashore in an eddy.

Weeping and shivering, having stared death in the face and barely escaped, the travellers had little enthusiasm for further exploration. The cargo and all their provisions were mostly gone and destroyed. They managed to rescue a bale containing eighty pounds of gunpowder, however, and they laid it out to dry in the sun. Mackenzie passed out the rum as he urged his indifferent guides to continue just a little farther. Perhaps he passed out too much rum. At one point he looked up to see an exhausted and intemperate voyageur strolling over to the swath of drying gunpowder while smoking his pipe. "I need not add," Mackenzie dryly noted in his journal, "that one spark might have put a period to all my anxiety and ambition."

Although they had salvaged barely a month's worth of food, Mackenzie exhorted them and appealed to their honour and reputation until they agreed to keep going. On June 17, they finally came to a river that could actually be navigated safely, McGregor River, and floated downstream until it intersected with an even bigger river, what would become known as the Fraser. Here Mackenzie sent two scouts ahead and they returned after being shot at with arrows. Making a wide berth of that particular patch of shore, they cruised until they rounded a bend and stopped to inspect an abandoned cedarwood lodge. The building was nine by six metres, with three separate rooms. It was a Dakelh-Carrier seasonal fishing lodge that also had a large drying rack for salmon.

As they continued poling down the Fraser, they were again shot at with arrows. Mackenzie was nothing if not brave. Deciding on his "adventurous project," he stepped ashore and walked alone along the bank of the river, displaying interesting trade goods in his outstretched arms. Eighteen men quietly came forward and sat down, and Mackenzie called his two interpreters over. Several dozen other people were nearby, including a captured Sekani man, several Shuswap from farther south and a woman who understood Cree because she had been sold as a slave twice, each time progressing farther west. She could converse with Cancre. Although communication was challenging, Mackenzie received a disheartening description of the river ahead. He learned that it was clearly not meant for canoe travel. This stretch of the Fraser is one of Canada's most chaotic and dangerous rivers. Riddled with rapids and falls, it is nearly impassable. These people also told him that the people to the west were apparently "a very malignant race, who lived in large subterraneous recesses; and when they were made to understand that it was our design to proceed to the sea, they dissuaded us from prosecuting our intention, as we should certainly become a sacrifice to the savage spirit of the natives. These people they described as possessing iron, arms, and utensils, which they procured from their neighbours to the Westward, and were obtained by a commercial progress from people like ourselves, who brought them in great canoes."

He convened a conference on June 23 to determine the best course of action—whether to continue along the river despite the forewarned danger or instead veer off to the west on an unknown tributary. Mackenzie's leadership style, bold and commanding, brooking no questions, and his pride had earned him a reputation among his fellow travellers as a know-it-all. Mackenzie was shocked when one of the Dakelh-Carrier men he was prodding for information jocularly questioned his authority. As the meeting began the man asked, "What can be the reason that you are so particular and anxious in your inquiries of us respecting a knowledge of this country: do not you white men know everything in the world?" Momentarily at a loss for words, and lacking the subtle sense of humour to appreciate the comment, Mackenzie belatedly launched into an earnest defence. "We certainly were acquainted," he said, "with the principal circumstances of every part of the world; that I knew where the sea is, and where I myself then was, but that I did not exactly understand what obstacles might interrupt me getting to it; with which he and his relations must be well acquainted, as they had so frequently surmounted them." Although Mackenzie lacked local knowledge, he did possess a global perspective of world geography not known to the Dakelh-Carrier or to others on his journey, and he was smug and self-important enough to boast of it. "Thus," he proclaimed, "I fortunately preserved the impression in their minds, of the superiority of white people over themselves."

The Dakelh-Carrier inhabited the sub-boreal inland forest regions of central British Columbia along the Fraser River and north as far as

Fur trader, explorer and lovable rogue Pierre-Esprit Radisson.

Prince Rupert of the Rhine, shown in his royal finery in an official portrait from 1670.

Pierre Le Moyne d'Iberville, the French explorer and naval commander who bedevilled the Company and captured their outposts in Hudson Bay in the late seventeenth century.

A foppish Samuel Hearne in the 1790s, after he returned to London.

An Iroquois warrior with musket, in a sketch from 1795 by J.G. de St. Sauveur. Iroquois were the preferred enforcers hired by both the North West Company and the Hudson's Bay Company during the turbulent years when the companies were warring.

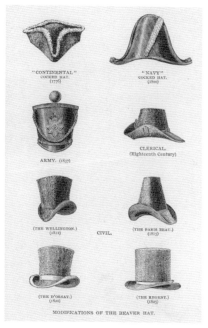

Collecting the bodies of plague
victims on a London street.

Hats in stylish beaver fur, from a
nineteenth-century monograph.

The *Nonsuch* returns to London in October 1669, in this imagined scene from
an early Hudson's Bay Company calendar. Painting by Norman Wilkinson.

A Debarquem.t des Munitions de guerre et de Bouche B. Camp de Bourbon .C. Mortie caché dans le Bois D Escarmouches . E. Fort de Nelson .

D'Iberville's attack on York Factory in September 1697.
Engraving by Jean-Baptiste Scotin.

Attickasish shows Anthony Henday the bison in 1754,
as imagined in this scene by Charles W. Jeffreys.

The drafty stone outpost of Prince of Wales Fort, in a sketch made circa 1770.

The spring brigade leaves Lachine for the west in the 1820s, in this imagined scene from an early Hudson's Bay Company calendar. Painting by Franklin Arbuckle.

Indigenous voyageurs heft ninety-pound packs of furs at a Company trading post in the 1800s. Painting by Henry Alexander Ogden, 1882.

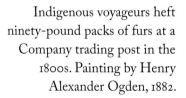

David Thompson,
in an artist's impression based
on historical accounts.

Cuthbert Grant,
the Scot-Cree elected military
leader of the Métis.

The Little Emperor: Sir George
Simpson, governor of the
Hudson's Bay Territories.

Dr. John McLoughlin,
the King of Old Oregon.

Sir James Douglas was simultaneously the
Company's chief factor at Fort Victoria and
the governor of the crown colony of
Vancouver Island.

Samuel Hearne builds Cumberland House, 1774-75, in this imagined scene from an early Hudson's Bay Company calendar. Painting by Franklin Arbuckle.

Winter fishing on the Assiniboine and Red Rivers, showing Fort Garry (Fort Gibraltar) in this 1821 watercolour by Peter Rindisbacher.

A Métis buffalo hunt on the prairies. Painting by Paul Kane, 1846.

A mid-nineteenth-century Métis family with Red River carts.

Métis drivers with Red River ox carts, circa 1860.

The idyllic Company settlement at Fort Vancouver, Washington.
Painting by Lieutenant Henry Warre, 1845.

Steamship *S.S. Beaver* anchored off Fort Victoria, circa 1846,
in this imagined scene from an early Hudson's Bay Company calendar.
Painting by A. Sherriff Scott.

modern-day Prince George, a rugged, hilly land of lakes and rivers, with cold winters and hot, sultry, bug-infested summers. They were hunters as well as salmon fishers. Throughout their territory there was extensive trade along the so-called grease trails, an exchange of dried meats and berries, furs and hides for the ubiquitous "grease," which was actually the oil extracted from eulachons (more prosaically known as candlefish), which were rotted or fermented in large vats, mixed with boiling water and the oil skimmed off the top. Extremely nutritious, the prepared oil, and the dried fish, was a mainstay of the coastal economy and considered a delicacy. Other prized goods from the coast were smoked eulachon and dried seaweed (similar to nori), a source of vitamin B_{12}.

On the advice of the people, Mackenzie decided to spurn the south-flowing Fraser and paddle along the smaller tributary, abandon their canoe, load their goods into packs and head on foot overland to the west along the clear broad path that then lay before them. It is a testament to Mackenzie's leadership and powers of persuasion that there was no dissent from his nine exhausted and weary fellow travellers. Mackenzie consulted his charts, took some readings to calculate longitude and concluded that he couldn't be far from the ocean, at least according to the information presented in Meares's book. He and his troop were at the head of one of the principal grease trails and now were assured of a good, easy road that avoided the defiles of the mountains, kept only to the low valleys and was clear of deadfall. This road was a well-worn, vital and long-standing traditional artery of commerce. Mackenzie learned that it would take him to a people with large wooden canoes who lived on a river that led to the ocean.

It was now July 4, and soon they were joined by four people from a Dakelh-Carrier tribe heading in the same direction on their own journey. In the evening they quietly sang wistful songs as everyone drifted off to sleep. Mackenzie noted that one man had a metal knife and another had a dressed sea otter pelt that had obviously originated from the coast. The next morning, Mackenzie, through his interpreter, offered to pay one of the men to guide them down the road for a while. As the days passed, they kept encountering people along the trail, primarily Dakelh-Carrier and Nuxalk (Bella Coola) from farther west. One large group consisted of five families travelling west with packs of goods for trade. The women had their hair neatly plaited and decorated and were clad in fine leather garments; they chatted amiably as they enjoyed a pleasant summer journey. Each person, including the children, shouldered suitably-sized packs as they meandered at a leisurely pace toward their destination.

At each new village, the foreigners were welcomed and they were able to hire new guides to keep them on track to the coast. Mackenzie grew excited with each promising new rumour about the nearness of the salt water. The land was now forested, and the trail followed the shores of lakes and rivers. News of their arrival preceded them and they no longer excited fear; instead they were presented with baskets of berries and delicacies such as salmon roe in strong aromatic oil as offerings of welcome. Unfortunately, salmon caviar was an acquired taste and some of the men, used as they were to the earthy fare of the interior aspen parkland, found the smell and taste repugnant, and they were pleased when a hunter shot a caribou and they roasted steaks for dinner.

On July 17 they were in sight of the mighty Coast Mountains, and soon after they began a long climb, struggling under the weight of their heavy packs. One mountain dominated the others, a rocky, snow-capped beast. "Before us appeared a stupendous mountain, whose snow-clad summit was lost in the clouds; between it and our immediate course, flowed the river to which we were going." It is still called Stupendous Mountain. They trudged along a path with snow packed hard by countless feet, unmelted even in the height of summer. Soon they reached the Bella Coola Gorge, a ninety-metre-deep plunge through forested ledges to the river below, into a land of cedar forests and turbulent glacier-fed waterways surrounded by looming mountains with overhanging ice fields. The trail wended through a forest of monstrous shaggy cedar, hemlock, spruce and fir, many of them larger than any tree any of them had ever seen, with the upper foliage lost in the mist.

From a vantage in the distance they had spied a village along a river, and once they had followed the path down to the valley bottom, Mackenzie went ahead and strolled right in and began approaching people and shaking their hands. The people were the Nuxalk, or Bella Coolas, part of the culturally and linguistically similar Salish culture that lived in the southern interior of B.C. and the Pacific coast from Oregon to northern B.C., including the territory where the cities of Seattle, Vancouver and Victoria are now situated. They are distinguished for their common architecture of large cedar longhouses that spaciously housed up to forty extended family, and are known for their intricate wood carving, particularly ornamental masks, and their elaborate dances and ceremonies.

Mackenzie dropped his pack and sat down upon it exhausted. Villagers came over, and he was welcomed without surprise and was pointed in the direction of the big cedar longhouse of the chief. He walked between great wooden posts and up a set of stairs, through a doorway and into an airy but dimly lit communal hall with three fires burning along its length. He was quietly offered a seat on a long wooden bench around a great board and waited for his companions to arrive. When the companions were seated, a man with a countenance of great dignity rose and clapped his hands and women arrived bearing woven mats upon which were displayed cedar platters of herbed roasted salmon. They ate in silence since they had no ability to understand each other's language. When the feast was over, attendants prepared a fire outside in the common ground and laid out sleeping boards made from the planks of giant trees. Mackenzie and his men were instructed to sit, and a dessert of pounded salmon roe mixed with berries and herbs was brought. "Regaled with these delicacies," they settled in for sleep. "I never enjoyed a more sound and refreshing rest," Mackenzie recalled.

For breakfast, the travellers supped upon more roasted salmon and bowls of ripe raspberries and gooseberries. The next day they toured the village, inspecting the stately cedar buildings and the communal weir across the river that seemed to provide unlimited fresh fish. The people of the village were muscular and vigorous, wearing colourful soft cedar bark robes trimmed in silky dark sea otter fur. The women's hair was neatly trimmed, while the men's was worked into long plaits. Mackenzie called the place Friendly Village, and indeed they were well received as novel travellers from a distant eastern land. The villagers even lent them two durable cedar canoes to continue their downstream voyage, along with seven young men to paddle and help guide them the fifty kilometres to the ocean inlet. During the voyage Mackenzie, no stranger to observing feats of canoe dexterity and skill, beheld athleticism that would have secured the respect of the most skilled voyageur. Approaching a salmon weir, the Friendly Villagers paddled furiously and the large canoe "shot up and over it without taking a drop of water." After several other displays of prowess, Mackenzie admitted that his voyageurs "were inferior to these people, as they themselves acknowledged, in conducting those vessels."

By the end of the day they came to Nooskulst, the "Great Village," an important trading centre and the largest town in the valley, situated at the mouth of the Noosgulch River. Its two hundred or so people dwelt in four thirty-by-twelve-metre cedar lodges. At first it seemed as if their arrival was causing tension, as many of the young men were armed. But then the chief came forward and gave Mackenzie a big hug, and then they were all hugging each other. The chief's bearded son draped a magnificent sea otter robe around Mackenzie's shoulders, and Mackenzie in turn presented him with a pair of scissors, with which he began trimming his beard. Communication was awkward, conducted in sign language, since no one present could translate between any of the languages spoken. Nevertheless, they were regaled with a three-hour feast of savoury flame-roasted salmon on cedar planks and cakes of tender sweet hemlock bark. The platters were artfully adorned with red-and-black paintings of stylized animals and fringed with intricate carvings.

Mackenzie was impressed in particular with the intricately crafted decorative cedar chests and great stockpiles of dried salmon. The voyageurs admired a finely crafted fourteen-metre-long cedar canoe carved from a single massive cedar log, adorned front and rear with black-and-white stylized images of fishes, while the gunwales were rimmed in gleaming white sea otter teeth. The canoe matched James Cook's 1778 description of huge cedar dugout canoes with "human" teeth. American and British sea otter traders had become frequent visitors to the coast by the mid-1780s, and Mackenzie noted many items that had come to these people through trade, particularly copper items. Copper was highly valued, especially sheets of raw metal that could be tooled into innumerable decorative and practical items.

In the morning, the magnificent cedar canoe was made ready and four young men, among them the chief's son, readied themselves to accompany Mackenzie to the coast. The language barrier had improved somewhat as dialects became more familiar, and they understood Mackenzie's desire. The travellers had to leave "dog" behind, which made them a little sad after all the adventures the little beast had accompanied them on. The next day, they pulled ashore and slept at another large village of six communal lodges that was unoccupied, as the inhabitants were inland. (The village was called Q'umk'uts or Komkotes and was at the site of the modern-day town of Bella Coola.)

The voyage down the turbulent, swift-flowing river finally led to a long, snaking inlet of the Pacific Ocean at the mouth of the Bella Coola River. They detected the tangy smell of the ocean and saw the seaweed-lined shores of present-day North Bentinck Arm. It was salt water but it wasn't the open ocean. As they continued along the winding inlet, the water became turbulent and the winds picked up. The hosts and guides became quiet and nervous-looking and were loath to continue. They paddled ashore for the night and ate a fire-cooked porcupine for dinner.

When they next paddled out into the inlet, they beheld three large canoes crowded with fifteen young male warriors bearing down quickly.

These people were Bella Bella (Heiltsuk, from the Wakashan language family), a group culturally and linguistically distinct from the Coast Salish, and also prevalent on and around Vancouver Island and the northern Pacific coast. They were renowned for their arts, carving and spiritual ceremonies, including the potlatch. The three canoes cruised up aggressively and surrounded the travellers, and the warriors reached into their canoe and grabbed items to inspect. These people were familiar with the European/American coastal traders. One man, Mackenzie recalled, told them that "a large canoe had lately been in this bay, with people like me, and that one of them, who he called 'Macubah' had fired on him and his friends." Mackenzie took Macubah to be Captain George Vancouver, who had been on a British government surveying and charting mission in the 1790s and, unknown to Mackenzie, had been in the region just sixteen days earlier. (None of the records from Vancouver's voyage mention any aggression or conflict, so historians suspect that the reference could have been to a conflict with other traders around the same time.)

When Mackenzie and his cohorts decided to paddle farther west along the Dean Channel, the Heiltsuk followed them to see what they were up to. Finally, a man whom Mackenzie called a "troublesome fellow" forced his way into their boat and began toying with Mackenzie's possessions and clothing. When he finally returned to his own canoe, he demanded that the travellers follow him up a smaller channel to his village. Feeling nervous and now surrounded, Mackenzie knew it was time to go.

They paddled across the narrow inlet as ten more canoes of Heiltsuk, each containing three to six men, paddled quickly toward them. Mackenzie, who had not experienced anything but welcome on his travels so far, became "very apprehensive that some hostile design was meditated against us." The shore here was very steep and rocky, and the travellers left their canoe and quickly scrambled up to the top of a defensive rock, while the Heiltsuk began yelling. Some of them asked to trade, but they appeared to not be interested in the meagre supply of items that Mackenzie had remaining. At sunset, the gathered Heiltsuk paddled back across the water, leaving the travellers to a miserable night eating dried rations while huddled around a sputtering fire atop the rocky promontory.

In the morning they spied two large cedar canoes similar to their own, with a great number of people in each, paddling swiftly toward them, and the Nuxalk guide, fearing for the worst, "renewed his entreaties for our departure as they would soon come to shoot their arrows, and hurl their spears at us." The man grew agitated and implored Mackenzie to escape before they were trapped and killed.

Mackenzie had been busy completing the astronomical observations to fix his latitude and longitude as proof of his accomplishment. Once he was done, he rushed over to a large rock and got out some materials he had brought along perhaps for this precise purpose. He quickly inscribed his famous epigraph in vermilion, a red pigment used to mark bales in the fur trade, mixed with bear grease: "Alexander Mackenzie, from Canada, by land, 22nd July, 1793."

Chapter Ten

THE COLUMBIA ENTERPRISE

Once Mackenzie had scrawled his famous words on the stone on July 22, he heeded the anxious and strenuous urgings of his Nuxalk guide and ordered the men to begin paddling back to Q'umk'uts at the mouth of the Bella Coola River. Paddling furiously all night, the ten adventurers managed to outrun their Heiltsuk pursuers. Once they passed this dangerous place where the formerly friendly chief was now brooding and sullen because he had erroneously believed his son injured by Mackenzie, the journey was challenging but uneventful. After three days of paddling and portaging east upstream they discovered their "lost friend," the dog, who was now skeletal and wary of them, whimpering and dodging away whenever anyone approached. Now on a well-trodden path, they lured him in by leaving a trail of food behind them as they trudged east until the poor beast was able to "recover his former sagacity."

During the remainder of the month-long trek through the Coastal Range, the weary travellers grew weak when their food ran out and they were racked by a series of unexplained colds and headaches. Mackenzie staggered along on swollen, aching ankles, while one of their guides even had to be carried intermittently. By early August they were ascending the upper reaches of the Fraser and circling the series of small lakes at the Continental Divide. Once they struck the banks of the east-flowing Peace River and followed it a little distance, herds of bison congregated in the grasslands and they hunted for food. The weather was hot and dry, and they wended their way through the foothills. Invigorated by a diet of roasted country meats, they reached Fort Chipewyan on August 24 after an odyssey of 107 days, the hectic return averaging an incredible fifty-eight kilometres a day.

The winter at Fort Chipewyan was uneventful and anticlimactic. Mackenzie chaffed at the bit to bring news of his adventures to his partners at Grand Portage. In the dark and cold he found himself growing listless and morose, a lack of energy he had never experienced before. His mind wandered when he tried to write an account of his adventures, and his isolated quarters brought on dark moods. Fur trading was boring compared with exciting travel, and he considered the daily routine of managing the fort mundane and beneath him. He resolved to quit the life of a field partner and become a strategist and manager. In a letter to a friend, he fumed with impatience and claimed, "I think it unpardonable in any man to remain in this country who can afford to leave it."

The next season at Grand Portage, he pressed his partners to push the trade to the Pacific, and over the next year voiced his ideas in Montreal and London, urging for a cessation of the increasing hostilities between the North West Company and the Hudson's Bay Company, perhaps even a merger. Energy was being wasted, he claimed, and progress thwarted as the companies grappled with each other. A consolidated monopoly, firmly controlled from London and Montreal, would be a great bulwark against American expansionism, a northern empire of commerce that would be an appendage of the British Empire. He became a managing partner in Montreal, buoyed by the faith placed in him by other wintering partners who hoped that he would understand their concerns and work to improve conditions.

Mackenzie's geopolitical musings were perhaps the first from a fur trade agent who assumed that Indigenous peoples had no inherent sovereignty and should naturally fall under the authority of Britain—that indeed the fur trade should not be a commercial enterprise but should have the political purpose of controlling the northern part of the continent. Mackenzie was never really a good fur trader and certainly not inclined that way by temperament. He was more of a big-picture planner and an imperial dreamer. He had no interest in Indigenous peoples or their culture or society, nor an interest in living off the land or having a country family. He wanted to make money, earn fame and return to a city life at the hub of political and cultural activity.

When Mackenzie's exhortations fell on deaf ears, and after he engaged Simon McTavish in a failed struggle for control of the North West Company, he resigned in 1799 and founded another fur trade enterprise, called the XY Company. The splinter enterprise gave stiff competition to the North West Company for a few years until it was absorbed by that company. These years were marked by great hostilities, an increase in the sale of hard liquor and guns, and the inducement to violence and theft against each other's property. The animosity of the competition presaged the growing conflict between the Hudson's Bay Company and the North West Company in the following decade as the Company followed the Nor'Westers inland, constructing their posts in the same locations and competing for the same furs. At the same time, as Mackenzie pointed out, it was becoming a logistical struggle to manage a supply line that stretched from Montreal to Athabasca, a distance of 4,425 kilometres. Mackenzie even tried to buy out the Hudson's Bay Company in 1803, unsuccessfully. He continued to advocate for the merger of the two companies so as to use Hudson Bay as a shipping route to avoid long supply lines and the exorbitant shipping duties paid on furs passing through Montreal.

In 1801, with the help of a ghostwriter, Mackenzie completed his famous book with the tongue-twisting title: *Voyages from Montreal, on the River St. Laurence, through the Continent of North America, to the Frozen and Pacific Oceans; In the Years 1789 and 1793. With a Preliminary Account of the Rise, Progress, and Present State of the Fur Trade of That Country.* The publication of the tome was a great success, and it was widely read by armchair adventurers and statesmen alike, including Napoleon Bonaparte and President Thomas Jefferson. Regarding the geographical importance of his revelations, he concluded that Pond's "assertion was nothing but conjecture, and that a Northwest Passage is impractical" and expostulated that his own expeditions had "settled the dubious point of a practicable North-West Passage; and I trust, it has set that long agitated question at rest, and extinguished the disputes respecting it for ever."

WHEN IN MONTREAL, MACKENZIE WAS usually the life of the party, a bon vivant and loquacious entertainer and teller of tales. That his social obligations with the elite of Montreal society—including Scottish entrepreneurs, British army officers, French upper civil officials and the judiciary, as well as visiting autocrats and other dignitaries—involved heavy drinking is well established. He was particularly fond of the infamous Beaver Club, a biweekly gathering held at upscale Montreal hotels and elevated taverns. Founded by Nor'Westers in 1785, its famous motto was "Fortitude in Distress." Drinking to a high level was the primary purpose, as clannish Scotsmen associated with the fur trade engaged in ritual bacchanalia in the months before the spring breakup. Evenings were notable for feasting, boasting and toasting of each other's successes, with whisky and wine, and the inebriated antics of the current and former Nor'Wester grandees—the wintering partners, agents, brokers and their rich cronies, but certainly not the lower-status voyageurs.

George Landmann, a lieutenant in the Corps of Royal Engineers, wrote of one such gathering of the Beaver Club. "In those days," he recalled, "we dined at four o'clock and after taking a satisfactory quantity of wine, perhaps a bottle each, the married men . . . retired, leaving about a dozen to drink their health. We now began in right earnest and true highland style, and by four o' clock in the morning, the whole of us had arrived at such a degree of perfection, that we could all give the war-whoop as well as Mackenzie and McGillivray, we could all sing admirably, we could all drink like fishes, and we all thought we could dance on the table without disturbing a single decanter; but on making the experiment we discovered that it was all a complete delusion, and ultimately, we broke all the plates, glasses, bottles, &c., and the table also, and worse than all the heads and hands of the party received many severe contusions, cuts and scratches." Other accounts recall prodigious meals of venison steaks, roasted beaver tails and pickled bison tongues, and revellers too drunk to stand or sit, slumped on the floor grasping for a final bottle of spirits. The evening often ended in the broken table being upended and the stagger-ing celebrants clambering aboard for a jolly re-enactment of a canoe shooting rapids, propelled by bellowing gentlemen paddling away with their walking sticks, fire pokers and soup ladles. It isn't hard to imagine that Mackenzie's later kidney issues stemmed from this life.

The fur trader and map-maker David Thompson later called Mackenzie a "gentlemen of enlarged views," which he didn't intend to be entirely complimentary. Mackenzie was a dominating personality who sought to bend other people to his will and expected them to labour in his interests with vigour and self-sacrifice. He was a difficult man to get along with since he always knew best, and was adept at tire-lessly promoting his interests, which in his later years were aligned with an expansion of the British Empire in North America.

In addition to making oodles of money from his fur trade interests, Mackenzie was proffered a knighthood from King George III for his patriotic geopolitical ruminations. For the remainder of his life, Mackenzie advocated for the merger of the two British fur companies and other commercial schemes but with less public flair, being mostly content to live a quiet life after he married a young kinswoman, Geddes

Mackenzie, with whom he raised three children as a laird on his Scottish estate. His hard-living youth caught up to him in his fifties. He wrote to a friend in 1819, a year before he died at the age of fifty-six of kidney disease, "I have been overtaken with the consequences of my sufferings in the North West. . . . I have in obedience of orders become a water drinker and a milk sop. I have not tasted wine, spirituous or malt liquor for several months which I think has been of service to me. . . . The exercise of walking, particularly if uphill, brings on a headache, stupor or dead pain which at once pervades the whole frame, attended with a listlessness and apathy which I cannot well describe."

Mackenzie had a flair for drama, a burning ambition and a near-prophetic vision of the importance of his accomplishment—the first ever cross-continental crossing—but his self-aggrandizing promotion begs the question: What constitutes geographical exploration and discovery?

It doesn't seem that an individual being led through a land by the land's occupants should count as discovering it, except in a personal sense. Mackenzie and his team should more accurately be called travellers. They were not exploring a land devoid of inhabitants; they were touring distant, populated lands for eastern economic interests. They were discovering new markets, which is not to be sneered at, as these were difficult and dangerous expeditions through geography unknown to them and into lands with people of foreign customs who were not necessarily friendly or welcoming to strangers. Mackenzie contributed greatly to the European geographical and social perception of the northern territories.

His documentation of the geography and peoples of the northwest in turn led to the accurate mapping of the Interior and the subsequent exploitation of the resources, which led to a permanent change in the prevailing social structure. To map something is to gain an overarching knowledge of how places and people interact that isn't known to anyone other than the mapper. It bestows a more global view of a place that enables a different sort of thinking—viewing the world like a game board rather than responding to local customs and daily interactions. Reasonably accurate maps enable planning by those who have no personal experience with a place—specialists who see a bigger picture or who create that picture and envision possibilities not obvious to those on the ground. Mackenzie's journey, first to the Arctic Ocean and then to the Pacific, changed forever the understanding of the continent by giving it boundaries, a limit on the previously unfathomably huge domain. The formerly mysterious world of unknown dimensions, populated with innumerable geographic and cultural mysteries, was now contained. Whatever mysteries remained were finite and could be systematically probed and documented. After Mackenzie's expedition, the land was no longer inestimably huge and bewildering but was like a jigsaw puzzle, with many of the edge pieces already in place and an increasingly large portion of the inside as well. As the shape and interior of the puzzle became clearer, those who possessed this information began to imagine controlling it. Empires exist because they can be conceived.

IN THE EARLY NINETEENTH CENTURY, eastern colonial civilization was centred chiefly in the United States, along the St. Lawrence River and in what is now southern Ontario. After the American Revolution, the population in Upper and Lower Canada had surged. Most people had no clear geographical concept of anything west of the Great Lakes, nor any moral or political claim to these lands. The lieutenant governor of the British colony had his headquarters at Niagara-on-the-Lake, near the border with the new country of the United States, which was expanding westward into the Midwest. Niagara was then the westernmost settlement of the British Empire in America. Along the New York–Albany–Illinois route farther south, the best fur lands in the United States were being opened west of the Mississippi, but the main markets were still on the Atlantic coast.

For anyone in the fur trade in the early nineteenth century, the increasingly complex logistics was a serious problem with a single obvious solution: establish a depot on the Pacific coast. Mackenzie had argued just this strategy in the late 1790s: that it would be more practicable for the North West Company to get their westernmost furs to the Pacific than to the St. Lawrence, particularly with the increasing number of American and British ships engaged in the sea otter trade with coastal Indigenous peoples and China making the voyages safer and predictable.

Before 1818, there was no international boundary between the United States and British-held territory west of the Mississippi River (the border, sketched out on rudimentary maps, ended in the northwest corner of Lake of the Woods, as set out in the Treaty of Paris in 1783). There were no British settlements or soldiers beyond that point, the land being occupied by dozens of independent Indigenous nations with a multitude of different cultures. But, as Mackenzie had argued, developing new trade routes and outposts in the West was significant for establishing a precedent for future sovereignty—which was in turn important for long-term commercial viability in the fur business, where trade, because of its territorial base, could be easily disrupted by international disputes. Captain George Vancouver, on his epic voyage for the British government in the early 1790s, snuffed out any lingering rumours of great western seas or east-leading waterways from the Pacific, and, along with the Boston sea captain Robert Gray, had marked the broad, navigable Columbia River on a chart of the Pacific coast. As a river highway into the heart of the area known as Old Oregon—today's Washington, Oregon, Idaho and British Columbia—the Columbia soon became the focus of both American and British fur traders searching for a Pacific outlet for their wares.

The downside was that finding a route to the Pacific was easier said than done. The Great Plains, after nearly fifteen hundred kilometres of open grassland and aspen parkland, rose into foothills and rugged ice-capped mountains that formed a seemingly impenetrable barrier to further travel to the West. Beyond this rocky blockade, what lay between the Pacific coast was, even after Mackenzie's travels, a mystery.

Mackenzie instinctively understood the importance of the Columbia, and in 1801 he urged the British government to establish a permanent fort and trading post at the mouth of the river to secure British political claims to the region. A more northern route was not viable, he suggested, for the Columbia was "the most Northern situation fit for colonization, and suitable for the residence of a civilized people." At the time, Britain was locked in a tectonic struggle with Napoleonic France.

In 1803, the British government in London gave colonial courts in Upper and Lower Canada jurisdiction over activities that occurred in the territory west of the Canadas, a land now being called the British Indian Territory, unbeknownst to the Indigenous population. Ostensibly the new jurisdiction was to provide a legal forum for the competing fur companies and the commercial operations of the handful of other traders in those lands, to prevent them from committing crimes against each other. But it was also the first instance of an outside political claim on these lands. Asserting legal and political authority had never been part of the operations of the Hudson's Bay Company in its previous 140 years, and had never featured in the planning and strategy of the early decades of the old North West Company.

At the same time, in 1803, President Thomas Jefferson, after reading Mackenzie's *Voyages from Montreal*, hastily commissioned a military and scientific expedition to explore the Louisiana Territory, which the United States had recently purchased from France. The expedition was then to press on over the Rocky Mountains to the Pacific coast to counter the British claims. Other imperial nations that had their eyes on Pacific America included Spain, looking north from Mexico, and Russia, looking south from Alaska. Called the Corps of Discovery and led by Meriwether Lewis and William Clark, the well-provisioned band of around forty-two struggled their way west over the Continental Divide at Lemhi Pass (on the Montana-Idaho boundary), followed the Clearwater and Snake Rivers to the Columbia and floated to the Pacific. But they, like Mackenzie in the north, were awed by the difficulty of their trek. After hammering together a rough-hewn stockade (naming the uninspiring dwelling Fort Clatsop) and spending the winter of 1805 cursing the weather—a dreary monotony of cloud, fog and drizzle—they returned east as soon as the snow melted from the mountain passes. "O! how disagreeable is our Situation during this dreadful weather," whimpered Clark before gleefully turning his back on the coast forever. The great obstacle to the Columbia as a thoroughfare to the Pacific, they reported, was the treacherous 550-kilometre seasonably impassable mountainous trail between the Missouri and Snake Rivers.

Despite the depressing reports, one prominent American fur baron believed he could use the Columbia River route as a gateway to the Orient. John Jacob Astor, broad featured and squat with sharp, penetrating eyes, held a virtual monopoly on the American fur trade. Astor was not born destined to dominate the American fur business. The younger son of a butcher in the sleepy town of Waldorf, Germany, it was not his early training as a crafter of flutes that gave him an edge in the competitive fur business. It was his keen business sense and limitless ambition. Astor arrived in America in January 1784, on a typical transatlantic voyage of the late eighteenth century—crammed into the dank steerage compartment of a bilgy wooden trading vessel for six weeks as it lurched across the ocean. His ship was then frozen in Chesapeake Bay for another two months. Here he chanced upon the unlikely information that would propel him into a world of riches and privilege. Sharing the voyage with the aspiring young man was a German fur merchant who, while they stared wistfully at the shore during their ignominious tenure in the icy bay, explained the rudiments of the fur business to the eager youth. From these conversations, Astor must have surmised that the fur trade was a business of high margins and extreme danger but, importantly, required comparatively little capital investment to get started; it was a business where, with a bit of luck, an independent, enterprising individual could make inroads even against the dominant North West Company.

With his cache of information, seven wooden flutes and a few dollars, Astor set out for New York, a city of forty thousand inhabitants spreading over the soggy marshland at the estuary of the Hudson River. It was a rudimentary outpost by sophisticated European standards, but it was growing quickly, and during Astor's lifetime it would emerge as one of the largest and pre-eminent cities of the Atlantic Seaboard. In 1784, only months after British troops had withdrawn from the city, Astor began his slow rise to prosperity with a job hawking sweet cakes from a vending stall in the dirty crowded streets. Within eighteen months he had left street vending behind forever and had wriggled his way into a position with a small independent trading company and was making trips up the Hudson River into the gloomy Catskill Mountains to deal directly with the Iroquois.

Astor was also busy wooing the hand of the daughter of his Scottish landlady. Sarah Todd helped her mother run a humble boarding house near the old Bowery. Of modest origins like Astor, she was reasonably pretty, sensible if dour. They were married in a simple ceremony in 1785, and opened a shop on Water Street selling flutes and violins from London, as well as furs. Sharing Astor's love of money, Sarah possessed great talent in assessing the market value of furs. With a keen business sense, she helped their fledgling enterprise divest itself from a dependence on importing musical instruments to concentrate fully on the fur trade. (The peculiar and loyal couple eventually had eight children together; five survived.) Sarah managed their small Water Street shop while John, with a musket, powder horn and sixty-pound pack, slogged his way by foot through the forests of upstate New York.

It was tedious, dangerous work, but Astor was a man driven by ambition. He quickly realized that the true secret to wealth in the fur business was volume, and turned his mind to increasing his role as a wholesaler. He moved from being a small-scale fur purchaser leading the wild, rustic life to a business manager, arranging for the exchange of furs at set locations along his torturous route. Soon, the sloops navigating the Hudson were frequently loaded with bales of fur destined for the small shop on Water Street, where they would be expertly appraised and distributed.

Their great breakthrough came in 1796, after Jay's Treaty between Britain and the United States closed the Ohio valley to the Canadian traders of the North West Company, leaving the region open to Astor, who had already established a distribution network leading from the eastern Great Lakes to New York. By the early nineteenth century, he had contacts throughout the United States (as it existed at the time) and in Montreal, the heart of the trade where he occasionally dined and celebrated at the Beaver Club. Eventually he held a stranglehold on nearly all the furs being pulled from the eastern woodlands, and his New York warehouse was a gigantic clearinghouse for the peltry of half a continent. He knew good business opportunities when they presented themselves, and possessed the ruthless, calculating, single-minded focus to persevere in spite of daunting obstacles and moral dilemmas.

By the time the young republic had purchased the Louisiana Territory from France in 1803, Astor had been in the fur business for the better part of twenty years. His enterprise, consolidated as the American Fur Company in 1808, was rivalled only by the Hudson's Bay Company and the North West Company. His influence, a near monopoly, extended from New York to the Mississippi River and made him one of the wealthiest Americans of his time. He lived in one of New York's grandest brownstone mansions, with his business premises a short walk away so he could keep a vigilant eye on his expanding enterprise (and sort and beat the pelts personally when the urge was upon him). He also had an opulent country estate on the eastern river frontage of Manhattan, alongside the rural retreats of New York's other emerging magnates. He later made a second, even greater, fortune in Manhattan real estate, buying vast tracts of suburban farmland and developing it as the city expanded with immigration from Europe. He was the founder of one of the wealthiest American dynasties of the nineteenth century, and the foundation of his fabulous fortune was fur.

(Despite the philanthropic generosity of Astor's heirs, time has not been kind to the original patriarch. His is one of the greatest success stories in a nation renowned for its rags-to-riches tales, yet it is also one of the greatest tragedies. To Astor, the charming youth from Germany who rose from the crowded dirty streets to the pinnacle of wealth and influence, confidant of presidents and aristocracy, the future should always have been open and expanding, full of endless possibility and opportunity. How it closed in on him, narrowing his increasingly dim view of life to the endless acquisition of wealth, often at the expense of others, is a tragedy of lost opportunity equal to the misery he caused the impoverished denizens of his ill-kept tenements. Tales of Astor's infamy are legion. Whether they can all be believed is debatable, but there is bound to be some truth in even the most unlikely tale. He reputedly was an uncouth boor lacking all social grace, and a cold and heartless tyrant who rode his carriage through the expanding suburbs of New York, foreclosing mortgages and evicting tenants unable to meet the escalating rent. On his deathbed at the age of eighty-five, in 1848, racked by palsy and digestive disorder, suckling nourishment at the breast of a wet nurse, he apoplectically demanded a final payment from a destitute old woman before he could expire in satisfaction.)

Astor's audacious, yet oddly sensible, scheme for western furs followed in a general way the pattern that Alexander Mackenzie suggested for the British in 1801. A central depot at the mouth of the Columbia River would receive shiploads of goods sent twenty-four thousand kilometres around Cape Horn from New York or Boston, which would then be hauled into the mountains to supply the many small trading posts scattered along the Columbia, Snake and their tributaries. The valuable pelts would be carted back to the coast, crammed into the holds of world-girdling ships that would ply the Pacific to China. The bales of furs would be bartered for Oriental luxuries worth a fortune in Europe, such as teas, porcelain and silk, and the European commodities would be shipped across the Atlantic to America. It would be a golden round of trade guaranteed to further enrich Astor, as well as to consolidate American territorial claims to the Columbia watershed.

In 1810 Astor formed the Pacific Fur Company as the commercial vehicle for his plans. Before sending his expedition to the Columbia—by sea from New York around Cape Horn, with a land contingent arriving later along the route pioneered by Lewis and Clark—he first sought the partnership of the North West Company, perhaps to avoid unnecessary competition. It was probably while feasting and boozing at the prestigious Beaver Club in Montreal in 1808 that Astor offered the partners of the North West Company a one-third option in his grandiose scheme. But the Nor'Westers, evidently secure in their position (and aware that their agent David Thompson was steadily searching for the inland origin of the Columbia River), refused. Why accept a one-third option on a venture when they believed they were already further advanced toward a similar goal? Other Nor'Westers had already established the first fur trade outpost west of the Continental Divide in 1805 along Mackenzie's route at the juncture of McLeod Lake and the Pack River.

Perhaps for revenge, Astor recruited five experienced field partners from the dissatisfied ranks of the Nor'Westers, including Mackenzie's lieutenant on his travels to the coast in 1793, Alexander MacKay, and selected another Canadian, Duncan McDougal, an experienced Scottish veteran of the fur trade, as the leader. He also hired many disgruntled French-Canadian and Iroquois voyageurs and clerks. In August 1810, the voyageurs sallied forth from Montreal, canoeing down to New York, where they presented a lively and novel scene paddling their canoes around the harbour before boarding a ship for the Pacific in early September. Washington Irving, whom Astor hired in 1830 to record the events of his enterprise, colourfully described the scene: "Down this river [the Hudson] they plied their course merrily on a fine summer's day, making its banks resound for the first time with their old French songs; passing by the villages with whoop and halloo, so as to make the honest Dutch farmers mistake them for a crew of savages. In this way they swept in full song and with regular flourish of the paddle, round New York, in a still summer evening, to the wonder and admiration of its inhabitants, who had never before witnessed on their waters, a nautical apparition of the kind." Ironically, for a company that was trying to establish American territorial claims on the distant Pacific coast, the majority of Astor's employees and partners were British citizens, most from the vicinity of Montreal. Irving described them as "men seasoned to hardship, who cared for neither wind nor weather. They could live hard, lie hard, sleep hard, eat dogs!—in a word they were ready to do and suffer anything."

But Astor, usually a shrewd judge of character, miscalculated. He hired Captain Jonathan Thorn, on leave from the U.S. Navy, to be in charge of his main ship, the *Tonquin*. Thorn was not the most suitable person to lead an expedition of more than twenty unruly voyageurs and fur traders, many of whom had never been on an ocean-going ship before, on a frightening and perilous six-month voyage around Cape Horn. A commendable military officer, he evidently lacked the diplomacy and patience to lead a risky civilian commercial venture. He was a typical naval officer of his day—he demanded respect, valued hierarchy and tyrannically enforced naval discipline. But he was so focused on keeping a tight ship that he failed to appreciate the commercial objectives of the expedition. His single-minded focus was precisely what impressed Astor, but to the fur traders he was a strutting martinet.

Trouble arose after only a few days at sea, when Thorn demanded lights out at eight o'clock. This was shocking news to McDougal and the three other proud and touchy ex-Nor'Westers who were engaged in an important game of cards. They haughtily informed Thorn that as the senior partners of the Pacific Fur Company that was paying his salary, they could do as they pleased. Thorn flew into a rage at having his authority challenged, and in the acrimonious quarrel threatened to blow off the head of anyone who disobeyed him. Although cooler heads prevailed, the incident set the atmosphere of hostility that eventually contributed to the ultimate failure of the expedition.

A few months later, when the ship put in on the Falkland Islands for fresh water, Thorn, accustomed to prompt obedience of orders, became irritated when a landing party failed to return at his call. He ordered the ship to sail, deserting the lingering group. Seeing the ship hoisting sails and putting to sea, the small band, including McDougal, leaped into their small boats and desperately rowed to catch up as the ship grew smaller on the horizon. Thorn, however, was prepared to abandon them, and believed he was right in doing so, until one of the traders forced him to return at the point of a pistol.

For the rest of the journey the voyageurs mostly spoke French around Thorn to irritate him. And Thorn, trying to retain control over an "insubordinate" group, made a series of poor decisions soon after arriving at the Oregon coast. When the *Tonquin* neared the mouth of the Columbia in March 1811, a menacing storm was brewing and the winds were whipping up great waves over the bar at the river's mouth. Thorn, against the urgings of his own officers and Duncan McDougal, ordered a small boat lowered into the roiling surf to search for a safe passage, stating to one of his officers, "Mr. Fox, if you are afraid of water, you should have remained at Boston." The boat was soon sucked under and the five men drowned. And then a second boat was swamped and another three men were lost, before the ship could be eased safely over the bar and into the river. It hardly augured well for the remainder of the expedition.

After dropping off the traders and their supplies in the shadowy forest along the Columbia, Thorn took the *Tonquin* up the coast to trade at Clayoquot Sound, on western Vancouver Island. He first met the Nuu-chah-nulth, then known as the Nootka, who were of the same culture as the people visited by James Cook in the 1770s as well as, in 1792, by British naval captain George Vancouver and his Spanish counterpart Juan Francisco de la Bodega y Quadra. The two had met to discuss the disagreements between their respective empires over who would lay exclusive claim to the Pacific coast of America north of California and south of Alaska. The name Nootka was an approximation of the term

Cook heard them yelling to him when his ships approached through the turbulent open ocean. Thinking it was their term for the entire inlet (now called Nootka Sound), it actually meant "come around" to the sheltered inner harbour.

Known for their distinctive textiles and conical cedar hats, and dwelling in mighty cedar longhouses fronted with totem poles along the magnificent beaches of the region, with the roar of the surf as the backdrop, the tribes of the Nuu-chah-nulth culture were concentrated on western Vancouver Island and the mainland to the east, and spoke a common language of the Wakashan family. Like other coastal peoples, they were known for their elaborate potlatch ceremonies, at which hosts seeking social status bestowed vast quantities of gifts on their guests. (By the early nineteenth century, several decades of contact with European mariners had introduced smallpox and other unknown diseases, and the population was already greatly reduced from around thirty thousand to only several thousand by mid-century.) They generally feasted upon seafood, such as halibut, herring, rockfish and salmon captured from boats and in rivers, and clams, sea urchins and mussels harvested during low tide. The Nuu-chah-nulth are famously known as one of the few peoples who routinely hunted whales, grey or humpback, paddling into the surging froth and swells of the open ocean in huge dugout cedar longboats and harpooning the monstrous mammals for meat, blubber and oil. Hunting leviathans was a dangerous communal activity that required a great deal of courage and cooperation, and it bred a fierce and brave culture accustomed to working together to achieve larger objectives.

Thorn, not familiar with fur trade protocol, or indeed common manners or common sense, lost his temper a final time. During negotiations with an important chief, he became enraged and slapped the man in the face with a discarded pelt. Stunned and humiliated, the people left the ship. Early the next morning a band of Nuu-chah-nulth canoed across the placid water and clambered aboard the ship, ostensibly to trade. Thorn ignored the anxious entreaties of the traders to flee immediately, and amazingly he traded dozens of knives to the very people he had gravely insulted the day before. As soon as they were armed with their new knives, they attacked, stabbing and slashing at the unwary mariners and flinging them from the ship. Thorn was quickly speared like a fish, and most of the others were killed before they knew what was happening. (Four sailors escaped in an open boat but were later captured and enslaved.) The mortally wounded company clerk, Mr. Lewis, sensing his imminent demise, dragged himself below deck, and then the next morning when the attackers returned to inspect and plunder the ship, he ignited the barrels of gunpowder deep in the hold. The entire vessel was blown to pieces in the quiet harbour, killing all on board and destroying all the trade goods. It was a critical blow to the Pacific Fur Company and a devastating loss of young men from Clayoquot Sound. With the loss of the *Tonquin*, Astor's outpost was left without supplies and without a means of bringing its furs to market.

MEANWHILE, BACK AT THE COLUMBIA, life was passing as planned. McDougal, his partners and the voyageurs immediately began the arduous trek into the forbidding cloud-capped mountains to let the local people know they were open for business, and began negotiating for the precious inland pelts. Others began chopping down gigantic cedar and fir trees to make a small clearing in the dense coastal rainforest. Once the trees cracked and thundered to the forest floor, they stripped the bark and hastily constructed a primitive stockade of pointed timbers, and named it Fort Astoria after their patron. Although this was a demanding and tiring job, the pleasant spring weather evidently made the task easier. "The weather was magnificent," wrote one pleased clerk, Gabriel Franchère, "and all Nature smiles . . . The forests looked like pleasant groves and the leaves like flowers."

Chapter Eleven

THE GREAT RIVER
OF THE WEST

W hile Fort Astoria slowly took shape in the clearing near the mouth of the Columbia in 1811, David Thompson, the dreamy astronomer and wanderer who had worked for both the Hudson's Bay Company and the North West Company, was making his leisurely way down that very waterway after constructing trading posts along many of the interior rivers during the previous few years. The partners of the North West Company had continued the quest for the headwaters of the Columbia River, but without success. The most famous expedition was undertaken by the fleshy-faced dour Scot Simon Fraser, who was propelled along the turbulent waters of what is now called the Fraser River to the coast near the present-day city of Vancouver. But the Fraser, with its mesmerizing whirlpools, terrifying gorges and precarious bridges clinging to the slippery spume-slickened rock, proved to be as treacherous and unnavigable as the Bella Coola River. "We had to pass where no human should venture," noted the undaunted Fraser with great understatement. After Fraser's return in 1808, the Nor'Westers knew beyond a doubt that no river other than the Columbia could be a viable route to the Pacific.

Compact and wiry, with long black hair cropped across his forehead, David Thompson did not present the picture of the intrepid adventurer pushing on to great feats of daring and sacrifice. And indeed, despite his thirty-year odyssey in the Far West, he was better known for his loyalty, pious clean living and devotion to his family. He was more interested in his ethnographic observations and filling in his detailed chart of the northwest than in amassing a fortune to swagger in eastern society as Mackenzie was then doing. He was a good fur trader, excelling at developing trading relationships with Indigenous peoples because of his knowledge and appreciation of their cultures.

His quiet competence and unheralded survival instincts were blended with a poetic appreciation of Indigenous cultures and way of life. While many of his fellow field traders were semi-literate, Thompson was a prolific and skilled writer, eventually turning his decades of journal notes into thirty-nine clear volumes and penning an amusing and perceptive narrative of his adventures. Many of these decades of adventure were shared with his wife, the multilingual Charlotte Small, whom he had married in 1799, when he was twenty-nine and she not yet fifteen, in a simple ceremony on the shore of a northern lake in present-day Saskatchewan. She was the daughter of a Cree woman and fur trader Patrick Small, who had abandoned his wife and three children and retired to London after fifteen years with the North West Company.

Thompson met Charlotte at Île-à-la-Crosse, a remote North West Company outpost near the headwaters of the Churchill River. "My lovely wife is of the blood of these people," he claimed, "speaking their language [Cree] and well-educated in the English language, which gives me a great advantage." She also spoke French and a smattering of other local languages and dialects. Short and compact, with dark eyes and copper-coloured skin, she was known for her boundless energy and her reserved and gentle character. They eventually had thirteen children, ten of whom survived to adulthood, and Thompson laboured additional years in the fur trade to fund his children's education. "It is my wish to give all my children an equal and good education," he remarked in 1810, "my conscience obliges me to it, and it is for this I am now working in this country." Thompson and Charlotte remained together their entire lives, eventually retiring to the outskirts of Montreal.

Thompson had earned a reputation as a fair and honest trader with the Indigenous peoples with whom he had spent many decades of his life. On one occasion "several old Indians made a bargain with me," he recalled. "If they should die in winter, I should not demand the debt due to me in the other world—namely, heaven. To which I always agreed." He also refused to trade liquor, having witnessed the social disruption it inflicted on Indigenous communities during his travels, an act of defiance that reduced profits but was nevertheless admired by some. "I was obliged to take two kegs of alcohol, overruled by my partners," he complained "for I had made it a law to myself that no alcohol should pass the Mountains in my company, and thus be clear of the sad sight of drunkenness, and its many evils: but these gentlemen insisted upon alcohol being the most profitable article that could be taken for the Indian trade. In this I knew they had mis-calculated; accordingly when we came to the defiles of the Mountains I placed the two Kegs of Alcohol on a vicious horse; and by noon the Kegs were empty, and in pieces, the Horse rubbing his load against the Rocks to get rid of it; I wrote to my partners what I had done; and that I would do the same to every Keg of Alcohol, and for the next six years I had charge of the fur trade on the west side of the Mountains, no further attempt was made to introduce spirituous Liquors." If he found liquor secreted among his annual supplies and gear, he simply got rid of it.

Toward his voyageurs, he was less understanding. Despite their protests, he would attempt to enlighten them with biblical parables and fables that he would read aloud from a French edition of the Old Testament as they lounged by a riverbank at the end of a tiring day or by the campfire as they digested their evening meal—and expressed amazement that they weren't enraptured by the scriptures. He didn't understand them, and their antics and motivation remained unfathom-able. Thompson raised his eyebrows at their simple contentment and mocked their slothful behaviour. "A French Canadian has the appetite of a Wolf, and glories in it. Each man requires eight pounds of meat per day or more," he wrote, astonished. "Upon my reproaching some of them for their gluttony, the reply I got was, 'What pleasure have we in life but eating?' A French Canadian, if left to himself, and living on what he has, will rise very early, make himself a hearty meal, smoke his pipe, and then lie down to sleep again for the rest of the day."

Thompson spent many decades of his life in the fur trade. He was born in London to Welsh parents in 1770. His father died when he was a small boy of three, and four years later his struggling mother enrolled him in the Grey Coat Hospital in Westminster, a school for poor boys where he was, he later wrote, raised with "piety and virtue . . . a founda-tion for a sober and Christian life." He was also taught useful skills such as basic Latin, mathematics, geography and navigation. In 1784, at the age of fourteen, he was recruited as an apprentice by the Hudson's Bay Company and sailed off to Hudson Bay, never to return to his native land. His tenure with the Company was not wasted, and he learned the skills of a trader and later a surveyor and map-maker along the stony beaches of Hudson Bay. For a while he worked under Samuel Hearne, sometimes writing out edited passages of Hearne's manuscript detailing his adventures with Matonabbee many years earlier. But he was not suited to the lethargic life of a Bayman, despite several officers lending him books on history and natural history. "Neither writing nor reading was required," he later remarked of those long, boring days, "and my only business was to amuse myself; in winter growling at the cold and in the open season, shooting Gulls, Ducks, Plover and Curlews, and quarrelling with Musketoes and Sand Flies."

In 1796, he was lured from the Hudson's Bay Company by their ener-getic archrival, the North West Company, with the promise of the opportunity to explore the vast continent spreading south and west from the isolated posts strung out along the shore of Hudson Bay. Beginning with a visit to the Mandan villages and a survey of the head-waters of the Mississippi River in present-day Minnesota, Thompson eventually roamed nearly ninety thousand kilometres in the sprawling lands west of the bay, equivalent to walking around the globe twice.

Even in these early years of wandering, he was methodically compil-ing the data for a ten-foot chart detailing the regions of his travels—travels that extended from York Factory in the north, to the Missouri River in the south, to Montreal in the east, and to the mouth of the Columbia River at the Pacific Ocean in the west. Every few days he would devote several hours to observing and recording astronomical minutiae, such as the eclipse of Jupiter's moons, in order to fix his lati-tude and longitude, and record it all in a weather-beaten logbook that he carried with him everywhere.

Thompson's lifelong effort to produce a detailed map of western North America was the continuation of the rudimentary cartographic revelations of Mackenzie. It represented a real change for European and eastern colonial cultures: from being minor players in the bewildering politics of a vast, mostly unknown land, to being the controllers of a compendium of powerful knowledge. Once Thompson's map was com-pleted, anyone could glance at it and gain a full portrait of the entire domain and its resources, a more universal geographic knowledge than was available to the people who lived there.

DURING MANY OF THE YEARS Thompson spent in the western Plains and aspen parkland, he was based out of Rocky Mountain House, at the edge of the grasslands along the North Saskatchewan River within sight of the mountains. The fort was founded in 1799, one year before Thompson first arrived. He quickly became familiar with the manners and customs and politics of the surrounding people, whom he described as "a fine race of men, tall and muscular, with manly features, and intel-ligent countenances, the eyes large, black and piercing, the nose full and generally straight, the teeth regular and white, the hair long, straight and black." As he did whenever he moved to a new post or region, Thompson spent much time with them on hunting forays and lingering about their lodges, spending a winter as a guest in a large camp in the vicinity of present-day Calgary, observing and writing about the people and their customs and politics: how the young men would paint their faces to attract the attention of women, the gambling games, the crushing work-load of the women, morality and religion—all fascinated him. He noted that many bore the scars of the smallpox epidemic that had raged in the interior during the 1780s and depleted populations, altering the social and political order.

With a keen appreciation for human nature, Thompson described the key Piegan leaders and their political structure, searching for an under-standing that would be vital to his success in his business and to satisfy his own curiosity. In Thompson's time, the Piegan had two principal leaders, the civil chief and the war chief. Thompson didn't know Sakatow, the civil chief, well. But he did observe how the man ruled and his gen-eral responsibilities. "In every council he presided, except one of War. He had couriers which went from camp to camp, and brought the news of how things were, of where the great herds of Bisons were feeding, and of the direction they were taking. The news thus collected, about two or three hours after sun set, walking about the camp, he related in a loud voice, making his comments on it, and giving advice when required. His language was fluent, and he was admired for his eloquence, but not for his principles and his advice could not be depended on." The war chief Kootenae Appee was a different character altogether, and had little to do with Sakatow. "He looked on the civil Chief with indifference as a garrulous old man more fit for talking than anything else, and they rarely camped together."

Thompson became friends with the renowned war chief, whom he called "my steady friend" and who worked with Thompson to increase trade and promote good relations between the traders and the Piegan on whose territory they operated. Kootenae Appee was an impressive character. Standing over six foot six tall, "he appeared to be of Bone and Sinew with no more flesh, than absolutely required; his countenance manly, but not stern, his features prominent, nose somewhat aquiline, his manners kind and mild; his word was sacred, he was both loved and respected, and his people often wished him to take a more active part in their affairs but he confined himself to War, and the care of the camp in which he was." On their first meeting, Thompson inadvertently committed a dire social transgression that could have ended his life. When Kootenae Appee entered the tent, he offered Thompson his left hand, "and I gave him my right hand, upon which he looked at me and smiled as much to say a contest would not be equal." According to Blackfoot custom of the time, offering one's right hand—the hand the warrior used for throwing spears, drawing a bow or pulling a trigger—was an invitation for a duel. Kootenae Appee was gracious enough to brush off the affront, since Thompson was clearly not a threat and was eager to learn their customs.

Kootenae Appee always lived and camped in a large settlement of fifty to one hundred lodges, if not more, and provocatively pushed the boundaries of Piegan territory by placing himself closest to his enemies on the far side of the mountains. He had five wives, twenty-two sons and four daughters. His grown-up sons were as tall as himself, and the others, Thompson noted, "promised the same." Kootenae Appee favoured keeping good relations with the fur traders and permitted them to operate within his territory, persuading others to do the same, "and in his speeches reminded his people of the great benefit of [which] the Traders were to them, and that it was by their means they had so many useful articles, and guns for hunting, and to conquer their enemies." Thompson also observed that the women's lives were made much easier by certain trade items: just see a woman "sewing their leather clothing with a pointed brittle bone or a sharp thorn and the time and trouble it takes," he wrote. "Show them an awl or a strong needle and

they will gladly give the finest Beaver or Wolf skin they have to purchase it."

Thompson noted that Kootenae Appee's position as war chief was
not hereditary but had been earned from his conduct in war and his
advice, strategies and leadership over many years. Kootenae Appee's
great strength was in diplomacy and persuasion, and he seldom engaged
in any battle unless he could secure the support of two hundred or more
warriors. By using his charisma and insight, he secured allies for every
endeavour "by which all might have a share of the honour and plunder,
and thus avoid those jealousies and envyings so common amongst the
Chiefs. He praised every Chief that in the least deserved it, but never
appeared to regard fame as worth his notice yet always took care to
deserve it, for all his expeditions were successful."

THOMPSON QUICKLY LEARNED THAT THE PIEGAN, or Piikani, were
in a general state of conflict with the people farther west on the other
side of the mountains, the Kutenai, a Plains tribe that had only two
generations earlier been pushed west by the Piegan and other tribes of
the Blackfoot Confederacy, the Siksika (Blackfoot) and the Kainai
(Blood). Since Henday's time nearly a half-century earlier, the confederacy of linguistically and culturally similar peoples had banded together
to become the most powerful military force in the region. They were
surrounded by many enemies, however, and consequently they were
fierce warriors. The political situation was always in flux, with an
ever-shifting series of alliances and enmities. There were the Crow,
Cheyenne and Sioux (Dakota, Lakota and Nakota) on the Great Plains.
There were the Shoshone, Flathead, Kalispell, Kootenai and Nez Perce
to the west and southwest in the mountainous regions. For a time, the
Blackfoot Confederacy's greatest challengers were the occasionally
allied Plains Cree, the Nakoda or Stony (Assiniboine) and the Saulteaux
or Plains Ojibwa of the loosely affiliated Iron Confederacy to the north
and east. (The Iron Confederacy also traded European manufactured

goods to the Mandan for beans, maize and tobacco.) Later in the nine-teenth century the Blackfoot Confederacy's adversaries included the Métis. The Piegan occupied the westernmost fringe of the Confederacy's territory and were a fierce people tasked with guarding the frontier from enemies coming over the mountains.

The Piegan, like the Blackfoot and the Blood, never used canoes but rode horses, of which they were masters, and kept dogs to haul their goods. They tended to dwell in concentrated semi-permanent commu-nities of at least one hundred lodges and lived by hunting bison herds and migrating with them, enlivening their diet with trout from the many cold streams that rushed down through the grassy foothills from the mountains. In the late summer and fall, after the chokecherries rip-ened and bison wandered west in search of better grasses, bands would congregate to drive vast numbers of bison over cliffs at places such as Head-Smashed-In Buffalo Jump in southwestern Alberta.

The Piegan for a time occupied the position as middlemen in the trade with the Kootenay (also spelled Kootenai and Kutenai) and other cultur-ally similar peoples to their immediate west, and were in direct opposition to the North West Company's plan to expand the trade over the moun-tains. In particular they sought to maintain a monopoly on guns to pre-serve their military superiority. In one instance, a band of mounted Piegan warriors followed Thompson when he travelled from Rocky Mountain House into the mountains to meet a band of Kootenay and escort them back to the fort. The intimidation wasn't entirely successful, and the Kootenay were able to trade pelts of wolverines, fishers, bears and over a hundred beaver. The Piegan did everything short of all-out war to prevent the commerce. Thompson persuaded the Kootenay to send a guide over the pass the following year to help him lead a pack train over the moun-tains, but the man was killed within a few miles of the fort.

Thompson's plans to expand the trade to the west were similarly thwarted the next year, when the North West Company retrenched to established fur trade regions to compete with the Hudson's Bay

Company and Mackenzie's new renegade XY Company. Thompson spent the next several years moving from place to place with Charlotte and his growing family until he was sent back to Rocky Mountain House in 1806.

In the summer of 1804, Simon McTavish, the head of the North West Company and Mackenzie's archrival, had died, at the age of fifty-four, paving the way for the merger between the North West Company and the XY Company, ending the destructive rivalry. As soon as Thompson returned to Rocky Mountain House, Kootenae Appee rode to the fort with an armed entourage. He wanted to visit Thompson, to exchange greetings but also to warn him off attempting to forge commerce with his enemies. In 1807, the Hudson's Bay Company built an outpost called Acton House very near to Rocky Mountain House and began spying on Thompson's preparations.

History conspired to give Thompson his opportunity to sneak west past the Piegan. The previous summer, members of the Lewis and Clark expedition had killed two Piegan warriors along the Marias River in what is now Montana. The conflict "drew the Piegan to the Missouri to revenge their deaths," Thompson wrote, "and thus gave me an opportunity to cross the Mountains by the defiles of the Saskatchewan River, which led to the head waters of the Columbia River, and we there builded Log Houses." Thompson first trekked over the Continental Divide in 1807, through the swampy, windblown route now known as Howse Pass, in today's Banff National Park. His brigade included ten pack horses loaded with trade goods, a troop of voyageurs and Charlotte, holding the hands of two young children while the youngest was yet a fifteen-month-old bundle strapped to her back. The expedition totalled eleven men, five women and nine children, a pack of yelping dogs, thirty horses and several canoes for later use. The descent into the verdant valley of the upper Columbia was a hellish slog through an overgrown tangle of deadfall, clusters of alders, willows and devil's club, and numerous creek crossings.

Beyond the mountains and in the valley, the forest opened up into a drier terrain of more widely spaced ponderosa pines, grassy clearings and marshy little lakes. Thompson constructed Kootenae House just north of Lake Windermere, in eastern British Columbia, and settled into the life of a travelling salesman, tramping over the hills, following numerous rivers and ascending within sight of the shining glaciers throughout eastern B.C., western Montana and Idaho, and inviting the people to trade at his new post. Trade in what was now called the Columbia Division doubled each year, and new posts were built, among them Kullyspell House and Salish House in Idaho and western Montana, respectively. Thousands of pounds of goods were packed over Howse Pass each year and bales of furs made their way east.

It was here that Thompson was introduced to a food that he had never encountered on the east side of the Continental Divide: moss bread. One of Thompson's men, Jaco Finlay, made some for him after being instructed how to do so by a band of Kootenay he met while fishing along a lake. "The manner of preparing it is as follows," Thompson wrote. The moss "is gathered from the trees and all the small dead twigs taken out of it, and then immersed in water until it becomes perfectly flexible, and afterwards placed on a heap of heated stones . . . and allowed to remain until cooked, which generally takes a night. Then before it cools it is compressed into thick cakes and is fit for use." Although Thompson ate a great many foods while roaming over much of north-central North America, sampling local delicacies and different cooking methods and herb variations, moss bread never suited his palate. It had a "lightly bitter insipid Taste," he wrote, and could be mainly appreciated in times of hunger and privation.

The people with whom Thompson sought to trade included primarily the Kutenai, Interior Salish and the Snake (Shoshoni), interior tribes who lived mostly along rivers and lakes in Idaho, Washington, Oregon and British Columbia and who had a similar way of life but spoke different languages. They were semi-nomadic hunters and salmon fishers who moved in a seasonal cycle through their river-riddled, hilly and mountainous territory. Some of these people, in particular the Kutenai, returned east of the Rockies each year to hunt bison and occasionally found themselves in violent conflict with the Piegan. The Piegan made frequent, if not annual, treks across the mountains to the valleys and rolling hills of the Kootenay country to raid, sow fear and to steal horses.

While expanding the North West Company's commercial network, Thompson began his four-year quest for the headwaters of the deceptively meandering Columbia. The great irony is that the first river he gazed upon when he descended from Howse Pass in 1807 was the Columbia, but since he was looking for a south-flowing river he dismissed it from consideration. The two-thousand-kilometre-long Columbia has its headwaters in the mountains of eastern British Columbia, and flows about 240 kilometres northwest before making a hairpin turn and descending south through gorges and broad valleys into Washington, and then west along the Washington-Oregon state boundary. It is one of the greatest drainage basins in North America, draining 668,000 square kilometers into the Pacific Ocean.

JUST AS THE VAGARIES OF HISTORY OPENED Howse Pass to Thompson and the Nor'Westers, it likewise closed it abruptly. The Piegan had been angered by the founding of Kootenae House and had been periodically sending small groups to investigate and harass the traders and their customers, and debated attacking it for years. Kootenae Appee's voice always rose to caution against an outright attack, anticipating that it would not bring the desired result and would give the fur traders reason to refuse to trade with the Piegan or raise their prices. An outright war was in no one's best interest.

But in early 1810, Thompson's partner Finan McDonald, a six-foot-four red-haired bearded giant, was travelling with a band of Kutenai on a bison-hunting expedition in disputed territory when they were ambushed by a group of Piegan warriors. McDonald and the Kutenai were armed with guns, courtesy of the North West Company, and seven Piegan were killed and dozens injured, but only five Kutenai. It was an unprecedented and humiliating military defeat for the Piegan. The simmering irritation over Howse Pass came boiling up—not only was it undermining the Piegan's role as middlemen in the trade, but by enabling arms to reach their enemies the pass was endangering their security and pre-eminence. Thompson was on a trip east of the mountains with his family during the summer of 1810, and when he set out to return in the fall, his plans were thwarted. While he waited for his brigade to catch up with him, it was met by Kootenae Appee and a mounted, well-armed Piegan war band at Shunda Creek, west of Rocky Mountain House. The canoes and horses of the annual supply brigade were stopped and escorted back to Rocky Mountain House. There was no peaceful way to get around the Piegan blockade. Knowing that he was the magnet for their wrath and fearing he would be killed, Thompson set off alone and hid out for nearly a month, living rough while the drama receded.

Earlier that summer, the Hudson's Bay Company had sent a spy through the pass to see what the Nor'Westers were up to and to determine whether it would be advantageous to follow them west. His name was Joseph Howse, an otherwise unremarkable employee who bequeathed his name to the pass, even though he never made it across to the other side. The Piegan lay in ambush, surrounded him and issued him an unambiguous warning: never attempt to cross again. "If they ever again met with a white Man going to supply their Enemies," Howse warned, "they would not only plunder and kill him, but they would make dry Meat of his body." Kootenae Appee may have been friends with Thompson and favourably disposed to the fur traders, but his loyalties lay first with his people.

Thompson of course had no intention of engaging in a gun battle with his customers, many of whom he had known for many years, but he had been ordered by the partners of the North West Company to quickly cross the Rockies, find the Columbia River and follow it to the coast. There was a renewed urgency for this objective: to pre-empt the arrival of Astor's Pacific Fur Company. Thompson, an amiable socializer with a strong facility in Indigenous languages, was always attentive to new geographical information and he had heard from an Iroquois man named Thomas that some people had crossed to the west by following the Athabasca River, the "Great River of the Woods," into the heart of the craggy mountains. He had proposed searching for the route years earlier, but the partners didn't want the expense.

Thompson regrouped and set off north through the grizzled and trackless terrain of the Front Ranges near today's Jasper National Park, searching for the alternative pass. His band included twenty-five men, three women, twenty-four heavily laden horses and the ubiquitous pack of dogs. It was November, and the journey "would put us in safety [from the Piegan], but would be attended with great inconvenience, fatigue, suffering, and privation, but there was no alternative."

Hemmed in by a wall of lodgepole pines and rugged uplifted rocky terrain, it took them many weeks of dangerous and tricky travel. Men set off in advance of the brigade with axes, chopping away deadfall so the horses could get through as the group slowly wended their way north to the Athabasca River and then followed it upstream through the valley into the mountains toward the narrow, wind-lashed pass. As late fall turned to winter and the snow fell, horses became mired in the turgid muskeg and slipped on mud-slickened stones. There was no game, and the men became exhausted and demoralized. Nor'Wester Alexander Henry, hearing of their journey, recorded their miserable fate in a letter: Thompson was "cutting his road through a wretched thick Woody Country, over Mountains and gloomy Maskagues and nearly starving with Hunger, Animals being very scarce in that quarter, and his hunter can only find a chance Wood Buffalo, upon which they sub- sist . . . in fact, their case is pitiful."

As winter gripped the land, the horses began slipping on ice. The cutting cold and gusting wind lowered the men's spirits and they began quarrelling and brooding and dreaming of retreat. Nevertheless, after spending three weeks hunting and building sleds and snowshoes in temperatures as cold as minus thirty-six Celsius, they pushed on upriver past the current-day Jasper townsite near the end of December, marking a supply line for future use and leaving some men behind to construct a fort. One voyageur named Du Nord was a darkly muttering complainer sowing discontent. Thompson, a perceptive individual, noted that "he is what we call a 'flash' man, a showy fellow before the women but a coward in heart, and would willingly desert if he had courage to go alone, very gluttonous and requiring a full ten pounds of meat each day. As I am constantly ahead, I cannot prevent his dog flogging and beating."

They loaded sledges with pemmican, grease, flour and hundreds of pounds of trade goods, harnessed teams of dogs and began the treacherous slog up the Whirlpool River. Soon a warm chinook flowed over the land from the west, bringing the fresh smell of spring and temperatures that rapidly turned the snow into a mess of slush that soaked their clothing during the day and then froze it at night. The exhausted dogs whimpered with the conditions, especially when their loads were increased with piles of chopped wood. According to Thomas, the Iroquois guide, there was no wood at the summit of the pass, so to avoid freezing to death they had to haul their own.

The pass, which they reached on January 10, 1811, was a place of otherworldly desolation: stunted trees surrounding a series of small pools bound on either side by tremendous walls of grey, icy rock and glaciers. It was gloomy, with the distant rumbling of avalanches. One voyageur remarked how close the brilliant stars were and that "he thought he could almost touch them with his hand." The land dropped away into a new valley with a river flowing far below, yet despite seeing their objective and the journey ahead downhill, the men were afraid and nervous. "When Men arrive in a strange Country, fear gathers on them from every Object," Thompson noted and urged them on to finish their journey.

By the end of January, Thompson had reached what he now thought must be the Columbia River (it was actually the Wood River that leads into the Columbia) and he sent the lazy Du Nord, who was threatening to desert, and some others back over the pass with instructions to be ready to bring over more supplies in the spring. He then set to building a log cabin, prosaically called Boat Encampment, which for fifty years became the staging ground for all goods shipped over the pass. He also began constructing a great clinker-built cedar canoe stitched together with spruce roots to rush downstream to the Pacific as soon as enough ice melted off the river to make paddling safe.

Athabasca Pass was the fifty-kilometre portage that connected the Columbia River system with the Athabasca River system—the land component of a complex transcontinental river transportation network over which thousands of people and many hundreds of tons of trade goods were to pass before it was abandoned in the 1850s. It never failed to impress its visitors. When the renowned Scottish botanist David Douglas made the trip in 1827, after pressing inland from Boat Encampment up to Athabasca Pass, he remarked, "The sensation I felt is beyond what I can give utterance to. Nothing, as far as the eye could perceive, but mountains such as I was on, and many higher, some rugged beyond any description, striking the mind with horror blended with a sense of the wondrous works of the Almighty." George Simpson later remarked that "it appears extraordinary how any human being should have stumbled upon a pass through such a formidable barrier . . . nature seems to have placed it here for the purpose of interdicting all communication between East and West sides of the continent." Though inefficient and dangerous, Athabasca Pass had one remediating quality: it was out of range of the Piegan.

In the spring of 1811, Thompson still couldn't believe that the north-flowing river was the Columbia, so he again set off south upstream. Had he gone north instead, he soon would have come to a 180-degree turn and been ushered downstream, eventually to the Pacific. He and his men spent two months canoeing and hiking through present-day southeastern British Columbia and northwestern Montana and Idaho to a point near

Spokane, Washington, consuming two months on a nearly one-thou-sand-kilometre detour before heading north to Kettle Falls and connect-ing with the Columbia again.

When Thompson finally located the elusive Columbia, he immediately set out to navigate it to the coast. In July, at a point near where the Snake River disgorges into the main channel of the Columbia, Thompson began to ponder the political ramifications of his expedition. He disembarked and chopped down a large tree, stripped the branches and some of the bark and nailed a primitive note to the contraption. "Know hereby," it intoned imperiously, "that this country is claimed by Great Britain as part of its territories and that the N.W. Company of Merchants from Canada, finding the Factory for its people inconvenient for them do hereby intend to erect a Factory at this place for the commerce of the country around."

Thompson and eight voyageurs rushed onward to the coast, paddling from dawn till dusk. In mid-July, as they smelled the fresh air of the ocean, they rounded a bend in the river only to have their hopes dashed. From a pole near a ramshackle village flew the Stars and Stripes, "four low Log Huts, the far-famed Fort Astoria of the United States." Former Nor'Wester and current Astorian Alexander Ross recorded their arrival: "On the 15th of July, we were rather surprised at the unexpected arrival of a north-west proprietor at Astoria, and still more so at the free and cordial reception given to an opponent. Mr. Thompson, northwest-like, came dashing down the Columbia in a light canoe, manned with eight Iroquois and an interpreter, chiefly men from the vicinity of Montreal." As they pulled up, Thompson and his exhausted men were clapped on the back and welcomed to the settlement.

During a week recuperating from their epic dash, as guests of Duncan McDougal, treated to hearty dinners of roasted salmon, duck and par-tridge, Thompson made the trip several miles west to observe the Pacific Ocean. But he always had someplace else to be. He had business to attend to and he missed his wife and children, and so he began prepar-ing for the slow upstream paddle back to familiar territory.

The significance of Thompson's arrival was far-reaching. By arriving at the mouth of the Columbia first, Americans had strengthened their territorial claim to the region—the first non-Indigenous settlement on the coast, rude and primitive though it was, was American, not British.

By now Thompson was thirty-eight and feeling his age. He was old for a field partner in the fur trade and for the uncertain, demanding and dangerous life he had been leading for many years. After quickly organizing the new Columbia District, he retreated over the mountains to the east and retired from the fur trade, packing up his entire family and moving to a rural estate in Glengarry County, Ontario, where he lived like a country gentleman managing his investments and business interests and raising his children. After his final trip east, in 1812, a committee of the principal partners of the North West Company at Fort William voted in favour of paying him a full share of profits for three years while he worked on his maps. For many years Thompson worked on transcribing his field notes into readable narratives and plotted his painstakingly collected astronomical observation points into a grand chart of all the regions of his travels.

Apart from the calculation of latitude, which was calculated on both land and at sea by measuring the angle of altitude of the sun, the techniques used on a land survey were quite different from those on a nautical survey. The greatest difference was in calculating longitude. The simplest way was to carry an accurate clock, or chronometer, set to Greenwich time and observe the difference between Greenwich time and local time at high noon. However, the prototype chronometers that James Cook and George Vancouver brought on their voyages were too finicky and bulky to survive years of exposure to the elements on a rough overland journey through the wilds.

Thompson used a far more time-consuming and error-prone method to calculate longitude that involved the observation of celestial bodies. He brought with him on all his travels a primitive watch that was accurate for around six hours at a time and that he set at high noon. He got out his telescope and squinted through it at the moons of Jupiter, awaiting the precise time of the eclipse of one of the moons at local time. He then consulted a book of tables that told him when the eclipse occurred in Greenwich. Based upon the earth's rotational speed, the time differences for the same eclipse was translated into degrees of longitude. When clouds blocked the stars from his view or the moons of Jupiter were hidden, Thompson measured the angle of the moon against two known stars, consulted a set of astronomical tables known as the *Nautical Almanac*, and then calculated Greenwich time to compare it with local time. Each of these methods could be accurate but painfully slow, particularly the lunar distances method, which could take up to three hours.

During the years of his travels, Thompson spent thousands of hours observing the sky and calculating latitude by the sun and longitude by the stars. The Salish people who observed him at his frequent stargazing gave him the nickname Koo Koo Sint, "the Man Who Looks at Stars." Once he had calculated the latitude and longitude of key locations, he marked these "peg points" in his journal and also perhaps on a crude field chart. He then track-surveyed, or estimated the terrain, to fill in the detail between his "peg points." When he set out to create his great chart after retiring from the fur trade, he began with such a well-balanced skeleton of astronomically fixed points that his accuracy was remarkable.

Thompson's ambitious cartography project consumed the first year of his retirement. From his volumes of notes of astronomical readings and his own estimates of distance and direction, he diligently created a great map of the land west of Hudson Bay. He drew it in with dark ink on twenty-five separate sheets of rag linen, and when fully laid out it measured three metres wide by two metres tall. The North West Company took possession of it and hung it in a prominent place on the wall of their conference and dining hall at Fort William. It could be consulted by senior officers to plot strategy and was also of interest to visiting travellers and dignitaries en route to the West. (Today the map hangs at the Archives of Ontario.) "Thus I have fully completed the survey of this part of North America from sea to sea," Thompson wrote, "and by almost innumerable astronomical Observations have determined the positions of the Mountains, Lakes and Rivers, and other remarkable places on the northern part of this Continent; the Maps of all of which have been drawn, and laid down in geographical position, being now the work of twenty seven years." His work became the standard yet unacknowledged base for all maps of the region for generations afterwards, traceable by several minor errors in Thompson's original.

Thompson also offered his services as chief astronomer and surveyor for the British contingent of the International Boundary Commission, demarcating the heavily forested, lake-littered territory between the St. Lawrence River and Lake of the Woods. After more than twenty years in the east, raising his children far from the rugged land where several of them and their mother had been born, and where he and their mother had spent many years of their lives, and seeing them educated and established in business and professions, he had the sad misfortune to lose a great deal of his savings in the stock crash of 1837. At the age of sixty-seven, and despite failing eyesight, he reluctantly took a job surveying the Muskoka district in Upper Canada. He and Charlotte spent the remainder of their days with one of their daughters and her husband near Montreal and died within months of each other in 1857, after a fifty-eight-year marriage.

After Thompson retired, the Nor'Westers, with a supply line connecting their operations in the Columbia District to Montreal, and the Astorians, based from their fort on the west coast, in the following years extended the fur trade throughout Old Oregon. Their agents trekked over vast tracts of terrain, following the valleys between monumental snow-capped peaks and rocky brown hills, the terrain sometimes bone-dry, spotted with cacti and red-tinged ponderosa pines, sometimes lush and loamy in the shadow of gigantic evergreens. They often pounded together their ramshackle forts across the river from each other and lugged in their goods along the same treacherous paths, competing for the business of the many people who lived in the region. A few of these posts later grew into cities, such as Spokane House, Fort Walla Walla and Fort Kamloops. While working out the geography of the region, they shivered in their tents at night, sweltered in the scorching summer sun and cursed the endless rain near the coast.

When the United States and Britain declared war in 1812, however, the repercussions were felt even on this far side of the Continental Divide. The traders were caught in the drama, since their business activities fell under the purview of their host nations, from whence capital and investment flowed. There was no universal law or custom governing the vast region, and so the companies inadvertently began to create one through their national allegiances. They began to view themselves as extensions of their nations, rather than as purely commercial-oriented guests of the peoples with whom they did their business. When war was declared, Astor must have cursed the day his fertile mind ever led him to implement his Columbia enterprise. He faced commercial losses if the venture failed (the capital investment was mostly his), which seemed very likely with a full-scale war disrupting regular commerce. (After his vociferous lobbying for an immediate end to the war yielded few results, Astor devoted himself to increasing his holdings by buying up merchant ships and businesses financially ravaged by the disruption of the trade. He also made a fortune later in the war by secretly buying North West Company furs at a discount and clearing them through his warehouse in New York City.)

For most of the Astorians, desperately low on provisions because Astor couldn't send his ships through the British naval blockade in the Atlantic, the problems were also personal. Many of them, including their leader, Duncan McDougal, were actually British citizens working for an American company. The war put them in an awkward position. Theoretically they were at war with their partners in the trade and their employer in New York.

When the Nor'Wester David McTavish floated down the Columbia at the head of a small private army numbering several dozen men in September 1813, the Astorians knew it wasn't business as usual. McTavish informed McDougal and the Astorians that a British warship was sailing around the Horn to seize everything that was American on the coast. McDougal, realizing their situation was bleak, and hoping to salvage what he could before the fort was taken by force, began negotiating for the sale of the entire operation—fort, inland posts, trade goods, provisions and the mounds of accumulated furs.

On October 16, the Pacific Fur Company was officially dissolved and sold to the North West Company for the paltry sum of $58,000, about a third of its value. Down went the Stars and Stripes and up went the Union Jack. Many of the Astorians, including McDougal, joined or rejoined the North West Company, and the others were offered passage back east. When he heard the news of his humiliating loss, Astor was furious. Using his enormous political influence, in 1817 he persuaded the U.S. government to ban all foreign companies from the fur trade on American soil. He then picked up all the North West Company outposts in American territory around the Great Lakes for a pittance.

ON NOVEMBER 30, 1813, about six weeks after the sale of the Pacific Fur Company, the twenty-six-gun HMS *Raccoon* sailed up the Columbia and began searching for a large American military base. (To ensure British naval support, the directors of the North West Company had exaggerated the size of Fort Astoria.) When Captain William Black stepped ashore and surveyed the sprawling cluster of huts, he was dismayed. Inside the primitive palisade, dwarfed by the surrounding firs and drooping cedars, traders from both companies lounged nonchalantly, as if they weren't at war. Where was the far-famed Fort Astoria, American stronghold on the Pacific? "What is this fort I have heard so much of?" he bellowed. "I could batter it down with a four-pounder in two hours!"

After pondering the disappointing turn of events for a few days, Captain Black, perhaps tipsy on wine, perhaps fearing that the prize money for capturing Astoria would be forfeited because it was no longer American, swaggered ashore with some armed marines. After calling everyone to witness his actions, he announced his intention to seize Fort Astoria for the British. But we just purchased it, claimed the Nor'Westers, so it already is "British." Ignoring their claims, Black lowered the Union Jack and raised the Stars and Stripes. After an appropriate delay he lowered the Stars and Stripes. "The chiefs of several Chinook and Clatsop bands who traded at Fort Astoria had been invited to the ceremony," wrote one observer, and shared some glasses of wine with the congregation. Then "the Captain took a British flag that he had brought for the purpose and raised it to the top of the staff; taking a bottle of Madeira, he smashed it against the pole, proclaiming in a loud voice that he took possession of the establishment and the country in the name of His Britannic Majesty and named it Fort George." After claiming Fort Astoria as a prize of war, he set to sea, believing that he had secured the Pacific Northwest for Britain, never knowing that his curious and overzealous actions may have done just the opposite.

Not long after Captain Black departed Fort George, a North West Company ship arrived to resupply McTavish and his men. (Astor still couldn't get a ship through because of the naval blockade.) Eight years after Lewis and Clark made their epic trek down the Columbia to the coast, the Columbia watershed was finally being serviced from the Pacific—but in control of the trade was a British company out of Montreal, not an American company. About a year later, on December 24, 1814, American and British commissioners in Europe settled the War of 1812 by signing the Treaty of Ghent. Most significantly, the main provision of the treaty required each side to restore any territory seized during the war. And hadn't Captain Black seized Astoria?

It was not until later that anyone in British and American diplomatic circles knew what had happened on the distant Columbia, but as soon as they found out, the legal squabbles began. Astoria was sold to the North West Company, claimed the British, and therefore had nothing to do with the Treaty of Ghent. It was captured by a British officer in December 1813, claimed the Americans, and as property seized during the war it must be returned. No one wanted another war over a few paltry huts, however, even if they were located on the Columbia, so both parties eventually agreed to abide by the terms of the treaty. In October 1818, a British ship slipped over the Columbia's bar and anchored off Fort George. British and American commissioners went ashore, exchanged documents, hoisted the Stars and Stripes and stood by as the transfer was consummated with a tremendous blast from the ship's guns. Fort Astoria was now American again, at least in the minds of the diplomats.

The question of sovereignty over the entire region, however, was not so simple. Not only had none of the independently governing Indigenous people of the territory been consulted or informed, but it was also out of the hands of the fur traders. Mighty global empires had set their eyes on territorial dominance, and the fur companies, puny even by business standards of the day and dwarfed by the power of their nations, were to act as the bulkhead of empire by obeying and coercing others to obey the laws of their nations. With the Convention of 1818, American and British negotiators agreed on a border along the 49th parallel east of the Rocky Mountains, but they did not extend the boundary farther west. They each felt they had valid political precedents in favour of their claims to the Far West—the Americans because Robert Gray first sailed up the Columbia River and because Fort Astoria (properly American again after the Treaty of Ghent) was the only permanent non-Indigenous settlement on the coast; the British because of the extensive coastal surveys of James Cook and George Vancouver, and because the only non-Indigenous people living in the Interior were fur traders with the North West Company (although many of them were undoubtedly of mixed heritage).

By the early nineteenth century, the land was already being haggled over by distant empires who studied large, detailed (but not perfectly accurate) charts of the entire North American continent. Life went on. Furs were still valuable, and the traders continued their relationships with the Indigenous people, their daily lives taken up with prosaic activities like hunting, raising their mixed-heritage children and finding enjoyment and meaning where they could. But others, viewing the land as a game board in an epic contest of strategy and hegemony, were scrutinizing rivers, lakes and mountains, scouring travellers' accounts of journeys and making plans to control the land, unbeknownst to the people who lived there. The story of Old Oregon now involved political agreements and treaties negotiated on the opposite side of the world, on foreign continents, by people who had never even travelled to the lands they haggled over and had little knowledge of the cultures and political structures of the people who would be most affected.

The European colonial settlement of eastern North America had progressed quickly in the last decade of the eighteenth century and into the nineteenth century. Cities like Boston, New York and Philadelphia had mushroomed after the revolution, and farmland expanded to feed the influx of people and increasingly encroached on the traditional territories of Indigenous peoples. The British, anxious to maintain against the United States a legal claim to the Columbia River, the artery of the fur trade west of the Great Divide, proposed extending the 49th parallel west to the Columbia and then following the Columbia as the border to the sea. To the American negotiators who had their eye on the large, deep harbours of Puget Sound (the only viable harbours for large ships north of San Francisco) this was not ideal. But in 1818, weary from years of inconclusive conflict during the War of 1812, neither the British nor the Americans were willing to grapple over who would lay claim to the land on the far side of the Continental Divide. So they agreed to jointly "occupy" the region, deferring more complicated, and politically charged, questions to the future. (The terms of the Convention of 1818 were reaffirmed indefinitely in 1827, with the provision that either country could cancel the agreement with one year's notice.)

In February 1819, the United States and Spain signed the Adams–Onis Treaty. In addition to selling the territory of Florida for $5 million, Spain also agreed to the northern boundary of California being set at the 42nd parallel and ceded any rights to the territory north of that to the United States. Russia, in two separate treaties—with the United States in 1824 and with Britain in 1825—bowed out of Old Oregon (but retained the right to trade in the region), agreeing to a southern boundary for Alaska roughly similar to the Canadian-American border today.

Old Oregon, now defined as the territory west of the Rocky Mountains, north of Spanish California and south of Russian Alaska, became a political no man's land, jointly claimed on paper by Britain and the United States, and open to settlement and commercial development from either nation, although neither had any tangible presence there and they had neglected to inform the local inhabitants of their decision. Of course, the only commercial development was the fur trade, and the traders were more likely to follow the customs of their Indigenous hosts and customers than those of Londoners, Montrealers or New Yorkers. The vast territory remained unchanged for decades, until the 1830s, when the first wagon trains began rolling west along the Oregon Trail.

The Hudson's Bay Company and the North West Company faced other challenges east of the Rockies that proved to be more of a threat—their own internecine quarrels.

Chapter Twelve

COMPANIES AT WAR

As the Nor'Westers fanned out across the northwestern interior, building many dozens of tiny, often temporary, ramshackle forts at promising river junctions, they were laying the groundwork for a network for intercontinental trade, travel and logistics. Although they were followed westward wherever they went by the Hudson's Bay Company, the future of the fur trade seemed to lie with the Montreal business model and not the London model that had steered the Company for over a century. Salaried workers, even with bonuses, suited a stable commercial landscape, while the commission-based compensation of the North West Company, where whole careers and fortunes could be made exclusively upon the number of furs obtained, suited a changing environment. The situation was similar to today's disruption in the news industry brought on by the internet, where the measured and stable subscription-driven outlets have been shattered by the quest for sensational stories and angles to generate clicks and hence advertising revenue.

Of course, the aggressive business model of the Nor'Westers had no concern for externalities such as overhunting or disruption of Indigenous societies. Nevertheless, hidebound traditions and social hierarchy imported from Britain, such as three different grades of tea served to different levels of employees depending upon their social status, were laughable examples of the Company's ossified and inefficient structure. The two enterprises seemed almost to be the inverse of each other. In the early nineteenth century, during the battle between the companies, the Company directly employed fewer than five hundred people, whereas approximately four times that number of employees and contractors were associated with the North West Company. The North West Company had expanded rapidly and was also doing four times the business. But by 1811, many of these men were neither exclusively labourers, traders or canoe or York boatmen—they were, whatever else they might be, also guerrilla warriors.

The competition between the companies became so intense that they often built their forts and outposts within sight of each other, each hoping to attract customers with their slightly different variation on the standard package of trade goods: the Hudson's Bay Company offered good wool blankets and copper pots; the North West Company offered higher-quality tailored coats. While the Company pushed inland from the bay, the Nor'Westers pushed north of the Great Lakes into the Company's traditional territory around the Bottom of the Bay and all but strangled the trade to many of the venerable posts along the coast. Soon there were dozens of posts across the land and virtually all Cree and Chipewyan transportation and resale agents were driven out of business.

As a consequence of these changing patterns of trade, the Company's multi-generational policies and customs, such as recognizing the status of Indigenous trade captains and advancing credit for necessities for the winter, were undermined by the proliferation of dozens of small inland trading posts. Collecting debts in this environment became more difficult to manage, as did maintaining long-term relationships.

After Mackenzie's upstart XY Company merged with the North West Company in 1804, the Nor'Westers and the Company had only each other to compete with. All the stable conventions of trade that had governed the Company's business for over a century were slowly abandoned—no more ceremonial affirmations of friendship, respect given to Indigenous trading captains and their lieutenants who brought in the furs to Hudson Bay. Company employees now did that job, many of them of mixed heritage. There were still plenty of jobs for hunters, trappers, labourers, but the career choices were becoming limited and the new environment was not conducive to building local business pyramids. Soon, the only role for Indigenous workers was as contract employees, which resulted in an increasing lack of agency.

The relationship between the Company and its customers changed from a meeting of peoples and cultures for mutually beneficial commercial exchange, with each side managing its own business and politics, to one where the terms of exchange were dictated increasingly by one party. Although the competition may have brought cheaper prices, these came at the cost of a truncated menu of career options, thus entrenching cultural and racial divisions of economic activity and stifling entrepreneurial ambition. In the short term the competition no doubt delighted the Indigenous fur trappers, who could bargain hard for their furs, visiting multiple posts easily to gain the best deal. But over time the culture that came with the North West Company undermined their freedom and economy.

At some point during the interminable struggle for dominance, the commercial war became an actual war. With no police force to enforce civil conduct, as would be the case in Britain or along the St. Lawrence, and no single Indigenous band or nation strong enough to enforce universal laws and regulations, the companies, at least in the field, turned into gangs of unscrupulous thugs who roamed northern North America without restrictions.

The lucrative region of the Athabasca country, essentially the Northwest Territories and northern Alberta and Saskatchewan, was first brought into the commercial orbit of the fur trade by Peter Pond, Mackenzie and others in the late eighteenth century and disrupted the commercial activities of Indigenous traders like Matonabbee. The Company hadn't sent anyone to the Athabasca country after Matonabbee and Hearne's journeys decades earlier. In 1790, their choice of agent, the surveyor Philip Turnor, left much to be desired. He was so ill prepared that he mostly wandered and hunted; he survived because of the good-will of local people who were positively disposed toward the Company.

Turnor reported that the Nor'Westers dominated the region but that the people harboured a dislike of them and their aggressive, disrespect-ful, atrocious customs such as demanding a woman as payment for her husband's or father's debts, and then selling or indenturing her until the debt was paid. He reported that certain Nor'Westers sometimes oper-ated more like a mafia protection racket than as commercial agents. The Athabasca region, home to the largest beavers with the most luxuriant pelts, lay outside the Company's monopoly in Rupert's Land and in the Arctic watershed, so the Company had no moral or legal grounds to push the Nor'Westers out, while the Nor'Westers in turn fought to keep the Company's envoys at bay, claiming the territory belonged to them exclusively, even threatening or assaulting Indigenous people who ven-tured near the Company's outposts.

The next Company employee to venture into Athabasca country was Peter Fidler, a young English recruit whom Turnor had trained, along with young David Thompson, in the skills of surveying and map-mak-ing. Fidler was sent west in 1802, with his Cree wife, Mary, and fifteen Orkney Island labourers, to establish a Company post at Lake Athabasca situated near the North West Company's Fort Athabasca. Fidler called it Manchester House, and it proved a miserable place to live, with freez-ing winters and roving packs of ravenous wild dogs. But Fidler's chief complaint was with the Nor'Westers, who he thought far worse than feral dogs. They marched over during the construction of Manchester House and boldly informed Fidler that he had no legal right to be in the region (apparently ascribing no authority to the Dene-speaking peoples in whose lands both companies were operating).

Fidler's chief adversaries were two younger clerks, Peter Ogden and Samuel Black. Black was later described as "a Ghastly, raw boned and lanthorn jawed" Scotsman, who was "equal to the cutting of a throat with perfect deliberation" and who was "a cold blooded fellow who could be guilty of any Cruelty." Together, Black and Ogden, the wild young son of a Montreal lawyer, earned a reputation as a dark duo when they worked together, ruthless blackguards.

With twenty-six people at Fort Athabasca, against only half as many at Fidler's disposal at Manchester House, the Nor'Westers threatened and assaulted Indigenous people whom they suspected of visiting Company posts, sometimes raiding their encampments, and they harassed Company employees, firing gunshots near them when they were on hunting expeditions. Black later burned down the Company post at Île-à-la-Crosse and was complicit in murder. Nevertheless, he had a long career in the fur trade even after the two companies merged in 1821. Indigenous people lived in dread of him whenever he took control of remote outposts. One wonders about the relationship he had with his two Métis country wives and eight children. When Black was finally killed, in 1841, by Tranquille, a chief of the Shuswap who was fed up with his terrorizing behaviour, Black's family in Scotland fought to disinherit his North American wife and children by claiming his marriage wasn't legal. Ogden also went on to a long but controversial career in the trade when he moved west to Old Oregon in the 1820s, leaving behind his flirtation with anti-social violence.

Despite Black's and later Ogden's torment over the years, Fidler, who was proficient in the Chipewyan, Piegan and Cree languages and customs, worked the remainder of his life with the Company at various posts throughout the interior and devoted himself to surveying and cartography. He was involved in establishing the Red River Settlement for a few years before he returned to the fur trade. He and Mary had fourteen children, eleven of whom survived to adulthood, before he died of a stroke at the age of fifty-one at Dauphin Lake House in central

Manitoba. Unlike Black, Fidler at least left a clear, legally recognized will for his family.

The chaos and social disintegration caused by the warring companies was the perfect environment for sociopathic personalities to express violence and to disrespect social norms—to engage in bullying, intimidation and psychological warfare—since there was no one to moderate their behaviour. They were in fact rewarded for defeating the competition—in a literal rather than a business sense. As the nineteenth century progressed, violence, threats and intimidation quickly became a viable commercial strategy. The companies ambushed and shot at each other along the main canoe routes, attacked each other's forts and plundered their trade goods and annual fur shipments, and moved artillery around and built batteries to threaten and control the key rivers. Forts were no longer euphemistically named places of business but were built with a view to defence. Most of the terrorist-style activities were initially undertaken by the Nor'Westers, such as cutting down stockades, stealing fishnets and threatening the competition's customers. In 1816, while stationed at Île-à-la-Crosse, Fidler fumed that "some people reading this Journal might very naturally suppose, that many of the ill actions that has been done was by people in a state of inebriety—but they are very sober people—it is a systematic plan that has been laid at Grand Portage to harass & distress us." A constant low level of violence prevailed throughout the entire region, and the underlying stress permeated all aspects of life for both traders and Indigenous peoples.

Both companies turned to Mohawk-Iroquois voyageurs, who were also good enforcers. In the early 1800s, the North West Company brought in hundreds of eastern Iroquois from near its headquarters at Montreal on three-year-long contracts to trap beaver in the Saskatchewan District in direct competition with the local hunters, and the combined harvest rapidly depleted the beaver in the region. The Iroquois emerged as the most efficient fur trappers in the northwest. They devoted themselves to it fully as an economic activity instead of merely trapping sporadically as part of seasonal life. With great and devastating effect, they made use of the newly designed steel-spring leg-hold traps and baited them with castoreum, made from the sex glands of beavers. By the 1820s, beavers in regions of the Saskatchewan District were severely depleted, whereupon the commercial trappers moved into the Athabasca and Peace River regions. It was the Company's hiring of Mohawk-Iroquois that in turn finally allowed it to break into the lucrative Athabasca District in 1815. The Iroquois were more aggressive and not as easily intimidated as the Company's Orkney Islander workforce. They did not back down from threats from Nor'Wester agents or their hired muscle from local Indigenous groups.

This new era of trade was carried out beyond the reach of legal restraint, in a region where it was possible to pursue any tactic that would afford advantage. As Alexander Mackenzie presciently noted, "The consequence was not only the loss of commercial benefit to the persons engaged in it, but of the good opinion of the natives, and the respect of their men, who were inclined to follow their example; so that with drinking, carousing, and quarrelling with the Indians along their route, and among themselves, they seldom reached their winter quarters; and if they did, it was generally by dragging their property upon sledges, as the navigation was closed up by the frost. When at length they were arrived, the object of each was to injure his rival traders in the opinion of the natives as much as was in their power, by misrepresentation and presents . . . who could entertain no respect for persons who had conducted themselves with so much irregularity and deceit. . . . The winter, therefore, was one continued scene of disagreements and quarrels . . . To such an height had they carried this licentious conduct, that they were in a continual state of alarm, and were even frequently stopped to pay tribute on their route into the country; though they had adopted the plan of travelling together in parties of thirty or forty canoes, and keeping their men armed; which sometimes, indeed, proved necessary for their defence. Thus was the trade carried on for several years, and consequently becoming worse and worse."

THE GREATEST PROBLEM OF THE CHAOTIC, warlike state of the inland commerce was the damaging effect liquor had on Indigenous cultures, particularly in the Saskatchewan District. (In the Athabasca District liquor never became a huge trade item and was never in demand, as Dene-speaking peoples had limited interest in it.) The pushing of rotgut liquor as an easy trade item had demoralizing and destructive results for the Indigenous peoples even while profits piled up in Montreal, the distillers flourished and the partners lived like lairds. In the early 1800s, up to one-third of the cargo in North West Company brigades was liquor; a decade later, tens of thousands of gallons flowed west from Montreal. Nor'Wester field partners shared directly in the profits of their goods and were inclined to maximize their returns, whereas most of the Company's field personnel were employees who didn't profit directly and were anyway more inclined to avoid disruptive practices. But although the Company had opposed the indiscriminate sale of hard liquor since 1670, believing it was bad for business, in the 1800s it too began to peddle its own variation of "brandy" and "rum"— gin tinted with iodine or tobacco juice.

York Factory and on occasion other forts established their own stills during the Napoleonic Wars, when the British government forbade domestic distillation as a form of rationing. There was far more profit to be had pushing concentrated and easy-to-transport booze than selling frying pans, beads and tools, which required a sophisticated distribution and stock-management system, such as the Company had developed over generations. Regardless of the views of individual traders (many of whom, it should be noted, were what we would today call problem drinkers, as were the partners at the Beaver Club in Montreal, if not the directors in London), the decision to push liquor was made farther up the chain of command. Also, as the Company found to its detriment, if liquor was not one of the goods on offer, most of the fur business migrated to the North West Company. Once in the field, both companies diluted the concentrated liquor with water, although this led to suspicious customers who devised a novel method to determine its potency. They would flick or spit a small quantity into a fire. If it flared up or sparkled it was deemed sufficiently pure; if it made the flames sputter, they wouldn't pay as much for it. Hence the origin of the term *firewater*.

By the second decade of the nineteenth century, both companies used liquor as a means of bringing people into their establishments. Free booze was distributed as an inducement to trade, and perhaps also to cloud judgment and weaken resolve. Free liquor soon became an expectation and was no longer restricted to special occasions or ceremonies. The quality of other trade goods declined in correlation.

This new style of business repulsed many of the older Company men. Alexander Henry had spent many years in the early nineteenth century, during the era of the warring companies, working at posts along the Pembina River, in the Plains and aspen parkland, and he had much to say on the topic of spirituous liquor and its dreadful effect on country life. When there were murders, beatings or abductions of women, he concluded it was because of excessive drinking. One haunting evening he recorded, "Tabashaw stabbed a near relation of his own, Missistaygouine, in six different places in the breast and sides; every stab went up to the handle; the poor fellow lingered an hour and died. Water Hen, in fighting with another Indian, was thrown into the fire and roasted terribly from his neck to his rump. . . . The Indians totally neglect their ancient customs; and what can this degeneracy be ascribed but to their intercourse with us, particularly as they are so unfortunate as to have a continual succession of opposition parties to teach them roguery and destroy both mind and body with that pernicious article, rum? What a different set of people they would be were there not a drop of liquor in the country. . . . We may truly say that liquor is the root of all evil in the North West."

Henry's journal describes frequent violence and fighting almost always precipitated by the distribution of hard liquor. "In a drinking match at The Hills yesterday, Gros Bras in a fit of jealousy stabbed Aupusoi to death with a hand-dague [knife]; the first stroke opened his left side, the second his belly, and the third his breast; he never stirred, although he had a knife in his belt, and died instantly." In revenge, Aupusoi's young brother grabbed a musket, loaded it, snuck over to Gros Bras's tent, stuck the gun through the opening and fired, killing him. Others, related to Gros Bras, soon came and stabbed to death the boys' mother, Little Shell. Then "the little fellow ran into the woods and hid . . . until they were all sober." Another entry records "Indians arriving daily and drinking the proceeds of the spring hunt . . . Le Boeuf quarreled with his wife and knocked her senseless with a club, which opened a gash on her head six inches long and down to the bone. She laid so long before she recovered her senses that I believed her dead."

Fur trader Daniel Harmon describes one lurid incident in 1800 that rivals those described by Henry: a woman was drinking and soon began brandishing a knife, until she stumbled, fell over and drove the blade two inches into her own abdomen. "To see a house full of Drunken Indians, as it generally consists of Men, Women and Children, is a truly unpleasant sight, for they in that condition often quarrel, fight and pull each other by the hair, and at times you will see ten or twelve or more all by the ears at one and the same time, till at last they all fall flat on the floor, one upon the top of the other, some spilling Rum out of a Kettle or Dish . . . while others are throwing up what they have just drank." Of course, Harmon, a sermonizing New Englander who moved back east to Vermont with his Cree wife, Elizabeth, and their children, also detested drunkenness in the Canadian voyageurs. "Of all the people in the world, I think the Canadians, when Drunk, are the most disagreeable . . . Indeed, I would rather have fifty drunken Indians in the fort, than five drunken Canadians." Alcohol abuse in the Saskatchewan District during these years was widespread and certainly contributed to the breakdown of the social customs that had governed Indigenous peoples and traders alike.

These and other reports are a dispiriting window into societies being shaken, the disintegration of social bonds and the reign of entropy, as structure was washed away by the twin forces of epidemic disease and hard liquor. No one had control over disease. But the hard liquor, which was both a symptom of and a further cause of the social disintegration, was a direct result of the cutthroat competition between the companies in their quest to control the fur trade. Liquor and private warfare, with all their attendant social ills, were also bad for the economy. Soon their own competition superseded the very business of trading for furs that justified their existence. The Company was unable to pay any dividend in 1809, and its expenses were increasing just as the value of furs flatlined during the wars with Napoleon and the closure of European markets. After years of deadly competition that drove both companies to the brink of bankruptcy, the war came to a head in the Red River valley in today's province of Manitoba.

THOMAS DOUGLAS, THE FIFTH EARL OF SELKIRK, was a Scottish philanthropist of vast fortune. Mercurial, whimsical and accustomed to the luxury of his parlour and library, he was a dreamer, broad-minded and educated in the liberal arts at the University of Edinburgh. A quiet, thoughtful man of around forty at the time of his colonizing scheme, he was noted for his fine clothing and his refined tastes, the opposite of the bombastic and boastful Mackenzie then prominent in public discourse about the fur trade.

While attending university in the 1790s, Douglas became aware of the distressing condition of Scottish Highlanders displaced from their lands during the infamous Highland Clearances, in which Scottish lairds, only a generation after the brutal conquest of the Highland clans by the English at the Battle of Culloden, evicted their sharecropping peasants so they could more profitably run sheep pastures. Tens of thousands of tenant farmers were forced off the land and relocated to other regions or overseas. Lord Selkirk then spent some time in revolutionary France, where he solidified his social conscience. After coming unexpectedly into a massive inheritance after the deaths of six older brothers, Lord Selkirk vowed to do something to improve the Highlanders' lot in life. His family, after all, was known for bold, romantic undertakings, for following their passions: their coat of arms featured a heart with a crown. He wrote a book, *Observations on the Present State of the Highlands of Scotland*, in which he argued that emigration was inevitable, and he began to think of the problem as one that he could personally solve.

On a trip to Montreal in 1803, Lord Selkirk dined at the infamous Beaver Club, where tales of the distant northwest inflamed his imagination. As a sort of test run for his more grandiose dream for Rupert's Land, he had organized the relocation and settlement to Prince Edward Island of nearly eight hundred Highlanders. He then tried a similar scheme in Upper Canada. Since these proved moderately successful, he thought these hardy folks would also thrive in the Red River region, where the Company had a fort, where herds of bison could be hunted for meat and where the land, according to Alexander Mackenzie, was fertile.

It was hard to come by free land for settlers in populated Upper and Lower Canada, and Lord Selkirk quickly discovered that if he intended to avoid territory that was claimed by the United States he was limited to Rupert's Land, a territory that was, according to British law at least, the commercial monopoly of the venerable Hudson's Bay Company. Therefore, he reasoned, if he could buy up the Company's stock, he then could influence the directors to grant him the right to establish his utopian agricultural colony in the territory of their grant. However, holding a commercial monopoly that hindered domestic competitors did not mean the Company and its several hundred inland employees held any political authority. Clearly, they did not, in practice or desire, a point that was to cause Selkirk and his settlers a great deal of trouble.

Selkirk's affiliation with the Company began with his marriage. His wife, Jean, was an heiress from the rich and influential Wedderburn family, which had large investments in Company stock. War was ongoing in Europe; dividends had been cut in half in 1801 and ceased altogether in 1809. As a result, and compounded by the continuing commerce-destroying struggle with its Canadian rivals, Company stock was depressed. The share price plummeted from £250 to £50 while paying no dividends for five years. Selkirk and his brother-in-law, Andrew Wedderburn, and other family members began quietly buying up the stock, which was seldom traded and not very actively scrutinized. Eventually they acquired enough shares to take a controlling interest, narrowly beating out a rival attempt by Alexander Mackenzie and the North West Company. Wedderburn took a position on the board of governors in London and began to reorganize the Company's finances into a "New System" of "Retrenching," to bring fiscal discipline to the complicated logistics the Company faced during its interminable conflict with the Nor'Westers.

A Company-owned colony, Wedderburn proposed, could help bring down the cost of importing goods, particularly for food and other products that were expensive to sail across the Atlantic to the frozen rim of the bay. An agricultural colony could provision posts for a fraction of the cost as well as provide a place for retiring fur traders to go with their country families as an alternative to returning to Britain or Montreal.

In May 1811, for the paltry sum of ten shillings and some other considerations, the Company gave Selkirk 116,000 square miles (300,438 square kilometres) of prime land at the forks of the Red and Assiniboine Rivers south of Lake Winnipeg, a broad swath of steppe, swamp and rocky lakeland between Lake Superior and the Rocky Mountains. Although the land was flood-prone and windy for most of the year, it was fertile. The main problem with the entire scheme was that the Nor'Westers, the Métis and various Indigenous peoples were already using the land, and they disputed that the Company had any right to give it away to its supporters. The proposed settlement site, not accidentally, was situated directly on the main transportation route used by the North West Company, between Montreal and the prime fur territory of the northwest.

Lake Winnipeg was the nexus of the intercontinental trade network. Connected by waterways that led in all directions, from there traders and travellers could paddle to much of northern North America with little more than a day's portage. It was also where the pemmican needed to feed the canoe and York boat brigades of both companies could easily be purchased. The Red River valley became the centre of the corporate battle, since its resources were vital for business.

By this time the logistics of the trade demanded great numbers of labourers and voyageurs. Stuffed into ninety-pound sacks, pemmican was a commodity that was the lifeblood without which the North West Company couldn't exist. The Nor'Westers had several depots that traded goods for pemmican in the Red River district and shipped it to Bas de la Rivière Fort on Lake Winnipeg, where it was then issued to canoe brigades heading to the distant but fur-rich Athabasca region. Pemmican was also shipped south and east to Fort William and used to feed canoe brigades heading back to Montreal. Though bison roamed in mighty herds on the open prairie, hunting was antithetical to farming. Selkirk's utopian colony was viewed as a vicarious attack on the North West Company. Simon McGillivray, a prominent partner in the North West Company, was very direct: "It will require some time and I fear cause much expense to us as well as to himself [Selkirk], before he is driven to abandon the project; and yet *he must be driven to abandon it*, for his success would strike at the very existence of our trade."

Selkirk had never been anywhere near Red River, but this didn't deter him. He was used to the privilege and luxury that accrued to one of the wealthiest people in Britain. He could afford to dream. But he also could afford ignorance, since he wouldn't be among the people initially travelling to these distant lands. Selkirk called his new domain Assiniboia. Five times the size of Scotland, it covered a large part of Manitoba and parts of Saskatchewan, North Dakota and Minnesota (states that did not yet exist). He hired Captain Miles Macdonell, a Scottish soldier who had fought in the American Revolution, to lead a party to scout the land in advance of the arrival of the Selkirk settlers.

But Selkirk wouldn't encounter smooth sailing. His nemesis Mackenzie was never one to shy from conflict; in fact he seemed to thrive on it. He denounced Selkirk's project as a "mad scheme" and vowed to fight the settlers or to urge Indigenous peoples to assault them. The battle wouldn't be waged by him personally, of course. Mackenzie had never returned to the northwest after earning his fame and fortune by reaching the Pacific decades earlier, and even then he had not had any influence over or respect for the Indigenous peoples. He would pay others to do his dirty work while he remained in England. This work involved printing and distributing pamphlets and taking out advertisements in newspapers that denounced the operation to prospective crofters in Scotland, warning them of the starvation and hard times they would face, as well as bribing customs officials to become extra-vigilant in vetting customs papers at Scottish ports and even paying potential émigrés not to sail. As a result of these bureaucratic impediments, Selkirk's settlers sailed late for York Factory and were late taking the York boats inland to Red River. Meanwhile, all along the Nor'Wester supply line, directives were issued to make life hard for the new settlers, to offer them no assistance and indeed to impede them whenever possible.

Although the Company and Selkirk's colony were theoretically independent entities, they were strongly linked. The colony was supposed to bring over from Scotland up to two hundred settlers each year, but many of them were initially signed on as Company employees or indentured servants in an effort to bring some order and discipline to them. Macdonell was also an officer with the Company.

The first contingent of Selkirk's settlers arrived in the harsh Canadian prairies in 1812 and met with immediate hostility from the North West Company and its bison-hunting Métis allies.

IN RUPERT'S LAND, generations of relationships between Scottish traders, French-Canadian and Iroquois voyagers and various other Indigenous peoples had resulted in a muddled mélange of customs, traditions and genetic ancestry—indeed a unique social life and identity. There had been children of mixed parentage since the first Europeans arrived from across the Atlantic, but these people had never lived in great numbers in any one region. Most of them resided in the vicinity of the St. Lawrence or along the western coast of Hudson Bay and were associated with the fur trade. By the early nineteenth century, however, thousands of these people had migrated to the vicinity of the Red River. One observer, Alexander Ross, who had resided in the region for many years, wrote that "not a tenth part of their number really belong to Red River, although they have from choice made it the land of their adoption. Hither, in fact have flocked the half-breeds from all quarters east of the Rocky Mountain ridge, making the colony their great rendezvous and nursing place."

With Indigenous mothers, and fathers or grandfathers of generally French or Scottish ancestry through the fur trade, these people had developed a powerful sense of separateness and distinctiveness from either of their backgrounds. They were often called *bois-brûlé*, "burnt wood," for their slightly lighter skin tone compared with the Indigenous peoples, and slightly darker complexion than Europeans. The French Catholic ones were called Métis, perhaps derived from the Spanish term *mestizo*, or "mixture," that was applied to people of mixed Spanish and Mexican heritage, and this term became more commonly applied throughout the century. (Nowadays the term *Métis* is often loosely applied to all people of blended European and Indigenous ancestry, but is distinguished from official political and legal category of the Métis Nation.) James Carnegie, a peripatetic English lord who travelled the prairies and Rocky Mountains in the nineteenth century, was impressed with their physique, calling the Métis "a fine race, tall, straight, well proportioned, lightly formed and extremely active and enduring. Their chests, shoulders and waists are of that symmetrical shape so seldom found among the broad-waisted, short-necked English or the flat chested, long necked Scotch." The Métis were noted for their pride and sense of honour, and for their generosity, hospitality and joy of dancing and celebration.

One of the distinctive commercial activities of the emerging Métis culture was the biannual bison hunt, which was made possible by the eponymous Red River carts, two-wheeled ox carts that, owing to ungreased axles, made such an ear-piercing screech, like thousands of fingernails on a thousand blackboards, that they could be heard for miles across the prairie. The Red River carts had been in use at least since 1801, and most likely for decades before then. The hunt, a month-long communal activity that demanded cooperation and strict rules, took place in June and September. Once the people had come together from their disparate communities, they elected an overall "chief" of the hunt and ten captains who would organize and manage the affair. Others were chosen as soldiers and guides. General rules changed from hunt to hunt depending on the leader, but often included no hunting on the Sabbath; no branching off or lagging or separating from the group for whatever reason; and no hunting until the order was given by the captain. The punishments for violating these rules were rooted in social pressure: having one's saddle or coat publicly cut up, flogging for a repeat offence (extremely rare) or being publicly humiliated by being called a thief in front of the congregation. The prohibition against theft and hunting ahead of the group were rules common of the Cree, while the rules that structured the actual hunt came from Plains Indigenous cultures who were accustomed to communal bison hunting.

Ross relates a particular story that illustrates the Métis communities' strong self-regulation. "On one occasion, a gentleman on his way to the

States forgot, in his camping place, a tin box containing 580 sovereigns in gold, and in silver and bills the amount of 450 more. The following night, however, a halfbreed named Saint Matte happened to encamp on the same spot, picked up the box, followed the gentleman a day's journey, and delivered box and contents into his hands to the utmost farthing, well knowing it was money. Considering their poverty, we might well speak of Saint Matte's conduct in the highest strains of praise. And this act might be taken as an index of the integrity of the whole body, generally speaking . . . Punishments here are scarcely more than nominal; and may well suggest the question to a more civilized community, whether it is always the severest punishments that have the best effect in reclaiming offenders."

After stocking up on goods purchased on credit at Fort Gibraltar (later renamed Fort Garry), the first contingent of the Métis camp would head south from Lake Winnipeg to Pembina and then branch west, picking up additional families on the way. They travelled twenty-five kilometres a day, enveloped by the piercing dirge of axles and wooden wheels with bison hide for tires. Whenever they came upon a river, they removed the wheels and floated their carts over like a boat. Each night they turned the carts into a defensive circle, within which sprung up a community of tents that hosted the evening's festivities around a great campfire, while guards patrolled the perimeter. Their enemies included the Plains Sioux, who claimed the territory as their own and who would frequently attack smaller or undefended groups. Each evening, the captain and principal lieutenants ascended a grassy knoll and squatted in a circle with their pipes, discussing the day's progress and the plans for tomorrow. Ross wrote of these nightly confers, "There is happiness and pleasure in the society of the most illiterate men, sympathetically if not intellectually, as well as among the learned: and I must say, I found less selfishness and more liberality among those ordinary men than I had been accustomed to find in higher circles. Their conversation was free, practical, and interesting."

The only thing that disturbed Ross was their vehement proclamations of independence and freedom. "They cordially detest all the laws and restraints of civilized life, believing all men were born to be free. In their own estimation they are all great men, and wonderfully wise; and so long as they wander about on these wild and lawless expeditions, they will never become a thoroughly civilized people, nor orderly subjects in a civilized community."

Each morning the camp would disband and move off to the west in search of the herds, each cart travelling abreast of the others rather than in a line to avoid the great clouds of dust. The families walked beside their oxen and carts the entire distance, thousands of kilometres on each hunt, and the entire congregation was followed by a braying pack of hundreds of dogs. These semi-feral beasts were kept all summer and were fed bison even as supplies dwindled so that in the winter they could be used for hauling sledges. Each Red River cart could carry as much as nine hundred pounds of cargo and go in any direction so long as the ground was level. They were not used for a family's personal items.

The purpose of these massive hunts was not personal sustenance, as was the case for most Indigenous societies, but the large-scale production of bison robes and pemmican to sell to the fur brigades and posts. Later on, during the eastern Industrial Revolution, the hides were used for machine belts. By the 1840s, bison had supplanted beaver as the most important fur for trade, but soon even the once endless herds were becoming "beavered out" by overhunting, which created tensions between peoples as their range shifted farther west. Before 1820, around five hundred carts set off on the hunt, but by 1840 there were over twelve hundred, and they had to range ever farther west on the prairie to locate the dwindling herds. From an estimated sixty million bison in 1600, the population had declined to forty million by 1830, and they were nearly extinct by the 1880s. Many millions were killed for sport with repeating rifles or by men hired to provide food for railway workers or machine belts, leaving the Métis with nothing to eat, no leather for clothing or shelter, no bones for tools, no hair for rope, and causing widespread starvation among the Plains peoples.

Alexander Ross witnessed one great hunt in 1840. After weeks of travel, scouts rode back and reported that they had spied a great herd, and the sprawling mass of carts slowly ground to a halt and set up camp for a longer stay. Early in the morning, hundreds of mounted hunters spread out in a line, readied their multiple guns, with their mouths stuffed with extra musket balls. After a suitably dramatic pause, the guide raised his arm and bellowed, "*Commencez!*" There was a slow bestirring down the line, and then "the whole cavalcade broke ground and made for the buffalo, first at a slow trot, then at a gallop and lastly at full speed. They had approached within four or five hundred yards before the bulls curved their tails or pawed the ground. In a moment more, the whole herd took flight and horses and riders were presently seen bursting in among them; shots are heard and all is smoke, dust and hurry." It was a wild melee of sport and slaughter. Riders dashed among the panicked beasts, guiding their horses with their knees amid blinding clouds of dust, steering to avoid the lurching, bellowing bison and fallen riders. In a stunning display of equestrian prowess, they reloaded as they manoeuvred around each downed beast through the heat and dust and sea of surging bison. Wielding their guns with both hands, they fired at close range, within three metres, below and behind the left shoulder, into the heart. Shaking a fresh powder charge into the muzzle, hunters spat the next ball from their mouths and tamped the shoulder stock on their saddle to settle it before again attending to the roiling mass of thundering hooves and thrusting horns that surrounded them.

When the herd outran the hunters and the dust settled, the grass-lands as far as the eye could see were covered in dark mounds of dead or dying animals. Riders trotted around surveying the field. "The surface was rough and full of badger holes," Ross reported. "Twenty-three horses and riders were at one moment all sprawling on the ground. One horse gored by a bull was killed on the spot; two more were disabled by falls. One rider broke his shoulder blade, another burst his gun and lost three fingers by the accident and a third was struck on the knee by an exhausted ball. These accidents will not be thought over-numerous considering the result, for in the evening no less than 1,375 tongues were brought into camp."

The hunt that Ross recorded resulted in an astonishing 225 pounds of meat per person. They immediately set to butchering the animals and cleaning the hides, while the women moved the carts and lodges of the camp into the middle of the carnage. In the days that followed, everyone, even the children, worked from dawn to dusk constructing racks and drying the meat in the sun and packing it onto carts for transport. Most of the meat would later be made into pemmican. Pemmican was made by placing the dried bison meat on a cured hide and pounding it into a grainy powder that was then mixed with buffalo grease and saskatoon berries before being packed into bison-skin bags. Pemmican was the ideal food for calorie-starved voyageurs who laboured incessantly with no time to hunt. Dense and calorie-rich, it could be easily transported and eaten straight from the bag if necessary, but was much more palatable when roasted over a fire or added to stews and soups. Once the day's work was over and the sun had set late in the evening, fires were lit, tea was brewed and pipes smoked. Bison tongues roasted over the fire, while the smell of sage and other herbs wafted in the cool air.

Once the meat was processed and hundreds of skeletons lay mounded on the prairie, the hunting brigade made their weary way back east with the squealing carts now heavily laden with meat and valuable hides. Both were sold to the North West Company and the Hudson's Bay Company and earned more money for the Métis than all their farming and other activities combined. The bison hunt was vital to the Métis way of life, while the food and other products of the bison were vital to the companies, but particularly the North West Company, which maintained a serpentine supply line across the continent all the way to the Pacific, where they had taken over the fur trade at Fort Astoria. The

Métis and the Nor'Westers would become natural allies in opposition to anything that threatened their livelihood, for no other reason than mutual self-preservation.

IN AUGUST 1812, GOVERNOR MILES MACDONELL and the first eighteen Red River settlers faced a hard life once they arrived at their not so utopian destination of Assiniboia, at the junction of the Red and Assiniboine Rivers, in what is now the city of Winnipeg. They had spent weeks at sea crossing from England to Hudson Bay on a Company supply ship, followed by a month travelling in York boats upstream—a distance of 620 kilometres with thirty portages—just to reach Lake Winnipeg. With them on this journey was a single cow and a single bull that they named Adam and Eve. Clambering from the boats, they must have stared in dismay at their new home: a flat grassland dotted with aspens along the streams and rivers. After disembarking they stood around while Macdonell made a speech in a simple ceremony, taking "possession" of the land for Lord Selkirk. Then he passed out some rum to the handful of curious Métis and Ojibwa onlookers. The most common Indigenous people in the Red River region were the Saulteaux, or Plains Ojibwa, who had moved west into the territory when the Cree and Assiniboine had moved farther west to take up bison hunting after their business as traders was undermined by the proliferation of inland trading outposts.

The ground was unbroken, which meant the settlers faced a staggeringly heavy workload to bust the sod and churn the earth with primitive hand-held tools and plows pulled by oxen. With nowhere to live, the settlers also had the task of making shelter before winter set in. The planting season had already passed before they had finished constructing a crude palisade they called Fort Douglas, provocatively situated adjacent to the North West Company's Fort Gibraltar. It was the first Company fort in the region.

In October, a second contingent of 120 settlers arrived, and over the next few years hundreds more. They froze, they starved, and locusts devoured their meagre crops, most of which had failed. Scurvy, which always arose in these situations, sucked the life from them. There was disease, grass fires and a flood. They would not have survived without the welcome given them by Chief Peguis and his Plains Ojibwa–Saulteaux followers. Peguis, one of the most influential leaders in the region, tended to side with the Company and the settlers. A short but powerfully muscled man with the booming voice of an orator, he had brought his band of Saulteaux from the Sault Ste. Marie region to settle west of the Red River in the 1790s. Although he was a renowned leader of his people, he was also key in helping Selkirk's settlers survive the early years by showing them how to hunt and by sharing food with them. He and his people even showed the settlers how to hunt bison. He warned them of the North West Company's aggressive intentions to destroy the settlement, but for some reason they ignored him, per-haps overwhelmed by the prospect of starting over. Some of the Métis then threatened Peguis, suggesting that if he made a treaty with the Selkirk settlers, he and his people would be attacked and driven from their lands. They were all living in volatile times, with enflamed passions, prey to ill-conceived actions.

The implacable antagonism of the North West Company made life nearly unbearable for the settlers, and their arrival marked the begin-ning of seven years of enflamed intercompany warfare. Macdonell's bel-ligerent edicts served only to fan the flames. He demanded that his settlers be given first right to purchase pemmican from the Métis and then demanded that the Métis stop hunting bison on horseback, osten-sibly to preserve the herds near his outpost. What right did he have to be making authoritarian edicts to people who had been living on the land for ages before he arrived? Whenever Macdonell issued a directive, it was ignored and mocked by the Métis, and they continued on with life as usual—but now with a kernel of resentment and anger at the arrogance of the foreigners who sought to command them. As Ross had noted, a strong belief that people were born free and were not subject to the arbitrary whims of anyone else was one of the key social traits that ran through the Métis community. In their view, Macdonell had no authority over them just because he claimed that an ancient paper across the ocean made him the boss.

Macdonell's actions became increasingly desperate, and on January 8, 1814, with his settlers facing starvation, he issued a decree that was to have dire consequences. Since the settlers of the colony needed food, the Pemmican Proclamation declared it illegal to export pemmican from the colony for one year. He sent out riders to the North West Company posts, including Fort Gibraltar and Fort La Souris (near Brandon House so as to trade with the Mandan in North Dakota), and nailed the proclamation to their gates. He then instructed his men to begin arresting Métis bison hunters for supplying North West Company outposts. He justified his actions by claiming they were for the benefit of "the welfare of the families at present forming settlement on the Red River . . . no person trading in furs or provisions within the territory . . . shall take out any provisions, either flesh, dried meat, grain, or vegetable."

Macdonell went even further that October when he invoked the Company's ancient charter and issued a demand to all the people currently residing at North West Company posts to vacate the land within six months. The North West Company posts along the Red, Assiniboine and North Saskatchewan Rivers employed hunters and labourers who produced great quantities of pemmican for the voyageurs coming and going from the farthest outposts. For the Métis of the Red River region, bison hunting and pemmican production was the lifeblood of their economy. This new regulation struck at the very heart of their existence and could not be tolerated. It was a decree that, if enforced, could destroy the North West Company's operations and endanger the livelihood of Métis hunters. It was a declaration of war.

The Métis responded by electing a Scots-Cree named Cuthbert Grant as their military leader, an ill-defined role that came with the sobriquet Captain of the Métis. Grant was a blunt-looking, direct man with dark hair and a swarthy complexion. Born to a Scottish father and a Cree mother at the North West Company's Fort Tremblant in Saskatchewan, he was orphaned at the age of six and sent to Montreal, or perhaps Scotland, for his education. There he was raised a Presbyterian, before returning to work for the Nor'Westers in 1812, at the age of nineteen. His upbringing was organized by William McGillivray, who ensured that Grant had a prominent position in the North West Company as the young man matured. Grant's sister had also married into the officer ranks of the North West Company, and, oddly, Grant was married to Elizabeth McKay, herself of mixed heritage, whose brother was in charge of the Hudson's Bay Company's Brandon House. The two companies might have been in conflict, but many of them knew each other.

Starting as a clerk along the Qu'Appelle River, Grant became one of the earliest Métis nationalist leaders. Along with Peter Bostonais Pangman, he was inspirational in rallying the Métis of the Red River region to see themselves as a distinct culture from both the fur traders and the Indigenous peoples who shared the land. Grant later led Métis settlers to new communities and was named Warden of the Plains by George Simpson in 1828. But he was overshadowed by the more famous leaders of the following generation such as Louis Riel and Gabriel Dumont. Grant's claim to historical fame lies with his leadership during several key skirmishes and raids during the chaos of the Pemmican War and particularly the Battle of Seven Oaks. The local Saulteaux–Plains Ojibwa, caught in the crossfire, were urged to join sides in the conflict, but, although Peguis was more favourably aligned with the Company and the settlers, he perceived that it was not often in his people's interest to strongly takes sides.

Duncan Cameron of the Nor'Westers began to incite the Métis to join with him and Grant to advance their mutual interests. With a long history of intimidation as a trade tactic, the North West Company urged the Métis to make use of their skills as horsemen and hunters to harass and threaten the settlers. The Métis began with a series of quick raids, knocking down fences, scattering cattle and sheep, trampling and even burning crops in the fields, and firing guns toward the settlement at night. They naturally ignored Macdonell's proclamations and continued to hunt bison as they always had, taking care to drive the herds farther away from the settlement. They also were happy to steal or "confiscate" furs, supplies and equipment from Company posts and from the farms. Macdonell complained that "repeated accounts reached us from Fort Daer [Pembina] that the cattle were driven from our hunters . . . and others running them on horseback that our hunters could not kill a sufficiency of cattle, that when they would be crawling on their bellies after a herd of buffalo on the snow, a party of horsemen would come before them and drive away the herd."

Attacks, reprisals and skirmishes characterized years of uneasy conflict during the Pemmican war, as the two companies sought to dominate the pemmican industry and thereby control the transportation routes vital to the fur trade. Guns and field artillery were captured and recaptured, and they burned and destroyed each other's forts and harassed one another's brigades. In the summer of 1815, armed bands of Nor'Westers and Métis attacked and burned down Fort Douglas, along with the mill, kitchen, smithy and stables. They captured 150 of Selkirk's settlers, including Macdonell. The remaining settlers retreated to the north of Lake Winnipeg, abandoning their fields of wheat, potatoes and barley. The next year, in retaliation, the new governor of Assiniboia and Rupert's Land, Robert Semple, an American businessman with little fur trade experience, seized and destroyed Fort Gibraltar, the North West Company post at the confluence of the Red and Assiniboine Rivers, thereby endangering every Nor'Wester canoe brigade coming and going along their regular travel and transportation circuit. Then Semple ordered the attack and destruction of the Nor'Wester post Fort La Souris, near Brandon House. Grant retaliated that same year by leading the Métis in the sacking of Brandon House, confiscating twenty-nine thousand pounds of pemmican. He flew the new Métis flag—a sky-blue background with a sideways figure eight. But neither company had sufficient resources to launch a complete military conquest of the other.

In the evening of June 19, 1816, Semple and twenty-eight men, settlers and Company employees, encountered Grant and about sixty Métis and some Indigenous riders associated with the North West Company as they took loads of pemmican overland in carts to supply the canoe brigades at Lake Winnipeg. They were trying to avoid the Company's artillery battery along the Assiniboine River. The two groups moved toward each other in a copse of trees near a ravine that was known as Seven Oaks. Grant got the Métis to spread out and deploy in a semicircle in front of Semple's men, most of whom were afoot, and began to press in, squeezing them against the banks of the ravine. The atmosphere was tense. They glared at each other.

Grant sent François-Firmin Boucher out to parley while he kept his gun trained on Semple, who also moved forward. Boucher swore and insulted Semple until Semple lost his temper and reached for Boucher's gun, or perhaps the reins of his horse, to arrest him. Boucher's horse reared and he fell. Grant raised his rifle and a shot rang out. Semple dropped to the ground, clutching his thigh, as Grant yelled at his Métis to dismount and begin firing from behind their horses. The Baymen and settlers rushed forward to help Semple and when crowded together, Grant's men, all skilled sharpshooters and bison hunters, fired en masse. Most of Semple's men fell injured. The Métis rushed forward and began killing the wounded, stripping them naked and defiling the corpses by smashing their skulls with their rifle butts and leaving the mangled mess for the wolves.

Grant strode up to the wounded Semple and saw him clutching his thigh and supporting his head on his hand. "I am not mortally wounded," Semple said to Grant, "and if you could get me conveyed to the fort I think I should live." Grant promised that he would do so, but as soon as he left to attend to other duties, one of his men came up and shot Semple in the breast. John Pritchard, the sole survivor from Semple's camp, was dispatched with a warning to Fort Douglas. "Captain Rogers, having fallen," he wrote, "rose up again and came towards me . . . I called out to him, 'for God's sake give yourself up.' He ran towards the North-West people for that purpose, myself following him.—He was without arms, and raised up his hands, imploring them in broken French, and in English, to be merciful, and spare his life:—but Thomas McKay (son of Alexander McKay a retired partner of the North-West Company) shot him through the head, exclaiming that he (Rogers) was an officer of the company and a dog.—Another man . . . cut open his belly with a knife."

The battle was over in twenty-five minutes, and when the smoke cleared, twenty-one Selkirk settlers and Company employees were dead, including Governor Semple, along with one wounded Métis affiliated with the North West Company. The next day, Peguis and some of his hunters retrieved the bodies of Semple and the other settlers, loaded them onto a cart and hauled them to Fort Douglas, where they were buried in a mass grave. Morale in the colony plummeted, and when Grant demanded they abandon the colony and leave him their possessions, up to 180 of the remaining settlers retreated from the settlement, going north toward Lake Winnipeg, leaving the North West Company in control of the region once again.

LORD SELKIRK WAS TRAVELLING WITH HIS large entourage along the northern coast of Lake Superior, near Sault Ste. Marie, in July, when a courier arrived and related the woeful tale that his colony had been attacked and destroyed. He had made the voyage from London to Montreal with his wife and children in the fall of 1815, with the plan to enlist troops to march west and defend his colony the next summer. While enjoying the hospitality of Montreal society, Lord Selkirk met William McGillivray, who presented him with an offer to merge the two companies: the Nor'Westers would become the senior partner, with two-thirds of the goods, capital and profits, while the venerable Hudson's Bay Company would become a junior partner, based on its current level of business. But Lord Selkirk rejected the notion that the Company's charter was worth only a third of the combined value. He continued with his preparations to personally visit his massive landholding. His private army consisted of about 180 men and an additional 150 hardened Swiss mercenaries who had fought with the British during the Napoleonic Wars. Lord Selkirk offered them free land in the new colony in exchange for their services.

Selkirk felt his actions were justified because the Company's governing charter gave it the right to raise armed forces and the "power and authority . . . to continue or make peace or war with any prince or people whatsoever, that are not Christians, in any places where the said company shall have any plantations, forts or factories." But the British government declined Lord Selkirk's request for government troops, apart from fourteen soldiers for a personal guard. Set on vengeance, and despite advancing tuberculosis that was now sapping his energy, Lord Selkirk ordered his war band onward to Fort William on Lake Superior to conquer the North West Company's inland headquarters, arrest the officers and release any prisoners who were being held there. Coincidentally, the British government had also just issued instructions to John Sherbrooke, the new governor-in-chief of British North America (which now had a population of over half a million, mostly along the St. Lawrence), to dispatch a delegation to the distant region and demand a cease to all hostilities, a stop to all blockades of transport routes, and the disbanding of all militias. All seized goods and equipment were to be returned. Sherbrooke deputized two men, William Coltman and John Fletcher, and bestowed upon them senior military rank and the power to investigate and also to arrest Lord Selkirk if needed.

Lord Selkirk, however, promptly led his private mercenaries to Fort William and deployed his soldiers and artillery. "Their number together must have exceeded 500 men and the place, though not properly a Fort, but merely a square of houses and stores, surrounded by a strong and lofty picket fence, contained an ample supply of guns and ammunition, and was capable of considerable resistance." There were about 250 people in the fort. Selkirk, backed by his overwhelming superiority in artillery and troops, demanded entry from William McGillivray, the head of the company who was then in the fort, having arrived from Montreal ahead of Selkirk. As soon as the gates were opened to allow a parley, Selkirk's troops dashed forward through the breach and swarmed into the fort. The voyageurs refused to fight, and the place was taken without incident. Selkirk arrested many of the trading partners and officers, including a young Quebec-educated medical doctor named John McLoughlin who still had an interesting career ahead of him, and sent them back to Montreal on charges of treason and accessory to murder. McGillivray was astounded and embarrassed to have been outwitted by what he termed this "piddling lord."

Selkirk's troops halted the incoming and outgoing canoe brigades, blockading the supply lines between Montreal and the inland territories and costing the Nor'Westers a small fortune with the entire year's trade disrupted. North West Company officers had been busy stuffing all their records into the big fireplace in the kitchen to destroy incriminating evidence, such as plans and orders to field operatives; the only incriminating paper that survived was a list of the rewards to be paid to the Métis warriors at Seven Oaks, but it was enough. Lord Selkirk dispatched soldiers to seize several other North West Company outposts on Lake Superior and inland at Fort Lac la Pluie. When an officer arrived from the east with an arrest warrant for Lord Selkirk, Selkirk had the man thrown in a storage house for several days. Selkirk would be charged with resisting arrest.

Throughout the fur regions, officials from each company began attacking and arresting one another on imaginary or trumped-up charges. Nor'Wester agents assaulted and burned several Company forts in Athabasca country and tried to starve out the Company men by seizing supplies and forcibly preventing Indigenous hunters from taking meat to Company forts. The Nor'Westers eventually expelled all the Company personnel from the region. But it was a pyrrhic victory. Their violence and their intimidation of local peoples came back to haunt them: Indigenous people shunned their enterprise, and their own trade declined. Waging war against your clients and customers is never a solid long-term business strategy. In the Red River region, Cuthbert Grant and his band of Métis firebrands were riding around sowing fear, and even contemplated raising a larger force to ride east to retake Fort William. The two companies were engaged in outright civil war.

After spending the winter at Fort William, Lord Selkirk set out for Assiniboia himself in 1817, leaving Fort William in the possession of the Nor'Westers again (although he "purchased" all their food supplies to feed his army). His troops retook Fort Douglas without firing a shot, and he called his settlers back from Norway House, north of Lake Winnipeg, where they had fled, and tried to bring some stability to the region. He negotiated a land treaty with the Cree and Saulteaux, through Peguis. The settlers agreed to pay them annually one hundred pounds of "merchantable" tobacco for the right to occupy a three-kilometre stretch of land along the banks of the Red and Assiniboine Rivers and at the forks of the Red River, although decades later Peguis became disillusioned with illegal settler encroachment on traditional territories. The Nor'Westers were taken aback at the determination of the liberal Selkirk, having initially believed him to be a squeamish wimp. But no sooner had Selkirk departed east after four months in the region than the battles resumed. Even the arrival in the summer of 1817 of Commissioner William Coltman and Major John Fletcher with the government's proclamation failed to halt the violence.

It was a crazy time. Samuel Black, Fidler's psychopathic nemesis at Fort Athabasca, again led the assault in the north, stabbing people and starving others until the Company abandoned their outposts in the region. After preventing the Indigenous people from hunting for the Company, Black and his gang placed pemmican and dried meat along trails in front of starving men, and then arrested them for theft when they ate it.

Nearly three dozen Company men died in that region, and a small fortune in capital was lost, before the Company sent in fur trade veteran

Colin Robertson at the head of nearly two hundred men. Robertson had success in cowing Black for a while, but Black soon received reinforcements, including one of the mixed-parentage children of Simon McGillivray, who shared his famous father's names. His arrival signalled that the conflict was not about to end, and indeed in October 1818 Robertson was captured while out alone near Fort Wedderburn and taken to Fort Chipewyan as a prisoner. In the spring of 1819, William Williams, the governor of Rupert's Land after Semple's death, blockaded Grand River at the northwest shore of Lake Winnipeg, by the series of portages that lay astride the main canoe route to Athabasca country. Not a timid man, and not a trader either but a former East India Company captain, Williams strategically placed cannons and swivel guns behind log ramparts and captured ten canoes of North West Company personnel, including five officers, and supplies before retreating to Norway House. Although there were a few other tit-for-tat skirmishes, this was the final gust of ill wind before the conflict died. At least in the field.

Meanwhile, the Pemmican War trials were beginning in Montreal (not in Quebec City or York, the respective colonial headquarters of Lower and Upper Canada). The witness evidence collected over several months resulted in an incredible thirty-eight charges of murder, sixty charges of larceny and thirteen instances of arson. But it was largely a political trial; many of the judges and magistrates had connections to the North West Company, one of the richest and most politically influential enterprises in Montreal. Only a small number of charges were ever brought to trial, purportedly because the alleged offences happened in such a distant land, and because the conflict was between two commercial entities. Whose law would apply in such a remote locale? The question of jurisdiction was unavoidable. No one who participated in Seven Oaks was convicted. Even Cuthbert Grant escaped punishment by fleeing back west to Red River when he was released on bail, and the charges against him were quietly dropped. Only one Nor'Wester was convicted of a crime, but was never sentenced.

Lord Selkirk, however, after countless days spent in consultation with his lawyers and holed up in stuffy courtrooms, quietly coughing blood into a cloth as his consumption worsened, was charged with theft, false imprisonment and resisting arrest and was levied a hefty fine. He personally spent nearly £100,000 in his defence and the Company also spent heavily. Selkirk was driven nearly mad with frustration. But he was stubborn and quixotic, and since he believed he was right he would never back down. "My honour is at stake in the contest with the North West Company and in support of the settlement at Red River," he declared to his brother-in-law James Wedderburn. "Till that can be said to be fairly out of danger and till the infamous falsehoods of the North West Company are finally and fully exposed, expenses must be incurred which it is utterly impossible to avoid, honour is at stake." In his stubborn adherence to the defence of his honour, Lord Selkirk was perhaps influenced by his wife, Jean, who had earlier taken on the role of his secretary, forwarding to him in the field dispatches from Montreal regarding the political situation. "If we are to be poor for three generations," she declared to him, "we must absolutely fight this out."

After another year in Canada, Lord Selkirk returned to England but quickly relocated to a drier climate in the south of France, where he died, in 1820, at the age of forty-eight. He battled to the end for his settlers, leaving a heavily indebted estate for his loyal wife to contend with. His, and the Company's, struggle with the North West Company over the right to colonize land that was already inhabited by Indigenous and Métis people ended only with his death.

With all the fighting and reprisals, the situation had become financially ruinous for both companies. To bring some order to the situation, the Hudson's Bay Company governors made the unorthodox decision, prompted by one of their prime investors, Andrew Colvile (formerly Wedderburn), to hire a new backup governor from outside the ranks. Colvile had the perfect person in mind.

PART FOUR

FALL

Chapter Thirteen

THE LITTLE EMPEROR

Everything was about the change at York Factory in the summer of 1821. It had been many years since the waterways had seen so many canoes heading downriver to the historic outpost, which now consisted of several dozen wooden and stone buildings that made up the Company's main depot on the shore of Hudson Bay. For decades much of the trade had been siphoned off toward the St. Lawrence and the Company's inland posts where the furs were collected and transported by smaller numbers of efficient York boats rather than flotillas of independent Indigenous traders. Now the Company had appointed a new inland governor of what was to be called the Northern Department, and he had ambitious plans to radically transform the business. A call had been sent out to all the senior officers of the North West Company and the Hudson's Bay Company to make the journey to York Factory to hear the news and receive their new instructions.

Nicholas Garry of the London Committee had sailed to York Factory to describe the practical details of the merger and to announce what was in general to be expected. This great concourse at York Factory was the first meeting of the new management team. There was to be no fighting among the erstwhile enemies. The new governor had invited them and they could not refuse. As they neared the coast and the fort, they heard the drumming from a community of Cree and Iroquois who camped on the level ground before the sprawling fort, and soon the population grew as canoes of Métis and voyageurs arrived. Despite the nervous apprehension, the makeshift community began to exude the atmosphere of a festival or large market. There were games and storytelling and soon singing as the tension dissipated. In the Great Hall, where the senior officers congregated, George Simpson, then in his late twenties, pre- sided over daily feasts of wild duck, arctic char and venison, while ser- vants filled cups with imported sherry, port and beer. People talked and laughed, stories were told, and animosities and grudges were forgotten, at least temporarily. According to John Todd's eyewitness report of Simpson's diplomacy, "their previously stiffened features began to relax a little; they gradually but slowly mingled together, and a few of the better disposed, throwing themselves unreservedly in the midst of the opposite party, mutually shook each other by the hand." The purpose of the great gathering was to forge a new common identity between the suspicious factions.

The stout young man who presided over the festivities exuded confi- dence and charisma. He was charming and persuasive when called for, yet caustic when it suited him, his behaviour always self-serving. Since his own interests nicely dovetailed with those of the Company, his ambitions became the Company's ambitions and the Company's ambi- tions became his own. He had a nearly insurmountable series of obsta- cles to overcome to bring rationality and profit back to the fur business. The years of violence and disorder had riven the interior, nearly ruining both companies and fracturing the lives of the tens of thousands of Indigenous peoples who depended upon their business and whose ter- ritories saw the brunt of the battles. Simpson instinctively knew that he had to make people believe they were on the same side, that their personal success was inextricably linked to the new Company's success, if he wanted to bring stability to the land and the fur trade. He spent his time at York Factory reading field journals, scouring maps and interviewing everyone, from the Home Guard Cree to the blacksmiths and labourers, boatmen, traders and clerks. He had to understand the big picture of how all the different components of the geographically vast and complex commercial operation worked.

Simpson, oddly, was a newcomer to the fur trade. He was a compromise candidate, someone who had minimal association with either company and no historical baggage, someone who could be perceived as belonging to neither side but who also could bring fresh insight to a business in desperate need of reorganization. He was born in the small Scottish town of Dingwall, in 1792, to the irresponsible scoundrel son of a Calvinist minister; little is known about his mother. They were not married, and Simpson was raised primarily by his aunt until the age of sixteen, when his uncle Geddes took an interest in him out of familial obligation and because the lad had shown an aptitude for mathematics.

He was shipped out to London in 1808 to apprentice at the sugar brokerage firm Graham and Simpson, which merged with another firm, Wedderburn and Company, in 1812. For twelve years he proved his mettle in the sugar industry. Reliable, intelligent and hard-working, he was a manly, likeable fellow in tune with the times. He was marked for promotion early on, and was an especial favourite of the senior partner Andrew Colvile, who had changed his name from Wedderburn to distance himself from the scandal of a mixed-heritage half-brother from Jamaica. Simpson was short and energetic, with a penchant for fine clothes, and liked to be seen as a man about town, dallying in coffee shops in his off-hours. He applied himself dutifully to the responsibilities of a clerk in the overseas trade, and was certainly astute enough to observe his boss's racist attitudes. The sugar trade was notorious for its racism, for the brutal and degrading treatment of black slaves in horrendous working and living conditions. Young Simpson made several trips to the West Indies, where he absorbed notions of superiority based upon skin colour and culture—that it was acceptable for people to have no rights or agency over their own lives; that women could be used without consequence. Simpson enjoyed the power, the feeling of superiority. These attitudes, not historically established in the Company's fur business in an institutional way, were part of the new corporate culture that Simpson would bring to North America in the coming decades.

When Thomas Douglas, Lord Selkirk, married Colvile's sister, Jean, and Colvile, along with his new brother-in-law, began buying Company stock, Simpson was introduced to a new career opportunity. Colvile, who was on the Company's board of directors, was well aware of the turbulent and precarious situation in which Rupert's Land found itself, and thought his young business clerk would thrive under the rugged conditions. Simpson knew not to waste an opportunity, so in the spring of 1820, when he was given five days' notice to wrap up his affairs and depart his sedate London life, he accepted immediately. He dashed off a note to a colleague that he was packing for a long and arduous journey and would be engaged in "important business connected with the affairs of Lord Selkirk, the Hudson's Bay & North West Compys." He would be the acting governor-in-chief of Rupert's Land, ready to assume command if the current governor, William Williams, was arrested or killed by agents of the North West Company, which at the time seemed likely.

Simpson carried two identical letters from Colonial Secretary Lord Bathurst, one to deliver to the Nor'Westers at Fort William and the other for him to abide by. They were demands, based on the 1817 order from John Sherbrooke, to cease all hostilities and return stolen goods. The British government was now serious about ending the commercially damaging wars between the two companies.

In early March, Simpson sailed for New York, a month-long voyage, and then proceeded north on poor roads to Montreal, where he was received with a hearty welcome that bode well for his mission and future prospects, despite being an agent of the Company. After enjoying his celebrity, he set off inland, ironically along the traditional voyageur trail of the North West Company, to Fort William, where he delivered his letter from Lord Bathurst. Simpson continued on to Red River and north to Norway House, where he met Williams. The Nor'Westers, it turned out, had not been keeping the peace but rather had just captured more Company officers. Simpson, a sponge for information and wanting an accurate picture of the extent of the fur territory, volunteered to lead the sixty-eight-man brigade to Fort Wedderburn on Lake Athabasca. He made sure they were armed.

Establishing a custom that he would maintain for decades, Simpson demanded a frenetic pace, waking his men early and urging them on after dark. In the shadow of the Nor'Westers' Fort Chipewyan, Simpson settled in for his first long, frigid winter in the fur country. Far from being cowed by the discomfort and freezing winter, something for which he could not have been prepared, Simpson seemed energized by his situation. Civilization may have had its perks, but everything in the great northwest seemed earthy and tangible. The primitive conditions didn't bother him, and neither did the weather or isolation. Even the danger and stress of dealing with the petty aggressions and threats of the Nor'Westers merely added zest to his life, like a bracing breath of cold air in the morning. Life was truly in his own hands here; his decisions mattered in a way they had not working in an office in London smothered by stultifying conformity. Here he was free. Unfortunately for others under his charge, Simpson's enjoyment of his freedom meant correspondingly less freedom for them, as he imposed his will on their behaviour and began to reorder their world.

One day Simpson was out inspecting the terrain around the fort. He had with him a pet dog that he had inherited along the way, a Scottish terrier named Boxer. When challenged by one of the Nor'Westers, Simpson puffed out his chest and stared. The world had changed from the conditions that prevailed even a year earlier. No one fired at him or dared to collar him and drag him in as a prisoner, and no one shot his dog. He simply stared them down. Simpson had read the government letters and knew the force behind them; for the first time in years a powerful authority was waiting to fall like a sword on the neck of anyone who broke the peace. While they might still bluster and puff, the bullies on both sides had had their day. Simpson himself would end up as the only bully, though it's doubtful he thought of it that way. So insightful into the character of others, he had a curious blind spot into his own.

That first winter, he learned as much as he could about the land he would soon govern and the people who lived there. He soaked up knowledge about the geography, the climate and the territory, the politics and customs of the various Indigenous peoples. He also seemed not to be concerned about the hardships of travel, despite never before having sat in a canoe or donned snowshoes or hauled a toboggan. Sleeping out in the open among clouds of mosquitoes didn't bother him, nor did freezing rain. He didn't even complain about the food, though it was basic and radically different from what he was accustomed to. Instead he revelled in his ability to make do with less to set an example for others. He claimed with jocular bonhomie in one letter to a friend that his cloak would "answer the purposes of a bed." He thrived on the tactile daily experiences and the control he exerted over his world. After he met Lieutenant George Back, of the overland Franklin expedition, who was expecting assistance and supplies from the Company, Simpson delivered his scathing assessment: "Franklin, the Officer who commands the party has not the physical powers required for the labour of moderate Voyaging in this country; he must have three meals p diem, Tea is indispensable, and with the utmost exertion he cannot walk above Eight miles in one day, so that it does not follow if those Gentlemen are unsuccessful that the difficulties are insurmountable." The expedition turned into a terrible ordeal of starvation, murder and cannibalism.

Simpson was a shrewd observer, quickly taking stock of the situation on the ground. He catalogued waste, inefficiency and incompetence and was already mentally restructuring supply lines and thinking about

logistics and money-making improvements. He had an instinctive practical sense of the entire supply and transportation system, with all its
flaws, problems and challenges, not the least of which was the competition. The Nor'Westers would be put down not by what he termed
"prize fighting," but rather through good business practices, better-quality trade goods and efficient management. These would prove far more
dangerous weapons. Simpson believed discipline and hard work, not
destructive violence, would win profits. This would not have been possible even one year earlier when prize fighting was the regular state of
affairs. Mismanagement was the other chief problem, as far as he was
concerned. He wrote that many of the men and officers were passing
their time inland "eating and Drinking the Compy's property, smoking
their Tobacco, and Sleeping their time away." He resolved to fix that. A
pugnacious manager with an unbendable will, Simpson usually prevailed in a dispute and was remarkably adept at banging some sem-
blance of order out of the mismanaged disarray that had overtaken the
trading enterprise during the previous decade of commercial war.

Simpson departed the Athabasca district at the end of May 1821 with
a great disgust for the incompetence, corruption and mismanagement
he had seen, and with a head full of ideas. A month later, while travelling south and east, he was surprised to hear from a former Nor'Wester
that the two companies had merged, or had been merged by the British
government. He had only just joined the war and was saddened that he
wouldn't have the opportunity to defeat his adversaries through practical superiority. "The information seems to disconcert both Officers and
Men," he wrote, "and I must confess my own disappointment that . . .
Our opponents have not been beaten out in the Field, which with one
or two years of good management I am certain I might have effected."
He quickly set off for York Factory with his entourage.

IT WAS LORD SELKIRK'S IMPLACABLE antipathy toward the North
West Company, which stemmed from the struggle over the Red River

Colony, that had been the main impediment to the two companies reaching some form of reconciliation or a merger of business activities. Although Selkirk had returned to England in late 1818, his health continued to deteriorate. In what many considered a foolish preoccupation with the colony, he continued to pump vast sums of money into the venture to keep it from collapsing and to mount a legal defence to the charges and claims of the North West Company, nearly pauperizing his estate. After he died, in April 1820, the negotiations between the companies finally began.

The costs of the seven-year conflict were staggering, with both parties crushed under the weight of debt. The Hudson's Bay Company owed over £100,000 to the Bank of England and other creditors, but still maintained its coterie of well-placed political advocates. As it did during previous iterations of turbulence wrought from conflict, the Company retrenched and waited for a time when they could return to profitability. Many of its shareholders were aristocratic or rich, or both, and could play the long game. The North West Company, on the other hand, was more vulnerable. The years of warfare and the interminable legal squabbles had drained its coffers. Trade had declined, and insolvency was a possibility. Its business model involved paying extravagant yearly dividends to its proprietors, who were also the managers, leaving little capital to finance longer-term goals; it had been less prepared to weather a prolonged commercial war. Although the Company enjoyed greater financial stability and could afford to forgo or shrink dividends, this was not a winning long-term strategy, and investors were growing impatient.

The North West Company, without access to stable long-term foundational credit, had been financing its battles with Lord Selkirk and the Company to the tune of nearly £50,000 by skimping on the pay to its wintering partners, those who did the actual trading and travelling throughout the interior. The split in loyalty between the Montreal agents, who organized the goods that were shipped to Fort William, and the wintering partners grew so strained that the winterers actually discussed using the hated Company as their supply agents instead of the Montreal merchants. Some of them, including Dr. John McLoughlin and Angus Bethune, travelled to Montreal and on to London to secretly test the waters and see whether the Company was interested in becoming their supply agent. They knew the enterprise was on unsound financial footing and were now looking out for themselves and their families. They carried with them the proxy votes of their fellow inland partners.

This brooding civil war in the Nor'Wester ranks undermined the Montreal partners' authority and bargaining power. Not surprisingly, the Company admitted that it would be glad to work with all but the most violent murderers and criminals, of which there seemed to be no shortage. As the carrot of motivation, Lord Bathurst made it known to the head managers and shareholders of both companies that a new entity would be granted even greater powers of monopoly than those found in the Company's original charter. The British government wanted one financially secure British company to counter American expansionism. Edward "Bear" Ellice, named for the jocular facade that glossed the greasy manner in which he always obtained what he wanted, was a towering financial and political operative associated with the Whig government. His extended family had commercial interests in the Montreal fur trade, and he offered his services as a mediator and broker between Andrew Colvile and Simon McGillivray. Unfortunately for McGillivray and the Nor'Westers, Bethune and McLoughlin's arrival in London was a blow, since they were offering the support of the wintering partners to whoever would give them the best deal. McGillivray's bargaining leverage undermined, Ellice chaired a meeting in an opulent office in the financial district and the deal was inked.

When the details of the contract between the two fur entities became known, eyebrows were raised. It was clearly favourable to the Company and its seventy-seven shareholders, and indeed the stock soared on news of the merger, which some likened to a takeover. The board was to be dominated by former Company members, as was the ownership, although many of the former North West Company winter partners were to be promoted to the position of chief factor, in charge of prominent posts.

On paper at least, the Hudson's Bay Company amalgamated with the North West Company in the spring of 1821, while Simpson was still in the field. The British Colonial Office had been pressuring both sides to form a financially stable entity that would spread British influence across the continent, as a bulwark to American expansion. The Company was now to be an appendage of British colonialism, like the East India Company: a branch of empire rather than an exotic way for financially endowed aristocrats to augment their fortunes.

As promised, the territory of the new Company's exclusive monopoly was empire-sized, defined, at least in Britain, as anywhere to which a Company employee or a Nor'Wester had ever travelled in the past 150 years. It would include the historical Rupert's Land, as well as the Athabasca, Peace and Mackenzie Rivers, and the New Caledonia and Columbia Districts of the former North West Company. It would extend from Hudson Bay north to the Arctic and west to the Pacific and encompass all the interior parkland. It was Alexander Mackenzie's dream realized, an exclusive British imperial trade monopoly that covered, or smothered, northern North America. Only the two Canadas and the Atlantic colonies weren't included in its dominion.

At the same time, the Company's new charter granted it political and criminal authority. The British government passed the Act for Regulating the Fur Trade, and Establishing a Criminal and Civil Jurisdiction Within Certain Parts of North America, which established a framework for regulating people's lives in a way never before done in the fur territories. It was a profound shift of attitude, and, eventually, balance of power.

The Red River Colony, still a controversial development even after Lord Selkirk's death, had grown too large to eliminate and had taken on a life of its own. After he had time to assess the situation, Simpson came to one of his usual cutting, yet prescient, conclusions. The population had plumped to nearly five hundred people, he wrote to his patron

Colvile, but unfortunately these people were a "mass of renegades and malcontents" whose "disruptions are not to be constrained without the assistance of civil & military power; I therefore conceive it indispensably necessary for its future welfare that a Code of Laws should be made, Magistrates appointed, constables sworn in and a small Military Establishment provided to give effect to the Civil Authorities." For the first time, the Company was governed by regulations that bestowed political authority and responsibility over settlements and over people who were now living inland in what had been, since the Company's founding a century and a half earlier, territory exclusively under the dominion and jurisdiction of the multitude of Indigenous peoples. Now Simpson would have control over Red River and other forts and factories where fur traders retired with their families.

Although the new fur trading monopoly retained the name Hudson's Bay Company, it was a mélange of styles, customs and structures inherited from both parent enterprises—the central planning and enviable financial backing of the Company, where all people were employees, and the cavalier profit-driven partnerships of the North West Company. The Company had already been moving in this direction during the later years of the war, as it drove ever farther inland. Other changes reflected common sense and confirmed the rationale behind Radisson and Groseilliers's original business plan. Shipping would be through York Factory, not Montreal, a drastic blow to the colonial business community, coupled with a precipitous reduction of liquor sales from Montreal. When Simon and William McGillivray disembarked from their canoe at Fort William later in the summer of 1821 and related the news, they were met with howls of outrage. Fort William's days of triumphant celebration and ceremony had ended. Soon the news spread throughout the land and led to the epochal meeting at York Factory where Simpson began his ascendancy toward becoming the little emperor of a vast domain.

Simpson initially was placed in charge one of the two new departments, or regional governorships, into which the new Company had been divided. Of the two, the Southern Department, basically most of northern Ontario, was more sedate and beavered out; it was in its mature phase of development. The Northern Department, by contrast, held the greatest potential for expansion and increased profits; Simpson was put in charge here. He set to work immediately to mould the swollen and culturally bifurcated commercial contraption toward a unified purpose that would bring stability and profit.

At the time of the merger the two companies had numerous overlapping forts and far too many workers. There were ninety-seven North West Company forts and outposts and seventy-six belonging to the Hudson's Bay Company. Many of them were within hailing distance of each other and in direct competition for the same business from the Indigenous traders, and hence unprofitable. In Simpson's opinion there were also many overpaid and underworked employees, an observation that didn't change much throughout his life. Renowned for his snap decisions, Simpson made his mind up on whom to fire and whom to keep or promote based on intuition and personal affinity, specifically if they showed him the proper deference. Over a thousand surplus personnel, as he termed them, were fired or replaced within his first four years. Those who weren't compulsive workaholics, and those who questioned his authority, had their wages trimmed by as much as a quarter.

He also grumbled about those who had large families near the forts that the Company might be obliged to support. Simpson reduced the two thousand or so employees from when the companies merged to just over seven hundred after five years (although the number increased steadily into the 1830s, more than doubling). The aging were also in his sights: "I consider it highly injurious to the general interest," he wrote to Andrew Colvile and the London Committee in 1826, "to have old worn out men in our councils, they are timid, indolent and helpless and would be of no manner of use in cases of difficulty, danger or emergency. Worn out Indian Traders are the most useless, helpless class of men I ever knew and the sooner the Company can get rid of them after their days of activity and labour are over the better." But getting rid of them could be a problem, he admitted, because they "become attached to the Country, to the half savage Life they have been accustomed to lead and to their women and Families and will not move unless actually forced away." Many, especially those of mixed parentage, migrated with their families to the vicinity of the Red River Settlement, where they took to part-time farming and bison hunting.

OVER THE NEXT SEVERAL YEARS TOURING his ever-expanding commercial empire, Simpson began the epic travels for which he became famous. For the next thirty-three years, he criss-crossed the sprawling domain in his executive birchbark travel canoes. Artful and light, his vessels were over nine metres in length and manned by a premier crew of Iroquois paddlers from the Montreal vicinity who routinely propelled him up to 160 kilometres a day. Simpson kept to a seemingly erratic routine, and this unpredictable schedule, coupled with speed, meant that he could swoop into outposts with little notice, catching the factors unaware and unprepared, the better to inspect their posts without their having the forewarning to clean things up. He swanned about the land while his voyageurs paddled machine-like under the watchful scowl of their new boss. Travelling eighteen hours in a single day in all weather was not uncommon. On one famous journey to the Pacific in 1824, the canoes were launched at Grand Portage, on the shores of Lake Superior, and the entourage of voyageurs paddled furiously across the prairies, ascended the Rocky Mountains and rushed southwest along the Columbia to the Pacific Ocean. The entire journey consumed only an astonishing eighty-four days, twenty days less than any other recorded crossing.

Simpson set speed records on nearly every canoe and boat route in the country, and he never stayed in one place for long. He crossed the Rocky Mountains to the Columbia and New Caledonia Districts, the administrative regions that divided the Company's territory west of the Rocky

Mountains, three times by different routes; he went back and forth to Montreal and York Factory dozens of times; and he visited every remote outpost. He made eight voyages back to London, eight journeys to New York or Boston, and in the 1840s completed an epic trip around the world. He was accompanied by secretaries who scrawled out his orders, suggestions and instructions while he stomped around posts, scanning for deficiencies and possible improvements. Of course he never did any paddling himself—he just sat imperiously in the middle. Nevertheless, he recalled later in life that all his ailments seemed to vanish as soon as he sat in his canoe.

Perhaps it was all the nap time that improved his health. A habitually early riser, he would bellow for his paddlers to awake while he splashed in the freezing water of whatever lake or river they had camped near. The men dragged themselves wearily to the canoe and set off paddling for several hours before stopping for breakfast. While the voyageurs gnawed on pemmican, Simpson, as befitting his exalted status, relaxed and nibbled at the dainties that his servant procured. Then it was back into the boat for hours more paddling until lunch, when he might take a glass of wine or port while resting against a tree. The pattern was repeated until dinner and then again into the dark when they made camp. Simpson often would doze while the paddles endlessly dipped into the water, lulling him to sleep. A devious man, sometimes he would wake but keep his eyes shut, slowly allowing his arm and hand to dangle in the water, by which he could gauge the speed of the canoe by the drag on his hand. No one would shirk when Simpson was around. The men never had time for naps, and had scant rest.

In what became a tradition when approaching a fort, Simpson's illustrious canoe, usually flanked by a couple of others, would put ashore nearby yet out of sight. The men would don clean clothes, Simpson his distinctive black beaver top hat, and the bagpiper or trumpeter would ready his instrument to announce the arrival. The coming of Simpson was always an event.

During these early years, there was something that Simpson pondered while his canoe rhythmically pressed onward. Reflecting on his former life in London, he realized that while he might toil and strive to advance himself in the hierarchy of society and business, and his chances were good to achieve moderate success, greatness would be forever beyond his grasp, particularly with his obscure heritage and bastard birth. In the old northwest, however, he was poised to leapfrog the lower and middle rungs of the social ladder and clamber right to the pinnacle. On the one hand, there were disadvantages to this wilderness life. There would be no social peers suitable to someone at the pinnacle of society, nor "civilized" entertainments and amusements of the sort to be found in London such as theatre, music and dining. There were no rarefied gentlemen's clubs to bolster his social status while puffing on cigars and sipping whisky. And perhaps most frightening to someone of Simpson's temperament and ambition, if things didn't work out, or he became injured or the fashion market changed, he would be far from the pulse of empire and unable to shift easily to a new career. But on the other hand, to balance these detractions, there were the compensating benefits of personal freedom; the beguiling ego-boosting perquisite of power over others; the deference that came to him by virtue of having other people's futures in his palm.

The balance of the equation led him to make a choice to abandon his former London life and gamble on the wilderness fur empire on the distant fringe of the British Empire. He would rather turn forever from his former life as a London dandy and instead rule the fur forts of Rupert's Land. Here he could preside as an emperor, the pre-eminent ruler of every social and business situation in which he would ever find himself.

THE COMPANY'S DOMAIN AFTER THE MERGER was enormous. At nearly 7.8 million square kilometres, it was equivalent in size to western Europe, or about 8 per cent of the earth's surface. Under Simpson's reign, as the nineteenth century progressed, the Company would grow so powerful that it dominated the lives of hundreds of thousands of Indigenous peoples as well as its own employees. The Company eventually would have posts as far away as Hawaii, and its warehouses in London became the global clearinghouse for most of the world's fur. But the members of the London Committee, the aristocratic entitled gentlemen who enjoyed most of the profits, had scant inclination to board a sailing ship for the month-long voyage across the Atlantic to York Factory, and certainly little enthusiasm for touring the dangerous lands to the west. Any knowledge they had of events in their distant domain came to them through letters or occasional interviews—they were essentially absentee landlords who, for all their power in London, had to rely on ruthless and charismatic men like Simpson to be their proxies. So long as Simpson kept the enterprise profitable, he would be granted an ever-greater degree of social, political and economic leeway. So, Simpson kept the enterprise profitable. This had the added benefit of keeping his senior managers focused and enthusiastic, since their success also depended upon these profits.

Within a few years, the Company more than doubled its dividend, to 10 per cent, then up to 20 per cent by 1828, and sometimes even higher but never dropping below 10 per cent for the next forty years. Although Simpson was technically beholden to the London Committee as the ultimate source of his authority, in North America he became a virtual dictator, his decisions unappealable owing to his smooth maintenance of the Company's profit-generating machinery. One disgruntled employee, John McLean, wrote disgustedly of his time squirming under Simpson's thumb, saying, "In no colony subject to the British Crown is there to be found an authority so despotic as is at this day exercised in the mercantile Colony of Rupert's Land; and authority combining the despotism of military rule with the strict surveillance and mean parsimony of the avaricious trade. From Labrador to Nootka Sound the unchecked, uncontrolled will of a single individual gives law to the land . . . Clothed with a power so unlimited, it is not to be wondered at that a man who rose from a humble situation should in the end forget what he was and play the tyrant."

Simpson's success was founded on his uncanny understanding of logistics, the seasonal movement of people and goods based upon the directional flow of rivers, how to get supplies exactly where they were needed in the precise quantities needed, and how to get the maximum quantity of furs out to the bay for speedy shipment to market. To him the land was not a series of immutable barriers that must be circumvented, but a malleable collection of circumstances that could be adjusted to his and his employer's benefit. To Simpson, as never before, the world of the fur trade was a giant game board, the forts, factors and voyageurs chits to be moved and placed each year for maximum advantage. Simpson deftly deployed his resources to maximize the number of furs from each district and to minimize the expenses; one without the other wasn't good enough.

The first step to making money, Simpson believed, was not wasting it on frivolous extravagances—even if those extravagances were compensation for the tedium and harsh conditions of the job and had been perquisites for many generations. He was preoccupied with petty things like cutting out "luxury" goods from the employees' lives, which involved changing the men's diets from meat to fish, regulating the amount of tea a chief factor was entitled to, stipulating the format of increasingly mandatory religious services, and detailing proper mealtime etiquette and utensils (tin plates; no tablecloths or wine glasses). It was a dramatic departure from past eras, when the evening meal was the focus of social life along the Bay. "I consider it quite unnecessary to indent for Sauces & Pickles on public account," he wrote in one of his general memoranda under the headline SAUCES. "I never use fish sauce in the country, and never saw anyone use it or pickles either. From the quantity of Mustard indented for, one would suppose it is now issued as an article of trade with the Indians!"

Suspicious by nature, Simpson nosed his way into every aspect of the business looking for things others might have missed. The overarching theme of his governorship was control, and he believed that improving the Company's efficiency involved not merely optimizing its operations but cutting expenses. Over the years, Simpson gradually phased out the use of transport canoes—apart from his own enormous and speedy executive canoe—and replaced them with the heavy but large York boats that the Company had been using on certain routes for decades. In keeping with Simpson's philosophy of economy, it was just a matter of math. The inelegant and tubby boats had a greater manpower-to-cargo ratio. They were also cheap to make and maintain and required less skill to use. The real clincher for Simpson was that he could have the boats made larger while the number of men to crew them was kept the same. One of his devious schemes to cut wages was to pressure labourers and officers to renew their contracts during the winter, when, because of their isolation, they had no idea what the prevailing rates and wages were, and they usually agreed to less in the absence of a competitive market.

Taken as a whole, Simpson's actions, including his preoccupation with the minutiae of people's lives, confirm the conclusion that he wielded an unwholesome authority over those who lived in his domain. He enjoyed knowing that he held power over people, that they could be kept in check by having no agency over the bread-and-butter aspects of their lives. Displaying deference and loyalty to him was the surest way of securing a promotion—that and not being Indigenous or of mixed heritage. Simpson rarely promoted the sons of his officers and their Indigenous wives above the position of labourer or interpreter, preferring to bring in Scots from overseas for officer ranks. By the 1830s, many of his officers fumed at this discrimination against their children and sought alternative opportunities for them. "It appears the present concern has stamped the Cain mark upon all born in this country," wrote trader Charles Mackenzie regarding his mixed-heritage son Hector. "Neither education nor abilities serve them. The Honourable Company are unwilling to take natives, even as apprenticed clerks, and the favoured few they do take can never aspire to a higher status, be their education and capacity what they may." But native-born people—whether Indigenous or of mixed heritage—were the ones who best understood the Company's operations and responsibilities, and they chafed at being relegated to positions of subservience beneath imported managers. It was an uphill battle, and by the 1860s the "half breeds" made up only a third of the officer ranks.

Simpson didn't care if he was liked or hated—he worked for his own benefit and to keep the London Committee satiated with profit. Beneath the surface, his was an information empire as much as a fur empire. The more profitable and secure things seemed, the less anyone was inclined to interfere with his methods or his personal life. Seeing in Simpson an uncommonly astute operative who appeared content to dwell in the hinterland, the Company promoted him to be in charge of both the Northern and Southern Districts in 1824. Simpson became the head of a personality cult that ran a complex commercial, and increasingly political, empire. He was the boss of the only general store for half a continent.

FROM HIS EARLIEST DAYS IN THE COUNTRY, Simpson began to think of the Indigenous peoples in a proprietary sense. He was often condescending, referring to them, regardless of culture, history and geography, as a "Savage race" and plying them with liquor when he wanted something from them, and then boasting how liquor worked like a charm to achieve his goals. After the merger, he sought to "reconcile them to the new order of things . . . I am convinced that they must be ruled with a rod of iron, to bring and keep them in a proper state of subordination, and the most certain way to effect this is by letting them feel their dependence upon us." On another occasion he wrote that "an enlightened Indian is good for nothing." He knew that they had grown dependent on manufactured trade goods, that a pre-industrial traditional life was not generally possible or desired, and that with no more competition he and the Company had much greater power. To Simpson, and increasingly to the Londoners who read his reports and letters, the Indigenous peoples were no longer the proprietors of their traditional lands, but rather middling cogs in the fur trading machine that was being imposed across the land, a machine that under Simpson's watch would run like clockwork, its rigid logistical imperatives imposed unilaterally without consideration for the cultural or political legacies of the people whose lands the Company operated in. Over time, Simpson shifted the balance of power not only in a practical sense but also in a psychological sense.

Sometimes when Simpson did the right thing, it was for the wrong reasons. When he banned the use of steel leg-hold traps in certain regions, it wasn't out of concern for animal cruelty or that overhunting might be harmful to Indigenous peoples in the long term; it was to correlate the Company's fur supply to European demand. Simpson cut out liquor as a freely available trade item in most regions, not because it wasn't profitable but because he felt it made people lazy and unproductive. The British government ordered the Company to implement the ban as part of the terms of the merger, first in the northern regions and then rolled out across the land so that liquor was strictly controlled even for use by Company employees, and used infrequently and in small quantities as a trade item. In that action Simpson was returning to the policies of an earlier era in an effort to alleviate the extreme devastation that alcohol had caused during the years of corporate warfare, but the policy was tinged with a sense of obligation and paternalism. Tea was introduced as a substitute drink, and later flour, from which people began making an unleavened pan-fried bread called bannock.

In 1826, Simpson placed strict limits on the number of beaver skins that could be traded in each region, ostensibly to conserve what by then was obviously a dwindling resource. But it also served as a method of control over people who had long considered themselves hosts rather than subservient workers toiling on the lower rungs of the social hierarchy. Under Simpson, Company authority was stretched to apply to Indigenous peoples as well as traders. He simply viewed Indigenous peoples as he did anyone else in his domain, not as independent masters of their own destiny but as somehow tied to the Company, chits to be moved around the board. During Simpson's reign Indigenous peoples increasingly fell under the Company's control, their lives shaped and patterned to improve the Company's trade efficiency. It was the beginning of the end of their autonomy.

Simpson also sought to manage the beaver supply by closing posts where he wanted to preserve beaver and opening new ones where he wanted to increase the haul, placing quotas on some fur species and paying more for others in an effort to balance populations. He implemented these policies, which sometimes had beneficial long-term results, without consultation with or concern for the immediate welfare of the affected people, whether those were the independent Indigenous people, the Company-affiliated Home Guard and those of mixed ancestry, or his own employees and their families. He thought and planned broadly and made overarching changes without regard for the impact on individual lives. In fact, he sought to distance the Company from owing any responsibility to any people. Because he was running a monopoly, these displaced people had no other options. They were being managed by Simpson in a way similar to how he managed the beavers.

Simpson thought the monopoly meant he had total control, but not all of his initiatives succeeded. One idea that failed spectacularly was his belief that, now that he held a monopoly, he could degrade the quality of trade goods while keeping the rate of exchange in beaver pelts the same, since the customers had no alternative. But in this his own London Committee sided with the complaints of the Indigenous peoples, claiming that it was a moral duty to supply long-standing customers with quality firearms and blankets. Simpson also was unsuccessful in changing some long-standing traditions and customs. He tried to get rid of gift giving but underestimated the entrenched value of the ceremony and was only able to direct the exchange toward less-valuable items such as tea, sugar or tobacco instead of firearms, knives, kettles and blankets. The credit system was also a burden Simpson felt would be better left in the past. "Heavy debts are ascertained to be injurious to the Trade and of little benefit to the Indians, it is therefore understood that no more shall be given than there is a reasonable prospect of being repaid." But he never was able to impose stricter regulations on credit because the custom, enduring for so many generations since the Company's earliest days in the seventeenth century, was entrenched as a sign of respect and faith.

DURING SIMPSON'S REIGN, Company forts and factories became more substantial and permanent. The most strategically situated posts, at important river junctions or trans-shipment locations, grew in size. And along with this new permanence in infrastructure came the growth of auxiliary economic activities such as agriculture, construction and black-smithing. At the same time, Simpson began creating a complimentary catalogue of the Company's human assets, principally of the key man-agers. Dating from his earliest days in charge of the Northern Department and continuing for decades, Simpson kept this secret book with him at all times, writing in code to prevent it from ever being read by the wrong eyes. His famous "Character Book" was an insightful col-lection of character sketches, blunt and unflattering, yet oddly percep-tive, of around 150 senior officers, or those whom he felt had potential. No names graced its pages, only a series of numbers that corresponded to words, and only he had the key, always kept separately. Reading it today provides a window into the astonishing rogues' gallery of miscre-ants, malcontents and downright peculiar people who made up the upper echelons of the Company's field managers. But the main problem with Simpson's assessments was that he never revised them. Once he made his assessment of a person and wrote it in his book, it forever became the basis for his dealings with them.

Angus Bethune, one of the Nor'Wester inland partners, who along with John McLoughlin had led the mutiny in 1820 and who had served during the early days at Fort Astoria, was described as "a very poor crea-ture, vain, self sufficient and trifling, who makes his own comfort his principle study; possessing little Nerve and no decision in anything: of a snarling vindictive disposition, and neither liked nor respected by his associates, Servants or Indians. His Services would be overpaid by the victuals himself and Family consume." Colin Robertson was "a frothy trifling conceited man, who would starve in any other country and is perfectly useless here: fancies or rather attempts to pass himself off as a clever fellow, a man of talents and refinement." John Clarke was "a boasting ignorant low fellow who rarely speaks the truth and is strongly suspected of dishonesty; his commanding appearance and pompous manner, however, give him a good deal of influence over Indians and servants." John Rowand, the legendary governor of Fort Edmonton and apparently one of Simpson's friends, was "of fiery disposition and as bold as a lion. An excellent Trader who has the peculiar talent of attracting the fiercest Indians to him while he rules them with a Rod of Iron," but although he "will not tell a lie (which is uncommon in this Country)," he "has sufficient address to evade the truth when it suits his purpose."

The damning character judgments make for amusing reading for their cutting insults. According to Simpson, his men came from the lowest dregs of society. While one was singled out as having "a cruel and Tyrannical disposition," another was "one of the worst and most dangerous men I ever was acquainted with. My presence alone keeps him sober, but when left to himself he will assuredly become a confirmed Drunkard." He offered grudging respect for the man who was "a tolerable bruiser. Can drink, tell lies and Swear," but dismissed another as being "not quite of Sound Mind." On one hand he gave us "a flippant, superficial, trifling creature who lies more frequently than he speaks the truth," while on the other we have a man who was "very slovenly both in business and in his appearance." One man "got into disgrace lately in consequence of having employed one of the Company's Servants in cutting off the Ears of an Indian who had had an intrigue with his Woman."

One suspects that Simpson's insights into the demeanour of his officers was not entirely truthful, dwelling as he did on the exaggerated negative aspects of their personalities. Yet his sketches provide a window into the turbulent, volatile and anti-social personnel of the two companies who, in the not too distant past, literally had been attacking each other. Some were dullards and thugs, others were master negotiators and traders, while others still were of questionable loyalty. As a group, there was not much that bound them together other than their distinctive peculiarities, a strong independent streak and perhaps an understanding and affinity with the Indigenous cultures into which most of them had married and with whom they worked on a daily basis.

Getting these disparate people to work together was like herding cats, and it took a man of unbending will and unifying vision to corral them and point them in the same direction. The fur business was like no other, dependent as it was on logistics and cultural diplomacy. The unusual skills of its field managers were the Company's greatest asset, something difficult to replicate without years of experience combined with a natural facility. Simpson understood this even as he sought to bring everyone, including the Indigenous peoples, under his control and management. His ultimate objective was to impose universal laws and hierarchy over an otherwise chaotic mélange of cultures and customs.

Simpson was the kind of man who always looked at himself from outside his own body—as if he wanted his life to appear as a painting, a painting for which he fabricated the composition to ensure no stray sunbeam banished the shadows and exposed the artful contrivance of his respectability. One wonders how he would have assessed his own character if he could have turned his razor-sharp perception onto himself. But he was a man curiously free from introspection, a man who believed that the rules that governed others did not apply to him.

IN 1826, SIMPSON ESTABLISHED HIS personal headquarters, and therefore the Company's, at Lachine, near Montreal, now a city of nearly fifty thousand, where he ensconced himself firmly at the pinnacle of Montreal society and the Anglo-Scottish business community. He used his home, whenever he was back that way in the off-season, for lavish dinners and parties for the political and business elite. He was certainly not afraid to mix business and pleasure, or perhaps saw no distinction between the two, for these social forays were as much for his amusement as for securing and consolidating the Company's position.

But although Simpson's mansion was in Montreal, he himself rarely was. His great passion was for near-continuous overland adventuring, touring the far-flung regions of his domain. He was ever on the move, showing his presence, issuing his decrees and keeping a tight control over the outposts across the continent. In 1828 Simpson boarded his executive canoe and embarked on another of his famous cross-continental epic treks, this one over eleven thousand kilometres, from York Factory to Fort Vancouver on the Columbia River: via Fort Chipewyan on Lake Athabasca, across the Rocky Mountains, down the Fraser River to the coast, south into Puget Sound and then finally overland to the Columbia. It was one of longest single-season canoe voyages in North American history. In the spring of 1829 he returned east again, met his councils and then returned to Lachine by the fall. He issued hundreds of decrees, chastised lenient traders, caught chief factors off guard and generally enjoyed the adulation and subservience that he demanded from his employees.

After this tour, Simpson sailed to London again, claiming the need to rest and rejuvenate after ten years in the trade. But it wasn't rest that animated him in Britain; it was his quest for someone he considered an appropriate bride. While wife-hunting across the ocean, he had abandoned one of his North American mistresses, Margaret Taylor, the daughter of a Cree woman and a skilled tradesman at York Factory, who was then pregnant with one of Simpson's many unofficial offspring. He left instructions for the child to be taken care of if "of the right colour," but otherwise to be bundled off along with the mother. Simpson had already fathered a host of children, including two in Scotland and many more in North America, conceived with the mixed-heritage daughters of fur traders under his command. He told John George McTavish at

York Factory to build a secret private entrance to his apartment so his dalliances would be undetected.

He referred to his mistresses as "bits of brown," "appendages" or "commodities." "The commodity," he wrote of one of his mixed-heritage mistresses, "has been a great consolation to me." When he had tired of Betsey Sinclair, his first mistress with whom he had a child, he left instructions with a subordinate to "dispose of the Lady . . . as she is an unnecessary and expensive appendage. I see no fun in keeping a Woman, without enjoying her charms which my present rambling life does not enable me to do." Some Canadian writers have waggishly referred to Simpson as "the father of the fur trade," but his pattern was to callously discard his mistresses when he was finished with the liaison, sending them back to their families. Also imagine the anger of the women's fathers, his own subordinate officers, who thought they were agreeing to an advantageous match for their offspring in accordance with long-standing custom. As far as is known, Simpson sired thirteen children with eight women, probably more, and he didn't take much responsibility for any of them; whatever success they had in life was their own.

Marrying within the trade was common practice, and these unions were respectable and accepted. Intermarriage between Indigenous peoples and fur traders was one of the social structures that had enabled the Company to succeed in the fur business and had moderated relations between peoples in the trade for generations. Simpson took advantage of the benefits while shuffling away from the responsibility and reciprocal obligations. His repeated violations of the traditions that regulated relationships in the fur country were disconcerting, insulting and demoralizing for the tone they set for the behaviour of others and the pall they cast upon the social institutions of the Company employees and their Indigenous families. As in so many other ways, Simpson did not fit into fur trade society. He ignored or subverted customs and seemed to have little regard for other people's lives. Simpson wasn't a tough-minded but judicious leader with a few embarrassing peccadilloes, he was a powerful cultural disruptor, saddling the future with his odious vision. Perhaps his world view had been tainted by his own tangential involvement in the slave trade. Certainly, he viewed and treated many of his various mistresses with cavalier contempt, mercenary usage and a callous disposal once his flighty eye had wandered.

Oddly, but not surprisingly, Simpson lived his life in accordance with his own desires, not the rules to which he expected others to adhere. Country marriages had existed informally for 150 years, but it was Simpson, soon after he became governor, who advised the London Committee to formalize the arrangement. He was concerned not about the welfare of women and children but for the Company's liability for dependents if they were abandoned at forts or if their husbands died. In 1821, he communicated his opinion to the London Committee that liaisons between employees and local women should be encouraged because they added stability to the relationship between the Company and its Indigenous customers. He said that the unions were diplomatic marriages that strengthened kinship ties, which of course had been known for ages. The Company even adopted a policy that family men had to reserve 10 per cent of their pay to be kept until they no longer had dependent children and that the men couldn't leave the country without making provision for their dependents. But then Simpson contradicted his own recommendations. He considered his native and mixed-heritage mistresses to be beneath his dignity as marriage partners (as he apparently also did with the white women of lower social status who had given birth to his children). To bolster his social standing, he wanted a white English wife comfortable in the salons of London and Montreal, where he perceived his interests as now lying.

While he was off wife-hunting in England, things were changing politically and economically. An intelligent if narrow-minded man, Simpson could envision a time when the fur trade's golden age, which he himself helped to create, would end. Despite his conservation efforts, many regions were no longer as plentifully endowed with beaver as they once had been, particularly surrounding major outposts and forts. The largest animals had already been trapped. The most profitable districts had been steadily moving west and north, and expansion would end once the land ended at the Pacific coast. Since the mid-1820s, Simpson had had his eye on the little-explored country west of the Rocky Mountains. This was a land where he did not yet reign supreme and where the Company did not yet have a large presence. But it was also a land where Simpson, though technically the governor, was not feared or treated with the deference he had come to expect.

Chapter Fourteen

THE KING OF
OLD OREGON

I n the summer of 1824, six years before his search in London for a suitable wife, George Simpson set off from York Factory on an epic three-month cross-continental canoe expedition to survey the far-thest-flung frontier of his sprawling fur empire: Old Oregon, the land west of the Rocky Mountains that was divided by the Company into the southern Columbia Department and the northern New Caledonia Department. The entire region had inexplicably failed to show a profit since the amalgamation of the two companies several years earlier, and his orders from the London Committee were to assess the region and bring some order to it. Simpson had yet to tour this Pacific province of his empire and he fully intended to shake it up and bring it in line with the other districts that he had so efficiently returned to profitability.

Simpson travelled in relative style in his own mighty birchbark canoe, colourfully decorated as befit its royal passenger and powered by an elite team of a dozen Iroquois voyageurs. Their machine-like sixty strokes a minute, sixteen hours a day, propelled him along the water highways of the continent up to 150 kilometres a day. Paddling down the Nelson

River, he was intent on setting speed records. He was particularly intent on overtaking one of his lieutenants who had also set off for the Columbia District three weeks earlier. To Simpson's delight and the new lieutenant's chagrin, after only six weeks Simpson's canoe rushed up to Dr. John McLoughlin's encampment along the shores of a river early one morning, catching them while they finished their breakfast.

McLoughlin was a curious, charismatic character, a six-foot-four, hulking giant, with a shaggy, prematurely white mane of hair, sharp grey eyes and a stern, creased face, hardened and angular from a life spent in the wilderness. The forty-year-old doctor was being shown his new fiefdom as superintendent of the Columbia District. He was to rule Old Oregon for the Company and keep it free from interlopers. Ostensibly under the authority of Simpson and the London Committee, McLoughlin, owing to the great distance from the Company's other operations, would essentially reign unfettered west of the Rockies.

A French-Scottish-Irish surgeon from Rivière-du-Loup, two hundred kilometres down the south shore of the St. Lawrence from Quebec, McLoughlin had spent most of his life employed in the fur trade. After two years studying medicine, he was granted his licence in Lower Canada and promptly signed on with the North West Company as the surgeon at Fort William, on Lake Superior, in 1803. He married the half-Cree Marguerite, the daughter of one of the early North West Company field partners and widow of Alexander McKay, the Nor'Wester who had gone with Mackenzie to the Pacific in 1793 and sailed on the *Tonquin* to the Columbia with Astor's Pacific Fur Company in 1810. Nine years older than McLoughlin and with four children already, she remained with him throughout his life, giving birth to four more children. Calm and gentle, she had the opposite characteristics to her husband's volatility and passion. McLoughlin mastered several Indigenous languages and quickly advanced to be one of the chief traders at Fort William. During the bitter war between the Hudson's Bay Company and the North West Company from 1814 to 1821, McLoughlin emerged as a respected diplomat and negotiator who helped ease the transition to a single company when he led the wintering partners in pressing for new terms with the Montreal agents. He had earned the trust of both the traders and the officers, and if a wilderness baron was needed to maintain the Company's hold on the distant domain, McLoughlin certainly looked the part, at least.

McLoughlin "was such a figure as I should not like to meet on a dark night in one of the bye lanes in the neighborhood of London," Simpson wrote warily in his journal after a long day on the trail, perhaps glancing across the fire toward his companion. "Dressed in clothes that had once been fashionable, but were now covered with a thousand patches of different colours, his beard would do honour to the chin of a Grizzly Bear, his face and hands evidently show that he had not lost much time at his toilette. He was loaded with Arms, and his own herculean dimensions formed a tout ensemble that would convey a good idea of the highwaymen of former days . . . [he was] ungovernable [with a] violent temper and turbulent disposition." An imposing figure, McLoughlin appeared the opposite of Simpson, who was short, plump and balding—although both had a hard-to-define magnetic charisma that drew attention to themselves and commanded respect and obedience.

McLoughlin was the logical choice for the key posts of New Caledonia and Columbia, despite Simpson's reservations about his independent and obstinate nature. Simpson both recognized McLoughlin's talents and disapproved of his independent temperament, grandiose schemes and defiance—traits that would eventually lead the two men into irreconcilable conflict when the Columbia Department hung precariously in the balance between American and British sovereignty in the 1840s. Deference was one of the key traits Simpson valued in his officers, and in this respect McLoughlin failed to satisfy.

Together the two men and their canoes crossed the aspen parkland following the Saskatchewan River and portaging over the wild and glacier-clad defiles of Athabasca Pass to Boat Encampment on the Wood River, following Thompson's route, and then canoeing down the Columbia to the coast, where Fort George (the former Fort Astoria) was the main depot for goods that were being shipped around Cape Horn. This was the route that would become known as the York Express, the Company's official cross-continental travel route that ran from York Factory on Hudson Bay to the Pacific. An advance canoe with a bugler announced their arrival and a bagpiper droned them into the fort's pullout. The place was a disappointment, ill-kept, with indolent men and a reputation for plying local Indigenous peoples with liquor. Simpson already had plans for its relocation.

Yet after inhaling the fresh coastal air and later travelling to see the white-capped ocean vista spreading before him, he knew he had for the first time reached the western boundary of his sprawling commercial domain—a territory that now was a monopoly that extended from the stony shore of Hudson Bay south to Spanish California, from the clear waters of Lake Superior to the sprouting agricultural community at Red River, and across the Rocky Mountains to the mouth of the Columbia River. The Company was now a conglomerate that had the greatest geographical reach of any in North America and was the only sanctioned non-Indigenous civil authority in most of western Canada and the states of Montana, Idaho, Washington and Oregon. Old Oregon was the most valuable beaver preserve yet remaining on the continent—the Columbia River basin alone was the size of France. It was also a magnet for the independent American trappers slowly pushing west over the Great Divide.

Although theoretically jointly "occupied" by the United States and Britain since the Convention of 1818, Old Oregon practically remained the sole commercial preserve of the Hudson's Bay Company. During the ten years since the North West Company purchased Fort Astoria from the Pacific Fur Company, Astor had abandoned his plans for the Pacific trade and focused his attention west of the Mississippi, along the Missouri River, so there was no competition for the Hudson's Bay Company west of the Rocky Mountains. The vast territory was loosely managed by a series of rude palisade forts strung together by established canoe routes along the principal waterways and, where topography made canoe travel impractical or impossible, a series of seasonal mule paths. The eighty thousand Indigenous inhabitants belonged to dozens of different tribes, spoke different languages, and other than trading at the forts, lived traditional lives.

The American free trappers were only just beginning to penetrate the Snake River country by the mid-1820s. West of the mountains, the usual pattern of the fur trade was inverted. Instead of Indigenous trappers bringing their haul of pelts to forts for exchange, it was just as likely that the trapping was done by white or mixed-blood trappers, who often traded for food or other provisions from well-ordered local societies. One of McLoughlin's tasks was to increase and expand the company's trade with coastal peoples.

These peoples included the Haida in the north, centred around the Queen Charlotte Islands (now Haida Gwaii); the Nootka (Nuu-chah-nulth) around Vancouver Island; the Tsimshian of western British Columbia and southern Alaska; the Kwakiutl (Kwakwaka'wakw) of northern Vancouver Island and the adjacent mainland; and the Coast Salish of western Oregon, Washington and southern British Columbia. These otherwise diverse peoples, with independent languages, customs and religions, had some cultural similarities that determined the nature of the fur trade on the coast. They were primarily marine-focused peoples who turned to the sea and rivers for their sustenance. They lived in permanent towns of impressive cedar longhouses such as those Mackenzie described on his journey to the coast in 1793. Instead of beavers, sea otters were the predominant source of fur, and the trade in this commodity had been conducted with independent American captains since the late eighteenth century. Their reliance on the fur trade was generally minimal and was centred on non-essential goods such as woollen blankets, beads and coloured cloth, and guns and ammunition. They did not unreservedly welcome foreigners into their territories, and in the case of the Haida they occasionally captured Russian, American, Spanish and British trading ships, plundering their cargo and enslaving their crews.

Slavery was widespread among the peoples of the Pacific Northwest coast, particularly among the Haida, who were known and feared for their Viking-like raids north and south of their homeland. "Those were stirring times," wrote the anthropologist Diamond Jenness, "when the big Haida war canoes, each hollowed out of a single cedar tree and manned by fifty or sixty warriors, traded and raided up and down the coast from Sitka in the north to the delta of the Fraser River in the south. Each usually carried a shaman or medicine man to catch and destroy the souls of enemies before an impending battle; and the women who sometimes accompanied the warriors fought as savagely as their husbands." There were small-scale semi-permanent slave markets at key places along the coast from Oregon to Alaska. Sometimes European and American trading ships would buy slaves at these markets and ship them to Haida Gwaii for resale.

Not yet ravaged by foreign diseases, these peoples were independent and confident, yet they had no knowledge of the expanse of the continent to the east of them or of the Company's bewilderingly complex logistical connections. Distant empires were discussing how to divide their traditional territory without involving them or even informing them of the discussions. There was Russian Alaska to the north, Spanish California to the south, and the large middle was to be divided between Britain and the United States.

SIMPSON AND MCLOUGHLIN SPENT the winter of 1824–25 debating the options for the Columbia Department. In between tours of outlying trading posts, they huddled around smouldering fires inside the leaky log huts at Fort George, stalked around the muddy compound in the dreary mist, and finally agreed on a strategy to preserve the territory for the British and the Company, not necessarily in that order.

To better secure the interior from the independent American fur trappers—still only a trickle that could easily be bought off or ruthlessly driven

out by cutthroat pricing—they decided to abandon Fort George and relo-
cate the central depot 140 kilometres upstream to a point Simpson had
chosen where the Willamette River wiggles into the Columbia (across
from the future city of Portland). The new depot, in a natural clearing
surrounded by massive hemlock, Douglas fir and cedars, facing the swift
waters of the Columbia and with the distinctive cone of Mount Hood to
the north, would be built on the north side of the river, as Simpson antic-
ipated that the river might become the international boundary, as Britain
had proposed in 1818. Perhaps having a keener perception of world events,
Simpson had originally favoured relocating the central depot "North of
this place, about Two or Three Degrees, at the mouth of Fraser's River."
To Simpson, the more northern river was the logical choice for the principal western depot because it undisputedly was first navigated by a British
explorer and was situated north of the 49th parallel—the boundary
requested by the Americans in 1818. If the American political claims prevailed, as he suspected they would, the Fraser would still be in British
territory. McLoughlin, however, felt that the Columbia was the great prize
and was loath to abandon it without a fight.

The new fort was at the head of navigation for ships sailing inland
and ideally suited for expeditions south along the Willamette Valley and
overland to Puget Sound. As a departing gesture, Simpson, without
much ceremony, christened the new fort by smashing a bottle of hooch
against the slippery wooden wall taking shape in a clearing and named
the dirty outpost Fort Vancouver—in honour of the British captain who
had been the second non-Indigenous mariner to discover the Columbia
River thirty years earlier, after Boston mariner Robert Gray, but who
was the first to map it. Fort Vancouver would become the central hub of
the entire fur trade enterprise west of the Rockies.

The fort would soon boast six-metre walls of solid beams enclosing
two large compounds containing over forty buildings, including a
church, schoolhouse, powder house and workshops for a blacksmith,
carpenters, millwrights and coopers. The grassy clearing surrounding

the fort was turned to agriculture and animal husbandry, with orchards, vegetable gardens and over a thousand cattle and hundreds of other domestic animals. A great central bell tolled to mark the start of the workday, to call people to church or school and to announce the arrival and departure of boats and brigades. Canadian French was the predominant language at the fort, while business was conducted in a pidgin language, Chinook Jargon, an amalgam of Chinook, French, English, Nootka, Chehalis and even Hawaiian. (Many Hawaiian Islanders worked for the Company at Fort Vancouver.)

Soon after Simpson headed east to return to the heart of his fur empire, McLoughlin began the difficult task of keeping American trappers and settlers east of the Snake River. Left to govern Old Oregon on his own, he took on legendary stature. After the company merger in 1821, the British government declared that the laws of Upper Canada would apply to British subjects in the Columbia District and delegated the authority to administer those laws to the Hudson's Bay Company. McLoughlin, as superintendent of Fort Vancouver, applied the law to British subjects, kept peace with the varied groups of Indigenous peoples and sought to maintain law and order over American settlers as well. He was known as the White-Headed Eagle to some of the Indigenous peoples, owing to his unruly mane of white hair, and the King of Oregon to the employees of the Company and the settlers who eventually trickled into his domain. At the height of the Company's operations in Old Oregon, McLoughlin held authority over thirty-four fur trade outposts, twenty-four small ports, six ships and over five hundred employees, as well as, after 1833, the subsidiary Puget Sound Agricultural Company and its farm and livestock operations centred around Fort Nisqually, between present-day Olympia and Tacoma, Washington.

For almost two decades McLoughlin presided over the region like a feudal lord, shrewd, manipulative, paternalistic and sometimes ruthless. He held court in an expansive timber hall behind the palisade of Fort Vancouver, and passed judgment on everyone within his domain, upholding the laws as he understood them and as he felt they applied in the outpost. Sometimes this meant fury and violence, other times unexpected understanding, depending upon his mood or local politics. McLoughlin's justice could be quick—he once flew into a rage and beat and publicly caned Herbert Beaver, a visiting British missionary. Beaver had written in a letter, which McLoughlin secretly read, claiming that Marguerite (his wife of over twenty-five years at the time) was "a female of notoriously loose character" and other insults related to her Indigenous ancestry and the fact that they hadn't been married in a Christian ceremony. The terrified and bloody Beaver escaped with his life only by the intervention of onlookers. Beaver had been sent out in the mid-1830s as part of the Company's new focus on evangelizing among the Indigenous people, as required by the British government to maintain its monopoly. Beaver, like nearly all the missionaries of this era, was sneering and condescending toward the Indigenous and mixed-heritage wives of the Company's officers, reflecting a new attitude that was creeping into Company culture under Simpson's reign.

McLoughlin's justice was equally meted out against Indigenous peoples whom he felt had transgressed his rigid code. Although he had no moral authority over them, other than force or arms, he felt that given the British government's claim of joint sovereignty over the region with the United States after 1818, it was his responsibility to dispense justice when it involved the Company, if not to intervene in any disputes between the various Indigenous tribes who outnumbered easterners of European descent twenty to one. Although the common punishment was to be flogged while strapped to a brass cannon followed by being chained in a dank cell, on one occasion, when some of his traders were killed near the Strait of Juan de Fuca, he ordered armed Company squads to level two encampments of the Clallam tribe, and twenty-three Clallam were killed in a prolonged conflict until they handed over the killers. McLoughlin was known not for leniency but for even-handed severity, an unusual sense of justice that earned him the fear, or at least the tolerance, of the Indigenous peoples in his commercial domain, and the fear of trappers, travellers and employees.

When McLoughlin visited the outlying regions of the vast territory, he travelled in style, with an entourage of wilderness courtiers and servants. "McLoughlin and his suite," wrote one observer, "would sometimes accompany the south-bound expeditions from Fort Vancouver, in regal state, for fifty or one hundred miles up the Willamette, when he would dismiss them with his blessing, and return to the fort. He did not often travel and seldom far; but on these occasions he indulged his men rather than himself in some little variety . . . It pleased Mrs. McLoughlin thus to break the monotony of her fort life. Upon a gaily-caparisoned steed, with silver trappings and strings of bells on bridle reins and saddle skirt, sat the lady of Fort Vancouver, herself arrayed in brilliant colours, and wearing a smile which might cause to blush and hang its head the broadest, warmest, and most fragrant sunflower. By her side, also gorgeously attired, rode her lord, king of the Columbia, and every inch a king, attended by a train of trappers, under a chief trader, each upon his best behaviour."

McLoughlin opened the gates of Fort Vancouver to all manner of travellers and wanderers, Indigenous, mixed-parentage or European, so long as they obeyed his rules and weren't directly threatening the Company or the fur trade in general. It became a multicultural enclave that included the Company officers, who were mostly Scottish or from around Montreal, and their predominantly Cree or mixed-heritage wives; French-Canadian, Métis and Iroquois voyageurs; Hawaiian labourers (who were called Kanakas or Owyhees); and at any time visiting dignitaries or travellers from up to thirty different Indigenous tribes. McLoughlin even sheltered three shipwrecked Japanese sailors. He hosted a nightly congenial dinner in the Great Hall that was renowned for its lively antics and conversation. The white-maned lord presided over the affair from an elevated head table, flanked by bagpipers braying out the ancient songs of the Highlands, while all dressed for the occasion and attended to his words. (The women dined separately and joined the men after dinner.) During interludes,

McLoughlin, a great talker who loved being the centre of attention, discoursed on politics, religion, the fur trade and other worldly topics. One of his famous visitors was David Douglas. A botanist affiliated with the Royal Horticultural Society of London, Douglas spent the years from 1825 to 1827 and from 1830 to 1833 roaming the vast forest domain of Old Oregon, sketching and categorizing thousands of wild and exotic plants of the Pacific Northwest, including the source of the region's future prosperity, the giant Douglas fir.

For twenty years McLoughlin tried to juggle his responsibilities to the Company with his personal inclination to provide aid, at the Company's expense, to the ever-increasing stream of American settlers arriving from the east. Simpson, on the other hand, was diametrically opposed to this, urging ill treatment or displacement of the settlers, knowing that non-Indigenous settlement would spell the end of the fur trade and, perhaps just as importantly, the end of his unsupervised reign over northern North America. Although Simpson visited Old Oregon only three times (in 1824–25, 1828 and 1841), his clashes with McLoughlin were legendary. For years, though, McLoughlin ruled virtually unchallenged, shaping Old Oregon as he saw fit, until he was undone by political and social events far beyond his control.

◇◇◇

TO ENTERPRISING YOUNG MEN.

The subscriber wishes to engage ONE HUNDRED MEN, to ascend the river Missouri to its source, there to be employed for one, two or three years.—For particulars, enquire of Major Andrew Henry, near the Lead Mines, in the County of Washington, (who will ascend with, and command the party) or to the subscriber at St. Louis.

Wm. H. Ashley
Missouri Gazette, February 13, 1822

WILLIAM ASHLEY, AN ASTUTE ENTREPRENEUR, gunpowder salesman and later politician based out of St. Louis, changed the fur trade
forever in the Pacific Northwest and set in motion events that would
change its politics as well. In the spring of 1823, Ashley and his partner
Andrew Henry organized a band of one hundred ragged and unruly
ramblers—some wastrels, some thugs, some adventurous youths from
the east, and quite a few former Nor'Westers disgruntled after the amalgamation with the Hudson's Bay Company in 1821. Ashley's small band,
based out of the ramshackle tavern town of St. Louis, poled their
unwieldy flat-bottomed barges upriver along the mud-coloured
Missouri River and into the mountains. From there they filtered into
the valleys and gulches of western Montana, Idaho, Wyoming and
Colorado to set traps for unwary beaver. They were the first American
"Mountain Men," and during the 1820s and 1830s they expanded their
operations westward toward the Pacific, nibbling at the fringes of
McLoughlin's domain and encroaching on the traditional lands of the
Indigenous peoples.

Ashley's "One Hundred Men" were not hauling into the wilderness
back-breaking burdens of trade goods to exchange with the Indians for
their furs. Instead they were laden with beaver traps and personal supplies. They had no intention of constructing a trading fort in the mountains. Ashley's scheme was to have his men do the actual trapping—a
role in the fur trade that had previously been the exclusive domain of
Indigenous peoples, particularly in the north.

Not surprisingly, the invasion of traditional territories did not help
relations between the two peoples. The various tribes didn't appreciate
hundreds of foreigners wandering around their territory trapping all the
beaver. Within a few years, a more or less constant low-level war existed
between the new trappers and the natives. Both the Mountain Men and
the Indigenous warriors proudly displayed the scalps of their vanquished
foes, sometimes wearing strings of the shrivelled flesh and hair as accoutrements to their outfits. The American senator Thomas Benton suggested

that nearly five hundred American trappers perished in combat with the Rocky Mountain peoples by the close of the 1820s. He made no estimate of the Indigenous peoples that they had killed.

The life expectancy of a "free trapper" could be short, and so for mutual protection as they invaded the traditional lands of proud and sometimes militant nations of the Blackfoot Confederacy and the Snake (Shoshoni) or Nez Perce, the free trappers travelled in brigades, or companies, of twenty men or more. Two of the greatest of these brigades were the Rocky Mountain Fur Company and the Missouri Fur Company, although both were later absorbed by the American Fur Company as John Jacob Astor tightened his grip on the American fur trade in the 1830s. Astor rapidly increased the trade along the upper Missouri River with the use of steam-powered ships. By the time the demand for fur had petered out by the 1840s, Astor had sold his interests in the fur trade, and the industry slipped into decline—the age of the Mountain Men was between 1822 and 1840. But the American Fur Company continued to flourish in the decades to follow, beginning the lucrative trade in bison hides that eventually drove the thundering herds to near extinction later in the century.

The old fur-post system of the Hudson's Bay Company did not suit the temperament of the Mountain Men; nor was it ideal in the torturous topography and foaming rivers west of the Great Divide, where horses rather than canoes were the ideal mode of transportation. Canoe brigades were all but useless to get furs to market. Rather, at an annual rendezvous in the mountains, the agents of the large fur companies carted in goods from St. Louis over the passes and arrayed them in a sprawling makeshift tent-encampment in the valley. The first rendezvous was held at Pierre's Hole in southern Idaho in 1823, and it immediately became an annual tradition, a sort of trapper trade fair where the lonely, bedraggled trappers, after a winter spent wandering up the uncharted valleys west of the Continental Divide, wading into freezing streams and ponds to set traps and haul in the bloated corpses of beaver, gathered for a few months of unbridled revelry and debauched celebration.

The Mountain Men, sometimes half-starved on a diet of roots, rosebuds, boiled moccasins and mountain berries, were often a sorry sight in the spring. At the rendezvous they could relax while they hawked their pelts for powder, shot, tobacco, guns, blankets, food and, most importantly, whiskey. Alcohol fuelled the bedlam for which the rendezvous were notorious, easing briefly the bush-fever-induced introversion that tainted life the rest of the year. Here they drank and gambled and drank, both Indigenous and whites; they held wild-horse races, barbaric wrestling contests, bleary-eyed duels and frantic buffalo chases until all their money and credit were used up. "There goes Hoss and Beaver!" was a common call for losing everything, as they did each year at the rendezvous. One of the few literate Mountain Men, George Ruxton, recorded a particularly grotesque game of skill he witnessed in 1832: two French Canadians gobbling opposite ends of a lightly toasted fatty buffalo intestine. "The two Canadians commenced at either end of the snake-like coil. As yard after yard slid glibly down their throats, and the serpent between them was dwindling from an anaconda to a moderate-sized rattlesnake, it became a great point with each feaster to hurry his operation . . . at the same time, whatever he did, each exhorted the other to feed fair, and every now and then, overcome by the unblushing attempts of his partner to bolt a vigorous mouthful, would suddenly jerk back his head, drawing out by the same movement, by the retreating motion, several yards of greasy Boudin from his neighbour's mouth and stomach, and, snapping up himself the ravaged portions, greedily swallowed them himself."

When they were finally broke, they begged the agents of the St. Louis trading companies for credit for a winter's kit, before wandering back to the wilderness for another stint. At the end of the summer and the rendezvous, the encumbered fur wagons, swollen with the yearly catch, lumbered east to St. Louis with the fortune.

Fur remained in great demand throughout the 1820s and 1830s in Europe and the American east, and the increased prices spurred the Mountain Men into the farthest corners of the continent in their quest the commodity that fuelled their brutish and curious way of life. As they wandered up every gulch and canyon with a pack horse or mule, they explored much of the interior of the Pacific Northwest. It was these early trappers who, for better or worse, "opened up" Old Oregon for the missionaries and settlers who ended the Hudson's Bay Company's thirty-year hegemony in the Far West and corroded the independence of the Indigenous societies. They were the forerunners of the American westward migration that would eventually pull the land into the American union.

AMONG ASHLEY'S "ENTERPRISING YOUNG MEN" was a young man destined to become a legend in his own time, Jedediah "Bible Man" Smith. Jedediah was one of the greatest Mountain Men, and one of the few literate members of this strange fraternity. Grizzled and wizened like an Old Testament prophet, he wore his lanky locks low over his shoulders to hide his mangled ear, chewed off by a grizzly bear on an early expedition to the Black Hills of Dakota. He reputedly carried a pistol in one hand and a Bible in the other for alternately battling competitors or preaching the Gospel.

When Jedediah Smith first ventured into the mountains searching for beaver in 1823, he was a twenty-four-year-old greenhorn from New York State. The west was the land of adventure and the unknown he had learned about possibly from reading Lewis and Clark's description of their epic foray to the Pacific, and the fur trade offered an outlet for the young man's imagination. Unlike many of his rough-hewn brethren, Jedediah was reputedly clean-shaven, humourless and stern, never using profane language, and frequently quoting from his Bible on the trail. He was teetotalling, educated, polite and stoutly Methodist, earning the epithet "Bible Man" for his temperate and considered demeanour.

He spent his first few years in the west, between 1823 and 1826, tra-
versing the gulches, canyons and valleys of eastern Oregon Territory in
pursuit of his lucrative quarry, warring with the Blackfeet and rising in
stature and respect within the unruly, semi-savage fraternity. Ironically,
his quest for the water-loving beaver led him on a great trek across
North America's driest deserts and eventually up the coast to Fort
Vancouver, where he was amazed at the fertile soil of Oregon around
the Columbia and Willamette Rivers.

By the time he was near thirty, he was a principal partner of the
Rocky Mountain Fur Company and renowned for having "a bump of
curiosity the size of a goose head." In 1826, he and fifteen trappers set
off from the Great Salt Lake on a grand adventure "for the purpose of
exploring the country S.W. which was entirely unknown to me, and of
which I could collect no satisfactory information from the Indians
who inhabited this country." He wandered across the blasted, sun-
baked alkali plains, eventually stumbling across the salt-pan-pocked,
shadeless waste of the Mojave Desert, and continued on to the sparse
Spanish San Gabriel Mission in Southern California, near present-day
Los Angeles. Here he and his troop were hospitably welcomed by the
Franciscan monks, and later held prisoner by the Spanish governor of
California. The presence of wandering Americans posed a serious
dilemma to the Mexican officials, who wanted both to prevent
American encroachment in California and to maintain good relations
with the expanding nation. After a month, Smith and his compatriots
were released and instructed to return east, so he set out north through
interior California before returning for the 1827 rendezvous along a
route near present-day Yosemite National Park (uncannily close to the
streams that would bear loads of gold-bearing ore twenty-five years
later) and through the Great Nevada Basin, 480 kilometres of crusty,
waterless salt flats. Back in Pierre's Hole, Jedediah observed casually,
"My arrival caused considerable bustle in camp, for myself and party
had been given up as lost."

Smith immediately set out on a second expedition, again crossing the rubble-strewn salty wasteland to the coast. This time he led his party north, into the monumental forests of interior western Oregon, where he was attacked along the Umpqua River by a band of Kalawatset (an Athapaskan-speaking tribal group of south-central Oregon) for trespassing and trapping on their lands. Fourteen of his band were slain, and only Smith and three others survived and fled north to Fort Vancouver. Here they recuperated as guests of John McLoughlin during the winter of 1828–29. McLoughlin used his considerable influence and the influence of the Company to retrieve the horses and furs taken in the attack—and then purchased the furs from Smith and resold them at a profit.

McLoughlin entertained Smith all winter and the two became friends despite their different allegiances. Smith was impressed with the fertile soil surrounding the fort: the gardens growing in the large clearing around the enclosure were flourishing with annual crops of grain and corn and with increasing numbers of apple trees and grape vines. Under McLoughlin's tutelage Fort Vancouver was beginning to look like a small community rather than a wilderness fur outpost. McLoughlin had also commissioned the construction of a gristmill and a sawmill, and kept herds of cattle and pigs. McLoughlin's "colonizing" efforts were so successful that he was shipping surplus produce to Spanish California and Russian Alaska. The Presbyterian missionary couple Henry and Eliza Spalding were delighted with the settlement when they visited in early September 1836, calling Fort Vancouver "the New York of the Pacific" and writing, "Here we find fruit of every description, apples, peaches, grapes, pears, plums and fig trees in abundance; also cucumbers, melons, beans, peas, beets, cabbage, tomatoes and every kind of vegetables too numerous to mention. Every part is very neat and tastefully arranged, with fine walks, lined on each side with strawberry vines. On the opposite end of the garden is a good Summer house [McLoughlin's] covered in grape vines."

That it was a lush and rich land was evident, and Jedediah suggested to his proud host, perhaps while feasting in the Great Hall, that it would be Americans who finally colonized the verdant valley, not British or eastern Canadians. It was not settlement that disturbed McLoughlin, though, who knew the land could not long remain un-tilled. It was the thought of losing Old Oregon to the United States, to "a people who will most probably feel very differently Inclined towards the Company."

After taking leave of McLoughlin and Fort Vancouver, Jedediah wandered back to southern Idaho for the 1829 rendezvous and spread his tale, both of his adventures and of the fertility and fur trade potential of western Old Oregon. Jedediah increasingly became aware that he was more than a mere trapper. He kept detailed journals of his travels and made intricate maps of the lands he explored, including information about passes, water sources, Indigenous peoples and their friendship or hostility to foreigners, and good locations for ranching or farming. He was smoothing the ancient trade and travel trails of the land, leading the way for the missionaries and settlers.

Jedediah died in 1831 at the age of thirty-two, speared, according to the hazards of his trade, by a lance in a battle with Comanche while leading a caravan along the Santa Fe Trail. After his death many of his notes and maps were passed around by the trappers, continuing the rumours of the wealth of the land west of the Snake River. One of the greatest explorers of his time, Jedediah saw more of the west than anyone before him, yet offered only this prosaic explanation for his roaming life, and perhaps the roaming life of the other Mountain Men: "I, of course, expected to find Beaver," he noted, "which with us hunters is a primary object, but I was also led on by the love of novelty common to us all which is much increased by the pursuit of its gratification."

McLoughlin may not have been altogether dismayed by Jedediah's prophetic pronouncement in 1829, but it didn't deter him from continuing his predatory tactics to preserve the majority of Old Oregon for himself and the Hudson's Bay Company. Ever since 1825, when he and

Simpson first developed a strategy for the Columbia District, a key component of the plan was to create a beaver-free zone to the south and east of the Columbia and Snake Rivers that would prevent or at least delay the encroachment of American free trappers. Simpson wrote a letter to McLoughlin explaining his reasoning: since "the first step that the American Government will take towards colonization is through their Indian Traders, if the country becomes exhausted in Fur-bearing animals they can have no inducement to proceed thither." He continued his reasoning when he wrote the London Committee stating that "The country is a rich preserve of Beaver and which for political reasons we should endeavour to destroy as fast as possible."

The weapon Simpson chose to wield in his battle against American encroachment into what he perceived as the Company's private domain was a fellow named Peter Skene Ogden. Of Loyalist stock, Ogden, a sturdy fellow with an unwavering gaze and a determined mouth, was the son of a prominent Montreal judge. His personal interest in the law, however, was scanty and he declined to follow his father and two older brothers into a legal career, although his interactions with the law in later years were a defining characteristic of his legacy. After a stint with the American Fur Company, he signed on as a clerk with the North West Company and was dispatched to Île-à-la-Crosse in 1810. Here, as we have seen, he encountered Samuel Black, a similarly young clerk who seems to have had a dark influence on Ogden, or the other way around. The two young men earned a reputation for belligerence, bullying and violence during the years of the wars between the companies. Their terrorism and intimidation of the Company's man Peter Fidler and their assault on Indigenous traders who frequented the Company's posts were legendary. In 1816, they and a small war band went too far when they stormed the Company fort at nearby Green Lake and demanded that the head clerk deliver to them a Cree man who had insisted on trading in defiance of Ogden's and Black's threats. Then, within sight of the fort, they "butchered" him "in a most cruel manner" as a warning to others.

Colonial authorities in Britain were disturbed at the revelation, and Ogden was charged with murder in a Lower Canada court in 1818. Rather than send him east for justice, the North West Company quietly shipped him out to the Columbia Department, where he worked at various posts—from Fort George (Astoria), Spokane House and Thompson's River Post (later Kamloops)—for the remainder of the war, leaving behind his Cree wife and young son. When the companies merged in 1821, both Ogden and Black were dismissed from service in the new monopoly because they were too violent and disorderly. Simpson described Ogden as "one of the most unprincipled Men in the Indian Country, who would soon get into habits of dissipation if he were not restrained by the fear of these operating against his interests, and if he does indulge in that way madness to which he has a predisposition will follow as a matter of course." Of course, Simpson also pegged him as "a keen, sharp, off hand fellow of superior abilities to most of his colleagues, very handy and active and not sparing of his personal labour." Simpson was astute at recognizing a good tool, and eventually Ogden was reinstated specifically to implement the scorched-earth policies beginning in 1824 with the Snake River expeditions based out of Spokane House.

Around this time, Ogden married Julia Rivet, a Spokane (Cayuse) from western Montana whom he reputedly bought from her father the chief for fifty ponies. There are stories about Julia dating from the time she followed her husband around on his beaver-killing rambles. Of the time she leaped into the raging torrent during spring runoff, roped herself to the raft piled with furs that was being swept away and hauled it ashore, saving them a fortune. Or in 1815, when American trappers stole Ogden's furs and then stampeded the Company's horses. When she looked up in horror to see her "first-born dangling from the saddle straps in a moss bag, she dashed into the American lines with a bound, she was in the saddle, she had caught up the halter to bring the horses back to the Hudson's Bay camp, when a drunken Yankee trader yelled, 'Shoot the damn squaw!'" Obscured by the billowing clouds of dust, she charged back to the Company camp, leading the stolen horses. Ogden and Julia had seven children and remained together until Ogden died in Oregon City in 1854, at the age of sixty-four. Ogden's will specifically recognized Julia and all of his children as the beneficiaries of his substantial estate. Because his wife was Indigenous and the marriage ceremony was according to the custom of the country and thus was not legally binding, Ogden's brother and sister in Montreal challenged the validity of the will, but they were only partially successful.

Between 1824 and 1830, Ogden led six expeditions into the Snake River territory, hunting beaver to the point of extermination for short profit and to create a fur desert. As usual for Simpson, his skill for choosing the right man for the job was unparalleled. A combative, aggressive man who seemed fearless and modelled his life around his saying that "Necessity has no laws," Ogden's first party was not the usual quiet group of trappers but rather consisted of more than seventy armed men, among them many Iroquois and French-Canadian voyageurs, each equipped with five iron-toothed leg-hold traps, over 370 horses, and dozens of sundry followers, including the wives and families of many of the men and some multilingual Indigenous traders. The young Jedediah Smith was also in his party. They trundled east and south through the foothills of the Wasatch Mountains of Utah to the Bear River, where they managed to trap over six hundred beavers and many hundreds more throughout the summer. They encountered some American Mountain Men trapping in the same vicinity, and Ogden watched impotently as many of his men abandoned him when they found out the Americans were being paid much more per beaver. The Mountain Men also told his trappers that, since they were now in American territory, they were freed of their debts to the Company, a compelling inducement particularly to the Iroquois, who despised being in debt each year after the Company lent them the funds to purchase their trapping outfit.

Ogden had dealings with nearly all of the different peoples during his expeditions through parts of Idaho, Utah, Wyoming, Nevada, Washington,

Oregon and California. He disliked and feared the prickly aggressive Blackfeet (Julia's father had been killed in a Blackfoot raid), appreciated others such as the Nez Perce and Cayuse (the people from whence his wife Julia came), hated the Snake of Oregon, with whom he was unable to have cordial relations, and fought a pitched battle with a war band of Mojave.

Ogden's forays were well organized, ruthlessly and efficiently hauling in many thousands of beaver every year, including females and young, even if the pelts were valueless. During these years his men nearly starved, were lost, nearly froze, were drowned and engaged in gun battles. "This life makes a young man sixty in a few years . . . A convict at Botany Bay is a gentleman at ease compared to my trappers," he wrote, but added that his men loved the roving dangerous life and that "they would regard it as a punishment to be sent to Canada." By the time he retired in the 1840s, after being transferred to Company posts on the coast and then inland to Fort St. James on Stuart Lake, nearly all of his original men had died in the field.

Although Ogden was mostly successful in creating a beaver desert, as the 1830s drew on, it became increasingly difficult for both the Company and the Indigenous peoples to keep out the free traders, missionaries and pioneers. The many glowing reports of Old Oregon's fertility had filtered east.

Chapter Fifteen

LOSS OF AN APPENDAGE

Hall Jackson Kelley was perhaps the most unlikely man to be interested in a pioneering expedition from his home in Boston to the dark and foreboding forests on the opposite side of the continent. A bookish, bespectacled grammar teacher born sometime around the end of the eighteenth century, his romantic visions of the West, inspired by reading the journals of Lewis and Clark, Captain Vancouver and other explorers, led him to zealously promote the Oregon Territory as the future crown jewel of the United States. His writings were a signpost leading to the end of the Company's monopoly in Old Oregon. That he had never been west of Boston did not deter him at all in his shameless promotion of and lobbying for government-backed support of his colonizing schemes.

Kelley did eventually make a solo trip to Oregon, but unknowingly took up with a group of horse thieves and so was treated coolly by McLoughlin when he arrived "penniless and ill-clad" at Fort Vancouver in 1833. He eventually cleared his name but never forgave McLoughlin for his treatment, and devoted his remaining days to pushing for an end to the British occupation of Oregon and lobbying for a government pension for his role in publicizing the region. He never returned to Oregon and died, a forgotten and broken man, in 1874.

Kelley was particularly incensed by the joint-occupation accord of 1818, taking his cue from another absentee Oregon promoter, John Floyd, an outspoken Virginia representative. Soon after the Convention of 1818 was signed, Floyd claimed that the British and the Hudson's Bay Company were stealing the region from the United States. He urged Washington to seize Oregon and oust the foreigners—he made no mention of the Indigenous owners of the land. Echoing the sentiments of manifest destiny in vogue following the Monroe Doctrine of 1822, Francis Baylies of Massachusetts seconded Floyd's opinions when he wrote, "Our natural boundary is the Pacific Ocean. The swelling tide of our population must and will roll on until that mighty ocean interposes its waters and limits our territorial empire. Then with two oceans washing our shores, the commercial wealth of the world is ours, and imagination can hardly conceive the greatness, the grandeur, and the power that await us."

Throughout the 1820s, Floyd repeatedly called for the annexation of Oregon, but his notions attracted little interest, other than providing fuel for Kelley's vision of a pious American settlement in the Edenic forests of Oregon—a vision Kelley later claimed was inspired by divine revelation: "The word came expressly to me," he announced, "to promote the propagation of Christianity in the dark and cruel places about the shores of the Pacific."

In 1829, Kelley founded the American Society for Encouraging the Settlement of the Oregon Territory, announcing, without a shred of evidence, that Oregon was a veritable Eden where crops flourished with little labour or attention. If only Congress would underwrite the costs of getting there and guarantee him title to the land. But there was little support for his initiatives in government circles, and membership in his society seldom exceeded five hundred. His evangelical proselytizing, magazine articles, letters to newspapers and self-published pamphlet did, however, stimulate a renewed interest in Oregon, particularly in one young Boston entrepreneur, Nathaniel Wyeth.

The twenty-nine-year-old Wyeth, who heard Kelley's inspirational oratory about the sunny prospects on the Pacific, was then engaged in a curious but lucrative enterprise cutting chunks of ice from ponds near his home in Cambridge and shipping them to the West Indies. In 1832, he became frustrated with Kelley's bureaucratic dithering and resolved to make his own colonizing expedition to the Far West. In the spring of 1832, he sent a ship loaded with supplies around Cape Horn to the Columbia River and set out in charge of a twenty-person overland expedition himself. His plan was similar to the scheme launched by John Jacob Astor in 1812, although not focused exclusively on the fur trade: from a commercial base (probably a stockade fort) on the lower Columbia, he and his followers planned to collect furs, dry and preserve salmon, and clear the forests for timber, in addition to founding an agricultural utopia.

Like Astor and his Pacific Fur Company, Wyeth's lofty dreams were crushed by natural calamity. He and his band of "industrious and temperate men," among them a blacksmith, farmers, fishers and two carpenters, eventually reached Fort Vancouver after an eight-month gruelling trek, following the old trapper trails across the crusty, windblown Plains and through the maze of mountains (now beginning to be beavered out with Ogden's efforts). They even survived the famous Battle of Pierre's Hole, where 150 Blackfoot warriors skirmished with the Mountain Men during the summer rendezvous.

Unfortunately, this was not the last of Wyeth's troubles. At Fort Vancouver he learned that a capricious Pacific storm had sucked under his supply ship containing all the accoutrements of colonization—beaver traps, trade goods, barrels for packing dried salmon, food and other sundry provisions. Fortunately for Wyeth, McLoughlin had a soft heart when it came to colonists (a fact that was beginning to disturb George Simpson as Fort Vancouver looked more and more like a prosperous settlement than a fur outpost) and welcomed the haggard emigrants to his humble abode. "I am now afloat," Wyeth speculated, "on the great sea of life without stay or support but in good hands i.e. myself and providence and a few of the H.B.Co. who are perfect gentlemen."

Although Wyeth took leave of Fort Vancouver and returned to Boston in the spring, many of his original followers, the first settlers to successfully travel the entire distance of the Oregon Trail, remained in Oregon. A few joined the Hudson's Bay Company; others began clearing land for homesteads in the nearby Willamette Valley where McLoughlin had directed them; and a former lawyer named John Ball founded the first Oregon school and began teaching the children of the Company employees and their Indigenous wives. Despite his initial ill fortune, soon after arriving in Boston the indomitable Wyeth began preparing for a second Oregon adventure, and he departed again in the spring of 1834.

Wyeth's second weary band arrived at Fort Vancouver in the fall of 1834 after a much less harrowing journey. They were welcomed with warmth by McLoughlin, and then politely directed south of the Columbia to the Willamette Valley. Although McLoughlin realized settlement was inevitable, he planned to keep the newcomers south of the Columbia, where he suspected the international boundary might run. Wyeth eventually constructed a trading post, Fort Hall, along the upper Snake River, against McLoughlin's warning, and was driven bankrupt in 1837 by the Company's cutthroat pricing. Despondently he returned to Boston. Wyeth's second band of over seventy emigrants included the tall and robust Methodist clergyman Jason Lee, who had been sent to Oregon with four evangelical disciples to tame the supposedly heathen hearts of the natives. He was to "live with them, learn their language, preach Christ to them and, as the way opens, introduce schools, agriculture, and the arts of civilized life."

Lee, decisive and hard-working, quickly began settling into a twenty-acre homestead, slapping together a crude cabin and clearing the land for crops the following spring. He wrote to his mission board informing them of his success and requesting more recruits—men with families and women, especially white women: "The Gov. and other Gentlemen of the H. B. Co. (though they have native wives) say that white females would be of the greatest importance to the mission," he reported, "and would have far more influence among Indians than males." That the Company's officers specifically requested white women seems doubtful, but nevertheless, two years later, a ship slid into the dock at Fort Vancouver and out stepped thirteen new colonists—men with families, including three unattended women, one of whom, Anna Maria Pittman from New York, married Lee three months later.

This was the beginning of long-term colonial settlement, just as it was in the Red River Settlement to the east, and other colonizers soon followed: the dour, tight-lipped Dr. Marcus Whitman and his plucky bride, the blonde Narcissa, crossed the country on their honeymoon in the companionship of the missionary couple Eliza and Henry Spalding. Narcissa and Eliza, the first two women to make the long trek to Oregon, had a dramatic influence at the rendezvous of 1836. They distributed Bibles to the intemperate trappers who sheepishly turned out for the morning devotions after taming their wilder inclinations. For twelve days the rendezvous took on a sedate charade before reverting to its chaotic glory. "This is a cause worth living for!" declared the energetic Narcissa, before pressing on to Fort Walla Walla. "If we had packed one or two animals with bibles & testaments, we should have had abundant opportunity of disposing of them to the traders & trappers of the mountains . . . Oh how many missionaries are wanted who will go into the highways & hedges & compel sinners to come in to the feast." McLoughlin was interested in their arrival, and offered them credit at the Company store and a gift of horses and cattle if they would settle south in the Willamette Valley, but they demurred and moved northwest to the territory near Fort Walla Walla to establish a Christian mission among the Cayuse.

The "plug-hat missionary" Samuel Parker and the Jesuit Pierre-Jean De Smet followed soon after, searching for lands for their eastern brethren, and within a few years missions of almost every denomination were scattered throughout the territory, but concentrated along the Willamette Valley. Despite the missionary zeal, the evangelizing results of the first preachers were not spectacular. Most converted Indigenous peoples abandoned the faith when it became apparent that it would not lead to the outward material prosperity enjoyed by other Christians, and Indigenous children adopted by the missionaries frequently succumbed to the usual diseases brought by missionaries, taking an increasing toll on the Indigenous communities in Old Oregon. After one particularly virulent "fever and ague" (perhaps a form of malaria) in 1830, the Scottish botanist and traveller David Douglas (who would himself die of fever a few years later in Hawaii) recorded, "Villages, which had afforded from one to two hundred effective warriors, are totally gone. Not a soul remains. The houses are empty and flocks of famished dogs are howling about, while the dead bodies lie strewn in every direction on the sands of the river." Within a handful of years most of the Indigenous inhabitants of the lower Columbia had succumbed to disease.

As it was in other regions where the Company operated in earlier eras, disease was the great killer of Indigenous peoples. In a darkly ironic twist, it was disease more than anything else that allowed for the white settlement of Old Oregon in the 1830s, by depopulating communities, and entire regions, with chilling efficiency, leaving vast tracts of land sparsely inhabited. In a similar pattern to what had occurred in the interior of the continent fifty years earlier, it was not uncommon for the afflicted to run delirious into the frozen mountain streams in a vain effort to cool their raging fever, or to stumble vomiting to the ground before their pocked bodies were still. McLoughlin wept at the suffering and death at Fort Vancouver, where a small number of people were afflicted. The skills of the most educated physicians were as ineffective as the Indigenous shamans in stemming the dark tide. Fear of smallpox was so great that one of Astor's partners in the founding of Astoria, Duncan McDougal, in 1812 threatened a band of hostile Chinook by holding aloft a small black vial, claiming that the mysterious killer was contained within, and that if they disobeyed his orders he would release it into their community. He later married Elvamox, the daughter of the local chief, and then abandoned her before returning east to a post near Lake Winnipeg, where he died in 1818.

The story of the black vial lingered and was sometimes the source of misinformation about the cause of disease in the region. In 1847, the Whitmans and twelve of their missionaries were killed by an enraged band of Cayuse near Fort Walla Walla after a measles epidemic flared through the community. When they saw Dr. Whitman hovering about the delirious sufferers in his dark robes, they thought he was secretly administering poison.

FAR FROM DISCOURAGED BY THEIR EARLY RESULTS, the missionaries turned to land promotion as a method of expanding their communities, and their glowing reports of the fertile lands of Oregon attracted greater numbers of prospective pioneers yearly. Another of McLoughlin's guests at Fort Vancouver was William A. Slacum, an American naval captain sent out to spy on the potential of the land and the activities of the Hudson's Bay Company. His intentions were obvious to McLoughlin, and the two developed a hatred of each other. Despite his hospitable stay at the fort, Slacum's report painted a dim view of the Company, which he claimed was harassing American pioneers, inciting Indigenous peoples to attack the missions and settlers and charging them outrageous prices for provisions.

Slacum's report, and other similar accounts, fostered an unsympathetic view of the Hudson's Bay Company in the minds of arriving pioneers that contributed to uneasy relations in the early days of settlement. With the increasing numbers of settlers arriving at Fort Vancouver, many of them suspicious of anything British, the unchallenged authority of the Hudson's Bay Company began to erode. The settlers heralded the end of McLoughlin's rule in Oregon and the end of fur trading (already by the early 1840s, the land south of the Columbia was showing declining returns), but to drive the settlers off the land was not something he would do, regardless whether it was in the best interests of the Company. Even a policy of peaceful non-interference did not sit well with the aging McLoughlin, who began to view the Willamette settlements as the beginnings of a new society, not pestering flotsam who were ruining the fur trade.

The flood of settlers increased dramatically after the Panic of 1837, when farm produce prices and land values plummeted in the eastern United States, leaving many farmers and land speculators without homes. The Willamette Valley, rhapsodized in song and tall tale, seemed like the golden land, a new frontier for a new beginning. The fact that Old Oregon was at least partly under foreign dominion, and was the traditional territory of thousands of self-governing Indigenous peoples, did not seem to disturb the thousands of emigrants, who in some ways had few other options. The stable and secure presence of the missions, well publicized by the late 1830s, and ironically the Company's Fort Vancouver both provided the nucleus for future settlement and the final incentive for thousands of pioneers to make the insurmountable cross-continental trek. For a brief time, the Oregon Trail was the longest road in the United States— 6,400 kilometres of rutted tracks winding west from Independence, Missouri, across the barren and windblown Plains toward the imposing wall of the Rockies, ascending to snow-plugged alpine passes that burst into bloom briefly in the summer, following the shores of surging rivers through red-rock canyons, bypassing foaming cataracts, before ending, more or less, at Fort Vancouver. There was an endless stream of baggy, cloth-covered wagons plodding their difficult way west toward a future the migrants could only dimly imagine.

BY THE 1840S OVER A THOUSAND SETTLERS a year were arriving at Fort Vancouver, destitute, on the verge of starvation and ill prepared for the coming winter. They presented McLoughlin with a great dilemma— it was not Company policy to extend credit except to certain trusted

Indigenous trappers, and particularly not to settlers, who undermined the Company's livelihood, yet he felt a growing sympathy toward the hopeful, ragged bands constantly arriving in his domain. Resolving his inner conflict, he generously extended aid to all incoming pioneers, and restrained Indigenous peoples and settlers alike from attacking each other. Company policy notwithstanding, he doled out over $30,000 in credit at the Company store by 1845, in no small part ensuring the survival of many of the settlers and their budding communities, and provoking the wrath of Simpson, who was taking an increasingly dark view of McLoughlin's support of foreign settlers who heralded the end of the Company's monopoly in Old Oregon.

Officially, the Company couldn't do anything to thwart the incoming settlers—politically the entire Oregon Territory was under joint administration of the British and American governments and was open to commercial development by both nations. That Oregon would be formally divided was not a question, but where it would be divided was a question without an easy answer. McLoughlin still hoped to hold the Columbia as the border, while Simpson, a more astute observer of the trends sweeping the continent, set his eyes on the Fraser River, just north of the 49th parallel, in accordance with his prediction in 1825. The ever-roving Simpson made his final visit to Fort Vancouver in 1841, and after a cursory tour of several northern posts, informed McLoughlin of his plans to finalize the relocation of the Company's central Pacific depot from Fort Vancouver to a new site farther north.

The two men had agreed to send James Douglas, a massive Scot of mysterious origin and McLoughlin's right-hand man for almost fifteen years, on an expedition to Vancouver Island to follow up on the many previous voyages searching for a good place for a large commercial outpost with agricultural potential, a good harbour and plentiful timber. Douglas departed in 1843 and founded Fort Camosun, soon renamed Fort Victoria, on the southern extremity of the sparsely inhabited rockbound coast. The new headquarters had a commanding view of the narrow Strait of Juan de Fuca (in case of future disputes) and was situated in a deep, safe harbour surrounded by agricultural and pasture land to supply the new community.

Simpson and McLoughlin quarrelled. Simpson could never brook a challenge to his authority, and McLoughlin was not a man to back down when he felt he was right. Simpson ordered McLoughlin to dismantle the coastal trading forts that McLoughlin had methodically built up over many years and that were running profitably. According to Simpson, there was no need for any Company outposts along the Pacific. Instead the entire coast could be serviced by a fleet of roving ships, with the backbone of the operation being the steam-powered paddlewheeler *Beaver*, which had been operating along the coast since 1835. As Simpson departed in a cloud of acrimony to continue on his tour of the world by heading west to Siberia, he made one final stop at Fort Stikine, a Company fort along what is now the Panhandle of Alaska at present-day Wrangell, in the territory of the Tlingit and the Haida. He arrived in April 1842, to hear that McLoughlin's son John Jr., who had been in command of the post as chief trader, had been murdered by his men five days earlier, among them the voyageur Urbain Héroux.

The younger McLoughlin had studied medicine in Paris, discouraged from entering the fur trade by his father, who noted the increasing disadvantage to mixed-blood employees under Simpson's reign. Never entirely successful at his endeavours, the young man had ended up with the Company after all, posted to one of its most dangerous forts. Simpson conducted a brief and lacklustre investigation into the murder and pronounced it "justifiable homicide," claiming that the younger McLoughlin was insane and a drunkard. Cold and vengeful, Simpson sent a heartless note to the senior McLoughlin noting the details of the case and blaming his son for mistreating his men until they murdered him in self-defence. McLoughlin devoted years to researching and proving his case that Simpson had no basis for his conclusions and that he had failed to interview anyone with a different explanation than the one put forth by the killers. Although McLoughlin was accurate, and later evidence paints a portrait of aggressive and violent men plotting to seize the fort with the aid of some local Tlingit, Simpson was too valuable to the Company and too powerful to face any repercussions, and the men responsible for the murder were never charged with the crime. After McLoughlin was ordered by his superiors in London to drop his accusations against Simpson or retire, he developed an implacable hatred for Simpson and the Company.

THE FINAL CRISIS FOR THE COMPANY IN Old Oregon could no longer be denied even by the optimistically blind McLoughlin, who could now clearly see his empire crumbling. When he informed officials in London of his inability to govern thousands of American citizens, he received no constructive reply and no instructions. He knew, however, that a private company could not long remain the only official authority in the region; that soon the unruly pioneers, the majority of them American citizens, would demand a more accountable government. It was in the best short-term interest of the Company to keep the territory free from colonists as long as possible, but this placed McLoughlin in conflict between the interests of his nation and the interests of his Company. Particularly without military help—and none was forthcoming from London or the Company—McLoughlin knew that holding Old Oregon would be nearly impossible. Remarkably, as late as 1844, he had somehow kept the majority of American settlers south of the Columbia, perhaps still hoping for a boundary along the mighty river.

The death, in 1841, of one of the original American settlers, Ewing Young, intensified the need for some form of political authority. Young died without a will, leaving a homestead and a herd of six hundred cattle in the Willamette Valley, and the distribution of his estate required a set of laws. In 1843, settlers along the Willamette united to form a provisional government that would recognize their land claims and stabilize their communities. Soon the provisional government was passing laws, levying taxes and vociferously pronouncing their affiliation with the United States. Initially, the non-American settlers, most of them retired fur traders and former employees of the Company, held aloof, but with an additional fourteen hundred American pioneers arriving in 1844 and another three thousand in 1845, their reservations were quickly swamped in the rising human tide.

In 1845, the settlers elected George Abernethy as governor of a new provisional state, and sent delegates to Washington, D.C., to request entry into the American Union. McLoughlin, left on his own, agreed on August 15, 1845, to "support the Organic Laws of the Provisional Government of Oregon" and cooperate with the new entity, as he explained to London, "to prevent disorders and maintain peace, until the settlement of the Boundary Question leaves that duty to the parent states." McLoughlin had declined to assert on behalf of the Company any political authority and accepted a subservient role under a national legal system.

The joint-occupancy agreement between Britain and the United States had never been fully resolved in a satisfactory manner. In 1826, the British proposed to hold all Old Oregon but allow the Americans a port in Puget Sound, while the Americans countered with the offer of free British navigation of the Columbia River but a boundary at the 49th parallel. In 1828, the joint-occupancy agreement was extended indefinitely, but by the mid-1840s it was almost moot—American citizens already were the primary inhabitants of the region (other than Indigenous peoples, who were always overlooked in the nineteenth century and who had been greatly damaged by disease), and they had only to make their wishes known. The weight of historical precedent was greatly diminished after the great influx of American citizens along the Oregon Trail. Partly owing to Company policy, the number of non-American settlers in the territory never amounted to more than several hundred, and they were greatly outnumbered by as early as 1843.

Meanwhile, American political interest in Oregon had crested in 1844 with the election of ardently expansionist president James Knox Polk on the Democratic campaign slogans "Fifty-Four-Forty or Fight" and the "re-annexation of Texas and re-occupation of Oregon." These were not ambiguous statements, and they didn't presage a healthy future for the Company monopoly or for British sovereignty in the Oregon Territory. The suggestion that American sovereignty should include the entire Pacific coast was not new. The Monroe Doctrine, based on President James Monroe's address to Congress in 1823, expressed American opposition to European interference in North America and stated that any foreign intervention in the affairs of the Americas (including the emerging states in South America) would be viewed as an assault on the United States. The ultimate extension of the Monroe Doctrine was the concept of manifest destiny as expressed by John L. O'Sullivan in the July–August 1845 issue of the *Democratic Review*: It was the nation's "Manifest Destiny," he pronounced, "to overspread the continent allotted by Providence for the free development of our yearly Multiplying millions." The belief that the United States was destined to control all of North America soon became the cry of expansionists, and was used as justification for the expropriation of Indigenous lands, the war with Mexico between 1846 and 1848, and Polk's slogan of "Fifty-Four Forty or Fight!" in Old Oregon. Congress ended the joint-occupancy accord with Britain in December 1845 and began whispering of war. A Royal Navy ship patrolled the Pacific coast, lingering in the Strait of Juan de Fuca.

To British officials it was all very complicated. It wasn't distant Oregon that was the issue but the possible invasion of other British territories in North America. The presence of the Company was the only claim that Britain could put forward to justify fighting for the territory. Apart from a handful of current and former employees and their families, the only non-Indigenous people in the territory were recently arrived American citizens. The United States was moving toward war with Mexico over the territory of Texas and had no desire for another conflict in the north. With their eyes set on California, the Americans offered up the 49th parallel, bisecting Vancouver Island but allowing the recently founded Fort Victoria to remain as a free port. The British countered with the proposal that, although the 49th parallel was reasonable, all Vancouver Island should remain British, with the border running through the Juan de Fuca Strait and out to sea. All of the Company's property would be legally recognized and the Columbia River would not be closed to the Company's ships for the duration of the fur trade. (The last Company fort shut its gates in 1871.) The agreement was accepted by both sides and formalized under the Oregon Boundary Treaty of June 1846. (Ironically, the boundary was almost identical to that proposed by American negotiators at the Convention of 1818.) In August 1848, the bill officially creating the Oregon Territory was passed in Congress, and five years later the region north of the Columbia River was designated Washington Territory. In 1863, the eastern portion of Old Oregon was organized as Idaho Territory (which included all of present-day Montana until 1864, when the Montana Territory was formed).

Less than a year before the Oregon Treaty was finalized, John McLoughlin, after a humiliating demotion, in no small part over his support of the pioneers, resigned from the Company. "Gentlemen," McLoughlin declared, probably thinking of Simpson, "I will serve you no longer." McLoughlin, now over sixty and stooped from his years in the trade, bitter with Britain for relinquishing the Columbia Department without a fight, and exhausted after his many years quarrelling with the hated Simpson, packed up and departed Fort Vancouver.

He did not return to Quebec, though, nor to Fort William, where his wife originated. After two decades at Fort Vancouver, Oregon was his only home, and his grown children were nearby. Across the Columbia, opposite the fort where he had lived and ruled for two decades, grew a bustling community named Oregon City. Here, in the new Oregon, the Oregon that he in no small way had helped to create, McLoughlin built a stately house and settled down with Marguerite into a life of comfortable obscurity with various family members and grandchildren living with them. He worked as a merchant and he established a mill, but he was sometimes viewed with suspicion by the people he had helped support, battling in court to secure his private land claims. He was granted American citizenship in 1851. The former King of Oregon, along with most of his former kingdom, had joined the American republic. And the Company had lost an appendage.

Chapter Sixteen

TWO FACES
OF THE COMPANY

Getting older is like climbing a mountain. The trail winds ever upwards, braiding and bifurcating along the journey. The farther you go, the steeper the track and the greater the struggle, but the grander the view. With a crane of the neck, you can glimpse the peak, usually obscured by false summits. When you pause for a rest and look back, you see many trails curving below on the slope; the branches that were fruitless detours, others that led to magnificent panoramas or restful meadows; there are the smooth, clear routes that were foolishly disregarded, the dangerous cliff that was avoided by mere chance rather than any great insight. Through the dips, crags and undulations that form the meandering trail below, people trudge upward on the same odyssey. They make their choices. Some go toward dead-end trails or dangerous washed-out stretches. They look up and see those farther along, above, enjoying the vista, not knowing the paths that led to such a quick ascent. Would they listen to advice?

George Simpson's life had many branches. The branch that led to his greatest personal triumph was his choice to forgo the variegated pathways of London for the seemingly mundane mud track that led him to the governorship of the distant yet venerable monopoly. But the choice that rippled through history and affected all the other people who dwelt within the Company's domain was the decision that led him to his wife, Frances. The daughter of Geddes Mackenzie Simpson, the uncle who gave George his start in the London sugar business, Frances was, at eighteen, twenty-six years younger than Simpson and renowned for her delicate beauty. They married in London in 1830, the same winter that Simpson's confrere, the old Nor'Wester John G. McTavish, married a Scottish woman, Catherine Turner, young daughter of a prominent lawyer. The two couples sailed together across the Atlantic and then travelled by canoe to Red River, on a sort of joint rugged honeymoon. Both Simpson and McTavish had country wives and numerous children around various fur posts who were whisked from sight and seldom acknowledged, though Frances was nervously apprehensive with the prospect of being confronted with "something disagreeable."

Frances had never left England before and was not prepared for the lack of creature comforts in the wilds or for the imperious and kingly role her husband played when surveying his domain. She did not thrive in this new environment. Simpson had commissioned a substantial stone fort to be built at Red River, the expense of which he tried to conceal from his governing council in London, but it wasn't completed for many years. The location of this new inland headquarters was off the flood plain, thirty-two kilometres north along the Red River, and was called Lower Fort Garry. It was distinct from Upper Fort Garry, at the junction of the Red and Assiniboine Rivers, which became the seat of the Company's administrative and judicial council, called the Council of Assiniboia. Simpson's big house was notable for its stately stone walls, well-tended grounds and an interior of ostentatious pretension that would have been at home in Montreal or London. The elegant furnishings, silver cutlery and china dinner set were imported by canoe and York boat from York Factory.

Many of the fur outposts now had collections of people living nearby who were not directly employed by the Company. The hinterland of Red River had grown to many thousands of people. For Simpson and Frances, their proper social circle included some of the wives of the early Selkirk settlers and the wives of the missionaries. After his own marriage to Frances, Simpson began to discourage marriage *à la façon du pays*, between his officers and Indigenous women, preferring they engage in unattached sexual liaisons, as if the women were second class. He and his wife refused to host the Indigenous wives of his officers as guests in their home, calling them disagreeable or savage. When one of his officers, Colin Robertson, introduced Frances to his long-standing country wife, Theresa Chalifoux, Simpson briskly reprimanded him for daring to bring his "bit of Brown with him to the Settlement . . . in the hopes she would pick up a few English manners."

Frances was a hothouse flower and struggled to take root in the less refined soil of Red River. When their first child died, Frances was desperately unhappy and lonely; Simpson brooded and ruminated and cast about for someone to blame. To Simpson, she was an elegant adornment, a symbol of higher social status, like a glorious feather in a mundane cap. After three years she and Simpson returned to England for the winter, and the next spring she remained, ostensibly to regain her health, and did not return to North America until 1838, when she travelled to Lachine for the summer, where Simpson had re-established his headquarters. She saw her husband in the off-season, until she moved to Montreal permanently in 1845. They would have four children together. Meanwhile, Simpson continued his restless roving about his domain.

Simpson's lieutenant, McTavish, likewise took on airs of pious snobbery when he settled at his new post, Moose Factory. He wouldn't tolerate his new bride mingling with the mixed-heritage or Indigenous wives of his officers, provoking confusion, animosity and discontent amongst the people of the fort. Nancy McKenzie Matooskie, McTavish's discarded country wife of seventeen years, mother of seven of his children, was paid a sort of dowry and was remarried against her wishes to a junior officer. One officer, James Hargrave, wrote, "The first blow [from the news] was dreadful to witness, but the poor girl is fast acquiring resignation." Born at Fort Chipewyan to Scottish trader Roderick McKenzie and an unnamed Chipewyan woman, Nancy had many highly placed uncles in senior fur trade posts, including Donald McKenzie, the governor of Red River, and her father had been Alexander Mackenzie's cousin. Previously she had been the pre-eminent lady of the fort when McTavish was the chief factor of York Factory. Now she was reassigned to Red River to be a servant in the Simpson household, one of only two mixed-heritage women allowed inside the manor. Frances sniffed that Nancy was "a complete savage, with a coarse blue sort of woolen gown, without shape & a blanket fastened around her neck."

Nancy eventually moved with her new husband to Fort Vancouver, but tragedy struck as they followed the York Express in 1838, when her husband and their three children perished in a boating accident and she was left alone with her youngest daughter, Grace, from her union with McTavish. John McLoughlin welcomed her into Fort Vancouver society and gave her a position. Grace later married a steamboat captain named Charles Dodd and the family moved to Fort Victoria, where Nancy lived with her daughter's family until her death, at the age of sixty-one, in 1851.

This sudden cold shoulder to Indigenous and mixed-heritage women introduced by Simpson and McTavish wasn't accepted without protest. One senior trader, her childhood guardian John Stewart, was appalled at McTavish's behaviour toward Nancy, a woman he had known since she was a girl. Her ill treatment did not pass without comment. "What could be your aim in discarding her whom you clasped to your bosom in virgin purity and had for 17 Years with you?" he demanded. "She was the Wife of your Choice and has borne you seven Children, now Stigmatized with ignominy. If with a view of domestic happiness you have thus acted, I fear the Aim has been Missed and that remorse will be your portion for life. I think it is well our correspondence may cease."

No one dared criticize Simpson, at least not publicly, since he controlled their careers, so the weight of opprobrium and censure fell on McTavish. At least McTavish, unlike Simpson, took responsibility for his children, sending some of them to school in Montreal.

Nevertheless, some officers took their cue from Simpson and McTavish. Chief Factor William Connolly, for example, abandoned his Cree wife, Suzanne, soon after their daughter Amelia had married an ambitious clerk named James Douglas (yes, the same; more on him later). The social order began to shift, and it became known that an Indigenous or mixed-heritage wife limited one's career, and more people, especially senior officers, began searching for white wives from Britain. Officer James Hargrave fretted, "This influx of white faces has cast a still deeper shade over the faces of our Brunettes in the eyes of many." Racial prejudice followed, and soon, at the urgings of newly arriving missionaries who claimed that country marriages were invalid, many, but certainly not all, officers began to cast off their spouses as being incompatible with the "civilized" society that was taking hold around Company forts, reducing the status of country wives to that of mistresses. As the nineteenth century progressed, the loss of kinship ties between Indigenous peoples, those of mixed-heritage and those of European descent began to disrupt the easy companionability that previously had flourished between the peoples of the fur trade.

Even Red River, a settlement that from its very beginning was a mixture of Indigenous, Métis and Scottish settlers, began to stratify. John Henry Lefroy, a British military officer who toured the Company's domain from Red River to Fort Chipewyan taking magnetic recordings on a scientific expedition, expressed mean condescension toward the mixed-heritage children of the Company's officers at school in Red River. "There were about 20 girls and nearly as many boys there, coarse looking animals, with little stamp of quality, not one pretty face." The trader John Todd wrote to a friend in 1843 offering his "scientific" evidence for why mixed-heritage children were no longer being promoted within officer ranks in the Company. "Well, have you observed that all attempts to make gentlemen of them, have hitherto proved a failure—the fact is there is something radically wrong about them all as is evidently shown from the Mental Science alone I mean Phrenology."

Cultural institutions that had presided over the land for generations now withered beneath the downward sneer of empire.

IN 1841, SIMPSON SET OFF FROM MONTREAL on a grand two-year romp around the world, leaving his wife behind in London, naturally. To ensure his grand tour was preserved for posterity, he had hired an English ghostwriter to accompany him and record the details, suitably embellished to reflect the august character of the leader. By the time he reached Red River, his entourage consisted of dozens of people who trundled on horse-drawn carts across the prairies to Fort Edmonton. At this time, Fort Edmonton was the largest and most important settlement beyond Red River, by then a sprawling wooden palisade with a collection of log buildings inside and surrounding it along the north bank of the North Saskatchewan River. The "Athabasca guides" informed Chief Factor John Rowand and Simpson of flooding in the valley of the iconic Athabasca Pass, and Simpson began to mull his options. His passion for fame and recognition rose one final time, and he instructed his guide on an alternative course. He had always suspected that an easier mountain crossing existed, one that would prove to be less burdensome and dramatic, and faster, than the treacherous pass discovered by David Thompson decades earlier. This was his opportunity to make his name resound again in the annals of fur trade history. If he discovered a new pass, it would bear his name and he would be feted.

Rowand hired Simpson a guide for the Rocky Mountains, bringing the party to at least twenty-two people with a cavalcade of forty-five horses to haul the gear. The chosen guide was "a half-breed . . . Chief of the mountain Crees" who had, Simpson noted, been "brought up among savages." Simpson called him Peechee, though his real name

was Pesew in Cree, or Louis Piché in French. Pesew had roamed as far
south as the Missouri River in previous years and was multilingual and
competent. He and his family lived to the southwest of Fort Edmonton,
and he knew of another pass by which the mountains could be traversed. As they wound their way through the golden grasses of the
gently undulating land, they came upon an encampment of Piegan
and decided to visit. Simpson recounted, in the arrogant twaddle that
passed for prose in his ghostwritten account, that these people "made
long prayers to me as a high and powerful conjurer" and begged for
boons and benediction, which he naturally bestowed upon the "savages." As if the fierce Plains warriors ever grovelled and simpered to
anyone in that manner.

By August the cavalcade was entering the mountains through pine
forests and a jagged gap, following the standard Cree and Assiniboine
route, where Pesew had arranged to meet his wife. The scenery here in
the mountain valley was "majestic." Simpson recorded that they emerged
from the woods on a ridge and beheld a valley below bounded "as far
as the eye could reach, mountain rose above mountain while at our
feet lay a valley surrounded by an amphitheatre of cold, bare, rugged
peaks." They were in the region of the Ghost River and Ghost Lakes
and, as they crossed the windswept dunes, Pesew told Simpson of the
epic battles between the Kootenay and the Piegan half a century earlier when the Kootenay were driven west of the mountains, from
which they only occasionally ventured east to hunt bison. It was a
mysterious region of unquiet spirits, where on certain nights the warriors from the burial grounds roamed, searching for the skulls of their
enemies. Simpson noted that only the "Demon of the Mountains
alone could fix his abode there."

After a couple more days of travel, they reached the long lake where
Pesew lived for parts of the year, and Simpson magnanimously bestowed
upon it the name Peechee Lake. It is now called Lake Minnewanka,
Nakoda-Assiniboine for "Lake of the Water Spirit." Pesew's wife was

not at the appointed spot. "Madam Peechee and the children had left their encampment," Simpson wrote, "probably on account of a scarcity of game." Simpson, no doubt for the edification of his reading audience, lectured, "What an idea of the loneliness and precariousness of savage life does this single glimpse of the biography of the Peechees suggest!" The entirety of Simpson's, or his British ghostwriter's, account is in a similarly bloated, pretentious and condescending vein, revealing not nearly as much about the life of Pesew and his family as it does about Simpson, the intended audience the publisher imagined for the book and the increasingly stultifying Victorian moral attitudes that were creeping into the lands where the Company operated. Simpson wanted to position himself as belonging to this new wave.

It was along the forested shore of Lake Minnewanka, however, that Simpson was told an interesting story while he lounged waiting for some of his weary men to round up lost horses and for the cook to prepare his evening repast, a "burgoo" of stewed partridges and pemmican. A young Cree couple had been exploring the lake when they noticed they were being followed by five armed and mounted enemy warriors. When the warriors spread out through the trees and galloped toward them, the man quailed at their ill fortune. Turning to his wife, he proclaimed that since "they could die but once, they had better make up their minds to submit to their present fate without resistance." She looked askance and replied that, since "they had but one life to lose, they were more decidedly bound to defend it to the last, even under the most desperate circumstances." We are young, she cried, "and by no means pitiful" and are duty bound to "prevent [our] hearts from becoming small."

"Suiting the action to the word," she grabbed a gun, aimed and fired, bringing "the foremost warrior to the earth with a bullet." Her shamed but hopeful husband, belatedly recruiting his courage, drew his bow and launched arrows, striking two of the charging warriors and knocking them from their horses. The fourth warrior was upon them and he leaped from his horse, raising his knife "to take vengeance" on the woman. He stumbled, and "in the twinkling of an eye" she lunged when he stumbled and stabbed him in the chest with her own knife. The fifth warrior, meanwhile, had raised his gun and fired at the man, sinking "a ball in the arm." Upon realizing he was outnumbered and likely to die, he reined in his horse and charged away, leaving his fallen comrades. The couple, delivered from what seemed certain death, then claimed the valuable weapons and horses of their vanquished foes.

THE REMAINDER OF SIMPSON'S round-the-world trip was uneventful, apart from his acrimonious meeting with McLoughlin in Fort Vancouver and his dismal investigation of the murder of McLoughlin's son at Fort Stikine. When he returned to his mansion at Lachine after his globe-girdling promotional tour, he settled into his role as the lionized pillar of the Montreal financial elite. He discouraged any investigation into his humble origins. Frances even moved from London to join him, and presided over formal dinners and functions with the grace of a chatelaine. Howsoever she tried, though, she could never entirely smooth the coarse edge to her husband's manners. On one occasion when she politely requested he say grace at a formal dinner, he reputedly groused, "Lord have mercy on what is now before us," and began eating.

Simpson was now a man of power, Victorian respectability and influence, and his home showed it: massive in proportions, it was plumped with carefully curated *objets d'art* and a potpourri of fur trade memorabilia, from paintings of wilderness scenes, stuffed animals, skins and Indigenous carvings to fine beadwork, elaborate cedar boxes and other crafts. The display rooms of his mansion were like a museum of his empire, which, like his wife, were accoutrements to the image he wished to project. He was also getting on in years. Now in his sixties, he had less energy for setting speed records on tours of his fur domain; he was now one of the old fur traders whom he had so derisively criticized and sought to dismiss from the Company's service in 1821. Nevertheless, in 1846 he was knighted by Queen Victoria for his, and the Company's, support and encouragement of exploration in the Arctic.

JAMES DOUGLAS WAS FORTY YEARS OLD in 1843 when, on orders from Simpson and McLoughlin, he sailed from Fort Vancouver and founded Fort Camosun, later named Fort Victoria. The future colonial capital began as a rude stockade, built around a cluster of whitewashed log buildings with two towers fitted out with nine-pounder cannons to establish and maintain authority. The staid little hamlet that grew around the fort, with gardens of imported English flowers flourishing in the mild climate, housed the retired traders who, as the years passed, settled down to the less strenuous occupations of farmers and dairymen. Under Douglas's watchful eye, life at the fort was tranquil and predictable. He maintained the fur trade, and the gold trade with Indigenous peoples along the Fraser River, while nominally promoting colonization in accordance with the new British policy for the Pacific slope, after securing the goodwill of the local Lekwungen, specifically the Songhees band whose village was about ten kilometres from the new trade fort. He read voraciously from his private collection of English classics and presided over orderly meals at the officers' mess, dining in style and guiding conversation toward proper subjects—such as British or American politics, the fur trade or scientific discovery. Douglas was proud of his cultured little outpost. Reporting to a friend in 1843, he noted that the region was "so different in its general aspect, from the wooded, rugged regions around, that one might be pardoned for supposing it had dropped from the clouds into its present position."

Douglas was an astute observer with a lifetime of experience on the far side of the Continental Divide. Sometimes called Black Douglas because of his swarthy complexion, the imposing six-foot-two governor had been born in 1803 in Demerara, then a Dutch colony and later part of British Guiana, the child of a Scottish sugar purveyor, John Douglas, and Martha Ritchie, "a coloured free woman." He was whisked away to

Scotland at the age of nine and spent the following decade at private boarding schools in Britain, where, among other things, he learned French, a language that would serve him well later in life. Here he remained until being struck by wanderlust and signing on as an apprentice with the North West Company. In 1819, he shipped out to Fort William and Île-à-la-Crosse, and once the two companies merged, went on to Fort St. James on the upper Fraser River.

His commanding presence and glacial countenance eased him quickly through the ranks of traders in the distant region. By 1828 he was respected enough to win the hand of sixteen-year-old Amelia Connolly, the daughter of chief trader William Connolly and his Cree wife Suzanne (Miyo Nipiy). The two were married "according to the custom of the country," and only later did they submit to a Christian ceremony at the insistence of Herbert Beaver, an English missionary who snubbed Amelia and sneered at their country marriage when he visited Fort Vancouver in 1837 (the very same Beaver whom McLoughlin had caned for his racist comments about McLoughlin's wife, Marguerite). The couple was transferred to Fort Vancouver, where Douglas worked his way up the ranks to the positions of chief trader and then chief factor, and presided as McLoughlin's right-hand man until 1849, when the Company's central depot was shifted to Fort Victoria. He moved there with his family after two decades along the Columbia. Over the years of their long marriage, they had ten children together, six of whom survived to adulthood.

In his youth Douglas earned a reputation for being "furiously violent when aroused," as George Simpson put it, and it was his temper that almost got him killed in a Dakelh-Carrier village near Stuart Lake in 1828. Hearing a rumour that Zulth-nolly, who was suspected of murdering two Company traders five years earlier over a dispute involving a woman, was holed up in an encampment along the upper Fraser River, Douglas and a band of men set out from Fort St. James in pursuit. Although details of the tale vary, Douglas's posse unwisely pursued Zulth-nolly into the cedar house of an elderly and respected chief named Kwah, or Kw'eh, who was absent at the time, and apprehended the outlaw in violation of a Dakelh-Carrier principle that held a chief's home to be a sanctuary. While struggling with his captors the man stabbed Douglas with an arrow in a vain attempt to escape. In a rage Douglas ordered the man hanged from a nearby tree, and then fed his corpse to the wolves before returning the short distance to Fort St. James.

A few days later, Kwah, hearing of the injustice, marched to the fort with a war party, burst through the gate and overwhelmed the traders' feeble resistance. Kwah's nephew held Douglas under the knife, awaiting his uncle's word. Luckily for Douglas, his wife, Amelia, was more astute and knowledgeable in local traditions. She rushed to the storeroom, returned and began flinging tobacco, clothing and other goods at Kwah's feet to pay her husband's blood debt to the family of the slain man. When the pile was large enough, Kwah suggested his warriors release her reckless husband. Visitors to Kwah's grave can read his epitaph, engraved into the stone tomb-marker: "Here lie the remains of Great Chief Kwah Born about 1755 Died spring of 1840. He once had in his hands the life of (future Sir) James Douglas but was great enough to refrain from taking it."

Either having mellowed with age or having learned from his brash misadventures, in later years Douglas suppressed his wilder inclinations and projected an air of cultivated disdain and unflinching dignity. He was inordinately proud of his position and numerous titles, occasionally signing his official correspondence "His excellency, James Douglas, Governor of Vancouver Island and its Dependencies, Commander-in-Chief and Vice-Admiral of the same," in case any should be in doubt of his august position. Over time, he became serious and stuffy, a champion of the cause of the British Empire, and he was a linguistic snob, fastidious and meticulously correct in his usage of the English language. He once returned a daughter's letter remarking that it had been "pruned of redundancies, as a study." Observe, he pronounced with authority, "how it is improved by the process."

Although Douglas was respected and obeyed throughout his life, Amelia experienced quiet coolness from white women in Fort Victoria after it had grown into the colonial capital. The more open and fluid society within the Company had changed under the baleful influence of George Simpson and British colonial expansion. Amelia was relegated to the backrooms of fashionable society, in part, at least, out of choice, but her Indigenous ancestry and accented English did not open many doors (her preferred languages were Cree and French). Some people mocked her accent and called her uncouth and of a "savage" race, but never to her face. One settler wrote to her brother in 1854 expressing her displeasure at Douglas and Amelia: "The Governor of Vancouvers Island has been in the Company out here ever since he was a Boy about 15 year of age and now he is a Man upwards of 60—so you may say he has been all his life among the North American Indians and has got one of them for a wife so how can it be expected that he can know anything at all about Governing one of Englands last Colony's in North America." One of Amelia's tactics for blending in was to outwardly present the image of model Victorian womanhood—dark formal ankle-length dresses buttoned tightly to her neck, with frilly lace protruding from full-length arms and an embroidered collar, hair pulled harshly back into a respectable bun. She is not smiling in these pictures, perhaps remembering freer days.

Douglas took his public responsibilities seriously (too seriously for some of his men, who called him Old Square Toes behind his back), but he wasn't above a little scheming to advance his position. He originally turned down the offer to be governor of the two combined colonies, claiming that the job didn't pay enough. He astutely couched his request for greater remuneration in the rhetoric of duty: "As a private individual," he noted, "I can live in a style befitting the fortune I possess; but as governor for the Crown, there is no choice: one must live in a manner becoming the representative of the Crown, and I could never consent to represent Her Majesty in a shabby way." He was offered a higher salary, and took on the governorship.

Douglas wasn't all business and Victorian formality, though. His wistful reminiscences of his halcyon days in the fur trade stand in contrast to his fearless and domineering public image. "I can recall nothing more delightful than our bivouac on a clear moonlit May night, near the Punch Bowls—the highest point of the Jasper Pass," he mused. ". . . Our camp was laid and our fire built, on the firm hard snow which was about 20 feet deep. As the daylight faded away, and the shades of night gathered over the Pass, a milder light shot up from behind the nearest Peak, with gradually increasing brilliancy until at last the full orbed moon rose in silent majesty from the mass of mountains shedding a mild radiance over the whole valley beneath." He also had a romantic streak. Of his wife Amelia he wrote: "To any other being less qualified, the vapid monotony of an inland trading Post, would be perfectly unsufferable, while habit makes it familiar to us, softened as it is by the many tender ties, which find a way to the heart."

SINCE THE INTERNATIONAL BOUNDARY agreement in 1846, Douglas had been running Vancouver Island and New Caledonia for the Hudson's Bay Company in much the same manner he and McLoughlin had run the Columbia Department. But after 1849, the British government took a much a greater interest in the colonization of lands it viewed in a proprietary sense, even without consulting the people who lived there. Britain's prime concern was to ensure that Americans didn't conquer it for themselves. "It is obvious," said Lord Grey shortly after the signing of the Oregon Treaty, "when an eligible territory is left to be waste, unsubdued to the use of man, it is impossible to prevent persons from taking irregular possession of the land. We have found it impossible in all our dominions to restrain such persons. The government of the United States will be equally unable to prevent such an occurrence."

To solidify British sovereignty north of the 49th parallel, the British Colonial Office created the Crown Colony of Vancouver Island in 1849 and made the Hudson's Bay Company's fur trade monopoly conditional on colonizing the region, leasing the entire island to the Company for ten years under condition it fulfill those obligations. The Puget Sound Agricultural Company, a subsidiary of the Company, was given large tracts of land around Victoria, thereby giving the Company control over the settlement. The Colonial Office appointed an English barrister named Richard Blanshard as the colony's governor, but Blanshard, who had no knowledge or experience of the local people or of the fur trade, soon discovered that the Company held all the power and that it was actually Douglas who was in charge. There were no civil resources or personnel, and everyone owed their livelihood to the Company, which meant Douglas. Blanshard showed a shocking ignorance of Indigenous customs and a proclivity for violent punishment of Indigenous offenders even when in their own territory, in one instance burning an entire village in retribution for crimes committed by three individuals. In 1851, Blanshard resigned and Douglas officially assumed control over the colony, while keeping his role as chief factor of the reigning fur monopoly.

Settlement, of course, was not the Company's business, and neither did the British government hold any moral or legal authority to dispense with the existing governments of the Indigenous inhabitants. While the Colonial Office might have preferred settlement as a hedge against American expansion, it was a death threat to the fur trade. The narrow interests of the Company rested on preserving lands unspoiled by extensive settlement, inhabited only by the Indigenous people. The Company might tolerate a limited number of settlements to supply food to its workers, but these would be kept under vigilant observation to ensure that they did not expand into larger and more independent communities that might escape the Company's control. Ever since the international border had been set along the 49th parallel in 1846, the Company had continued its leisurely pursuit of its primary objective—trading for furs.

It was the same conflict that had played out in Oregon in the 1840s. To preserve fur trade profits, the Company only half-heartedly pursued colonization, yet it was that colonization that would provide the foundation for sovereignty, which was the prime objective of the British government, and as such the British government took an increasingly focused interest in the Company's affairs. By charging nominal fees for land (when it was being offered free in the United States) and refusing to dispose of land in anything less than twenty-acre parcels, the Company discouraged all but a handful of gentleman farmers. Not surprisingly, during the 1850s fewer than a hundred people had arrived from Britain and less than five hundred acres had been cleared and tilled around Victoria, barely enough to feed the people who lived there. When the rush of gold seekers flooded north in 1858, Vancouver Island and New Caledonia were still the domain of the many Indigenous nations, except for the immediate area surrounding Fort Victoria, a small coal-mining outpost at Nanaimo on eastern Vancouver Island, and a handful of fur forts in the interior. There was nothing to distinguish the land from Washington Territory to the south, since the 49th parallel hadn't even been demarcated.

To avoid conflict and violence, in 1850 the British government had instructed Douglas to negotiate with the people of southern Vancouver Island for the right for the Company, and the British colony, to use the land for farming. He negotiated fourteen "purchases" or "deeds of conveyance" that theoretically sanctified the acquiescence of the Coast Salish peoples, specifically the Songhees, Sooke, Saanich, Klannam and Nanaimo tribes, that they held legal title only to the land surrounding their villages.

Naturally there were conflicts. Douglas ensured that all Indigenous peoples had full legal status before the courts, including the same rights as white settlers to hold land and property, although his philosophy was to not intervene in the disputes or issues of any of the Indigenous peoples so long as no Company employees, and later settlers, were involved. Sometimes Indigenous peoples, either out of innocence or to be provocative, would hunt domestic cattle, claiming they were wildlife that they were entitled to hunt according to their agreements. When other northern Indigenous peoples, such as the Haida and Tsimshian, began to visit Fort Victoria in search of economic opportunity and adventure, they were coolly received by the small numbers of settlers, who feared them.

But Douglas was also criticized for paying too much attention to the Indigenous population. "The Government is a perfect farce," wrote one disgruntled colonist. "Though the Governor is a wonderfully clever man among the Indians, he does not seem to be governing a white population at all." Early in 1858, Douglas welcomed around eight hundred "Black Pioneers" from California. Arriving with money and skills, they included tradesmen, teachers, business people, miners and farmers who wanted to escape persecution, and perhaps re-enslavement, after the Fugitive Slave Act was passed in the United States. At one time they were the largest non-Indigenous population on Vancouver Island and Salt Spring Island where they settled.

In the late 1860s, Joseph Trutch, a racist British-born engineer and land surveyor who would later serve as British Columbia's first lieutenant governor after the colony joined the country of Canada in 1871, was adamantly opposed to Indigenous land claims and refused to accept Douglas's treaties, resurveying the lands and shrinking them by up to 90 per cent in some cases. The Douglas Treaties, as they have become known, are fraught with problems and have led to numerous legal disputes.

Obviously Douglas, as the head of a monopoly corporation and with no legal training, was not a suitable person to be negotiating land treaties on behalf of the British Crown. He just happened to be the only remotely suitable person at hand. Douglas's treaties called to life a mélange of overlapping conflicts of interest—the peculiar situation of the local head of a chartered monopoly corporation representing the British government in land negotiations with Indigenous peoples concerning a territory that had never been part of Britain. That Douglas was able to weave a way between all these competing interests is a testament to his political acumen and his even-handed respect for different peoples and cultures—traits that were increasingly at odds in the Victorian colonial atmosphere of the mid-nineteenth century.

The land was vast, rugged and mostly unsuitable for settlement or agriculture, and no one could have envisioned the influx of millions of people, just as no one could have envisioned the majestic ancient trees in the Fraser delta entirely sawed down and a massive city smothering the former rainforest. At the time, the Salish peoples retained their rights to hunt and fish as they always had, so it seemed like nothing would change.

Chapter Seventeen

THE MONOPOLY DIES

As the nineteenth century progressed, other commercial activity unrelated to the dwindling fur trade expanded as communities and settlements sprung up around Company forts, which were magnets for retired fur traders and their Indigenous families as well as the grown children from earlier generations. Red River was originally conceived as a place where retired traders, with their unique culture and customs, could be comfortable. It was now home to thousands, including Indigenous peoples and Métis, who were related to the Company's employees and officers but who had been denied opportunities because of their ancestry and the Company's limited need for workers. They were increasingly annoyed with the monopoly that was strangling the economy and limiting their access to goods and provisions. Southern traders from the populous American territories, who had links to more efficient transportation networks, began infiltrating the Company's domain. The many people of Red River who were unaffiliated with the Company naturally began to do business with them.

As the economy grew, new commercial activities presented themselves at Red River, such as the plains bison trade, small-scale retail of goods from the U.S., logging, construction, cattle ranching, raising sheep for wool, growing hay and grain, and running hotels for the increasing number of travellers. The greatest industry to emerge mid-century was making leather and bison robes, which were too bulky and heavy for the Company to ship to York Factory. Prepared by Métis and Plains nations women, many thousands of these valuable garments were shipped south to supply the American market. The economy was taking on a life of its own, and George Simpson believed that it was to the Company's detriment.

As early as 1841, Simpson had attempted to put a damper on Red River's growth. He hired James Sinclair, the brother of Betsey, one of his cast-off mixed-heritage mistresses, Sinclair's Métis brother-in-law Jimmy Jock Bird and the Cree pathfinder Maskepetoon to lead twenty-three families away from Red River to Fort Vancouver. But the settlement continued to grow nonetheless. After his expedition for the Company, Sinclair, in an inveterate iconoclast with a stubborn streak, continued to pursue an adventurous life, leading more groups of emigrants over the Rocky Mountains into Oregon and Washington. Having his business interests undermined by the Company, he sold his cattle and land at Red River and moved to St. Paul, Minnesota, with his second wife, Mary Campbell, the Métis daughter of chief trader Colin Campbell, and their children, and became a U.S. citizen. The family returned briefly to Red River before he was hired again by the Company to improve trade at Fort Walla Walla, where he died at the age of forty-five, in 1856, and his family remained.

Simpson had relaxed the monopoly restrictions minimally in the 1840s to allow settlers to privately trade small numbers of furs with Indigenous peoples, hoping that this would prevent smuggling, but it had the opposite effect. Once people realized how much money could be made when they were free to pursue their own interests, more private traders went into business, testing the Company's resolve to shut them down.

Norman Wolfred Kittson, a Lower Canadian who had gone to work with the American Fur Company a decade earlier, found himself in Pembina, North Dakota, which was only about a hundred kilometres south of Red River and was a traditional destination of the Métis. He married Élise Marion, a Métis from St. Boniface, and formed a lifelong association with the Métis. In the later 1840s he formed an alliance with local free traders, including Andrew McDermot, a disgruntled Company clerk, and James Sinclair, to direct the Red River trade south to Pembina and later to St. Paul. They also enlisted the services of Pierre-Guillaume Sayer, another mixed-heritage son of a former Nor'Wester, who was then fifty-three years old and a respected member of the community. By this time, much of the Red River trade was being siphoned away, threatening the viability of the settlement and realigning the trade to shut out the Company. The growing population was transforming Red River just as settlers had transformed Fort Vancouver a few years earlier. Free trade with the Americans was a defiance of the monopoly so flagrant, in fact so dire, that it couldn't be ignored.

At the same time, there were complaints against the Company's belligerent behaviour, which included searching carts and houses for contraband, and general harassment. A petition signed by 570 residents of Red River, and dispatched to the Canadian Parliament and the British Legislature, described how "Hudson's Bay Company clerks, with an armed police, have entered into settlers' houses in quest of furs, and confiscated all they found. One poor settler, after having his goods seized, had his house burnt to the ground, and afterwards was conveyed prisoner to York Factory . . . On our annual commercial journeys into Minnesota we have been pursued like felons by armed constables, who searched our property, even by breaking open our trunks; all furs found were confiscated."

Simpson persuaded the London Committee to pressure the British government to send in several dozen soldiers to keep the peace, by which he meant defend the monopoly. But what did arbitrary lines on a map drawn by foreigners, maps that no one had seen in any case, have to do with Assiniboine, Ojibwa, mixed Scottish-Indigenous or Métis wandering their traditional territory? The Company should have been able to coexist with the Métis, since the Métis wanted nothing much other than to be left alone to pursue their business, but, fixated on monopoly, Simpson and the Company kept making rules and edicts designed to restrict personal freedoms and rights, the most egregious of which was a no-trading rule south of the imaginary 49th parallel.

In 1849, Métis free trader Sayer was arrested, taken to Lower Fort Garry and placed on trial for smuggling. Long disgruntled with the Company's blockade of business activities in the settlement, over three hundred armed and mounted Métis, led by Métis nationalist Jean-Louis Riel, father of the famous future freedom fighter, congregated at the St. Boniface church and then rode over to the primitive courthouse and surrounded it. Some of the hunters boasted of their ability to shoot through the window at the judge. James Sinclair served as Sayer's counsel, and through him Sayer admitted to trafficking in furs. But, Sinclair posited, Sayer believed he was within his rights to do so since he was merely giving presents to his relatives in a form of Indigenous trade that fell outside the Company's monopoly. The proceedings were overseen by the Scottish Adam Thom, a noted bigot who held the title Recorder of Assiniboia, but Thom dared not act on his inclinations with an armed and restive mob milling about the courthouse, occasionally peering in at him through the windows. The nervous jury found Sayer guilty but suggested he receive no punishment. As Sayer walked out of the courthouse, he was thronged with supporters cheering, firing their guns in the air and chanting, "*Le commerce est libre! Le commerce est libre! Vive la liberté!*"

But the Company didn't give up. It dropped prices in an attempt to drive the malcontents bankrupt and regain control. Nevertheless, the number of carts trundling and screeching their way between Pembina and Red River grew rapidly in the years that followed, from nearly five hundred a year to nearly two thousand by the late 1860s, when the demand for bison hides soared after the end of the American Civil War. The free traders were in ascendance.

In 1856, Kittson felt confident enough to open his own general store in St. Boniface to compete with the Company. An elegant and finely dressed man with a genial temperament, and respected by many, he later became the mayor of St. Paul and one of the most prominent financiers of the city, growing the transportation business—with carts, steamboats and later railways—between St. Paul and the Red River Settlement that eventually became Winnipeg. There was still no easy route from the western end of Lake Superior to Red River that did not involve travelling through the United States—the old voyageur routes had mostly become overgrown from lack of use, and never were conducive to trade and travel by anyone less hardy than the legendary canoemen from Montreal.

By 1858, Minnesota was recognized as a state and had a population of nearly 150,000, settlers who had flooded west along with American steamships and railroads. Soon, an American entrepreneur named Anson Northup piloted the first steamboat, complete with lengthy portages, along the Red River from St. Paul to Fort Garry. "In 1860, there will be rail all the way from New York and the sea coast to Pembina on the Red River," stated the petition from the Red River settlers to the British government. "In eighty to ninety hours, when the Americans will be rivals to the Company in the fur trade, sending their furs to London in twenty days, while the company only make one shipment from York." It was now a three- or four-day journey from New York to Red River through the United States and its rapidly increasing network of rail and steam lines. When Simpson set off on his round-the-world voyage in 1841, the same journey took him, despite speed records, thirty-eight days. After 1858 it could be done in ten. By the 1860s, Red River and Fort Garry had replaced York Factory as the Company's primary distribution centre, and the entrance and exit to the Company's realm was by rail and steamer from St. Paul. The great fear in Britain was that the entire region would become consumed by the ravenous geographical appetite of the United States.

In 1856, Simpson wrote a letter to the London Committee identifying what he felt was another overwhelming problem: the growing population of the "Halfbreed race." Despite Simpson's growing infirmity, he retained a keen grasp of how things worked in his domain. In the first century and a half after the Company was founded, its authority extended only to its overseas employees. Once it amalgamated with the North West Company and Simpson assumed the governorship, its authority began additionally to be imposed over a growing number of its customers, the Indigenous peoples. But when its territories, despite Simpson's active efforts to prevent it, were increasingly inhabited by English-speaking peoples of at least partial European descent who had nothing to do with the fur trade—including the "halfbreeds" that so discomfited him (despite most of his own descendants being of mixed race)—the Company's monopoly could no longer be tolerated. In fact the Company became despised by the Métis, the mixed-heritage Scottish, the Plains Indigenous peoples and the European settlers, who all found their economic aspirations blocked by the Company's monopoly.

Simpson's concern with "halfbreeds" was that there were by the year increasing numbers of them and that most of them had no economic function in the Company's closed-system economy. Many of them worked outside of the Company's economic orbit, and hence posed an existential threat to the Company's interests. Under Simpson, the Company tried to have a hand in all commercial transactions, but the Métis, with their blended culture, and a good number of whom were the sons of prominent officers who had been educated in Montreal or Britain, had ideas for business that did not involve the Company and the fur trade, with inputs and outputs that could not be supplied by or consumed by the Company. Soon they would demand an independent government too. The Company enforced a planned or centralized economy, while the Métis valued freedom and independence, a form of decentralized free enterprise that was to form the defining ethos of Canada's Prairie provinces. These were not compatible systems.

With improved travel and communication, the Company could no longer control the reports of activities from within its domain. Opinions were being aired denouncing the Company for behaving like an absentee landlord, of the sort who had exacerbated the problems of the Irish Potato Famine during the 1840s and caused the migration of millions to the United States. An editorial by George Brown in the Toronto *Globe* in 1856, one of his many inflammatory screeds hammering on a similar idea, concluded, "There can be no question that the injurious and demoralizing sway of that Company over a region of four millions of square miles, will, ere long, be brought to an end, and that with the destinies of this immense country will be united with our own. It is unpardonable that civilization should be excluded from half a continent, on at best but a doubtful right of ownership, for the benefit of two hundred and thirty-two shareholders." In another editorial along the same vein, Brown fumed, "Surely this project is the very madness of monopoly! Do the Hudson's Bay Company think that they can shut out people from the direct road to the great West forever?" Of course, Brown's and the *Globe*'s antipathy to the Company's monopoly was founded not on altruism, fighting for the freedom of a fellow people, but to derive a benefit in the form of new markets for their own manufactured products, to stimulate the moribund factories of Upper Canada by creating a colonial hinterland to exploit. Petitioners in Red River asked the British government to allow them to either join the Canadas or establish their own government. Others echoed the same refrain both in Canada and, more importantly, in London.

During the 1850s, Simpson's annual tours of his domain became truncated and symbolic. The days of surprise inspections and lightning reorganizations were over. His wife, Frances, died in 1853, and his own declining health limited his physical activities. His personal business interests had shifted more to Montreal's expanding industrial economy rather than Red River or the Athabasca country. While he continued to lobby high officials on the Company's behalf, his own investments were in railways, mines, banks and steamships. He was powerful and respected, yet not above ethically questionable manipulation of political and financial figures to further his interests or those of the Company. But the Company's monopoly and Simpson's power had begun to erode.

ON THE PACIFIC COAST, on the sleepy Sunday morning of April 25, 1858, a small cluster of devout Fort Victorians emerged from their church to observe a bewildering sight. The American sidewheeler *Commodore*, railings jammed with a motley, pack-burdened band of prospectors, and mounds of supplies clogging the deck, chugged into the placid harbour and disgorged its bright-eyed human cargo onto the small Hudson's Bay Company wharf. Clad in dungarees and red flannel shirts, and loaded with spades, pans, pickaxes and provisions, the unruly swarm began pitching tents in the fields surrounding the fort and clamouring for a ship to cross the island-studded Salish Sea and up the Fraser River where, rumour had it, an abundance of gold lay scattered along the sandy bars.

The first group of 450 prospectors, the forerunners of a vast migration of dream-deluded would-be millionaires, nearly doubled the population of Fort Victoria in one afternoon. In the following months the tide of fortune seekers inundated the tiny settlement with over twenty thousand, many from San Francisco, but others from Oregon, Washington and other American states. The great Rush of '49 in California was slowing, and anxious drifters were seeking new hunting grounds. On one afternoon, two separate steamships deposited almost three thousand boisterous miners and camp followers. Victoria swelled from a sleepy fur outpost into a chaotic, sprawling garden of canvas tents, the commercial centre for a lightning gold rush, inundating the Lekwungen people of the Coast Salish culture who traditionally occupied most of the region.

The price of building lots increased from $50 to $3,000 within months as businesses and supply depots sprouted like weeds around the fort. The hills surrounding Victoria were stripped of trees, becoming a stump-scarred moonscape as the logs were dragged to the waterfront and sawed and hammered into buildings and boats. The ill-prepared flotilla of skiffs, rafts, canoes, cockleshell craft and other unseaworthy scows immediately set out for the mainland, and many were capsized in the sea, swamped by the tides, grounded on the sandbars or blown off course searching for the inlet to the golden river. At the centre of it all, and faced with the dilemma of his life, was the imperial James Douglas, the fort's founder, the chief factor of the monopoly Hudson's Bay Company west of the Rockies and also, incongruously, governor of the Crown Colony of Vancouver Island.

The rush was no surprise to Douglas, who had seen the small shipments of gold being brought in from Indigenous miners along the Fraser River during the past few years. "It appears," he wrote to London in 1857, "that the auriferous character is becoming daily more extensively developed, through the exertions of the native Indian tribes who, having tasted the sweets of gold mining, are devoting much of their time and attention to that pursuit. The reported wealth of the . . . mines is causing much excitement among the population of the United States territory of Washington and Oregon, and I have no doubt that a great number of the people from those territories will be attracted thither with the return of fine weather in the spring." That he was right was some consolation, but it also left him very little time to devise a scheme to maintain the peace, enforce British sovereignty and defend the Company's interests, in a vast swath of rugged terrain to which the only access was a few mule paths used by the fur traders, and two rivers, the Columbia from the south and the Fraser from the west.

Fortunately for Britain, their independent-minded representative on the Pacific coast was a pragmatic and quick-acting man. Soon after the first hopeful boatloads of prospectors cleared Victoria, scurried up the Fraser past the point of navigation at Yale and began sifting through the sediment along the rushing river, Douglas declared all mines to be government property and began issuing licences to "dig, search for, or remove gold." Mining licences were not only a pleasant source of income for the fledgling government at Fort Victoria; they were also a tacit assertion of authority.

Although the Colonial Office was generally relieved to have the competent Douglas guiding things in New Caledonia, difficulties arose nonetheless over the touchy issue of his dual allegiance to the Crown and the Company, a seemingly clear case of conflict of interest. On one occasion, for example, even the diplomatic Douglas went too far: he began demanding that all prospectors destined for the mainland via Victoria not only had to pick up a mining licence but had to purchase their provisions, equipment and tools from the Company's monopoly store or from Company ships that lurked near the entrance to the Fraser River. Eventually, the Colonial Office politely slapped his wrist and told him to stop it. Even the most generous interpretation of the Company's fur trade monopoly did not extend to the sale of goods to American prospectors. Douglas's directive was later replaced with something more reasonable, a 10 per cent tariff on American goods.

Douglas knew he had little real power, and no official legal authority on the mainland other than his stature as a representative of the Company, but hearing him make a proclamation was to know he was not a man of bluster. He created both law and authority by his very claim that it existed. "The law of the land," he stated, "will do its work without fear and without favour." He also proclaimed into existence the Colony of British Columbia, replacing the old Company department of New Caledonia, creating the new British colony utterly without authority or precedent (a colony that was only later recognized by Britain).

THE COMPANY'S LICENCE WAS UP FOR RENEWAL in 1859, and in 1857 the British government established a select committee of the House of Commons to weigh the evidence and come to a conclusion on whether the venerable monopoly still served a purpose or whether it should be cut loose, its exalted status toppled in favour of other politically expedient objectives. Simpson, then aged seventy and worn out from his years of canoe travel, sailed to London for the select committee's hearings. In the great room, he was hammered for days with hundreds of detailed questions about the Company's activities and territories. Ever the loyal Company man—he had been governor for thirty-seven years—he defended the Company's record and practices, pointing out that even in hard times the Company supplied blankets, ammunition and other basic supplies to remote Indigenous peoples, that the Company served a vital humanitarian function and it could do so only if its monopoly was preserved. While this was accurate in some ways, it failed to address the fact that sometimes it was Company policies that caused the hard times that it then graciously set out to alleviate. Simpson also mentioned the missionaries the Company was now sending into the country, civilizing the people, and fulfilling another of the Company's requirements to maintain its monopoly. The comments of Upper Canada–born George Millward McDougall, who would establish several Methodist missions throughout present-day Saskatchewan and Alberta in the 1860s, give some flavour of the attitudes of the missionaries in general. He pronounced that "pestiferous and godless" Paganism "must be enervated and annihilated, with all the inane superstitions, and corruptions, and savagism of every debased tribe of the frigid North."

The item of most interest to the committee members, however, was the land's suitability for agriculture and settlement. For decades Simpson and the Company had been trying to prevent the settlement even of its own retired employees, going so far as to export settlers from Red River to Oregon and harassing the Métis in order to make the pursuit of their economic interests a challenge. Simpson strategically shuffled his papers, coughed, paused and sipped. Most of the land under the Company's charter, he pronounced, was unsuitable for any type of settlement owing to "the poverty of the soil." But the committee members referenced his own book from 1843 wherein he boasted of the great agricultural potential of the very lands he now denigrated as being suitable only for beaver trapping. Simpson had described the soil of Red River as being dark and

rich, conducive to producing "extraordinary crops . . . the wheat produced is plump and heavy; there are also large quantities of grain of all
kinds, besides beef, mutton, pork, butter, cheese, and wool in abundance." His earlier reports and opinions contradicted his short answers
to the committee, as did the Company's own reports on the agricultural
success of farms at Red River and at Fort Langley, near present-day
Vancouver. Once a man of domineering will with a precise grasp of his
objectives and the strategy to achieve them, now Simpson rambled, dis-
sembled and obfuscated. His performance was poor, and he and everyone knew it. The Company's credibility was damaged, and about it now
clung an aura of stagnant doom.

Dozens of others also gave testimony, either in favour or against. But
the problem the committee faced was a lack of unbiased information.
True, there had been peace and order under the Company, but perhaps
also a smothering of the independent spirit of the people. The population of the Company's territory was now around 160,000, almost all
culturally Indigenous, with perhaps 10,000 identifying as Métis, an
indeterminate but significant number of others of mixed heritage, and
3,000 white Europeans spread over 152 posts, with more than half of
them at Red River—considerably less than the region's population two
hundred years earlier.

Henry Youle Hind and John Palliser were sent out as the heads of
two independent expeditions between 1857 and 1859, to travel the land
and provide unbiased opinions on its current state and its potential for
agriculture and settlement. After years of touring the territory, they had
insightful observations but no clear answers. On the one hand Palliser
wrote, "I feel persuaded that the Greatest Calamity that could befall the
Indian would be to distroy the present fur trade . . . The traders thoroughly know their work and how to do it, with their system they convey
within the reach of every Indian in the territories the means of hunting
and the necessaries for his existence and their annihilation wd produce
the misery and distruction of thousands of Indians." But he also wrote

that, particularly at Red River and about those of mixed heritage, "Unfortunately for the monopoly, the people engaged in this trade are inhabitants of the Indian land and born on its soil. These people most of them Half Breeds are British subjects and whatever the rights and privileges of the Hudson Bay Company may be under the Charter, *They think it a very hard case* that they should be debarred from trading in the land of their birth, and that Foreigners (as the British company undoubtedly are to them) should have a vested priviledge which as British subjects the inhabitants are not permitted to enjoy." Most important, Palliser reported favourably on the agricultural potential of the southern portion of the Company's monopoly, calling it the Fertile Belt, though much of the western part of this territory, north of the arid plains along the 49th parallel and south of the aspen wooded regions farther north, were under the dominion of the fierce Blackfoot Confederacy, which had, since soon after David Thompson's and Kootenae Appee's era, mostly resisted the encroachment of foreign fur traders by burning the forts, particularly those of the American whiskey traders, when they became too numerous.

The select committee recommended that the Company's monopoly be curtailed and that certain territories, in particular the Red River and Saskatchewan region and Vancouver Island, be removed from the Company's jurisdiction, perhaps to become part of Upper and Lower Canada. Since no money was available to pay the Company for its loss of markets if this were to happen, nor money for the British government to defend the territory from Americans, the Company, at least temporarily, retained its rights. In any case there was no easy way of reaching the territories efficiently except through the United States, the political implications of which were anxiety-inducing.

AS THE SELECT COMMITTEE CONDUCTED its hearings in the spring of 1858, Douglas sailed across the unquiet waters of the Salish Sea and chugged up the Fraser to observe the mining camps first-hand. He was shocked at what he saw. An army of ragged prospectors, Indigenous and foreign, were toiling on their primitive claims in the shadow of the massive Coast Range. Chaotic shantytowns, with clusters of lopsided, leaning structures, had sprouted around the Company forts of Yale and Hope and were strewn out along the muddy banks of the mighty Fraser. These sprawling towns were not at all of a nature pleasing to Douglas. One early resident, David Higgins, recalled Yale during that turbulent time. It was, he observed with disdain, "a city of tents and shacks, stores, barrooms and gambling houses. The one street was crowded from morning till night with a surging mass of jostling humanity . . . miners, prospectors, traders, gamblers and painted ladies mingled in the throng . . . A worse set of cutthroats and all-round scoundrels never assembled anywhere . . . Night assaults and robberies, varied by an occasional cold-blooded murder or a daylight theft, were common occurrences."

Fortunately, Douglas's own assessment wasn't quite as harsh. These miners, he wrote cautiously after his tour of the primitive camps in May, "are represented as being, with some exceptions, a specimen of the worst of the population of San Francisco; the very dregs, in fact, of society. Their conduct here would have led me to form a very different opinion." Most of them turned out to be industrious, knowledgeable and hard-working. They were not American desperadoes come to annex the region for the republic, although an invasion nonetheless owing to their numbers. Douglas, with the memory of Oregon haunting him, knew full well the power of self-determination. If thirty thousand people in a region were American, dwarfing the Company employees and dominating the various Indigenous people as well, how long would it be until they declared that the land was also American? The names of the bars along the Fraser, still on the map today, are revealing: American Bar, Boston Bar and Sacramento Bar, to list a few.

And there was always the fear of violence between peoples. The eager, overzealous prospectors, in their haste to garner the golden nuggets, were advancing over Indigenous salmon weirs, destroying villages, molesting women and desecrating burial grounds. When Douglas first heard that Indigenous peoples—the Nlaka'pamux (Thompson Salish), centred around their town of Camchin (now called Lytton) at the confluence of the Fraser and Thompson Rivers, along with their Secwepemc (Shuswap) and Syilx (Okanagan) allies—were harassing and attacking the miners, he was amused. He wrote that he couldn't help but admire their wisdom and foresight. But soon he realized that without an overarching legal and political authority, there would be bloodshed. One British government official, Edward Bulwer-Lytton, the secretary of state to the colonies, remarked that "the Indians, being a strikingly acute and intelligent race of men, are keenly sensitive in regard to their own rights as the aborigines of the country, and are equally alive to the value of the gold discoveries." Miners' cries for protection from the American government would lead to that government coming to their aid. There was nothing Douglas or the Company could do to prevent the influx of miners, and he feared war and bloodshed would be the outcome, upending both the Company's business and the future of the region.

When the headless bodies of two French prospectors floated down the Fraser near Fort Yale in mid-August 1858, killed by people who, in Douglas's view, were "naturally annoyed at the large quantities of gold taken out of their country," he rushed to the scene, arriving just after vigilante committees had hunted down and shot Indigenous people in retribution. A truce had been agreed at Camchin between Captain Henry Snyder, one of the level-headed miners from California, and the Nlaka'pamux chief David Spintlum (Sexpínlhemx) for access to some land in exchange for peace. Douglas was in a vile temper. After lecturing the Indigenous villagers, whom he suspected could easily be overrun and murdered by the violent and well-armed miners (who were nearly all foreigners representing "almost every nation in Europe" as well as Mexicans and thousands of Chinese), he turned on the grumbling mob of miners and coldly admonished them for their foolhardy behaviour, pointing out that they were in the country "merely on sufferance, that no abuses would be tolerated and that the laws would protect the rights of the Indian, no less than those of the white man." He stared them down, leaving no room for dispute, before returning downriver, leaving justices of the peace to try to maintain order. There are no accurate figures, but it is known that dozens of people on both sides were killed. Certainly, the situation to the south, in Douglas's old haunting ground of Old Oregon, was sobering, with chaos sweeping the region as armed forces of the new American government shot and killed Indigenous peoples.

After his first tour in the spring, Douglas had urgently requested help from the British Colonial Office in London, and was no doubt anxiously awaiting it as summer drew to a close. The British government gave him "much credit for acting as he has always done—with promptitude and intelligence," and had created the new Crown colony of British Columbia on the mainland and put Douglas in charge of it. They also promised him dozens of Royal Engineers to help maintain the peace and preserve British autonomy over the American interlopers. His only recourse until they arrived, however, was to levy a licence fee for each saloon and order a survey of townsites at Hope and Yale, to avoid transition and ownership disputes, and hope that nothing bad happened.

On a drizzly, grey day in November 1858, Douglas again boarded a ship and crossed the Salish Sea, navigated up the turgid Fraser to Fort Langley, and scrambled up the muddy bank along with an entourage of dignitaries from Fort Victoria. As a condition of his acceptance of his new position as governor of both the colonies of Vancouver Island and British Columbia, Douglas had renounced his official allegiance to the Hudson's Bay Company and resigned his commission. The Company's monopoly on the fur trade west of the Continental Divide also was eliminated, technically reducing it to the status of any other business enterprise in the new colonies. But it certainly had a commanding lead as the only significant commercial presence of any size on the coast, and Douglas was still associated with the Company in everyone's mind. In his own mind, the interests of the Company and the colonies were still much the same.

For the first arrivals early in the spring of 1858, the gold literally had been strewn on the muddy riverbank, snuggled in beds of moss or lying in the silt just below the water's surface, but by late summer the easy deposits had been plundered; many of the latecomers were just earning "wages," while others had already pushed farther inland past the Fraser's gorge to scour smaller streams and lakes. As the surge of miners pressed deeper into the interior, Douglas could sense potential trouble. He knew that many had been too busy hunting gold to hunt anything else, so to prevent starvation during the winter and ensure a British presence in the remotest outposts, he devised a plan to circumvent the Fraser's treacherous gorge at Hell's Gate.

The existing canyon supply line was precarious and inadequate for the great demand and would be almost useless after the first snow. The cost of goods hauled through the raging defile by industrious Indigenous packers was ruinous. The system was also too slow. So Douglas commissioned a new route, called the Harrison Trail, to reach the goldfields. But about a year after the Harrison Trail was completed, before the winter freeze of 1859–60, the Fraser was pronounced a "humbug" and the disgruntled tide of prospectors retreated to the lower Fraser, Oregon and California. When their golden dreams failed to materialize, few had the temerity to suffer through another monotonous winter surviving on beans, oatmeal and greasy trail bread. As soon as the easy gold was scoured from the bars, many of the makeshift river towns were mostly deserted, leaving their primitive foundations sliding into the mud, while the weary proprietors of Fort Victoria had little else to do but lounge in their doorways and spit into the empty streets. The excitement receded, leaving Fort Victoria, if not as sleepy, staid and tiny as it had been, at least enjoying some respite from the frenetic pace of the past year and a half.

The mysterious interior of the mainland colony, however, was not entirely abandoned by the gold seekers. While thousands of erstwhile treasure hunters began to settle along the lower Fraser and start new lives farming and salmon fishing, continuing a sometimes uneasy coexistence with many of the local peoples, a few hundred optimistic or dream-deluded prospectors still scoured the hinterland for the elusive mother-lode. Glistening and sparkling, it lay sequestered in some secluded cave along the canyon, or perhaps unguarded just below the surface of a quickly flowing stream, shielded by a steely-grey sheet of clay. As the prospectors worked their weary way inland through the pine-covered hills of the intermontane plateau, they could almost smell the gold. The topography was right, similar to the gold zone in California, entirely unlike the bars of the Fraser, which contained mere tailings from a larger source. They found it just before the winter freeze in 1860.

Four ragged men who had pushed inland to Quesnel Lake decided to pole their flimsy raft around its shallow, swampy shore. Following a southbound creek, the weary band found golden flakes at the entrance to nearby Horsefly Lake. With pans and picks they waded through the shallows, shovelling and sifting gravel and clay, plucking lumpy golden nuggets from the stream until they dropped from exhaustion. Stuffing their deflated pokes with chunks of glittering ore, they lay down for the night, and awoke under a blanket of snow. With winter almost upon them, few provisions and far from the nearest trading post, they huddled around a smouldering fire and agreed that two should go out to buy supplies and the other two would search for the best claims. At the closest Company fort, the two men, giddy with excitement, either purchased their goods too energetically under the curious eyes of other patrons or were a little too eager to get back to camp, or they simply told just two special friends. Regardless, soon the rush was back on.

Fort Victoria again flourished as a supply base, along with the mainland towns of Fort Langley and New Westminster, as the hordes swarmed back up the Fraser. The Cariboo find, named after the Cariboo Mountains in central British Columbia, put to shame the paltry flash-in-the-pan Fraser rush. The miners quickly moved beyond panning for gold and burrowed beneath the blue-grey clay to discover streaks of dazzling golden colour. Soon a strange, wobbly shantytown materialized near the astoundingly rich mine claim of a Cornish ex-sailor named Billy Barker, who had deserted ship at Fort Victoria; it was named Barkerville in his honour.

Barkerville was a wild jerry-built concoction of erratic architecture and tumbledown barn-like structures with fantastic facades. A wood-planked boardwalk suspended above the muddy mire of Main Street was the only safe promenade for sauntering miners, ladies and other denizens of the sloppy community. One old photo shows a cattle drive rumbling through town while uninterested onlookers, secure on the boardwalk, go about their business. A single erratic avenue split the rows of saloons, stores, hotels, brothels, dance halls and a roaring opera house. It was lusty, lawless and expensive, until it burned to the ground in 1868. At its height it boasted a population of over ten thousand and claimed the dubious and transitory distinction of being the largest city west of Chicago and north of San Francisco.

The question of how to provision Barkerville and the goldfields, and how to remove the precious but weighty ore, weighed heavily on Douglas's mind. The treacherous paths of the Fraser and the ragged Harrison Trail were woefully inadequate to service the yearly multiplying throng that scrambled north and east from the coast to seek their fortunes.

Douglas knew that the fur trade was finished as a primary industry, and so in spite of the negative impact on the trade, he was determined to construct a winding wagon road from the head of navigation near Yale and going the entire distance to Barkerville. It was a monumental project, and he hastily wrote a dispatch to the Colonial Office informing them of his scheme. He wanted to "push rapidly with the formation of roads during the coming winter," he said, "in order to have the great thoroughfares leading to the remotest mines, now upwards of five hundred miles from the seacoast, so improved as to render travel easy, and to reduce the cost of transport, thereby securing the whole trade of the colony for Fraser's River and defeating all attempts at competition from Oregon." Thus spoke a true geopolitician. Competition from the Washington and

Oregon Territories was Douglas's great fear, especially since the natural geographic flow of the region was north–south along the broad, rolling hills and dry plateaus of the interior valleys.

Many of the American miners couldn't believe their ears when they heard of Douglas's outrageous proposal, and volunteered their services to show him many easier, more efficient southern routes into Washington. The natural route followed the lie of the land north–south, and Douglas knew it from his early days in the fur trade, when he had tramped along the Okanagan Trail down the middle of B.C., from Fort George to Fort Kamloops, and south to the big bend of the Columbia in Washington. Only grudgingly had the Company abandoned this obvious line of transport after 1846, and Douglas wanted to make sure it was not revived, particularly after he heard news of a new American trading post being built by a man named "Okanogan" Smith along the old trail just south of the border at the end of Osoyoos Lake. The hopeful entrepreneur, who, suspiciously in Douglas's view, was a U.S. land commissioner, had also planted a huge apple orchard and was digging irrigation ditches in his new community.

Smith faced the same problems with the east–west transportation route, however. To get from his lonely outpost to Olympia, the new capital of Washington Territory, it was easier to travel north into British Columbia, cross the mountains to Yale, float down the Fraser to the coast and then take a ship through Puget Sound. But the U.S. Army was then constructing its own monumental highway system, from Fort Benton, the head of steam navigation on the Missouri River, to the Dalles on the Columbia (a series of rapids and falls now submerged beneath a hydro reservoir). A branch was to link up with Fort Walla Walla, and another branch could easily be pushed north to Smith's outpost. Douglas feared that trade would drain to the south, sucking the economic vitality from British territory and perhaps strengthening American influence in the region—things that would not bode well for a British company.

Douglas pressed on with his highway scheme without waiting for a reply from Britain, financing the project by borrowing money from Victoria banks, probably without the official authority to do so. Nevertheless, he knew the ways of distant government officials; an answer to his request would likely have been in the form of a delaying motion. His grand road would circumvent the Harrison Trail and follow the old Indigenous routes along a precipitous narrow ledge blasted into the otherwise impassable Hell's Gate of the Fraser's terrifying chasm. Bored through solid rock or propped up by slippery logs and railings, with timber cribs filled with stones as a foundation, Douglas's highway hung precariously from the sides of sheer cliffs before surging north through lumpy brown grasslands with Jack pines on the hilltops, rolling on to Summit Lake and the golden hinterland. Stagecoaches clattered down the new highway at breakneck speeds, hauling people and supplies to the goldfields and hauling precious ore to the outside world.

The first tourists to travel the new road in 1863, the bungling duo of pale and reedy Lord Milton and his energetic protector Dr. W.G. Cheadle, remarked frightfully, "The road is very narrow, the mountainside terrifically steep. We rattled down at a fearful pace—a wheel coming off, the brake giving way, or a restive horse being almost certain death." Nevertheless, it was a vast improvement over the muddy, rutted and circuitous trail that had previously served the region. By 1868, fewer fortune hunters and gold brigades travelled the highway, but they were replaced by families bound for homesteads and ranches in the farming and grazing country of the high, dry interior plateaus.

Douglas had bucked monumental obstacles and run a highway over jagged mountain ranges counter to geographical sense, in opposition to the forces of nature and economics. All the gold from the Cariboo left the region entirely within what Britain called British territory, to the great benefit of the Company, and all the traffic and administration continued on this tortuous trek through mountains and canyons in a geographically preposterous route to the sea, where the Company also dominated. Had a less resolute man been in charge, the Cariboo traffic, as a matter of course, would have gone up the Okanagan Trail through Kamloops; freight destined for Barkerville would have been loaded at the docks at Fort Benton, and the out-flowing bullion would have enriched banks and businesses south of the 49th parallel. With no line of communication between the administration at Victoria and the Interior, the territory might not now be *British* Columbia.

In April 1864, before his great highway was completed, Douglas was forced somewhat reluctantly from his exalted position in charge of the two colonies, and he set off on a grand tour of the British Isles with his family. He had long resisted both the Colonial Office and his own citizens in moving toward a more democratic and accountable government. His opposition to any form of responsible government finally made him a political anachronism in the changing times of the later nineteenth century. He had resisted for years establishing an accountable legislature, only grudgingly allowing the slightest infringement of his authority. He even took to setting the property requirements to hold office so high as to eliminate all but the wealthiest citizens, many of whom happened to be his relatives or former Company officers. They said he was autocratic, and he was. They accused him of nepotism and they were right. He ran what was derisively called the "family-company compact." He manipulated land titles to amass a fortune in real estate, favoured Victoria over New Westminster and positioned the Company to take advantage of the rapidly changing situation. But ironically, many of the same traits that eventually drove him from office were the very qualities that had enabled him to maintain order throughout the gold rush and to guide the Company's New Caledonia Department into a new era.

Douglas lived out his final days in quiet prosperity, honoured more after he left office than he had been while he held it. He was knighted the year he was removed from office. He was the richest person in British Columbia when he died of a heart attack, at the age of seventy-four, in 1877. His estate was enormous, and he provided a legacy for all of his family members, and left property and an annuity for Amelia, who died in Victoria in 1890. Their children prospered, particularly their daughter Martha Douglas Harris, who drew on her mother's Cree stories and her relationship with local Indigenous peoples to become British Columbia's first published female author, writing *History and Folklore of the Cowichan Indians* in 1901.

Douglas lived to see his original rudimentary fur fort transformed into a stable seaport capital with a population of almost six thousand and a growing economy based on lumbering, fishing and shipping. Victoria was paved, and had gaslit streets with stately homes, banks, hotels, churches, schools, parks and government buildings. On the other hand, the rapid influx of foreign settlers caused innumerable conflicts with Indigenous peoples along the coast and interior of the mainland. In particular, smallpox and other diseases worked their way north. One epidemic that began in 1862 near Fort Victoria wildly spread north along the coast and killed around twenty thousand Indigenous people, a third of the population, from all culture groups, and, as epidemic disease did throughout North America, permanently shifted the demographics of the entire region. Given the shockingly high rate of mortality, there was a belief that it wouldn't be long before nearly all of the Indigenous people would be gone. The fur trade era, or at least the monopoly era, was coming to a close.

Other storied British monopolies were fading as well. The East India Company was becoming more of a branch of the British government, and the Royal African Company had declined along with the slave trade. It was obvious that, as it was in Old Oregon, the natural communication route linking Red River to the east was from the American rivers to the south and not the arduous York boat route with its interminable portages and harsh weather. Fort Garry soon replaced York Factory as the Company's distribution centre. Even Simpson's final journey west, in 1860, was by rail and steamer, not by executive canoe. He only made it as far as St. Paul before ill health and failing eyesight forced him to retreat to Lachine.

Simpson had written a letter to the London Committee in 1859 informing them that they should look for his replacement, since he would soon be coming up on forty years in the Company's service, nearly all of it serving as governor. "During that very long period," he wrote, revealing the obsessive dedication he had toward his position, "I have never been off duty for a week at a time, nor have I ever allowed Family ties and personal convenience to come in competition with the claims I considered the Company to have on me."

There is no more metaphorical conclusion to the Company's final phase than Simpson's death the following year, in 1860. Befitting his penchant for status-affirming display, his death occurred unexpectedly after he hosted at his estate the visiting Prince of Wales, the future Edward VII, and a congregation of prominent dignitaries, in a lavish reception featuring ten painted transport canoes, each manned by twelve extravagantly garbed Iroquois performing tricks and chanting voyageur songs while propelling the prince and the little emperor on a pleasure paddle. Soon after this final grand display, Simpson expired from apoplexy and was taken to Montreal for burial next to Frances.

No other individual put his stamp on the Company as George Simpson had, changing its culture and practices. But history has not been kind to Simpson. His boorish, sexist and racist attitudes infiltrated the Company's culture, upending long-standing customs and ushering in a new harsh intolerance. He managed his own affairs in a similarly off-putting manner. When he drafted his last will and testament, for example, he excluded from his vast estate all of his numerous children with Indigenous mothers, and he instructed his executor to assess the appropriateness of the suitors of his "legitimate" daughters and to withhold their portions if they failed to meet the standards he considered appropriate for one of his wealth and social standing.

Throughout the 1860s, the eastern British colonies were negotiating their merger into a new country called Canada. The Company was tangentially involved in these plans, as the monopoly proprietor of a vast hinterland that Britain did not want to be subsumed into the United States, which was hungry again after the Civil War ended in 1865. In 1867, Russia sold Alaska to the U.S., and the only thing blocking American political domination of all of western North America was the Company. But by this time, it was obvious that the Company had no moral authority to govern the land or its people. It was a monopoly trading enterprise riddled with conflict of interest and lacking political will or skill. In London, officials were in a quandary, and various schemes were floated, but the problem was sidelined during the negotiations between eastern colonies leading to Confederation.

The country's first prime minister, John A. Macdonald, sought to claim the rights to the Company's lands, and the Company's logistical infrastructure, for his new Dominion of Canada. Arguments were forwarded to merely brush aside the Company, its workers and the Indigenous peoples and seize the territory. But in 1869, the Company agreed to surrender its land rights to the British Crown, which would then transfer them to Canada. The Company would receive £300,000 in compensation, far less than the directors had hoped for, and retain its numerous forts and factories and the land surrounding them. Most advantageously, they were also granted ownership of 5 per cent of all the territory of the southern Fertile Belt, the tall grass prairie and the aspen parkland that weren't even the Company's traditional field of operation.

The many tens of thousands of Indigenous peoples were not consulted in the monumental business transaction between the British Company and a distant colonial government that had never sent a representative west into the lands it now imagined it owned, as if the whole affair was an uncomplicated real estate transaction between two parties with clear title and involving unoccupied land. The Riel uprising of 1869–70 forced the recognition of at least the prior occupancy of the Métis and some of the Indigenous peoples, and resulted in the formation of the "postage stamp province" of Manitoba. The challenging legacy of dealing with Indigenous title to traditional territories was left to the new Canadian government. In the following decades, Ottawa sent delegations west to negotiate seven treaties with Indigenous nations in an attempt to gain their consent to the new nation's sovereignty, to become part of the process that was transforming Canada from a country along the St. Lawrence and southern Ontario into a sprawling semi-empire that stretched across the continent.

On July 15, 1870, the entire remaining territory of the Hudson's Bay Company became part of the new nation of the Dominion of Canada. The Company would now have to float or sink as a regular business, albeit one powerfully entrenched, with sprawling landholdings in western Canada, a web of efficient supply lines and depots and forts spanning half a continent. The Company's interest, and indeed the interest of eastern financiers and boosters, was now in land speculation for an influx of settlers who the Canadian government hoped would create new markets for eastern manufactured goods. Trading for furs with Indigenous peoples was now a secondary side business, and most of the fur traders from the old days were by now retired or dead.

Epilogue

THE DUST OF EMPIRE

George Simpson was the greatest tragedy to befall the Company, and northern North America, since its founding in 1670. Although he may have made a select group of people a lot of money, in the end he cost them their honour. Rather than helping to prepare its employees, contractors and customers for the tectonic changes that were shaking the land in the later nineteenth century, Simpson, not surprisingly considering his past, turned on them, hastening and exacerbating the damage. The period of the Company's greatest unchallenged commercial success correlated to its period of greatest moral turpitude.

It didn't have to end that way. The reputation of such a venerable institution should have counted for more. Simpson was merely the first wave of betrayal, but he set a powerful precedent for the settlers who came during and after his tenure, brushing away a more open corporate culture and customs that had evolved over countless generations. Simpson consumed the Company's goodwill for his own advancement, and the material gain of a select handful of wilfully blind absentee investors, like a rabid dog gnawing on its own leg all the while thinking it was a great triumph.

But the final years of the Company's monopoly shouldn't taint its first one hundred and seventy, which were more dynamic and surprising. During that time, the Company evolved from a band of bewildered foreigners eking out their lives in trading posts along the sparsely inhabited rugged rim of a vast unknown continent, to a mostly domestic entity of blended cultures and customs dealing among themselves. Although most of the profits ended up in London, most of the drama occurred in western and northern North America. The land was changed, and people's lives were altered in the pursuit of the fur of the beaver and other animals. Apart from the technical minutiae, the Company's business, like all business, was fundamentally about managing people and relationships. It was these relationships over the generations that had such a profound influence on the course of history.

The rascally bushrunners Radisson and Groseilliers conceived of the idea for the Company but were driven from New France and peddled their scheme to England's King Charles II; Pierre Le Moyne d'Iberville led an overland assault from New France and seized York Factory and all the accumulated furs, bedevilling the Company with his raids for over a decade; Thanadelthur brokered peace between the Cree and the Chipewyan and pioneered the trade into the Athabasca region; James Knight sailed north from Fort Churchill in a doomed search for gold and a Northwest Passage; Matonabbee and Samuel Hearne ventured inland northwest from Prince of Wales Fort searching for copper and a route to the elusive Cathay, while scouting and developing lucrative new markets thousands of kilometres to the west; Attickasish took Anthony Henday with him on his multi-year commercial circuit as far west as the Rocky Mountains, into the lands of the Blackfoot Confederacy; Alexander Mackenzie had a dream to travel to the Pacific Ocean and, once he found the path, was welcomed in the villages along the trade routes in the mountainous Interior and escorted to his destination;

David Thompson, along with Charlotte Small, pioneered routes over the Rockies to the Columbia River and mapped most of western Canada and the Pacific Northwest over decades of travel; the quixotic Lord Selkirk dreamed of a colony for displaced Scottish crofters after the Highland clearances but unwisely situated it athwart the supply lines of the North West Company; Peter Skene Ogden explored most of the Pacific Northwest of the United States while under orders to exterminate the beaver population and deter American pioneers from travelling west into the region; Cuthbert Grant led Métis firebrands to the fateful battle defending their rights at Seven Oaks; Dr. John McLoughlin managed the company's territory in Old Oregon and transformed Fort Vancouver into a thriving multicultural settlement; Pierre-Guillaume Sayer sparked the struggle for free trade at Red River; and James and Amelia Douglas presided over the growth and evolution of Fort Victoria from a fur factory into a colonial capital.

Thousands of others ghosted through the annals of the Company's history, some taking their memories with them when they died, others leaving behind families or just their stories. They had their time, made their choices, saw something of the world and left their disappearing footprints across the land. A company is nothing other than a legal entity for tax and accounting purposes. It has no life of its own. It is a bloodless thing, an imaginary construct that can unify and motivate people to a common endeavour. The Company was merely a vessel for the dreams, aspirations, hopes and ambitions of the thousands of men and women whose contributions animated it for two centuries, in the process transforming a continent. The Company was nothing other than its people and their stories; everything else is now dust. And we live in their world, just as they live in ours.

NOTES

INTRODUCTION

"by meanes whereof there may probably arise very great advantage": The full text of the charter can be found at "The Royal Charter Incorporating The Hudson's Bay Company 2 May 1670," Canada History, http://canadahistory.com/sections/documents/empire/hbc_charter.html and "Text of HBC's Royal Charter," HBC Heritage, http://www.hbcheritage.ca/things/artifacts/the-charter-and-text. See also, the Solon Law Archive: https://www.solon.org/Constitutions/Canada/English/PreConfederation/hbc_charter_1670.html .

CHAPTER ONE

"apparelled more like a savage than a Christian": Captain Godey, quoted in Beckles Willson, *The Great Company*, 113.

"greatly beaten with the great concours of that people": Pierre-Esprit Radisson, *The Collected Writings*, vol. 1, 161.

"desirous to have seen their country": Ibid., 124.

"To tell the truth," he admitted, "I was loathsome to do them mischief":
   Ibid., 131.

"my new parents that weare so good and so favorable to me": Ibid., 159.

"was my destiny to discover many wild nations, I would not strive against
   destinie": Ibid., 159.

"a towne faire enough for a new country": Ibid., 163.

"It is a strange thing," Radisson mused, "when victuals are wanting, worke
   whole nights and days": Ibid., 211.

By 1660, the entire French presence in New France was barely 3,200 people:
   Jean Talon, "Statistics for the 1666 Census," https://web.archive.org/
   web/20120225232904/http://www.statcan.gc.ca/kits-trousses/jt2-eng.htm.

It is estimated that before European contact, the population of Indigenous
   Canada and the northern portions of the United States was over
   500,000: Arthur Ray, *I Have Lived Here Since the World Began*, p. 21.

"were soe strong and so to be feared, that scarce any body durst stirre":
   Pierre-Esprit Radisson, *Collected Writings*, Volume I, 115.

"were rare and precious in those countries": Ibid., p. 275.

"The women also, by having a nosegay in their hands, and dance very
   modestly": Ibid., 282.

"on their shoulders uppon which were represented all maner of figurs":
   Ibid., 282.

"Every one brings the most exquisit things to shew what his country
   affoards": Ibid., 282.

"We weare well beloved, and [they] weare overjoyed that we promissed
   them to come": Ibid., 287.

"This is a wandring nation," Radisson observed, "and containeth a vast
   countrey": Ibid., 288.

"old howse all demolished and battered with boulletts": Ibid., 286

"The bougre [bugger] did grease his chopps": Ibid., 300–301.

"We weare Cesars, being no body to contradict us": Ibid., 265

"nights were long and cold, and the earth covered with snow": Henry
   Hudson, *Henry Hudson the Navigator*, 110.

"without food, drink, fire, clothing, or any necessaries": Thomas A. Janvier, *Henry Hudson: A Brief Statement of His Aims and His Achievements*, III. See also http://www.ianchadwick.com/hudson/hudson_05.htm for an interesting discussion of events and documents related to Hudson's voyage.

"If the Passage be found," Hudson observed, "I confess there is something gain'd in the Distance": William Monson, *Sir William Monson's Naval Tracts in Six Books*, 431.

"Many a Storme, and Rocke, and Mist, and Winde, and Tyde, and Sea, and Mount of Ice": Thomas James, in Miller Christy, ed., *The Voyages of Captain Luke Foxe of Hull, and Captain Thomas James of Bristol*, 453.

"more required (I meane) in discovery," he wrote, "who is so pleased may set forth": Luke Foxe, Ibid., 415.

"I do confidently believe there to be a passage, as I do there is one between Calais and Dover": Thomas James, Ibid., 179.

"further search of a passage this way was hopeless": Luke Foxe, ibid., 364.

"with great pains in the loins, as if a thousand knives were thrust through them": Jens Munk, in C.C.A. Gosch, editor, Danish Arctic Expeditions, 47.

"the very place where the Passage should be, as it was thought": Thomas James, Miller Christy, ed., *The Voyages of Captain Luke Foxe of Hull, and Captain Thomas James of Bristol*, 597.

"the miserable groanings, and lamenting of the sicke men all night long": Ibid., 542.

CHAPTER TWO

"brave and courageous even to rashness, but cross-grained and incorrigibly obstinate": Anthony Hamilton, *Memoirs of Count Grammont*, 306.

"use the said Mr. Gooseberry and Mr. Radisson with all manner of Civility and Courtesy": quoted in Pierre-Esprit Radisson, *The Collected Writings*, Volume I, 62.

"sudden great storme did rise and put us a sunder": Ibid., 305.

"deluded and privately married": quoted in ibid., 67.

"Sole Trade and Commerce" of Hudson's Bay as "true and absolute Lordes and proprietors": The full text of the charter can be found at: http://www.hbcheritage.ca/things/artifacts/the-charter-and-text or http://canadahistory.com/sections/documents/empire/hbccharter.htm.

"by meanes whereof there may probably arise very great advantage to us and our kingdome": Ibid.

"say that [beaver] is the animal well-beloved by the French, English and Basques": Reuben Gold Thwaites, *The Jesuit Relations and Allied Documents*, 297.

"This poor animal, searching for something to eat, gets caught": Ibid., 301.

"two stories high, and round. The materials of which it is composed are wood and mud": Ibid., 300.

"these poor animals, which are sometimes in great numbers under one roof": Ibid., 301.

"Prior to the discovery of Canada": David Thompson, *The Writings of David Thompson*, Volume I, 190.

"There are sometimes three of four hundred of them in one place": Pierre Charlevoix, *Histoire de la Nouvelle France*, 159.

"I cannot refrain from smiling when I read the accounts of different authors": Samuel Hearne, *A Journey to the Northern Ocean*, 157.

"It would be as impossible for a beaver": Ibid., 157.

"they were remarkably fond of rice and plum pudding": Ibid., 164.

"in order to acquire a prodigious memory and never to forget what one had once read": Quoted in "The Beaver: A Cure for All Ills," *The Beaver*, September 1931, 284.

"There is an animal called Castor the Beaver, none more gentle, and his testicles make a capital medicine": T.H. White, ed., *The Book of Beasts*, 28–29.

CHAPTER THREE

"scornfully rejected all our advice in order to follow that of others":
   Pierre-Esprit Radisson, *The Collected Writings*, vol. 2, 7.

"though only after having resisted doing so for a long time": Ibid., 7.

"All my friends know that I loved my wife tenderly": Ibid., 7.

"They made us wait fruitlessly for a very long time": Ibid., 11.

"could see that I still had English sentiments": Ibid., 15.

"all his life he had frequented the lands of the wild men": Ibid., 19.

"While making him the gifts I told him that I took him for my father": Ibid., 27.

"seize his ship, which was a lawful prize, since it had no commission to
   trade": Ibid., 33.

"I am a Frenchman who tells you to withdraw": Ibid., 35.

"in a pitiful state, having drunk himself into a stupor": Ibid., 65.

"to cross over into England forever, and to commit myself so steadfastly to
   His Majesty's service": Ibid., 103.

"For Severall tymes Wee asked him if Wee should fire or Contrive some
   meanes to oppose the French": Quoted in Glyndwr Williams, *Highlights
   of the First 200 Years of the Hudson's Bay Company*, 10.

"taken an English Fort and three ships whereof one of good force with
   divers prisoners": Ibid., 11.

"will not have far to go, and will find goods at a much lower rate than with
   us": Harold Innes, *The Fur Trade in Canada*, 50.

CHAPTER FOUR

"the place as wee are come to is nothing but a confused heap of old rotten
   houses": James Knight, in K.G. Davies and A.M. Johnson, eds., *Letters
   from Hudson Bay, 1703-1740*, 38.

"to call, encourage, and invite, the remoter Indians to a trade with us":
   Henry Kelsey, *Kelsey Papers*, 1-3.

"the best lodging as ever Man had in this country": James Knight, in K.G.
   Davies and A.M. Johnson, eds., *Letters from Hudson Bay, 1703-1740*, 39.

"Monopolies are absurd, inconsistent, and destructive": Sir Matthew
Decker, *An Essay on the Causes of the Decline of the Foreign Trade*, 43.

**"she tells me that they promised her when she was there last that they
would get a great deal of copper"**: James Knight, in K.G. Davies and
A.M. Johnson, eds., *Letters from Hudson Bay, 1703–1740*, 64.

"Large presents of Powder, Shot & tobacco with other necessaries":
Ibid., 412.

"to take care that none of the Indians Abuse or Misuse the Slave Woman":
Ibid., 412.

**"one of such Spirit in his Life. She kept all the Indians in awe as she went
with"**: Ibid., 412.

**"she made them all stand in fear of her as she scolded at some and pushing
of others"**: Ibid., 412.

"ketcht him by the nose Push'd him backwards & call'd him a fool.":
James Knight, in Arthur Ray, ed., *Life and Death by the Frozen Sea: The
York Fort Journals of Hudson's Bay Company Governor James Knight*, 235.

"She did rise in such a passion as I never did see the Like before":
Ibid., 235.

**"Ye northern Slave Woman has been dangerously Ill and I expect her
Death every Day"**: Ibid., 341.

**"She was one of a Very high Spirit and of the Firmest Resolution that I
ever see in any Body in my Days"**: Ibid., 355.

**"they found it so badd that After they had built it I believe they was so
Discouraged"**: James Knight, in K.G. Davies and A.M. Johnson, eds.,
Letters from Hudson Bay, 1703-1740, 406.

**"Here is now Such Swarms of Small Sand flyes that wee can hardly See the
Sun through them"**: James Knight, *The Founding of Churchill*, 147.

"Cruseables, Melting Potts, Borax &c for the Trial of Minerals": Ibid., 152.

"Sickness and famine occasioned such bitter havock among the English":
Samuel Hearne, *A Journey to the Northern Ocean*, 5-6.

"some of the Company said upon this occasion": Joseph Robson, An *Account
of Six Years Residence in Hudson's-Bay*, 15.

CHAPTER FIVE

"The Wall's of our housses we here Live in are 2 foot thick of stone": James Isham, *James Isham's Observations, 1743–1749*, 173.

"a violent snow came on the NNW and lasted four days without intermission": Samuel Hearne, fort journals, in Timothy Ball, *Climate Change in Central Canada: A Preliminary Analysis of Weather Information from Hudson's Bay Company at York Factory and Churchill Factory, 1714-1850*. PhD Dissertation, University of London, 1983, Online.

"more like Beasts than men," he noted, with "a bag upon the back, with a tin pot and hatchet by the side": James Isham, *Isham's Observations, 1743-1749*, 117.

"sand fly's are so thick a man Can not see his way for them.": Ibid., 143.

"where they light is just as if a spark of fire fell and raises a little bump which smarts": James Knight, *Founding of Churchill*, 148.

"We know very well Governor Nixon before you Did it. But we never did approve thereof": Letter to Governor Henry Sergeant, in E.E. Rich, ed., *Copy-book of Letters Outward, 1679-94*, 185.

"made most excellent salled to our roast geese": William Wales, *Journal of a Voyage*, 126.

"that Juyce that you tap out of the trees which you mixt with your drink": Quoted in Douglas Leechman, "Fractious Farming at the Fur Trade Posts," *Canada's History (The Beaver)*, Winter 1970, 4.

"We are over run with mice and have a boar cat who can do nothing among them": Ibid., 5.

"is always handsomely supplied with provisions, very seldom having less than three dishes": Andrew Graham, *Andrew Graham's Observations*, 297.

"to send me Some country lads that are not acquainted with strong drink": John Nixon, in E.E. Rich & Alice M. Johnson, eds., *Minutes of the Hudson's Bay Company, 1679–1684: First Part, 1679–1682*, 251.

"are given very much to Quarrelling when in Liquor": James Isham, *Isham's Observations, 1743-1749*, 92.

"**Upon Hayes Island where our grand Factory is, you may propagate Swine**": Letter to John Nixon, in E.E. Rich, ed., *Copy-book of Letters Outward, 1679-94*, 9.

"**We are very sensible that the Indian Weoman resorting to our Factories are very prejudicial**": Ibid., 40.

"**The Company permit no European women to be brought within their territories**": Andrew Graham, *Andrew Graham's Observations*, 299.

"**pretty numerous" and that they tended to be "fine Children . . . streight lim'd, Lively active**": James Isham, *Isham's Observations, 1743-1749*, 79.

"**my old friend the mother of all my [seven] children**": Quoted in Van Kirk, *Many Tender Ties*, 158.

"**The union which has been formed between us, in the providence of God**": Daniel Williams Harmon, *Sixteen Years in the Indian Country*, 175.

"**I now pass a short time every day, very pleasantly, in teaching my little daughter Polly to read**": Ibid., 167.

CHAPTER SIX

"**The Silence is then broken by degrees by the most venerable Indian**": Andrew Graham, *Observations on Hudson's Bay*, 317.

"**smoking the calumet is necessary to establish confidence**": Ibid., 319.

"**a few simple medicines such as the powders of sulphur, bark, liquorice**": Ibid., 320.

"**I can from personal experience**": Ibid., 318.

"**are a good natured people and very susceptible of wrongs done them**": Ibid., 321.

"**a person of prime consideration . . . and his influence is very extensive**": Andrew Graham, *Observations on Hudson's Bay*, 149. Also Anthony Henday, edited by Barbara Belyea, *A Year Inland: The Journal of a Hudson's Bay Company Winterer*, 149.

"**All gentlemen that are acquainted with the natives in Hudsons Bay**": Andrew Graham, *Observations on Hudson's Bay*, 265.

"the Frenchmen of Canada made gifts to them in order to oblige them":
Pierre-Esprit Radisson, *The Collected Writings*, vol. 2, 121.

"On taking the necessaries which they require for the winter season":
David Thompson, *The Writings of David Thompson, Volume 1*, 276.

"And having noticed that one of them used a small piece of flat iron":
Pierre-Esprit Radisson, *The Collected Writings*, vol. 2, 27.

"came amongst them and bought up their furs, giving them a gun for fifty
wolves or beaver": Andrew Graham, *Observations on Hudson's Bay*, 257.

"he did not like to sit in the canoe and be obliged to eat fish and fowl":
Ibid., 257.

"The Standard of Trade at Fort Albany in 1733": See www.hbcheritage.ca
/history/fur-trade/standard-of-trade.

"for it is impossible for an Indian to carry them [big kettles] in their
canoes": Thomas McCliesh, in K.G. Davies and A.M. Johnson, eds.,
Letters from Hudson Bay, 1703-1740, 49.

"I have had several complaints from the Indians of the badness of our cloth
this year": Ibid., 49.

"Never was any man so upbraided with our powder, kettles and hatchets":
Ibid., 49.

"if your honours do not conceive the difference, the natives do": Richard
Norton, Ibid., 84.

"much afflicted with sickness" etc.: See Paul Hackett, *A Very Remarkable
Sickness*.

"they are frightened of going nigh one to another as soon as they take bad":
William Walker, *Cumberland and Hudson House Journals, 1779-82*, edited by
E.E. Rich and Alice Margaret Johnson, 265.

"this morn Eight Curnoes of our home Inds fitted out from here in order
to goe to war": Quoted in Paul Hackett, *A Very Remarkable Sickness*, 115.

"country is very much altered to what it was formerly": Anthony Beale, in
K.G. Davies and A.M. Johnson, eds., *Letters from Hudson Bay, 1703-1740*, 24.

"one cannoe came down the River, brought the unwelcome news of 2 Indns
Dying": Quoted in Paul Hackett, *A Very Remarkable Sickness*, 152.

"Esinepoet, his wife, 2 girls & a boy": Chart reproduced in ibid., *A Very Remarkable Sickness*, 161.

"they have seen but one Indian during the Winter": Quoted in Ibid., 197.

"keep a strict look out, that none of the Home Guards come to the factory": Matthew Cocking, quoted in ibid., 196.

"Those who escaped made a stop and threw into the river, according to their custom": Pierre Gaultier de Varennes et de La Vérendrye, *Journals and Letters of La Vérendrye and His Sons*, edited by Lawrence Burpee, 258.

CHAPTER SEVEN

"to return to their service, and not to go the Voyage": Arthur Dobbs, *An Account of the Countries Adjoining to Hudson's Bay*, 99.

"The Company have for eighty years slept on the edge of a frozen sea": Joseph Robson, quoted in Glyndwr Williams, "Arthur Dobbs and Joseph Robson: New Light on the Relationship between Two Early Critics of the Hudson's Bay Company," 132-135.

"the Musketoes were intolerable giving us no peace day nor night": Anthony Henday, *York Factory to the Blackfeet Country: The Journal of Anthony Henday, 1754-55*, edited by Lawrence Johnson Burpee, 325.

"I don't very well like it," Henday noted, "having nothing to Satisfy Them": Ibid., 325.

"smiled and said they dared not": Ibid., 326.

"berries the size of black currents and the finest I ever eat": Ibid., 327.

"I gave their leader half a foot of Brazile tobacco": Ibid., 321.

"a great many dried Scalps with fine long black hair, [were] displayed on poles": Ibid., 339.

"Great Leader who lives down at the Great Waters": Ibid., 337.

"They think nothing of my tobacco": Ibid., 338.

"their clothing is finely painted with red paint; like unto English ochre": Ibid., 338.

"they follow the Buffalo from place to place: & that they should not be
     surprised by the Enemy": Ibid., 339.

"I went with the young men a Buffalo hunting": Ibid., 338.

"If the Archithinues and Assinepoets could be brought down to trade":
     Ibid., 350.

"The French talk several Languages to perfection": Ibid., 350.

"I am sure of killing two or three of you, and if you chuse to purchase my
     life at that price": Samuel Hearne, *A Journey to the Northern Ocean*, 230.

"furnished me with a good warm suit of otter and other skins": Ibid., 48.

"made a grand feast for me in the Southern Indian [Cree] style": Ibid., 48.

"In stature, Matonabbee was above the common size, being nearly six feet
     high": Ibid., 229.

"when all the men are heavy laden, they can neither hunt nor travel to any
     considerable distance": Ibid., 49-50.

"are maintained at a trifling expense; for as they always stand cook": Ibid., 50.

"In conversation he was easy, lively, and agreeable, but exceedingly modest":
     Ibid., 229.

"As no man is exempt from frailties, it is natural to suppose that as a man
     he had his share": Ibid., 229.

"everything that would contribute either to facilitate or retard the ease of
     progress of travelling": Ibid., 54.

"some with the figure of the sun, others with that of the Moon": Ibid., 109.

"did not care if they rendered the name and race of the Esquimaux extinct":
     Ibid., 87.

"I came to consider that it was the highest folly for an individual like me":
     Ibid., 87.

"The shrieks and groans of the poor expiring wretches were truly dreadful":
     Ibid., 112.

"when the bullets struck the ground, they ran in crowds to see what was
     sent them": Ibid., 113.

"put a final end to all disputes concerning a North West Passage through
     Hudson's Bay": Ibid., 197.

CHAPTER EIGHT

"was known to live in open defiance of every law, human and divine":
Samuel Hearne, *A Journey to the Northern Ocean*, 73.

"God d——n you for a b——h, if I live I'll knock out your brains": Ibid., 74.

"good and amiable quality, in a most eminent degree": Ibid., 104.

**"during their approach, a most inviting opportunity offered itself to be
revenged"**: Edward Umfreville, *The Present State of Hudson's Bay*, 127.

**"without one officer being consulted . . . To a half-starved, wretched group
of Frenchmen"**: Ibid., 128.

"an honour to his nation, and an ornament to human nature": Ibid., 134.

"for bringing her up in the tender manner which he did": Samuel Hearne,
A Journey to the Northern Ocean, 104.

"This is more to be wondered at, as he is the only Northern Indian who":
Ibid., 232.

"The death of this man was a great loss to the Hudson's Bay Company":
Ibid., 232.

"a most delicious morsel": Ibid., 102.

"it has always been the custom among those people for the men to wrestle":
Ibid., 80.

"object of the contest" sat **"in pensive silence watching her fate"**: Ibid., 81.

"A murderer is shunned and detested by all the tribe": Ibid., 82.

"the Continent of America is much wider than many people imagine": Ibid., 15.

**"the natives, my guides, well knew that many tribes of Indians lay to the
West of us"**: Ibid., 15.

**The population was about 70,000 in 1765; by 1790 it was over 160,000; and
by 1806, 250,000"**: Wikipedia, demographic history of Quebec.

There were 9,000 people in 1800; 23,000 by 1825; and 58,000 by 1852:
Montreal archives: http://www2.ville.montreal.qc.ca/archives/500ans
/portail_archives_en/rep_chapitre6/chapitre6-2.html.

**"we builded Log Huts to pass the winter, the chimneys were of mud and
coarse grass"**: *David Thompson, The Travels of David Thompson: Volume I*,
157.

"I have frequently heard the Canadian and Iroquois voyagers": Quoted in
  Bruce Hodgins, *The Canoe in Canadian Cultures*, 113.

"I have been 24 years a canoeman and 41 years in service": James H. Baker,
  Lake Superior, 342.

"It however must be owned," he mused, "that the Hudson's Bay traders
  have ingratiated themselves more into the esteem": Edward Umfreville,
  The Present State of Hudson's Bay, 209.

"have become slaves to every vice which can corrupt and debase the human
  mind": Ibid., 211.

"Not at all to the ulterior advantage of the natives": Ibid., 207.

"liquors, bread, pork, butter, and cheese are sold": Gabriel Franchère,
  Franchere's Narrative of a Voyage, 387.

"The wintering hands who are to return with their employers": Ibid., 389.

"They are short, thick set, and active, and never tire": Thomas Loraine
  McKenney, *Sketches of a Tour to the Lakes*, 417.

"For musick we had the Bag-Pipe, the Violin, the flue & the Fife":
  Daniel Williams Harmon, *A Journal of Voyages and Travels*, 42. See also,
  Daniel Williams Harmon, *Harmon's Journal, 1800-1819*, edited by W. Kaye
  Lamb, 13.

"obscured by the cloud of ignorance that darkened the human mind":
  Alexander Mackenzie, *Voyages from Montreal*, v.

"favourite project of my own ambition": Ibid., iv.

"We were accompanied also by an Indian who had acquired the title of
  English Chief": Ibid., 2.

"It was, indeed, a very wild and unreflecting enterprise": Ibid., 64.

"I had to watch the savage who was our guide": Ibid., vi.

"that I had come a great way, and at a very considerable expense": Ibid., 100.

"that the Natives [there] are Big and very wicked, kill Common Men with
  their Eyes": Ibid., 83.

"the frost was so severe that the axes of the workmen became almost as
    brittle as glass": Ibid., 132.

"the atmosphere became so warm that it dissolved all the snow on the
    ground": Ibid., 136.

"Her dimensions were twenty-five feet long within": Ibid., 151.

"This magnificent theatre of nature has all the decorations which the trees
    and animals": Ibid., 154.

"The whole country," he proclaimed, "displayed an exuberant verdure":
    Ibid., 155.

"It was with the utmost difficulty," Mackenzie wrote, "we could prevent her":
    Ibid., 173.

"the river above us, as far as we could see": Ibid., 173.

"small prickles which caught our trousers": Ibid., 179.

"a carrying place to another large river": Ibid., 186.

"brandishing their spears, displaying their bows and arrows": Ibid., 198.

"a fearful detail of rapid currents, fallen trees and large stones": Ibid., 217.

"requested me to re-think, declaring, at the same time, that if they perished":
    Ibid., 217.

"I need not add," Mackenzie dryly noted in his journal, "that one spark
    might have put a period to all my anxiety and ambition": Ibid., 222.

"a very malignant race, who lived in large subterraneous recesses": Ibid., 245.

"What can be the reason that you are so particular and anxious": Ibid., 259.

"We certainly were acquainted," he said, "with the principal circum-
    stances": Ibid., 259.

"Before us appeared a stupendous mountain": Ibid., 316.

"Regaled with these delicacies": Ibid., 319.

"were inferior to these people, as they themselves acknowledged": Ibid., 324.

"a large canoe had lately been in this bay": Ibid., 344.

"renewed his entreaties for our departure": Ibid., 348.

CHAPTER TEN

"recover his former sagacity": Alexander Mackenzie, *Voyages from Montreal*, 368.

"I think it unpardonable in any man to remain in this country who can afford to leave it": Letter to Roderick McKenzie, in William Lamb, ed., *The Journals and Letters of Sir Alexander Mackenzie*, 340.

"assertion was nothing but conjecture, and that a Northwest Passage is impractical": Alexander Mackenzie, *Voyages from Montreal*, v.

"In those days," he recalled, "we dined at four o' clock": George Thomas Landmann, *Adventures and Recollections of Colonel Landmann*, 234. See also Lawrence J. Burpee, *The Beaver Club: Report of the Annual Meeting* 3, no. 1 (1924), 73–92. https://doi.org/10.7202/300038ar.

"gentlemen of enlarged views": David Thompson, *Narrative*, 170.

"I have been overtaken with the consequences of my sufferings in the North West": Letter to Roderick McKenzie, in William Lamb, ed., *The Journals and Letters of Sir Alexander Mackenzie*, 355.

"the most Northern situation fit for colonization, and suitable for the residence of a civilized people": Alexander Mackenzie, *Voyages from Montreal*, 411.

"O! how disagreeable is our Situation": Captain William Clark, November 28, 1805, in *Journals of Lewis & Clark Expedition*, edited by Gary E. Moulton. See also, online: Journals of the Lewis and Clark Expedition, https://lewisandclarkjournals.unl.edu/item/lc.jrn.1805-11-28.

"Down this river [the Hudson] they plied their course merrily on a fine summer's day": Washington Irving, *Astoria*, 43.

"Men seasoned to hardship, who cared for neither wind nor weather": Ibid., 44.

"Mr. Fox, if you are afraid of water, you should have remained at Boston": Alexander Ross, *Adventures*, 76.

"The weather was magnificent": Gabriel Franchère, *Franchere's Narrative*, 119.

CHAPTER ELEVEN

"We had to pass where no human should venture": Simon Fraser, *Letters and Journals*, 96.

"My lovely wife is of the blood of these people": David Thompson, *The Writings of David Thompson*, Volume I, 124.

"It is my wish to give all my children an equal and good education": David Thompson, letter to Alexander Fraser, in *Columbia Journals*, 254.

"several old Indians made a bargain with me": David Thompson, *Narrative*, 309.

"I was obliged to take two kegs of alcohol, overruled by my partners": Ibid., 396.

"A French Canadian has the appetite of a Wolf": Ibid., 443.

"piety and virtue . . . a foundation for a sober and Christian life": Ibid., xxiv.

"Neither writing nor reading was required": Ibid., 27.

"a fine race of men, tall and muscular, with manly features": Ibid., 348.

"In every council he presided, except one of War": Ibid., 346.

"He looked on the civil Chief with indifference as a garrulous old man": Ibid., 347.

"he appeared to be of Bone and Sinew with no more flesh": Ibid., 347.

"and I gave him my right hand": David Thompson, *The Writings of David Thompson*, vol. I, 67.

"and in his speeches reminded his people of the great benefit": David Thompson, *Narrative*, 347.

"sewing their leather clothing with a pointed brittle bone or a sharp thorn": David Thompson, *The Writings of David Thompson*, vol. 1, 59.

"by which all might have a share of the honour and plunder": David Thompson, *Narrative*, 347.

"drew the Piegan to the Missouri to revenge their deaths": Ibid., 375.

"The manner of preparing it is as follows": David Thompson, *Columbia Journals*, 235.

"If they ever again met with a white Man going to supply their Enemies": Ibid., 250.

"would put us in safety [from the Piegan], but would be attended with
   great inconvenience": David Thompson, *Narrative*, 441.

"cutting his road through a wretched thick Woody Country": David
   Thompson, *Columbia Journals*, 251.

"he is what we call a 'flash' man, a showy fellow": David Thompson,
   Narrative, 446.

"When Men arrive in a strange Country, fear gathers on them from every
   Object": David Thompson, *Columbia Journals*, 138.

"the sensation I felt is beyond what I can give utterance to": David Douglas,
   Journal, 259.

"it appears extraordinary how any human being should have stumbled
   upon": George Simpson, *Fur Trade and Empire*, 33.

"Know hereby," it intoned imperiously, "that this country is claimed by
   Great Britain": David Thompson, *Narrative*, 488.

"four low Log Huts, the far-famed Fort Astoria of the United States":
   Ibid., 501.

"On the 15th of July, we were rather surprised at the unexpected arrival":
   Alexander Ross, *Adventures*, 101.

"Thus I have fully completed the survey of this part of North America":
   David Thompson, *Narrative*, 502.

"What is this fort I have heard so much of": Gabriel Franchère, *Franchère's
   Narrative*, 134.

"The chiefs of several Chinook and Clatsop bands who traded at Fort
   Astoria": Ibid., 133.

CHAPTER TWELVE

"a Ghastly, raw boned and lanthorn jawed": "The 'Character Book' of
   Governor George Simpson, 1832," in Glyndwr Williams, ed., *Hudson's Bay
   Miscellany*, 192.

"some people reading this Journal might very naturally suppose": Peter Fidler,
   in Samuel Black, *A Journal of a Voyage from Rocky Mountain Portage*, xxxii.

"the consequence was not only the loss of commercial benefit": Alexander Mackenzie, *Voyages from Montreal*, x.

"Tabashaw stabbed a near relation of his own, Missistaygouine": Alexander Henry, *The Red River of the North*, 209.

"In a drinking match at The Hills yesterday": Ibid., 194.

"Indians arriving daily and drinking the proceeds of the spring hunt": Ibid., 210.

"To see a house full of Drunken Indians, as it generally consists": Daniel Williams Harmon, *Harmon's Journal*, 1800-1819, 28.

"Of all the people in the world, I think the Canadians, when Drunk, are the most disagreeable": Ibid., 53.

"It will require some time and I fear cause much expense": Simon McGillivray, in Thomas Thorner, ed., *A Few Acres of Snow: Documents in Pre-Confederation Canadian History*, 148.

"Not a tenth part of their number really belong to Red River": Alexander Ross, *Red River Settlement*, 83.

"a fine race, tall, straight, well proportioned": James Carnegie, Earl of Southesk, *Saskatchewan and the Rocky Mountains: A Diary and Narrative of Travel, Sport*, 359.

"On one occasion, a gentleman on his way to the States forgot, in his camping place": Alexander Ross, *Red River Settlement*, 250.

"There is happiness and pleasure in the society of the most illiterate men": Ibid., 252.

"They cordially detest all the laws and restraints of civilized life": Ibid., 252.

"the whole cavalcade broke ground and made for the buffalo": Ibid., 256.

"The surface was rough and full of badger holes": Ibid., 257.

"the welfare of the families at present forming settlement on the Red River": Miles Macdonell, quoted in Samuel Hull Wilcocke, Simon McGillivray and Edward Ellice, *A Narrative of Occurrences in the Indian Countries of North America*, 26.

"Repeated accounts reached us from Fort Daer [Pembina] that the cattle were driven": Miles Macdonell, quoted in Arthur J. Ray, *I Have Lived Here Since the World Began*, 108.

"I am not mortally wounded": Robert Semple, quoted in *Narratives of John Pritchard, Pierre Pambrun, and Frederick Damien Heurter, Respecting the Aggressions of the North-West Company*, 30.

"Captain Rogers, having fallen," he wrote, "rose up again and came towards me": John Pritchard, Ibid., 28-29.

population of over half a million, mostly along the St. Lawrence: Statistics Canada. https://www150.statcan.gc.ca/n1/pub/98-187-x/4064809-eng.htm

"Their number together must have exceeded 500 men and the place": Samuel Wilcocke, quoted in Samuel Hull Wilcocke, Simon McGillivray and Edward Ellice, *A Narrative of Occurrences in the Indian Countries of North America*, 67.

"My honour is at stake in the contest with the North West Company": Thomas Douglas, Earl of Selkirk, in *The Collected Writings of Lord Selkirk, 1810-1820*, edited by J.M. Bumstead ixxv.

"If we are to be poor for three generations": Letter from Lady Selkirk to Lord Selkirk, in George Simpson, *Journal of Occurrences*, xxix.

CHAPTER THIRTEEN

"their previously stiffened features began to relax a little": John Todd, quoted in Arthur Morton, *A History of the Canadian West*, 626.

"important business connected with the affairs of Lord Selkirk": George Simpson, quoted in James Raffan, *Emperor of the North*, 62.

"Franklin, the Officer who commands the party has not the physical powers required": George Simpson, *Journal of Occurrences*, 261.

"eating and Drinking the Compy's property, smoking their Tobacco": Ibid., 366.

"The information seems to disconcert both Officers and Men": Ibid., 349.

"mass of renegades and malcontents": George Simpson, in Harvey Fleming, ed., *Minutes in Council*, 394.

"I consider it highly injurious to the general interest": George Simpson, letter to Andrew Colvile, quoted in Peter Newman, *Caesars of the Wilderness*, 313.

"In no colony subject to the British Crown is there to be found an authority so despotic": John McLean, *Notes of a Twenty-Five Years' Service in the Hudson's Bay Territory*, 236.

"I consider it quite unnecessary to indent for Sauces & Pickles on public account": George Simpson, quoted in Margaret Macleod, ed., *Letters of Letitia Hargrave*, 159.

"It appears the present concern has stamped the Cain mark upon all born in this country": Charles Mackenzie, quoted in George Bryce, *The Remarkable History of the Hudson's Bay Company*, 175.

"reconcile them to the new order of things ... I am convinced": George Simpson, letter to Andrew Colvile, quoted in Harold Innis, *The Fur Trade in Canada*, 287.

"an enlightened Indian is good for nothing": George Simpson, letter to Andrew Colvile, in *Journal of Occurrences*, xl.

"Heavy debts are ascertained to be injurious to the Trade and of little benefit to the Indians": George Simpson, quoted in Arthur Ray Jim Miller and Frank Tough, *Bounty and Benevolence: A History of Saskatchewan Treaties*, 12.

"a very poor creature, vain, self sufficient and trifling": Glyndwr Williams, ed., *The Character Book of Governor George Simpson, 1832*, in *Hudson's Bay Miscellany, 1670–1870*, 178.

"A frothy trifling conceited man, who would starve in any other country": Ibid., 169.

"A boasting ignorant low fellow who rarely speaks the truth": Ibid., 171.

"Of fiery disposition and as bold as a lion": Ibid., 182.

"Got into disgrace lately in consequence of having employed one of the Company's Servants": The collection of quotes in the whole paragraph are from Ibid., 169-183.

"The commodity," he wrote of one of his mixed-heritage mistresses": George Simpson, letter to John George McTavish, in George Simpson, *Fur Trade and Empire*, 136.

"dispose of the Lady ... as she is an unnecessary and expensive appendage": George Simpson, letter to John George McTavish, in Harvey Fleming, ed., *Minutes in Council*, 424.

CHAPTER FOURTEEN

"was such a figure as I should not like to meet on a dark night in one of the bye lanes in the neighborhood of London": George Simpson, *Fur Trade and Empire*, 23.

"Those were stirring times": Diamond Jenness, Canadian Museum of Civilization: https://www.historymuseum.ca/cmc/exhibitions/aborig/haida/havwao1e.html.

"North of this place, about Two or Three Degrees, at the mouth of Fraser's River": George Simpson, *Fur Trade and Empire*, 73.

"a female of notoriously loose character": See W. Kaye Lamb, "The James Douglas Report on the Beaver Affair," in *Oregon Historical Quarterly*, 19-28.

"McLoughlin and his suite": Hubert Howe Bancroft, *The Works of Hubert Howe Bancroft: History of the Northwest Coast, vol. 2, 1800-1846*, 586.

"The two Canadians commenced at either end of the snake-like coil": George Ruxton, *Adventures in Mexico and the Rocky Mountains*, 255.

"for the purpose of exploring the country S.W. which was entirely unknown to me": Robert Richmond and Robert Mardock, *A Nation Moving West: Readings in the History of the American Frontier*, 138.

"my arrival caused considerable bustle in camp": Ibid., 139.

"Here we find fruit of every description, apples, peaches, grapes, pears, plums and fig trees": Henry and Eliza Spalding, in *The Letters of Narcissa Whitman*, 74.

"a people who will most probably feel very differently Inclined towards the Company": John McLoughlin, *The Letters of Dr. McLoughlin*, edited by E.E. Rich, 174.

"I, of course, expected to find Beaver": Jedediah Smith, *The Travels of Jedediah Smith*, edited by Maurice S. Sullivan, 26.

"the first step that the American Government will take towards colonization": Harvey Fleming, ed., *Minutes of Council*, ixviii.

"The country is a rich preserve of Beaver": George Simpson, in *Fur Trade and Empire*, 46.

"one of the most unprincipled Men in the Indian Country": "The Character Book of Governor George Simpson, 1832," in Glyndwr Williams, ed., *Hudson's Bay Miscellany*, xix.

"first-born dangling from the saddle straps in a moss bag": Agnes C. Laut, *Conquest of the Great Northwest*, 267.

"Necessity has no laws": Peter Skene Ogden, *Peter Skene Ogden's Snake Country Journals, vol 1*, xxxvii.

"This life makes a young man sixty in a few years": Peter Skene Ogden, "Ogden's Journals," *Oregon Historical Quarterly*, vol. 11, 217.

CHAPTER FIFTEEN

"our natural boundary is the Pacific Ocean": Charles H. Ambler, *The Life and Diary of John Floyd, Governor of Virginia, and the Father of the Oregon Country*, 67.

"The word came expressly to me": Hall Jackson Kelley, *A History of the Settlement of Oregon and the Interior of Upper Columbia*, quoted in Tim McNeese, *The Oregon Trail: Pathway to the West*, 42.

"I am now afloat," Wyeth speculated, "on the great sea of life": Nathaniel J. Wyeth, *The Correspondence and Journals of Captain Nathaniel J. Wyeth*, edited by F. G. Young, 178.

"live with them, learn their language, preach Christ to them": Dr. W. Fisk, Letter to the Editor of the *Christian Advocate and Journal*, March 9, 1833. Quoted in Rev. John O. Choules and Rev. Thomas Smith, eds., *The Origin and History of Missions*, 537.

"The Gov. and other Gentlemen of the H. B. Co. (though they have native wives)": Jason Lee, quoted in Albert Furtwangler, *Bringing Indians to the Book*, 63.

"This is a cause worth living for": Narcissa Whitman, *Letters and Journal of Mrs. Narcissa Prentiss Whitman, 1836–1847, Mountain Men and the Fur Trade*, online: https://user.xmission.com/~drudy/mtman/html /nwhitman.html.

"Villages, which had afforded from one to two hundred effective warriors, are totally gone": David Douglas, in *Companion to the Botanical Magazine: Being a Journal, Volume 2, 1836*, edited by Sir William Jackson Hooker.

"support the Organic Laws of the Provisional Government of Oregon": See the full text of "Dr. John McLoughlin's Last Letter to the Hudson's Bay Company, as Chief Factor, in charge at Fort Vancouver, 1845," https://archive.org/stream/jstor-1836705/1836705_djvu.txt. See also Robert Carleton Clark, "The Last Step in the Formation of a Provisional Government for Oregon in 1845," in *Quarterly of the Oregon Historical Society* 16 (March 1915–December 1915).

CHAPTER SIXTEEN

"bit of Brown with him to the Settlement": George Simpson, quoted in Jennifer Brown, *Strangers in Blood*, 129.

"The first blow [from the news] was dreadful to witness, but the poor girl is fast acquiring resignation": James Hargrave, *The Hargrave Correspondence*, 67-8. See also Sylvia van Kirk, "Hargrave, James," *Dictionary of Canadian Biography*.

"a complete savage, with a coarse blue sort of woolen gown": Frances Simpson, in Letitia Hargrave, *Letters of Letitia Hargrave*, 36.

"What could be your aim in discarding her": John Stewart, quoted in Sylvia Van Kirk, *Many Tender Ties*, 188.

"this influx of white faces has cast a still deeper shade": James Hargrave, quoted in Sylvia Van Kirk, *The Custom of the Country*, 83.

"There were about 20 girls and nearly as many boys there": John Henry Lefroy, quoted in Glyndwr Williams, *The Hudson's Bay Company and the Fur Trade*, 76.

"Well, have you observed that all attempts to make gentlemen of them": John Todd, letter to Edward Ermatinger, quoted in Jennifer Brown, *Strangers in Blood*, 188.

"a half-breed . . . Chief of the mountain Crees": George Simpson, *An Overland Journey*, 70.

"made long prayers to me as a high and powerful conjurer": Ibid., 70.

"as far as the eye could reach, mountain rose above mountain": Ibid., 75.

"Demon of the Mountains alone could fix his abode there": Ibid., 76.

"Madam Peechee and the children had left their encampment": Ibid., 76.

"they could die but once, they had better make up their minds to submit to their present fate without resistance": Ibid., 77.

"so different in its general aspect, from the wooded, rugged regions around": James Douglas, "Diary of a Trip to the Northwest Coast, 1840," quoted in John Adams, *Old Square Toes and His Lady: The Life of James and Amelia Douglas*, 61.

"pruned of redundancies, as a study": James Douglas, quoted in W. Kaye Lamb, "Letters to Martha," *British Columbia Historical Quarterly* (January 1937).

"the Governor of Vancouvers Island has been in the Company out here": Annie Deans to her brother and sister, February 29, 1854, letter reprinted in Barry Gough, ed., *Sir James Douglas as Seen by His Contemporaries: A Preliminary List*, 35.

"As a private individual": James Douglas, quoted in Margaret A. Ormsby, "Douglas, Sir James," in *Dictionary of Canadian Biography*.

"I can recall nothing more delightful than our bivouac": James Douglas, *Diary of a Trip to York Factory*. Online. https://search-bcarchives. royalbcmuseum.bc.ca/uploads/r/null/4/3/8/4381d8b7f71242f1c5780edf-d6512ef3a1c96ea2a8f67dcdbf6676181ef29dbf/MS0678.1.1.pdf, 9.

"To any other being less qualified": James Douglas to James Hargrave, March 24, 1842, in G. P. de T. Glazebrook, ed., *The Hargrave Correspondence, 1821–1843*, 381.

"It is obvious," said Lord Grey shortly after the signing of the Oregon Treaty, "when an eligible territory": Hansard's Parliamentary Debates, 1848, 473.

"The Government is a perfect farce": Charles Wilson, *The Frontier: Charles Wilson's Diary of the Survey of the 40th Parallel*, edited by George Stanley, 29.

CHAPTER SEVENTEEN

"Hudson's Bay Company clerks, with an armed police": Petition, in W. Kernaghan, *Hudson's Bay and Red River Settlement: with a Short Account of the Country and the Routes in 1857*, 13.

"In 1860, there will be rail all the way from New York and the sea coast": Ibid., 4.

"There can be no question that the injurious": See John Lewis, *George Brown*, 214.

"It appears," he wrote to London in 1857, "that the auriferous character is becoming daily": James Douglas, in *Copies or Extracts of Correspondence Relative to the Discovery of Gold in the Fraser River District*, 9.

"dig, search for, or remove gold": James Douglas, in *Papers Relative to the Affairs of British Columbia*, volumes 1-4, by 33.

"pestiferous and godless" Paganism "must be enervated and annihilated": George Millward McDougall, Missionary Notices, November 1854, quoted in James Ernest Nix, *Mission Among the Buffalo*, 12.

"extraordinary crops . . . the wheat produced is plump and heavy; there are also large quantities of grain": Great Britain, Report of the Select Committee on the State of British Possessions in *North America Which Are under the Administration of the Hudson's Bay Company*, 50.

"I feel persuaded that the Greatest Calamity that could befall the Indian would be to distroy the present fur trade": John Palliser, *Observations on the Proposed Annexation of Rupert's Land and the Monopoly Rights of the Hudson's Bay Company*.

"a city of tents and shacks, stores, barrooms and gambling houses. The one street was crowded": David Higgins, *The Mystic Spring, and Other Tales of Western Life*, 31.

"are represented as being, with some exceptions, a specimen of the worst of the population of San Francisco; the very dregs, in fact, of society": James Douglas, *Copies or Extracts of Correspondence Relative to the Discovery of Gold in the Fraser's River District*, 259.

"The Indians, being a strikingly acute and intelligent race of men": Edward

Bulwer Lytton, *Papers Relative to the Affairs of British Columbia*, volumes 1-4,
  59.

**"naturally annoyed at the large quantities of gold taken out of their
  country"**: Ibid., 16.

"merely on sufferance, that no abuses would be tolerated": Ibid., 16.

"push rapidly with the formation of roads during the coming winter":
  James Douglas, quoted in Report of the Department of *Commercial
  Transport*, 7.

"the road is very narrow, the mountainside terrifically steep": Walter
  Cheadle, *Cheadle's Journal of a Trip Across Canada*, 230.

"During that very long period," he wrote, revealing the obsessive dedication":
  George Simpson, letter to the London Committee, quoted in John S.
  Galbraith, *The Little Emperor*, 203.

SELECTED BIBLIOGRAPHY

Adams, John. *Old Square Toes and His Lady: The Life of James and Amelia Douglas.* Victoria, BC: TouchWood Editions, 2011.

Ambler, Charles H. *The Life and Diary of John Floyd, Governor of Virginia, and the Father of the Oregon Country.* Richmond: Richmond Press, 1918.

Backhouse, Frances. *Once They Were Hats: In Search of the Mighty Beaver.* Toronto: ECW Press, 2015.

Ball, Timothy. *Climate Change in Central Canada: A Preliminary Analysis of Weather Information from Hudson's Bay Company at York Factory and Churchill Factory, 1714-1850.* PhD Dissertation, University of London, 1983. Online.

Baker, James H. *Lake Superior: Its History; Romance of the Fur Trade; Physical Features, Treaties, Voyageurs, etc.* Saint Paul: Minnesota Historical Collections, volume 3, Minnesota Historical Society, 1879.

Bancroft, Hubert Howe. *The Works of Hubert Howe Bancroft: History of the Northwest Coast, vol. 2, 1800-1846.* San Francisco: The History Company Publishers, 1886.

The Beaver. "The Beaver: A Cure for all Ills." September 1931.

Beaver, Herbert. *Reports and Letters of Herbert Beaver, 1836-1838.* Edited by
W.W. Sage. OR: Portland, Champoeg Press, 1961.

Black, Samuel. *A Journal of a Voyage from Rocky Mountain Portage in Peace
River to the Sources of Finlays Branch and North West Ward in Summer 1824.*
Edited by E.E. Rich. London: Hudson's Bay Record Society, 1955.

Bourrie, Mark. *Bush Runner: The Adventures of Pierre-Esprit Radisson.*
Windsor, ON: Biblioasis, 2019.

British Columbia, Legislative Assembly. *Report of the Department of
Commercial Transport, containing the reports on Railways, Aerial Tramways,
Pipe-lines, Industrial Transportation, , and Commercial Vehicles.* Victoria:
Government Printer, 1969.

Brown, Jennifer S. H. *Strangers in Blood: Fur Trade Company Families in
Indian Country.* Vancouver: University of British Columbia Press, 1980.

Bryce, George. *The Remarkable History of the Hudson's Bay Company Including
that of the French Traders of North-western Canada and of the North-West,
XY, and Astor Fur Companies.* Toronto: Gilbert and Rivington, 1900.

Bumstead, J.M. *Fur Trade Wars: The Founding of Western Canada.* Winnipeg:
Great Plains Publications, 1999.

Burpee, Lawrence J., ed. *Journals and Letters of Pierre Gauthier De Varennes De
La Verendrye and His Sons, with Correspondence between the Governors of
Canada and the French Court, Touching the Search for the Western Sea.* The
Publications of the Champlain Society, vol. 16. Toronto: Champlain
Society, 1927.

Carnegie, James, Earl of Southesk. *Saskatchewan and the Rocky Mountains: A
Diary and Narrative of Travel, Sport.* Edinburgh: Edmonston & Douglas,
1875.

Charlevoix, Pierre. *Histoire de la Nouvelle France, 1744, 3 volumes.* Ottawa:
Editions Elysee, 1976.

Cheadle, Walter. *Cheadle's Journal of a Trip Across Canada, 1862-1863.* Victoria,
BC: TouchWood Editions, 2010.

Choules, Rev. John O. and Rev. Thomas Smith, eds. *The Origin and History of
Missions: A Record of the Voyages, Travels, Labors, and Successes of the Various*

Missionaries, who Have Been Sent Forth by Protestant Societies and Churches to Evangelize the Heathen; Compiled from Authentic Documents. New York: Gould, Kendal & Lincoln, 1848.

Christy, Miller, ed. *The Voyages of Captain Luke Foxe of Hull, and Captain Thomas James of Bristol, in Ssearch of the North-West Passage, in 1631—1632.* London: Hakluyt Society, 1894.

Clark, Robert Carleton. "The Last Step in the Formation of a Provisional Government for Oregon in 1845." *Quarterly of the Oregon Historical Society* 16 (December 1915).

Cocking, Matthew. *An Adventurer from Hudson Bay: Journal of Matthew Cocking, from York Factory to the Blackfeet Country, 1772–73.* Edited by Lawrence Johnstone Burpee. Ottawa: Royal Society of Canada, 1908.

Daschuk, James W. *Clearing the Plains: Disease, Politics of Starvation, and the Loss of Aboriginal Life.* Regina: University of Regina Press, 2013.

Davies, K.G. and A.M. Johnson, eds. *Letters from Hudson Bay, 1703-1740.* London: Hudson's Bay Record Society, 1965.

Decker, Sir Matthew. *An Essay on the Causes of the Decline of the Foreign Trade.* Dublin: George Faulkner, 1739.

Dickason, Olive Patricia, with David T. McNab. *Canada's First Nations: A History of Founding Peoples from Earliest Times, Fourth Edition.* Don Mills, ON: Oxford University Press, 2009.

Dobbs, Arthur. *An Account of the Countries Adjoining to Hudson's Bay, Their Methods of Commerce, etc., Showing the Benefit to Be Made by Settling Colonies and Opening Trade in These Parts; Whereby the French Will Be Deprived in a Great Measure of Their Traffick in Furs.* London: J. Robinson, 1744. Online.

Douglas, David. *Journal Kept by David Douglas During His Travels in North America 1823-1827.* London: William Wesley & Son, 1914.

Douglas, David. *In Companion to the Botanical Magazine: Being a Journal, Volume 2.* Edited by Sir William Jackson Hooker. London: 1836.

Douglas, James, W. Kaye Lamb, editor. "Letters to Martha." Edited by W. Kaye Lamb. *British Columbia Historical Quarterly* 1, no. 1 (January 1937).

Douglas, Thomas, Fifth Earl of Selkirk. *The Collected Writings of Lord Selkirk,*

1810-1820. Edited by J.M. Bumstead. Winnipeg: The Manitoba Record Society, 1987.

Fenn, Elizabeth A. *Pox Americana: The Great Smallpox Epidemic of 1775-82*. New York: Farrar, Straus & Giroux, 2002.

Fleming, R. Harvey, ed. *Minutes in Council, Northern Department of Rupert Land, 1821-31*. Toronto: Champlain Society, 1940.

Foster, Martha Harroun. *We Know Who We Are: Métis Identity in a Montana Community*. Norman: University of Oklahoma Press, 2006.

Fournier, Martin. *Pierre-Esprit Radisson: Merchant Adventurer, 1636-1701*. Montreal: McGill-Queen's Press, 2002.

Franchère, Gabriel. *Narrative of a Voyage to the Northwest Coast of America in the Years 1811, 1812, 1813, and 1814*. Translated by J. V. Huntington. New York: Redfield, 1854.

Franchère, Gabriel. *Journal of a Voyage on the North West Coast of North America During the Years 1811, 1812, 1813, and 1814*. Edited by W. Kaye Lamb. Toronto: Champlain Society, 1969.

Fraser, Simon. *The Letters and Journals of Simon Fraser, 1806-1808*. Edited by W. Kaye Lamb. Toronto: Macmillan of Canada, 1960.

Furtwangler, Albert. *Bring the Indians to the Book*. Seattle: University of Washington Press, 2005.

Galbraith, John S. *The Little Emperor: Governor Simpson of the Hudson's Bay Company*. Toronto: Macmillan of Canada, 1976.

Geiger, John, and Owen Beattie. *Dead Silence: The Greatest Mystery in Arctic Discovery*. Toronto: Viking, 1993.

Girard, Philip, Jim Phillips, Blake Brown. *A History of Law in Canada, Vol. 1: Beginnings to 1866*. Toronto: University of Toronto Press, 2018.

G. P. de T. Glazebrook, ed. *The Hargrave Correspondence, 1821-1843*. Toronto: Chaplain Society, 1938.

Gordo, Elizabeth Ternier. *Letitia Hargrave: Mistress of York Factory*. Winnipeg: TG Publishing, 2017.

Gosch, C. C. A., ed. *Danish Arctic Expeditions, 1605 to 1620: Volume 2, The Expedition of Captain Jens Munk, 1619-1620*. London: Hakluyt Society, 1897.

Gough, Barry. *First Across the Continent, Sir Alexander Mackenzie*. Toronto: McClelland & Stewart, 1997.

———. "Sir James Douglas as Seen by His Contemporaries: A Preliminary List." *BC Studies*, no. 44 (winter 1979–80).

Graham, Andrew. *Andrew Graham's Observations on Hudson's Bay*. Edited by Glyndwr Williams. London: Hudson's Bay Record Society, 1969.

Great Britain, Parliament. *Hansard's Parliamentary Debates*. London: G. Woodfall & Son, 1848.

Great Britain, Colonial Office. *Copies or Extracts of Correspondence Relative to the Discovery of Gold in the Fraser's River District, in British North America*. London: George Edward Eyre and William Spottiswoode, 1858.

Great Britain, Colonial Office. *Papers Relative to the Affairs of British Columbia, Volumes 1-4*. London: George Edward Eyre and William Spottiswoode, 1858-1862.

Great Britain. *Report of the Select Committee on the State of British Possessions in North America Which Are under the Administration of the Hudson's Bay Company with Minutes of Evidence, Appendix and Index*. London: British Parliamentary Papers, 1857.

Grob, Gerald N. *The Deadly Truth: A History of Disease in America*. Cambridge, MA: Harvard University Press, 2002.

Hackett, Paul. *A Very Remarkable Sickness: Epidemics in the Petit Nord, 1670 to 1846*. Winnipeg: University of Manitoba, 1999.

Hamilton, Anthony (Count). *Memoirs of Count Grammont*. Philadelphia: Grebbie & Co., 1888.

Hargrave, James. *The Hargrave Correspondence, 1821-1843*. Edited by G.P. de T. Glazebrook. Toronto: Champlain Society, 1938.

Hargrave, Letitia. *Letters of Letitia Hargrave*. Edited by Margaret Arnett Macleod. New York: Greenwood Press, 1969.

Harmon, Daniel Williams. *A Journal of Voyages and Travels in the Interior of North America*. Andover, MA: Flag and Gould, 1820.

———. *Harmon's Journal, 1800-1819*. Edited by W. Kaye Lamb. Victoria, BC: TouchWood Editions, 2006.

Harris, Martha Douglas. *History and Folklore of the Cowichan Indians.* Victoria, BC: Colonist Printing and Publishing Co., 1901; reprint by Marquette Books, 2004.

Hayes, Derek. *First Crossing: Alexander Mackenzie, His Expedition Across North America and the Opening of the Continent.* Vancouver: Douglas & McIntyre, 2001.

Hearne, Samuel. *A Journey to the Northern Ocean: The Adventures of Samuel Hearne.* 1795. Victoria, BC: TouchWood Editions, 2007.

Henday, Anthony, edited by Lawrence Johnson Burpee. *York Factory to the Blackfeet Country: The Journal of Anthony Henday, 1754-55.* Ottawa: Royal Society of Canada, 1907.

Henday, Anthony. *A Year Inland: The Journal of a Hudson's Bay Company Winterer.* Edited by Barbara Belyea. Waterloo, ON: Wilfrid Laurier University Press, 2000.

Henry, Alexander. *The Red River of the North.* Edited by Elliott Coues. New York: F. P. Harper, 1897.

Higgins, David Williams. *The Mystic Spring, and Other Tales of Western Life.* Toronto: William Briggs, 1904.

Hodgins, Bruce, John Jennings, Doreen Small, eds. *The Canoe in Canadian Cultures.* Toronto: Dundurn, 2011.

Hudson, Henry. *Henry Hudson the Navigator: The Original Documents in Which His Career Is Recorded, Collected, Partly Translated, and Annotated, with an Introduction by G.M. Asher.* London: Hakluyt Society, 1860.

Innes, Harold. *The Fur Trade in Canada.* Toronto: University of Toronto Press, 1999 reprint.

Irving, Washington. *Astoria. Or, Anecdotes of an Enterprise Beyond the Rocky Mountains.* New York: Henry W. Rees, 1836.

Janvier, Thomas A. *Henry Hudson: A Brief Statement of His Aims and His Achievements.* New York: Harper and Brothers, 1909.

Jenish, D'Arcy. *Epic Wanderer: David Thompson and the Mapping of the Canadian West.* Toronto: Doubleday, 2003.

Kelley, Hall Jackson. *A History of the Settlement of Oregon and the Interior of Upper Columbia.* Springfield, MA. 1868.

Kelsey, Henry. *Kelsey Papers.* Edited by John Warkentin. Regina: University of
    Regina Press, 1994.

Kernaghan, W. *Hudson's Bay and Red River Settlement: with a Short Account of
    the Country and the Routes in 1857.* London: Algar and Street, 1857.

Kirk, Sylvia Van. *Many Tender Ties: Women in Fur-trade Society, 1670-1870.*
    Winnipeg: Watson & Dwyer, 1980.

Kirk, Sylvia Van. "The Impact of White Women on Fur Trade Society." In
    Susan Mann and Alison L. Prentice, eds., *The Neglected Majority: Essays in
    Canadian Women's History.* Toronto: McClelland & Stewart, 1977.

Komar, Debra. *The Bastard of Fort Stikine.* Fredericton: Goose Lane, 2015.

Knafla, Louis A., and Jonathan Swainger, eds. *Laws and Societies in the
    Canadian Prairie West, 1670-1940.* Vancouver: University of British
    Columbia Press, 2006.

Knight, James. *Life and Death by the Frozen Sea: The York Fort Journals of
    Hudson's Bay Company Governor James Knight, 1714-1717.* Edited by Arthur
    Ray. Toronto: Champlain Society, 2018.

———. *The Founding of Churchill, Being the Journal of James Knight.* Edited by
    James F. Kenney. Toronto: J. M. Dent, 1932.

Lamb, W. Kaye, ed. *The Journals and Letters of Sir Alexander Mackenzie.*
    Toronto: Macmillan of Canada, 1970.

Lamb, W. Kaye. "The James Douglas Report on the Beaver Affair," *Oregon
    Historical Quarterly* 18 March 1946.

Landmann, George Thomas. *Adventures and Recollections of Colonel
    Landmann, Late of the Corps of Royal Engineers, volume 1.* London: Colburn
    and Co., 1852.

Lault, Agnes C. *Conquest of the Great Northwest.* New York: Outing
    Publishing Company, 1908.

La Vérendrye, Pierre Gaultier de Varennes et de. *Journals and Letters of La
    Vérendrye and His Sons.* Edited by Lawrence J. Burpee. Toronto: Champlain
    Society, 1927.

Leechman, Douglas. "Fractious Farming at the Fur Trade Posts." *The Beaver,*
    Winter 1970.

Lewis, John. *George Brown.* Toronto: Morang& Co., 1906.

Lytwyn, Victor P. *The Fur Trade of the Little North: Indians, Pedlars, and Englishmen East of Lake Winnipeg, 1760-1821.* Winnipeg: Rupert's Land Research Centre, 1986.

Mackenzie, Alexander. *Voyages from Montreal, on the River St. Laurence, Through the Continent of North America to the Frozen and Pacific Oceans, in the years 1789 and 1793.* Edinburgh: R. Noble, 1801.

McGoogan, Ken. *Fatal Passage: The True Story of John Rae, the Arctic Adventurer Who Discovered the Fate of Franklin.* Toronto: HarperCollins, 2001.

———. *Ancient Mariner.* Toronto: HarperCollins, 2004.

McKenney, Thomas Loraine. *Sketches of a Tour to the Lakes, of the Character and Customs of the Chippeway Indians, and of Incidents Connected with the Treaty of Fond du Lac.* Baltimore: F. Lucas, 1827.

McLean, John. *Notes of a Twenty-Five Years' Service in the Hudson's Bay Territory.* Edited by William Stewart Wallace. Toronto: Champlain Society, 1932.

McLoughlin, John. *The Letters of John McLoughlin from Fort Vancouver to the Governor and Committee, 1825-1844, 3 volumes.* Edited by E.E. Rich and W. Kaye Lamb. Toronto: Champlain Society, 1941-1944.

McNeese, Tim. *The Oregon Trail: Pathway to the West.* New York: Chelsea House, 2009.

Meares, John. *Voyage Made in the Years 1788 and 1789 from China to the North West Coast of America.* London: Forgotten Books, 2012 reprint of a 1790 original.

Monson, William. *Sir William Monson's Naval Tracts in Six Books: The Whole from the Original Manuscript.* London: A. and J. Churchill, 1703.

Montgomery, Richard Gill. *The White-Headed Eagle: John McLoughlin, Builder of an Empire.* New York: Macmillan, 1934.

Morton, Arthur. *A History of the Canadian West to 1870-71, 2nd edition.* Toronto: University of Toronto Press, 1973.

———. *Sir George Simpson: Overseas Governor of the Hudson's Bay Company.* Toronto: J.M. Dent, 1944.

Moulton, Gary E., ed. *The Lewis and Clark Journals: An American Epic of Discovery: The Thridgment of the Definitive Nebraska Edition.* Lincoln: University of Nebraska Press, 2003.

Newman, Peter C. *Caesars of the Wilderness.* Toronto: Penguin, 1988.

Nicol, Paul, C. *Discipline, Discretion and Control: The Private Justice System of the Hudson's Bay Company in Rupert's Land, 1670- 1770.* PhD thesis. University of Calgary, 2001.

Nix, James Ernest. *Mission among the Buffalo: The Labours of the Reverends George M. and John C. McDougall in the Canadian Northwest, 1860-1876.* Toronto: Ryerson Press, 1960.

Nute, Grace Lee. *Caesars of the Wilderness: Medard Chouart, Sieur des Groseilliers and Pierre Esprit Radisson, 1616-1710.* London: D. Appleton-Century Company, 1943.

Ogden, Peter Skene. *Peter Skene Ogden's Snake Country Journals.* Vol. 1, 1824–1825 and 1825–1826, edited by E.E. Rich. Vol. 2, 1826–1827, edited by K.G. Davies. Vol. 3, 1827–1828 and 1828–1829, edited by Glyndwr Williams. London: Hudson's Bay Record Society, 1950, 1961, 1971.

———. "Ogden's Journals." Oregon Historical Quarterly 11, no. 2 (1911).

Ormsby, Margaret A. "Douglas, Sir James," *Dictionary of Canadian Biography*, www.biographi.ca/en/bio/douglas_james_10E.html.

Palliser, John. *Observations on the Proposed Annexation of Rupert's Land and the Monopoly Rights of the Hudson's Bay Company. Confidential Despatch to the Secretary of State for the Colonies, 1858.* Edited by Marijan Salopek, 1993. Online: http://victoria.tc.ca/history/etext/palliser .observations.1858.html.

Payne, Michael. *The Most Respectable Place in the Territory: Everyday Life in the Hudson's Bay Company Service, York Factory, 1788 to 1870.* Ottawa: National Historic Parks and Sites, Canadian Parks Service, 1989.

Podruchny, Carolyn. *Making the Voyageur World: Travellers and Traders in the North American Fur Trade.* Toronto: University of Toronto Press, 2006.

Porter, Stephen. *The Great Plague of London.* Gloucestershire: Amberley Publishing, 2012.

Pritchard, John, Frederick Damien Heurter and Pierre Chrysologue Pambrun. *Narratives of John Pritchard, Pierre Pambrun, and Frederick Damien Heurter, Respecting the Aggressions of the North-West Company, Against the Earl of Selkirk's Aettlement upon Red River.* London: John Murray, 1819.

Radisson, Pierre-Esprit. *Pierre-Esprit Radisson: The Collected Writings.* Edited by Germaine Warkentin. 2 vols. Montreal and Kingston: McGill-Queen's University Press, 2012, 2014.

Raffan, James. *Emperor of the North.* Toronto: HarperCollins, 2007.

Ray, Arthur, and Donald Freeman. *Give Us Good Measure: An Economic Analysis of Relations between the Indians and the Hudson's Bay Company before 1763.* Toronto: University of Toronto Press, 1978.

Ray, Arthur, Jim Miller and Frank Tough. *Bounty and Benevolence: A History of Saskatchewan Treaties.* Montreal: McGill-Queen's University press, 2002.

Ray, Arthur, ed. *Life and Death by the Frozen Sea: The York Fort Journals of Hudson's Bay Company Governor James Knight, 1714-1717.* Toronto: Champlain Society, 2018.

Ray, Arthur. *Indians in the Fur Trade: Their Roles as Trappers, Hunters, and Middlemen in the Lands Southwest of Hudson Bay, 1660-1870.* Toronto: University of Toronto Press, 1988.

———. *I Have Lived Here Since the World Began: An Illustrated History of Canada's People.* Toronto: Key Porter Books, 1996.

Rich, E.E., ed. *Copy-Book of Letters Outward 1679-94.* Toronto: Champlain Society, 1948.

———. *James Isham. Isham's Observations on Hudson's Bay, 1743.* Toronto: Champlain Society: 1949.

Rich, E.E., and Alice Margaret Johnson, eds. *Introduction by Richard Glover. Cumberland and Hudson House Journals, 1779-82.* London: Hudson's Bay Record Society, 1952.

———. *Minutes of the Hudson's Bay Company, 1679–1684: First Part, 1679–1682.* Toronto: Champlain Society for the Hudson's Bay Record Society, 1945.

Rich, E.E. *The History of the Hudson's Bay Company 1670-1870.* Toronto: McClelland & Stewart, 1960.

Richmond, Robert W. and Robert Mardock. *A Nation Moving West: Readings in the History of the American Frontier.* Lincoln: University of Nebraska Press, 1966.

Roberts, Strother. "The Life and Death of Matonabbee: Fur Trade and Leadership Among the Chipewyan, 1736-1782." *Manitoba History*, no. 55 (June 2007).

Robson, Joseph. *An Account of Six Years Residence in Hudson's-Bay, From 1733 to 1736, and 1744 to 1747.* London: J. Payne and J. Bouquet, 1752 original. Project Gutenberg ebook 2008.

Ross, Alexander. *Adventures of the First Settlers on the Oregon or Columbia River, 1810-1813.* Lincoln: University of Nebraska Press, 1986, reprint of 1849 original.

Ross, Alexander. *Red River Settlement: Its Rise, Progress, and Present State. With Some Account of the Native Races, and Its General History, to the Present Day.* London: Smith, Elder, 1856.

Ronda, James. *Astoria and Empire.* Lincoln: University of Nebraska Press, 1990.

Ruggles, Richard I. *A Country So Interesting: The Hudson's Bay Company and Two Centuries of Mapping, 1670-1870.* Montreal: McGill-Queen's University Press, 1991.

Ruxton, George Frederick Augustus. *Adventures in Mexico and the Rocky Mountains.* New York: Harper & Brothers, 1848.

Smith, Jedediah Strong. *The Travels of Jedediah Smith: A Documentary Outline Including the Journal of the Great American Pathfinder.* Edited by Maurice S. Sullivan. Lincoln and London: University of Nebraska Press, 1934.

Simpson, George. *The Character Book of Governor George Simpson, 1832, in Hudson's Bay Miscellany, 1670-1870.* Edited by Glyndwr Williams. Winnipeg: Hudson's Bay Record Society, 1975.

Simpson, George. *Journal of Occurrences in the Athabasca Department, 1820 and 1821.* Edited by E.E. Rich. Toronto: Chaplain Society for the Hudson's Bay Record Society, 1938.

Simpson, George. *An Overland Journey Round the World, During the Years 1841 and 1842, 2 vols.* Philadelphia: Lea and Blanchard, 1847.

———. *Fur Trade and Empire. George Simpson's Journal; Remarks Connected with the Fur Trade in the Course of a Voyage from York Factory to Fort George and back to York Factory 1824-1825.* Edited by Frederick Merk. Cambridge, MA: Harvard University Press, 1931.

Stark, Peter. *Astoria: John Jacob Astor and Thomas Jefferson's Lost Pacific Empire.* New York: Ecco, 2015.

Swaggerty, William R. "Indian Trade in the Trans-Mississippi West to 1870." In *A History of Indian-White Relations. Handbook of North American Indians.* Washington, D.C.: Smithsonian Institution, 1988.

Thompson, David. *The Writings of David Thompson, Volume 1 and Volume 2: The Travels.* Edited by William E. Moreau. Montreal: McGill-Queen's University Press, 2009.

———. *David Thompson's Narrative, 1784-1812.* Edited by J.B. Tyrell. Introduction by Richard Glover. Toronto: Champlain Society, 1962.

———. *The Travels of David Thompson: Volume I and Volume II.* Edited by Sean T. Peake. Bloomington, IN: iUniverse Inc, 2011.

———. *Columbia Journals.* Edited by Barbara Belyea. Montreal: McGill-Queens Press, 1994.

Thorner, Thomas, and Thor Frohn-Nielsen, eds. *A Few Acres of Snow: Documents in Pre-Confederation Canadian History.* Toronto: University of Toronto Press, 2009.

Thwaites, Reuben Gold. *The Jesuit Relations and Allied Documents: Travels and Explorations of the Jesuit Missionaries in New France, Vol. VI, Québec 1633–1634.* Cleveland: Burrows Brothers, 1896.

Van Kirk, Sylvia. *Many Tender Ties: Women in Fur Trade Society, 1670-1870.* Winnipeg: Watson & Dwyer, 1980.

———. "The Custom of the Country: An Examination of Fur Trade Marriage Practices." In *Canadian Family History: Selected Readings*, ed. Bettina Bradbury. Toronto: Copp Clark Pitman, 1992.

Wales, William. *Journal of a Voyage, Made by Order of the Royal Society, to Churchill River, on the North-West Coast of Hudson's Bay: Of Thirteen Months Residence in That Country: and of the Voyage Back to England: In the Years 1768 and 1769.* Oxford, UK: Philosophical Transactions of the Royal Society, 1770. Online.

White, T.H., ed. *The Book of Beasts: Being a Translation from a Latin Bestiary of the Twelfth Century.* New York: Putnam, 1960.

Whitman, Narcissa. *The Letters of Narcissa Whitman, 1836-1847*. Fairfield, WA: Ye Galleon Press, 1986.

Wilcocke, Samuel Hull, Simon McGillivray and Edward Ellice. *A Narrative of Occurrences in the Indian Countries of North America*. London: B. McMillan, 1817.

Williams, Glyndwr. *Highlights of the First 200 Years of the Hudson's Bay Company*. Winnipeg: Peguis, 1976.

———. "Arthur Dobbs and Joseph Robson: New Light on the Relationship between Two Early Critics of the Hudson's Bay Company." *Canadian Historical Review* 40, 1949.

———. "The Hudson's Bay Company and the Fur Trade: 1670-1870." In *The Beaver: Exploring Canada's History* autumn 1983. 1993 Special Edition reprint.

Willson, Beckles. *The Great Company, Being a History of the Honorable Company of Merchants-Adventurers Trading into Hudson's Bay*. New York: Dodd, Mead, 1900.

Wilson, Charles. *The Frontier: Charles Wilson's Diary of the Survey of the 40th Parallel, 1858-1862, While Secretary of the British Boundary Commission*. Edited by George F.G. Stanley. Toronto: Macmillan of Canada, 1970.

Wyeth, Nathaniel J. "The Correspondence and Journals of Captain Nathaniel J. Wyeth." Edited by F. G. Young. *Sources of the History of Oregon* 1, no. 3, 1899.

Umfreville, Edward. *The Present State of Hudson's Bay: Containing a Full Description of That Settlement, and the Adjacent Country; And Likewise of the Fur Trade, With Hints for Its Improvement, &C. &C.; To Which Are Added, Remarks and Observations Made in the Inland Parts*. Toronto: Ryerson Press, 1954. 1790 original.

FURTHER READING

Archive.org and Google Books have digitized many old books, as well as modern reprints. The wealth of information available is astonishing and easy to access.

For a general interest economic history from a First Nations perspective, see *I Have Lived Here Since the World Began* by Arthur Ray (Key Porter, 1996).

For an overview of the culture and history of Indigenous peoples across northern North America, see Olive Patricia Dickason's *Canada's First Nations: A History of Founding Peoples from Earliest Times* (Oxford University Press, 2008).

For a discussion of women in fur trade society, see Sylvia Van Kirk's *Many Tender Ties* (Watson and Dwyer, 1996) and Jennifer Brown's *Strangers in Blood* (University of British Columbia Press, 1980).

For more information on disease in the Company's territory during the fur trade era, see Gerald N. Grob's *The Deadly Truth: A History of Disease in America* (Harvard University Press, 2002) and Paul Hackett's *A Very Remarkable Sickness: Epidemics in the Petit Nord, 1670 to 1846* (University of Manitoba Press, 2002).

For an excellent biography of Pierre Esprit Radisson, see Marc Bourrie's *Bushrunner* (Biblioasis, 2019).

For information on Thanadelthur, the origin of the name and the represen-
tation over time, see Patricia A. McCormack's essay at http://www.mhs.mb.ca
/docs/mb_history/55/thanadelthur.shtml.

On James Knight, see John Geiger and Owen Beattie's *Dead Silence: The
Greatest Mystery in Arctic Discovery* (Bloomsbury, 1993).

For the full story of Samuel Hearne, and Matonabbee, see Ken McGoogan's
Ancient Mariner (Phyllis Bruce Books/Perennial, 2004). Also by McGoogan is
Fatal Passage (Phyllis Bruce Books/Perennial, 2002), about John Rae, the great
overland explorer of the Arctic and the Northwest Passage, who was a Company
employee. Rae's story didn't fit within this book's narrative, but his personal
explorations are incredible and McGoogan's story telling is first-rate.

On Matonabbee, see Strother Roberts's "The Life and Death of
Matonabbee: Fur Trade and Leadership Among the Chipewyan" in *Manitoba
History*, http://www.mhs.mb.ca/docs/mb_history/55/matonabbee.shtm.

On Alexander Mackenzie, see Derek Hayes's *First Crossing: Alexander
Mackenzie, His Expedition Across North America, and the Opening of the Continent*
(Douglas & McIntyre, 2003).

For a good biography of David Thompson, see D'Arcy Jenish's *Epic Wanderer*
(Doubleday Canada, 2003).

For a good biography of George Simpson, see James Raffan's *Emperor of the
North* (HarperCollins, 2008).

For a fascinating investigation into the murder of John McLoughlin Jr. in
1842, see Debra Komar's *The Bastard of Fort Stikine* (Goose Lane Editions,
2015).

For greater details on James and Amelia Douglas, see John Adams's *Old
Square Toes and His Lady* (TouchWood Editions, 2011).

For a quirky and informative history of beavers, see Frances Backhouse's
Once They Were Hats: In Search of the Mighty Beaver (ECW, 2015).

For a fascinating narrative of John Jacob Astor's Pacific Fur Company and
Fort Astoria, see Peter Stark's *Astoria: Astor and Jefferson's Lost Pacific Empire*
(Ecco, 2015).

ACKNOWLEDGEMENTS

I have long been interested in the North American fur trade, particularly the early days during the first tentative meetings between peoples, when the world was a very different place socially, scientifically and technologically. For whatever reason, it seems that this period is often misrepresented and misunderstood. While the data—statistics and numbers and facts—are obviously a fundamental background to understanding the history, it has always been the people who have fascinated me. People who were biologically the same as you and me—just as intelligent and motivated by the same basic urges—but who lived their lives and made their decisions within the boundaries of different cultural and geographical constraints.

I wish to heartily thank Tim Rostron, senior editor, and Scott Sellers, associate publisher, at Doubleday Canada for enthusiastically embracing this project and my approach to the telling of this great story. It was my good fortune that John Pearce and Chris Casuccio at Westwood Creative Artists approached me several years ago. Since then we have shared many productive and interesting conversations about this project and others along its route from idea to manuscript. I also wish to thank copy editor Shaun Oakey for his historical knowledge and thorough attention to detail, and the many dedicated people at Penguin Random House who worked to transform my manuscript into a beautiful book, including Andrew Roberts, who designed the marvelous cover and elegant pages within. I'd also like to thank Halle Flygare, an explorer in his own right who during his youth blazed the trail of Mackenzie's route to the coast, for his detailed reading of the Mackenzie chapters.

Thanks to my neighbours Rosemary and Eric for lending me some splendid prints from an old HBC calender. Thanks also to Doubleday Canada intern Geffen Semach for her assistance.

Last but never least, thanks as ever to my wife, Nicky Brink, who, over the course of our twenty-five years together, has developed an interest in narrative history. A clear thinker and writer herself, she read the entire manuscript long before I dared to share it with anyone else.

INDEX

Note: HBC = Hudson's Bay Company; NWC = North West Company